THE NEW CAMBRIDGE SHAKESPEARE

GENERAL EDITOR
Brian Gibbons, *University of Münster*

ASSOCIATE GENERAL EDITOR
A. R. Braunmuller, *University of California, Los Angeles*

From the publication of the first volumes in 1984 the General Editor of the New Cambridge Shakespeare was Philip Brockbank and the Associate General Editors were Brian Gibbons and Robin Hood. From 1990 to 1994 the General Editor was Brian Gibbons and the Associate General Editors were A. R. Braunmuller and Robin Hood.

TROILUS AND CRESSIDA

Troilus and Cressida, long considered one of Shakespeare's most problematic plays, is both difficult and fascinating. Largely neglected during the eighteenth and nineteenth centuries, it has recently proved popular and rewarding on the stage as well as in the study. This edition questions certain received ideas about the play's text, especially the relationship between Quarto and Folio, and offers several new readings of old problems. Dawson's textual choices are often surprising but at the same time carefully grounded. He views the play from a performance perspective – frequently in the Commentary as well as in the detailed section on stage history in the Introduction. The Introduction also covers the cultural context in which the play was written, probes the controversy about its early performance, and provides extensive analysis of character, language, genre, and contemporary significance.

THE NEW CAMBRIDGE SHAKESPEARE

All's Well That Ends Well, edited by Russell Fraser
Antony and Cleopatra, edited by David Bevington
As You Like It, edited by Michael Hattaway
The Comedy of Errors, edited by T. S. Dorsch
Coriolanus, edited by Lee Bliss
Hamlet, edited by Philip Edwards
Julius Caesar, edited by Marvin Spevack
King Edward III, edited by Giorgio Melchiori
The First Part of King Henry IV, edited by Herbert Weil and Judith Weil
The Second Part of King Henry IV, edited by Giorgio Melchiori
King Henry V, edited by Andrew Gurr
The First Part of King Henry VI, edited by Michael Hattaway
The Second Part of King Henry VI, edited by Michael Hattaway
The Third Part of King Henry VI, edited by Michael Hattaway
King Henry VIII, edited by John Margeson
King John, edited by L. A. Beaurline
The Tragedy of King Lear, edited by Jay L. Halio
King Richard II, edited by Andrew Gurr
King Richard III, edited by Janis Lull
Macbeth, edited by A. R. Braunmuller
Measure for Measure, edited by Brian Gibbons
The Merchant of Venice, edited by M. M. Mahood
The Merry Wives of Windsor, edited by David Crane
A Midsummer Night's Dream, edited by R. A. Foakes
Much Ado About Nothing, edited by F. H. Mares
Othello, edited by Norman Sanders
Pericles, edited by Doreen DelVecchio and Antony Hammond
The Poems, edited by John Roe
Romeo and Juliet, edited by G. Blakemore Evans
The Sonnets, edited by G. Blakemore Evans
The Taming of the Shrew, edited by Ann Thompson
The Tempest, edited by David Lindley
Timon of Athens, edited by Karl Klein
Titus Andronicus, edited by Alan Hughes
Troilus and Cressida, edited by Anthony B. Dawson
Twelfth Night, edited by Elizabeth Story Donno
The Two Gentlemen of Verona, edited by Kurt Schlueter

THE EARLY QUARTOS

The First Quarto of Hamlet, edited by Kathleen O. Irace
The First Quarto of King Henry V, edited by Andrew Gurr
The First Quarto of King Lear, edited by Jay L. Halio
The First Quarto of Othello, edited by Scott McMillin
The First Quarto of King Richard III, edited by Peter Davison
The Taming of a Shrew, edited by Stephen Roy Miller

TROILUS AND CRESSIDA

Edited by
ANTHONY B. DAWSON

CAMBRIDGE
UNIVERSITY PRESS

CAMBRIDGE UNIVERSITY PRESS
Cambridge, New York, Melbourne, Madrid, Cape Town, Singapore, São Paulo, Delhi

Cambridge University Press
The Edinburgh Building, Cambridge CB2 8RU, UK

Published in the United States of America by Cambridge University Press, New York

www.cambridge.org
Information on this title: www.cambridge.org/9780521376198

First published 2003
Reprinted with corrections 2008

Printed in the United Kingdom at University Press, Cambridge

A catalogue record for this publication is available from the British Library

ISBN 978-0-521-37477-4 hardback
ISBN 978-0-521-37619-8 paperback

CONTENTS

ILLUSTRATIONS

Illustrations 1, 3, 4, and 5 are reproduced by permission of the Folger Shakespeare Library; 6 and 7 from the Theatre Museum (London) collection by permission of the Board of Trustees of the Victoria and Albert Museum; 2, 8, 9, 10, and 12 by permission of the Shakespeare Centre Library, Stratford-upon-Avon; 11 by permission of the photographer; 13 and 14 by permission of the British Library.

ACKNOWLEDGEMENTS

This edition has been gestating for a long time and it is gratifying now to be able to thank those many people who have helped bring it to the light of day. I have learned a great deal from the many previous editors of the play, most especially H. N. Hillebrand, whose monumental Variorum edition offers so much valuable information and keen analysis; I would also like to single out Alice Walker, the editor of the previous Cambridge Shakespeare version, G. B. Evans, my thesis supervisor of long ago, and Kenneth Palmer and David Bevington, editors of the second and third series Arden Shakespeare editions. Gratitude is due also to the Oxford editors, Stanley Wells and Gary Taylor, with whom I often found myself in fruitful disagreement; their work on the text and in *William Shakespeare: A Textual Companion* has proved indispensable to later editors. On a more personal level, I want to thank a number of people who have contributed in various ways to this drawn-out project, especially Roger Apfelbaum (who kindly sent me a copy of his excellent thesis on text and staging), Patricia Badir, Matthew Dawson, Brian Gibbons, Paul B. Harvey Jr, Barbara Hodgdon, Peter Holland, Laurie Maguire, Gordon McMullan, Carol Rutter, Stanley Wells, and Sarah Werner. I owe a special debt to Al Braunmuller, my wonderfully genial general editor, who combed carefully through evolving versions of text, collation, and Commentary, saving me on numerous occasions from error, solecism, stylistic infelicity, and logical deficiency. His hundreds of suggestions for improvement have made this a better edition than it could ever have been without him. Paul Yachnin, my good friend and colleague, provided a willing ear and many thoughtful responses when I was first puzzling out the intricacies of the text, and read, with his usual shrewd sympathy, versions of the Introduction and parts of the Commentary. More than any other person, Gretchen Minton helped bring this edition to fruition. She began as my research assistant, but soon became a partner in the enterprise, catching me up not only on the minutiae of editorial consistency, but on larger questions of meaning, staging, textual policy, etc. Her humour and commitment, her attention to the messy office she laughingly called 'The Troilus Institute', her sharp-eyed attention to every detail of the enterprise, were invaluable. Let me thank as well the staff of the Folger Shakespeare Library and the Shakespeare Centre Library in Stratford, who, as they have frequently been in the past, were brilliantly helpful. Sarah Stanton, the editor at Cambridge University Press, has once again proven her managerial and human skills, patiently moving the manuscript along and offering help and encouragement at just the right moments. Margaret Berrill, my amiable, sharp-eyed, and altogether exemplary copy-editor, not only spotted numerous errors, but also steered the project around various technological obstacles and through to print.

Lucie Sutherland tracked down a number of photos for me in London, Lisa Grekul, my current research assistant, has worked carefully on bibliography, references, and illustration-hunting, and Gudrun Dreher helped with German translation. As always, I have been lucky enough to enjoy the affectionate support of Honey Halpern. To all, my thanks.

ABBREVIATIONS AND CONVENTIONS

Shakespeare's plays, when cited in this edition, are abbreviated in a style modified slightly from that used in the *Harvard Concordance to Shakespeare*. Other editions of Shakespeare are abbreviated under the editor's surname (Evans, Bevington) unless they are the work of more than one editor. In such cases, an abbreviated series name is used (Cam.). When more than one edition by the same editor is cited, later editions are discriminated with a raised figure (Rowe²). All quotations from Shakespeare, other than those from *Troilus and Cressida*, use the lineation of *The Riverside Shakespeare*, under the textual editorship of G. Blakemore Evans.

1. Shakespeare's works

Ado	*Much Ado About Nothing*
Ant.	*Antony and Cleopatra*
AWW	*All's Well That Ends Well*
AYLI	*As You Like It*
Cor.	*Coriolanus*
Cym.	*Cymbeline*
Err.	*The Comedy of Errors*
Ham.	*Hamlet*
1H4	*The First Part of King Henry the Fourth*
2H4	*The Second Part of King Henry the Fourth*
H5	*King Henry the Fifth*
1H6	*The First Part of King Henry the Sixth*
2H6	*The Second Part of King Henry the Sixth*
3H6	*The Third Part of King Henry the Sixth*
H8	*King Henry the Eighth*
JC	*Julius Caesar*
John	*King John*
LLL	*Love's Labour's Lost*
Lear	*King Lear*
Luc.	*The Rape of Lucrece*
Mac.	*Macbeth*
MM	*Measure for Measure*
MND	*A Midsummer Night's Dream*
MV	*The Merchant of Venice*
Oth.	*Othello*
Per.	*Pericles*
PP	*The Passionate Pilgrim*
R2	*King Richard the Second*
R3	*King Richard the Third*
Rom.	*Romeo and Juliet*
Shr.	*The Taming of the Shrew*
Son.	*The Sonnets*
STM	*Sir Thomas More*

Temp.	*The Tempest*
TGV	*The Two Gentlemen of Verona*
Tim.	*Timon of Athens*
Tit.	*Titus Andronicus*
TN	*Twelfth Night*
TNK	*The Two Noble Kinsmen*
Tro.	*Troilus and Cressida*
Wiv.	*The Merry Wives of Windsor*
WT	*The Winter's Tale*

2. Other works cited and general references

Abbott	E. A. Abbott, *A Shakespearian Grammar*, 3rd edn, 1870 (references are to numbered paragraphs)
Adams	J. N. Adams, *Latin Sexual Vocabulary*, 1982
Adams, H.	Howard C. Adams, 'What Cressid is', in *Sexuality and Politics in Renaissance Drama*, ed. Carole Levin and Karen Robertson, 1991, pp. 75–93
Adelman	Janet Adelman, *Suffocating Mothers: Fantasies of Maternal Origin in Shakespeare's Plays, 'Hamlet' to 'The Tempest'*, 1992
Alexander	Peter Alexander, '*Troilus and Cressida*, 1609', *Library* 9 (1929), 267–86
Alexander, *Works*	*William Shakespeare: The Complete Works*, ed. Peter Alexander, 1951
Apfelbaum	Roger Apfelbaum, ' "Author's pen or actor's voice": a performance history of editorial problems in Shakespeare's *Troilus and Cressida*'. Unpublished PhD dissertation, Shakespeare Institute, University of Birmingham, 1996. Revised version to be published under title *Shakespeare's 'Troilus and Cressida': Textual Problems and Performance Solutions*, 2003
Beale	Simon Russell Beale, 'Thersites in *Troilus and Cressida*', in *Players of Shakespeare 3: Further Essays in Shakespearean Performance*, ed. Russell Jackson and Robert Smallwood, 1993, pp. 160–73
Bednarz	James P. Bednarz, *Shakespeare and the Poets' War*, 2001
Berger	Harry Berger, Jr, '*Troilus and Cressida*: the observer as basilik', *Comparative Drama* 2 (1968), 122–36
Bevington	*The Complete Works of Shakespeare*, ed. David Bevington, 3rd edn, 1980
Bevington²	*Troilus and Cressida*, ed. David Bevington, 1998 (Arden Shakespeare)
Blayney	Peter W. M. Blayney, 'The publication of playbooks', in Cox and Kastan, pp. 383–422
Bowen	Barbara E. Bowen, *Gender in the Theatre of War: Shakespeare's Troilus and Cressida*, 1993
Bowers	Fredson Bowers, *On Editing Shakespeare and the Elizabethan Dramatists*, 1955
Bradshaw	Graham Bradshaw, *Shakespeare's Scepticism*, 1987
Burns	M. M. Burns, '*Troilus and Cressida*: the worst of both worlds', *S.St.* 13 (1980), 105–30
Bullough	*Narrative and Dramatic Sources of Shakespeare*, ed. Geoffrey Bullough (8 vols., 1957–75), vol. VI, 1966
Cam.	*The Works of Shakespeare*, ed. W. G. Clark, J. Glover, and W. A. Wright (9 vols., 1863–6, Cambridge Shakespeare), vol. VI, 1865

Capell	*The Works of Shakespeare*, ed. Edward Capell (10 vols., 1767–8), vol. IX, 1768
Caxton	*The Recuyell of the Historyes of Troye* (written in French by Raoul Lefèvre, translated and printed by William Caxton, 1474), ed. H. Oskar Sommer, 1894
Chambers	E. K. Chambers, *William Shakespeare: A Study of Facts and Problems*, 2 vols., 1930
Chapman, *Iliads*	*The Iliads of Homer* (1611), in *Chapman's Homer: The Iliad*, ed. Allardyce Nicoll, 1984, pp. 3–499
Chapman, *Seven Books*	*Seaven Bookes of the Iliades* (1598), in *Chapman's Homer: The Iliad*, ed. Allardyce Nicoll, 1984, pp. 503–39
Charnes	Linda Charnes, *Notorious Identity: Materializing the Subject in Shakespeare*, 1993
Chaucer	Geoffrey Chaucer, *Troilus and Criseyde*, in *The Riverside Chaucer*, ed. Larry D. Benson, 1987
Collier	*The Works of William Shakespeare*, ed. J. P. Collier (8 vols., 1842–4), vol. VI, 1842
Collier²	*Shakespeare's Comedies, Histories, Tragedies, and Poems*, ed. J. P. Collier (6 vols., 1858), vol. IV
Collier³	*The Plays and Poems of William Shakespeare*, ed. J. P. Collier (8 vols., 1875–7), vol. V, 1876
conj.	conjecture, conjectured by
corr.	corrected
Cox and Kastan	*A New History of Early English Drama*, ed. John D. Cox and David S. Kastan, 1997
Crosse	Gordon Crosse, unpublished MS. theatre diaries, Birmingham Public Library
Dawson and Yachnin	Anthony Dawson and Paul Yachnin, *The Culture of Playgoing in Shakespeare's England: A Collaborative Debate*, 2001
Deighton	*Troilus and Cressida*, ed. K. Deighton, 1906 (Arden Shakespeare)
Delius	*The Works of William Shakespeare*, ed. Nicholas Delius (7 vols., 1864), vol. II
Dent	R. W. Dent, *Shakespeare's Proverbial Language: An Index*, 1981
Dent, *PLED*	R.W. Dent, *Proverbial Language in English Drama Exclusive of Shakespeare, 1495–1616*, 1984
Donaldson	E. Talbot Donaldson, *The Swan at the Well: Shakespeare Reading Chaucer*, 1985
Dryden	John Dryden, *Troilus and Cressida*, ed. Maximillian Novak and George Guffey, in *The Works of John Dryden* (California Edition, 20 vols., 1956–94), vol. XIII, 1984
Dyce	*The Works of William Shakespeare*, ed. Alexander Dyce (6 vols., 1857), vol. IV
Dyce²	*The Works of William Shakespeare*, ed. Alexander Dyce (9 vols., 1864–7), vol. VI, 1865
ed., eds.	editor(s), edited by
edn	edition
Ellis-Fermor	Una Ellis-Fermor, *The Frontiers of Drama*, 1946
Elton	William R. Elton, *Shakespeare's 'Troilus and Cressida' and the Inns of Court Revels*, 2000
Engle	Lars Engle, *Shakespearean Pragmatism: Market of His Time*, 1993

Evans	*The Riverside Shakespeare*, ed. G. Blakemore Evans, 1974
F	*Mr. William Shakespeares Comedies, Histories & Tragedies*, 1623 (First Folio)
F 2	*Mr. William Shakespeares Comedies, Histories & Tragedies*, 1632 (Second Folio)
F 3	*Mr. William Shakespear's Comedies, Histories & Tragedies*, 1663–4 (Third Folio)
F 4	*Mr. William Shakespear's Comedies, Histories & Tragedies*, 1685 (Fourth Folio)
Foakes and Rickert	*Henslowe's Diary*, ed. R. A. Foakes and C. T. Rickert, Cambridge, 1961
Freund	Elizabeth Freund, ' "Ariachne's broken woof": the rhetoric of citation in *Troilus and Cressida*', in *Shakespeare and the Question of Theory*, ed. Patricia Parker and Geoffrey Hartman, 1985, pp. 19–36
Gaudet, 'Troilus'	Paul Gaudet, ' "As true as Troilus", "as false as Cressid": tradition, texts, and the implication of readers', *English Studies in Canada* 16 (1990), 125–48
Gaudet, 'Father'	Paul Gaudet, 'Playing father: Q and F versions of *Troilus and Cressida*, 4.5' (unpublished paper)
Girard	René Girard, 'The politics of desire in *Troilus and Cressida*', in *Shakespeare and the Question of Theory*, ed. Patricia Parker and Geoffrey Hartman, 1985, pp. 188–209
Godschalk	William Godschalk, 'The texts of *Troilus and Cressida*', *Early Modern Literary Studies* 1 (1995), 1–54
Greene	Gayle Greene, 'Shakespeare's Cressida: "a kind of self" ', in *The Woman's Part: Feminist Criticism of Shakespeare*, ed. Carolyn Lenz, Ruth Swift, Gayle Greene, and Carol Thomas Neely, 1980, pp. 133–49
Greg, *Documents*	W. W. Greg, *Dramatic Documents from the Elizabethan Playhouse*, 2 vols., 1931
Greg, *First Folio*	W. W. Greg, *The Shakespeare First Folio: Its Bibliographical and Textual History*, 1955
Greg, *Principles*	W. W. Greg, *Principles of Emendation in Shakespeare*, 1928
Greg, 'Printing'	W. W. Greg, 'The Printing of Shakespeare's *Troilus and Cressida* in the First Folio', *PBSA* 45 (1951), 277–82
Hanmer	*The Works of Mr William Shakespear*, ed. Thomas Hanmer (6 vols., 1743–4), vol. VI, 1744
Henryson	Robert Henryson, *The Testament of Cresseid* (1532), in *The Story of Troilus*, ed. R. K. Gordon, 1964
Heywood	Thomas Heywood, *The Captives* in British Library (London) MS. Egerton 1994
Hinman	Charlton Hinman, *The Printing and Proof-Reading of the First Folio of Shakespeare*, 2 vols., 1963
Hodgdon	Barbara Hodgdon, 'He do Cressida in different voices', *English Literary Renaissance* 20 (1990), 254–86
Holland	Peter Holland, *English Shakespeares: Shakespeare on the English Stage in the 1990s*, 1997
Honigmann, 'Date and revision'	E. A. J. Honigmann, 'The date and revision of *Troilus and Cressida*', in *Textual Criticism and Literary Interpretation*, ed. J. McGann, 1985, pp. 38–54
Honigmann, *Myriad-Minded*	E. A. J. Honigmann, *Myriad-Minded Shakespeare: Essays, Chiefly on the Tragedies and Problem Comedies*, 1989

Honigmann, 'Reviser'	E. A. J. Honigmann, 'Shakespeare as a reviser', in *Textual Criticism and Literary Interpretation*, ed. J. McGann, 1985, pp. 1–22
Honigmann, Stability	E. A. J. Honigmann, *The Stability of Shakespeare's Texts*, 1965
Hortmann	Wilhelm Hortmann, *Shakespeare on the German Stage: The Twentieth Century*, 1998
Howard-Hill	Trevor Howard-Hill, 'The problem of manuscript copy for Folio *King Lear*', *Library* 4 (1982), 1–24
Hudson	*The Works of Shakespeare*, ed. H. N. Hudson (11 vols., 1851–9), vol. VII, 1854
Hudson²	*The Works of Shakespeare*, ed. H. N. Hudson (20 vols., 1880–1, Harvard edn), vol. XVI, 1881
Hulme	Hilda Hulme, *Explorations in Shakespeare's Language*, 1962
ILN	*Illustrated London News*
Jackson	Z. Jackson, *Shakespeare's Genius Justified*, 1819
James	Heather James, *Shakespeare's Troy: Drama, Politics, and the Translation of Empire*, 1997
Jensen	Phebe Jensen, 'The textual politics of *Troilus and Cressida*', *SQ* 46 (1995), 414–23
Johnson	*The Plays of William Shakespeare*, ed. Samuel Johnson (8 vols., 1765) vol. VII
Jones	Katherine Duncan-Jones, *Ungentle Shakespeare: Scenes From His Life*, 2001
Kellner	Leon Kellner, *Restoring Shakespeare: A Critical Analysis of Misreadings in Shakespeare's Works*, 1925
Kennedy	Dennis Kennedy, *Looking at Shakespeare: A Visual History of Twentieth-century Performance*, 1993
Kermode	Frank Kermode, ' "Opinion" in *Troilus and Cressida*', in *Teaching the Text*, ed. Susanne Kappeler and Norman Bryson, 1983, pp. 164–79
Kimberly	Michael E. Kimberly, *'Troilus and Cressida' on the English Stage*, 1968 (unpublished MA thesis, University of Birmingham)
Kimbrough	Robert Kimbrough, *Shakespeare's 'Troilus and Cressida' and Its Setting*, 1964
Kinnear	Benjamin G. Kinnear, *Cruces Shakespearianae: Difficult Passages in the Works of Shakespeare*, 1883
Kittredge	*The Complete Works of Shakespeare*, ed. George Lyman Kittredge, 1936
Knight	Charles Knight, *The Complete Works of W. Shakspere* (9 vols., 1839–44, pictorial edition), vol. IX, 1843
Knutson	Rosalyn Knutson, 'The repertory', in Cox and Kastan, pp. 461–80
Lancashire	Ian Lancashire, 'Probing Shakespeare's idiolect in *Troilus and Cressida*', *University of Toronto Quarterly* 68 (1999), 728–67
Leiter	*Shakespeare Around the Globe: A Guide to Notable Postwar Revivals*, ed. Samuel L. Leiter, 1986
Lettsom	W. N. Lettsom, 'New readings in Shakespeare', in *Blackwood's Edinburgh Magazine* 74 (1853), pp. 181–202, 303–24, 451–74
Long, 'John a Kent'	William B. Long, 'John a Kent and John a Cumber: an Elizabethan playbook and its implications', in *Shakespeare and Dramatic Tradition: Essays in Honor of S. F. Johnson*, ed. W. R. Elton and William B. Long, 1989, pp. 125–43

Long, 'Stage-directions'	William B. Long, 'Stage-directions: a misinterpreted factor in determining textual provenance', *Text 2* (1985), 121–37
Long, 'Woodstock'	William B. Long, ' "A bed/for woodstock": a warning for the unwary', *Medieval and Renaissance Drama in England* 2 (1985), 91–118
Lydgate	*Lydgate's Troy Book AD 1412–20*, ed. Henry Bergen, 1906, 1908, 1910 (Early English Text Society)
Mallin	Eric S. Mallin, *Inscribing the Time: Shakespeare and the End of Elizabethan England*, 1995
Malone	*The Plays and Poems of William Shakespeare*, ed. Edmond Malone (10 vols., 1790), vol. VIII
Marlowe	Christopher Marlowe, *Doctor Faustus, A- and B-Texts*, ed. David Bevington and Eric Rasmussen, 1993
Maus	Katharine E. Maus, *Inwardness and Theater in the English Renaissance*, 1995
Montaigne	Michel de Montaigne, *The Essayes of Montaigne* (1603), trans. John Florio, 1933
MS., MSS.	manuscript, manuscripts
Muir	*Troilus and Cressida*, ed. Kenneth Muir, 1982 (Oxford Shakespeare)
Muir, 'Note'	Kenneth Muir, 'A note on the text of *Troilus and Cressida*', *Library* 1 (1979), 168
Muir, *Sources*	Kenneth Muir, *The Sources of Shakespeare's Plays*, London, 1977
Mulvey	Laura Mulvey, 'Visual pleasure and narrative cinema' (1975), in *Feminism and Film Theory*, ed. Constance Penley, 1988, pp. 57–79
n., nn.	note, notes
Newlin	Jeanne T. Newlin, 'The darkened stage: J. P. Kemble and *Troilus and Cressida*', in *The Triple Bond: Plays, Mainly Shakespearean, in Performance*, ed. Joseph G. Price, 1975, pp. 190–202
Noble	Richmond Noble, *Shakespeare's Biblical Knowledge and Use of the Book of Common Prayer*, 1935
Norbrook	David Norbrook, 'Rhetoric, ideology, and the Elizabethan world picture', in *Renaissance Rhetoric*, ed. Peter Mack, 1994, pp. 140–64
Nosworthy	J. M. Nosworthy, *Shakespeare's Occasional Plays: Their Origin and Transmission*, 1965
Oxford	*The Complete Oxford Shakespeare*, ed. Stanley Wells and Gary Taylor, 1986
OED	*Oxford English Dictionary*, 20 vols., 1989
Orgel	Stephen Orgel, *Impersonations: The Performance of Gender in Shakespeare's England*, 1996
Ovid	*Ovid's Metamorphoses*, trans. Arthur Golding [1567], ed. J. F. Nims, 1965
Palmer	*Troilus and Cressida*, ed. Kenneth Palmer, 1982 (Arden Shakespeare)
Parker	Patricia Parker, *Shakespeare from the Margins: Language, Culture, Context*, 1996
Peele	George Peele, 'The Tale of Troy', in *The Life and Minor Works of George Peele*, ed. David H. Horne, 1952, pp. 183–202
Pope	*The Works of Shakespear*, ed. Alexander Pope (6 vols., 1723–5), vol. VI, 1725
Pope[2]	*The Works of Shakespear*, ed. Alexander Pope (8 vols., 1728), vol. VII
Q	*The Historie of Troylus and Cresseida*, 1609 (the quarto)
Rann	Joseph Rann, *Dramatic Works* (6 vols., 1786–94), vol. III, 1789

rev.	revised, revised by
Ritson	Joseph Ritson, *Remarks, Critical and Illustrative, on the Text and Notes of the Last Edition of Shakespeare*, 1783
Rossiter	A. P. Rossiter, *Angel with Horns and Other Shakespeare Lectures*, 1961
Rowe	*The Works of Mr. William Shakespear*, ed. Nicholas Rowe (6 vols., 1709), vol. IV
Rowe²	*The Works of Mr. William Shakespear*, ed. Nicholas Rowe (8 vols., 1714), vol. V
rpt	reprint, reprinted
RSC	Royal Shakespeare Company
Rutter	Carol Rutter, *Enter the Body: Women and Representation on Shakespeare's Stage*, 2001
Schmidt	Alexander Schmidt, *Shakespeare Lexicon*, 2 vols., 1874, rpt 1971
SD	stage direction
Sedgwick	Eve Kosofsky Sedgwick, *Between Men: English Literature and Male Homosocial Desire*, 1985
SH	speech heading
Singer	*The Dramatic Works of William Shakespeare*, ed. S. W. Singer (10 vols., 1856), vol. VII
Singer MS.	A copy of F2 formerly in S. W. Singer's possession, with seventeenth-century marginal corrections (cited in Variorum, pp. xv and 177)
Sisson	*William Shakespeare: The Complete Works*, ed. C. J. Sisson, 1954
Sonnets	Katherine Duncan-Jones, ed. *Shakespeare's Sonnets* (Arden edition), 1997
Spevack	Marvin Spevack, *A Complete and Systematic Concordance to the Works of Shakespeare*, 9 vols., 1968
SQ	*Shakespeare Quarterly*
S.Sur.	*Shakespeare Survey*
S.St.	*Shakespeare Studies*
Staunton	*The Plays of Shakespeare*, ed. Howard Staunton (3 vols., 1858–60), vol. III, 1860
Steevens	*The Plays of William Shakespeare*, ed. Samuel Johnson and George Steevens (Variorum, 10 vols., 1773), vol. IX
Steevens²	*The Plays of William Shakespeare*, ed. Samuel Johnson and George Steevens (Variorum, 10 vols., 1778), vol. IX
Steevens³	*The Plays of William Shakespeare*, ed. Samuel Johnson and George Steevens (Variorum, 15 vols., 1793), vol. XI
subst.	substantively
Swinburne	Algernon C. Swinburne, *A Study of Shakespeare* (1880), 1965
Tannenbaum	Samuel A. Tannenbaum 'Notes on *Troilus and Cressida*', *Shakespeare Association Bulletin* 7 (1932), 72–81
Tatlock	J. S. P. Tatlock, 'The siege of Troy in Elizabethan literature, especially in Shakespeare and Heywood', *PMLA* 30.4 (1915), 673–770
Taylor, 'Compositor A'	Gary Taylor, 'The shrinking Compositor A of the First Folio', *Studies in Bibliography* 34 (1981), 96–117
Taylor, 'Bibliography'	Gary Taylor, '*Troilus and Cressida*: bibliography, performance and interpretation', *S.St.* 15 (1982), 99–136
Textual Companion	Stanley Wells and Gary Taylor, with John Jowett and William Montgomery, *William Shakespeare: A Textual Companion*, 1987

Theobald	*The Works of Shakespeare*, ed. Lewis Theobald (7 vols., 1733), vol. VII
Theobald²	*The Works of Shakespeare*, ed. Lewis Theobald (8 vols., 1740), vol. VII
Thirlby	Styan Thirlby, *Letters to Theobald*, cited in the latter's edition, 1733
TLS	*Times Literary Supplement*
Tylee	Claire M. Tylee, 'The text of Cressida and every ticklish reader: *Troilus and Cressida*, the Greek camp scene', *S.Sur.* 41 (1989), 63–76
Tyrwhitt	Thomas Tyrwhitt, *Observations and Conjectures upon Some Passages of Shakespeare*, 1766
uncorr.	uncorrected
Variorum	*Troilus and Cressida*, New Variorum edition, ed. Harold N. Hillebrand and T. W. Baldwin, 1953
Walker	*Troilus and Cressida*, ed. Alice Walker, 1957 (New Shakespeare)
Walker, *Textual Problems*	Alice Walker, *Textual Problems of the First Folio: Richard III, King Lear, Troilus and Cressida, 2 Henry VI, Hamlet, Othello*, 1953
Walton	J. K. Walton, *The Quarto Copy for the First Folio of Shakespeare*, 1971
Warburton	William Warburton and Alexander Pope, eds., *The Works of Shakespear* (8 vols., 1747), vol. VII
Werstine, 'Narratives'	Paul Werstine, 'Narratives about printed Shakespeare texts: "foul papers" and "bad" quartos', *SQ* 41 (1990), 65–86
Werstine, 'Plays'	Paul Werstine, 'Plays in manuscript', in Cox and Kastan, pp. 481–98
White	*The Works of William Shakespearre*, ed. R. G. White (12 vols., 1857–65), vol. IX, 1862
White²	*Mr. William Shakespeare's Comedies, Histories, Tragedies, and Poems*, ed. R. G. White, 1883 (Riverside)
Williams, 'Calchas'	G. W. Williams, 'The entrance of Calchas and the exit of Cressida', *Shakespeare Newsletter* 44 (1994), 5, 18
Williams, *Dictionary*	Gordon Williams, *A Dictionary of Sexual Language and Imagery in Shakespearean and Stuart Literature*, 3 vols., 1994
Williams, *Glossary*	Gordon Williams, *A Glossary of Shakespeare's Sexual Language*, 1997
Williams, 'Second issue'	Philip Williams, 'The "second issue" of Shakespeare's *Troilus and Cressida*, 1609', *Studies in Bibliography* 2 (1949), 25–33
Williams, '*Troilus*'	Philip Williams, 'Shakespeare's *Troilus and Cressida*: the relationship of quarto and folio', *Studies in Bibliography* 3 (1950), 131–43
Woodbridge	Linda Woodbridge, *Women and the English Renaissance*, 1986

Unless otherwise noted, quotations from the Bible are taken from the Geneva Bible (1560).

INTRODUCTION

Style and genre: heap of rubbish, salty comedy, or what?

Troilus and Cressida is set during the Trojan War and tells a story of passionate loss, but it is neither heroic nor romantic. Failure and human weakness are its subject, and its multi-voiced tone combines corrosive scepticism, witty satire, idealised lyricism, prophetic foreboding, chatty humour, philosophical speculation, and windy political rhetoric. It has always and steadfastly refused categorisation and, for centuries, neither the study nor the theatre knew what to do with it. In 1679, in an attempt to make the play palatable for Restoration audiences, John Dryden rewrote it, determined to eliminate the 'heap of Rubbish, under which many excellent thoughts lay wholly bury'd'.[1] Dryden's version sought to turn the play into a proper romantic tragedy, exonerating Cressida from the taint of betrayal and making Troilus into a more palatable tragic lover. In accordance with literary tradition, Shakespeare's Cressida betrays Troilus, but Dryden's, for complicated reasons related to her father's desire to return to Troy, only *pretends* to accept Diomedes as her suitor. Unfortunately, Troilus overhears, and is misled into murderous rage. At the climactic moment of challenge, Cressida declares her innocence, but is viciously slandered by Diomedes. Troilus, tormented by Diomedes' sexual boasts and haunted by the 'betrayal' he has witnessed, refuses to believe her. She then stabs herself as proof of her faith and dies happy in the knowledge that Troilus is now convinced. Troilus slays the villainous Diomedes and is in turn killed by Achilles in battle. Shakespeare's conclusion is much more open-ended: though Troilus and Diomedes meet on the battlefield, neither dies, and of course Cressida too lives on. What Shakespeare leaves inconclusive, Dryden gives conventional tragic shape.

In a move to add ethical weight to his masculine protagonists, Dryden builds the action around a heroic quarrel between Hector and Troilus, modelled partly on the quarrel in *Julius Caesar*, and partly on a similar scene in Euripides in which private 'affection' is opposed to 'publick safety' (Preface, p. 228). In the original, Shakespeare stages a debate between Hector and Troilus (2.2), but Hector ends up weakly capitulating to his brother, even though he has the stronger argument. By contrast, Dryden keeps Hector heroically firm while Troilus is led to realise that his personal desire had been intruding on his social responsibility. Dryden also conventionalises the cowardice of Thersites, who thus becomes mainly comic, and pumps up the lurid voyeurism of Pandarus, thereby coarsening what Shakespeare had taken pains to twist and darken.

---

[1] 'Preface to the Play' (Dryden, p. 226).

Figure 1. An unwilling Cressida is delivered to Diomedes and the Greeks, while Troilus looks on helplessly (4.4). This engraving by H. F. Gravelot, made from a drawing by Francis Hayman, is the frontispiece to Thomas Hanmer's imposing edition of 1744.

Despite his efforts, Dryden's version was only occasionally performed, and after 1734 the play sank into obscurity. It remained unstaged till 1898.[1]

While Dryden's play may look silly to us today, we would be wrong to patronise it; better, I think, to see it as a living response of a sensitive poet, playwright, and critic to a text whose virtues, for historical more than personal reasons, were simply not visible to him. The play seemed to him shapeless and haphazard – as it still does

[1] Dryden's version was revived on four occasions between 1679 and 1734, each time for a small number of performances (Variorum lists ten in all). The first modern production was in Germany in 1898, the first English version in 1907.

to many readers. Its characters lacked personal stature, its language was knotted, difficult, and unpalatable. There was too much digressive philosophising, not enough concentrated action, and no clear public theme. All this is what Dryden meant by 'rubbish'. And it is indeed true that the play is more explicitly philosophical than is usual for Shakespeare, full of debate and grandiloquent abstraction, much of which has little direct bearing on the action. But Dryden must also have sensed something valuable (those 'excellent thoughts') in Shakespeare's text or he would, presumably, have left it alone. While the original play explores the near-impossibility of construct-ing a rational system of values in a world where values have lost their purchase, Dryden builds from it a tragic conflict between personal desire and the public good, marking the pain involved in personal sacrifice but stressing the necessity of subordinating private to public: Troilus rages against Hector but then tearfully agrees to support the decision to exchange Cressida. From our current vantage point, Dryden's attempts at repair only make the original characters' failures to be heroic or glamorous, their self-deluding protestations of virtue, their pathetically trivial desires, stand out more prominently. But our own cultural predilections are at work in any such perceptions. One reason we may now find Dryden's revisions inadequate is that they obscure the play's potential to speak discomfitingly of the world that most of us inhabit.

Though our sensibilities have changed, the play's complexities can still pose some of the same problems that they did for the Restoration and the eighteenth century. The play remains both difficult and fascinating, confronting the reader, the actor, and the spectator with more obstacles and richer opportunities than almost any other Shake-speare text. Its language, while extraordinarily inventive and rich, is frequently obscure. The plot is inconclusive, trailing off without the kinds of resolution we are used to from most of Shakespeare's work. The characters are both unsympathetic and inconsistent – indeed their inconsistency often interferes with our ability to sympathise, as when Hector, after marshalling a compelling argument for returning Helen and ending the hostilities, abruptly changes his mind about continuing the war (2.2), or when he puts his cupidity ahead of his honour to chase after an anonymous soldier in fancy armour (5.6). These features, while they troubled Dryden and many succeeding commentators for centuries, have proved a source of the play's appeal to twentieth-century readers and producers attuned to the uncertainties, ironies, and open-endedness of modernist novels or absurdist drama. Significantly, they also seemed to appeal to at least some members of the *original* audience and readership, as the author of a prefatory epistle added to the first edition of the play (1609) attests: 'Amongst all [of Shakespeare's comedies] there is none more witty than this.' So here we have a case of a text whose sceptical satire and unusual shape is grounded in the historical period from which it arose, but which soon lost that grounding as tastes and sensibilities changed; only much later, as the twentieth century brought critical irony and generic experimentation into conjunction, did the elements of the play that attracted some early readers and theatregoers regain a footing.

Dryden's response alerts us to one of the play's most enduring puzzles – its pecu-liar shape, the trouble we have in identifying exactly what kind of thing it is. 'Now expectation, tickling skittish spirits', announces the Prologue, 'sets all on hazard.' He is talking about the warriors, but the phrase applies as well to the audience and our expectations, which are provocatively tickled throughout. The play tends to put us off balance, not least because we are uncertain whether it is best regarded as comedy, tragedy, or satire. It seems, to adopt Swinburne's term, a strange 'hybrid'.[1] Does it even have an identifiable main character or pair of characters? Troilus and Cressida themselves are but two of many candidates (in *Romeo and Juliet* and *Antony and Cleopatra*, there is no doubt who the protagonists are). Many critics have considered Hector the tragic hero, one of the two plots revolves around Achilles, Ulysses has the second longest role,[2] and, especially in modern productions, Pandarus and/or Thersites have frequently dominated the stage.

The problem of genre goes back to the earliest days of the play's existence. The quarto title page (1609) calls it a 'Historie' but the prefaced epistle to the reader ('A never writer to an ever reader: News') refers to it repeatedly as a comedy.[3] In the 1623 Folio, it is designated a 'Tragedie', and was originally designed to follow *Romeo and Juliet*, though in the end it was slotted in between the Histories and Tragedies sections. The reasons for this have to do with the printing history of the Folio, but the awkward placement coincidentally marks the play's generic instability.

The play keeps gesturing towards tragedy – for example, in the dilemma of Cressida, the pain of Troilus, and the death of Hector – but it never goes the whole way there. And, though it is often very funny, especially in the way it mocks and deflates both heroes and lovers, it is certainly not a comedy in the usual sense. Shakespeare's comic lovers always move towards marriage; by contrast, Troilus and Cressida never mention marriage and end by betraying each other. Any expectations of the kind we entertain at the outset of more typical comedies are here quickly knocked off course, nor are we ever allowed the empathy with the characters common, in different ways, to both comedy and tragedy. All of this suggests satire, though the word seems inadequate to describe the multiple effects the play can generate. As I have already indicated, the writer of the 1609 epistle clearly regarded the play as a comedy, and displays an admiration of the satiric tone and verbal by-play: 'So much and such savoured salt of wit is in his [Shakespeare's] comedies that they seem (for their height of pleasure) to be born in that sea that brought forth Venus. Amongst all there is none more witty than this.' The writer is less alert to the pathos of the narrative or the struggles of the characters, though he does observe that Shakespeare's comedies in general 'are so framed to the life that they serve for the most common commentaries of all the actions of our lives'.

---

[1] Swinburne called it 'this hybrid and hundred-faced and hydra-headed prodigy . . . [which] defies and derides all definitive comment' (*A Study of Shakespeare*, 1880, p. 200).

[2] According to the Spevack concordance, Troilus has 537 lines, Ulysses 488.

[3] The quarto exists in two 'states'; the epistle to the reader, along with a new title page, was added after some copies of what is now known as the 'first state' had been produced. See Textual Analysis, pp. 234–42, for a full discussion of the puzzles concerning both the quarto and the Folio texts.

In the modern theatre, savage satire has often been the modish choice, the bitter invective of Thersites dominating the director's vision. But this neglects the genuine hunger for meaning and significance that afflicts so many of the play's figures. In 3.3 for example, Achilles, who till then has seemed little more than an aging athlete worried about his reputation, is led by the wily Ulysses into a surprising discussion of the fleeting nature of honour, its reliance on 'reflection', and its susceptibility to time's ravages; in the scene just before this, Troilus and Cressida, meeting for the first time and about to tumble into the bed conveniently provided by Pandarus, seek to come to terms with the 'monstrosity of love' and the delusions that attend desire (3.2). In many other scenes characters display a similarly inquiring spirit: Hector and Troilus argue cogently about value (2.2), Agamemnon and Nestor confront the collapse of order and Ulysses spins out a lengthy prescription to remedy it (1.3), Troilus turns to an ethic of violence in response to loss (5.3, 5.11), and even Pandarus, rubbing his syphilitic wounds at the end, desperately seeks an explanation for his isolation. Most of the characters reach for, even if they never achieve, some sort of significance beyond themselves.

In 1833, Coleridge wrote that 'there is none of Shakespeare's plays harder to characterize'[1] and a few years later the German poet Heinrich Heine faced the generic difficulties head-on: '*Troilus and Cressida* is neither a comedy nor a tragedy in the usual sense; it belongs to no special kind of poetry, and still less can it be judged by any received standard: it is Shakespeare's most characteristic creation.' This is an extraordinary statement about a play usually regarded as distinctly *un*characteristic, but Heine was also fully alert to the play's dazzling uniqueness: 'We can acknowledge its great excellence only in general terms; for a detailed judgment we should need the help of that new aesthetics which has not yet been written.'[2]

Such an aesthetics began to be written in the twentieth century, and with it has emerged a finer appreciation of this paradoxically most distinct and most representative of Shakespeare's works. The structural and thematic fragmentation, the instability of character, the frequently bitter or ironic tone, the edgy incongruity of marrying romance to satire or heroism to bombast, the appeal to the grotesquely physical in the midst of high-flying idealism – such features of *Troilus and Cressida* have been recognised as congruent with the discontinuities of much twentieth-century literature and art. And indeed they have been recognised as features of Shakespeare's work more generally, and of the work of many of his contemporaries. What was for historical reasons difficult to discern during the eighteenth and nineteenth centuries has, in the wake of cataclysmic wars and modernist aesthetics, opened once more. And so the play has come into its own. Again Heine led the way; appreciative of the 'clamorous bitterness' and 'withering irony' of the play, he remarks that it presents us with 'Melpomene', the muse of tragedy, determined to 'act the clown . . . dancing the *cancan* at a ball of *grisettes*,

---

[1] *Coleridge's Criticism of Shakespeare*, ed. R. A. Foakes, 1989, p. 171.
[2] Heine in Variorum, p. 523.

with shameless laughter on her pallid lips, and with death in her heart'. The play now appeals to readers with a sceptical eye and to theatre producers with a bent for social criticism. It is still full of puzzles, but that fact has been recognised as a virtue rather than a defect – its difficulties are generative, its obstacles fruitful. In some circles at least, it has become Shakespeare's most admired, maybe even his most 'characteristic' play.

The play in its time

DATE

Although the play was only published in 1609, near the end of Shakespeare's career, it was almost certainly written several years earlier. In February 1603, it was entered in the Stationers' Register, the official minute-book of the Stationers' Company that oversaw publishing and copyright in early modern London. The entry, made for James Roberts, reads in part: 'The booke of Troilus and Cresseda as yt is acted by my lo: Chamb*er*lens Men'.[1] No author is mentioned, but there is general agreement among scholars that this entry refers to Shakespeare's play. Thus it had clearly been completed and, presumably, performed before February 1603: the entry suggests, though it doesn't explicitly assert, public performance by Shakespeare's company (which was still under the patronage of the Lord Chamberlain – it became the King's Men later that year).

Further evidence indicates a performance date in the late summer of 1601, and hence a date of completion sometime shortly before that. The armed Prologue, though he appears only in the Folio and not in the quarto, seems to be a satirical thrust at Ben Jonson's *Poetaster*, which was produced in the summer of 1601.[2] Jonson's play features a similarly attired 'Prologus' who drives off Envy and declares that a 'well-erected *confidence* / Can fright [the] pride' of lesser poets. The *Troilus* Prologue wittily remarks, with a jab at Jonson, that *he* 'comes not in *confidence* / Of author's pen or actor's voice'. Thus Shakespeare's Prologue must have been written after June or July 1601, though the text itself may have been completed somewhat earlier.[3] On 11 August 1602, a play on the life of Thomas Cromwell was entered in the Stationers' Register and printed soon after, its title page linking it with the Lord Chamberlain's Men. This play includes lines that allude to the killing of Hector by 'Mirmidons', a feature of the

---

[1] Publishers frequently made entries without any clear intention of publishing the book they entered, which seems to have been the case here. Roberts probably sold the right to print *Tro.* to George Eld, who published the 1609 quarto. See Blayney, pp. 416–17, Bevington[2], pp. 398–406, and the Textual Analysis, pp. 234–6, for discussions of the early publishing history of the play.

[2] In a book published just as I was completing this edition, James Bednarz argues for detailed relations between *Tro.* and the so-called 'war of the theatres'. He suggests that Shakespeare was attacking Jonson and Marston, and indeed the whole 'poets' war', through his portrayals of Ajax and Thersites and their fruitless quarrels.

[3] The fact that the Prologue only appears in the Folio does not, of course, mean that it was written much later than the rest of the play. It could, however, have been added at the last minute to take advantage of the current vogue for satirical topicality.

story seemingly original to *Troilus and Cressida*.[1] Moreover, a speech in Middleton's *Family of Love* (1602) appears to parody Ulysses' famous discourse on degree.[2] These allusions suggest at least one Globe performance (and probably more) of Shakespeare's play in 1601 or early 1602. A possible reference in *The Return from Parnassus*, Part 2, a play acted at Cambridge in 1601–2, supports this dating: 'O that *Ben Ionson* is a pestilent fellow, he brought vp *Horace* giuing the Poets a pill [an allusion to *Poetaster*], but our fellow *Shakespeare* hath giuen him a purge that made him beray his credit.' The 'purge' referred to is sometimes thought to be the portrayal of Ajax.[3] Overall, then, the weight of evidence suggests a date in the second half of 1601. Eight years later, styles had changed and the play had no doubt fallen out of the repertoire. Hence the quarto blurb-writer, afflicted perhaps by the tendency towards 'oblivion' that Ulysses depicts in his warnings to Achilles (3.3.145 ff.), could claim, incorrectly, that the play was 'new' and back up his claim with the statement that it had never been publicly acted.

FIRST PERFORMANCES

That anonymous critic who penned the 1609 epistle touts *Troilus and Cressida* as a superior example of Shakespeare's characteristic comic mode, hence implying its stage-worthiness, and declares that those 'grand censors' who castigate plays and playing, should 'flock to . . . this author's comedies'. But at the same time, he says flatly that the play 'was never staled with the stage, never clapper-clawed with the palms of the vulgar . . . nor sullied with the smoky breath of the multitude'. How we should interpret this latter claim is uncertain. As we have seen, the play was written several years before it was published in 1609. Had it never been performed? Or was it perhaps written for private performance, such as an entertainment at one of the Inns of Court – the London law schools known for their witty, abrasive, and satirical style? If it was staged, did it prove to be, in Hamlet's words, 'caviar to the general', unappreciated by the mass of theatregoers, the script left to languish in the cupboard where the actors left their out-of-date playbooks?

Many editors and critics have adopted the position that *Troilus and Cressida* was indeed written for private performance and never publicly staged.[4] The argument, first

---

[1] See John Velz, 'An early allusion to *Troilus and Cressida*', *Notes and Queries* 33 (1986), 358–60.

[2] See Kimbrough, p. 19 (though *Family of Love* was not registered till 1607, scholars have tentatively dated it in 1602 or 1603). In the play, Middleton's Dryfat argues that if the Family of Love is not suppressed, 'each man's copyhold will become freehold, specialities will turn to generalities, and so from unity to parity, from parity to plurality, and from plurality to universality'. Compare the declension to 'universal' wolfishness in 1.3.114–26.

[3] This view is bolstered by the fact that at the end of the year Jonson added an 'apologetical dialogue' to *Poetaster* in which he expressed regret that 'some better natures' (quite possibly an allusion to Shakespeare) had got involved in the satirical attacks and counter-attacks of the so-called 'war of the theatres'. Many critics nowadays are wary of such direct identifications, but some kind of link between the *Parnassus* allusion and *Tro.* seems plausible. Bednarz offers extensive, though often circumstantial, evidence for these and other identifications; see especially pp. 19–54, 273–5.

[4] See Alexander and Elton, and also Taylor ('Bibliography'), Nosworthy, and Honigmann ('Date and revision'); for a critique of this view, see Kimbrough, pp. 21–2, Textual Analysis, pp. 234–5, 242–5, and Jensen.

made by Peter Alexander and recently bolstered by W. R. Elton's detailed comparison of the play to the kinds of entertainment in vogue at the Inns of Court, depends partly on an assumption about Globe audiences – that they were insufficiently sophisticated to appreciate the kind of wit that the play offers. This squares exactly with the opinion of the epistle-writer, whose claim about the 'vulgar' never 'clapper-clawing' *Troilus* is of course the basis for the argument in the first place. Both early modern and modern critics, though for different reasons, are probably underestimating the Globe audience, which was after all capable of responding to the complexities of *Hamlet* or *King Lear*. And recent commentators may be relying too credulously on an epistle which is essentially a publisher's blurb aimed at selling a 'witty' comedy to a discriminating reader, just the sort of reader who harbours elitist feelings about the vulgar and who might have been present at, or heard rumours about, a private performance. Such a potential buyer would have been especially tantalised by a claim that the play was never publicly performed.

Furthermore, the epistle's claim is contradicted by the original title page of the same 1609 edition, which states: 'THE / Historie of Troylus / and Cresseida. / *As it was acted by the Kings Maiesties* / seruants at the Globe'. This, in concert with the Stationers' Register entry, appears to provide clear testimony that the play *was* performed by Shakespeare's company in their home theatre, the Globe.[1] However, nothing concerning this play is ever simple. The original title page was quickly revised (see figures 13 (p. 236) and 14 (p. 237)), the reference to public performance expunged, and the epistle to the reader added. So what exactly happened? Though we will never know for certain, it seems highly unlikely that Shakespeare, busy writing and acting in plays in the public theatre – where he made his living and where his plays were a crucial component of the success of the theatrical company of which he was a shareholder – would have taken a few months off to produce a play for a single occasion. Moreover, Pandarus, in his direct addresses to 'tongue-tied maidens' (3.2.188) and 'sisters of the hold-door trade' (5.11.49) among the spectators, seems to be speaking to a public theatre audience. Since the Inns of Court were all-male precincts, there would have been neither 'maidens'[2] nor 'sisters' in the audience; nor would the Epilogue's glances at prostitution within the confines of the south bank area controlled by the Bishop of Winchester, where the Globe was located, have carried as much weight if they were spoken on the north bank of the river, in a more respectable location. I think it is reasonable to conclude, therefore, that the play was produced at the Globe shortly after it was written.

None of this precludes a special performance of some kind at one of the Inns of Court (as indeed happened with *Twelfth Night* in 1602), nor does it mean that Shakespeare was unaffected by, or uninterested in, the vogue for satire around the turn of the seventeenth century. Satire was a mark of sophistication among the young men associated with the Inns of Court, whose ironic and irreverent wit expressed itself in

---

[1] See the Stationers' Register entry cited above (p. 6).
[2] While 'maidens' in Elizabethan English can refer to either sex, the context here suggests either only women or both sexes.

numerous poems and parodies, as well as in a whole raft of plays written for the boys'
theatre companies after 1600. Shakespeare was a friend of one of the most active and
vociferous of satirists, John Marston of the Middle Temple.[1] In his plays of this period,
in *Hamlet*, *Measure for Measure*, and especially in *Troilus and Cressida*, he adopts the
prevailing tone of satirical invective and outdoes the railers at their own game. He joins
in the deflation of heroic pretension common in the works of other playwrights and
satirists, and participates, though only marginally, in the game of allusions indulged
in by a group of young playwrights who hurled insults at each other, using the actors
as their weapons.[2] Not only his fraternising with Marston and other members of the
Inns of Court, but especially his quick ability to extend and transform the intellectual
and moral interests of his associates, no doubt contributed to the special qualities of
this play. We don't have to posit an exclusive Inns of Court performance to mark the
influence of Inns of Court culture.

AUDIENCES

One reason that commentators have inclined towards the idea that the play was written
for one of the Inns of Court is the odd attitude it adopts towards its audience. One
might best describe it as cheeky: 'And Cupid grant all tongue-tied maidens here / Bed,
chamber, pander, to provide this gear' (3.2.188–9). At times, the play goes farther,
deliberately courting rejection, challenging us, as the Prologue says, to 'Like, or find
fault, do as your pleasures are, / . . . 'tis but the chance of war' (Prologue 30). This
strategy of estrangement is decidedly different from Shakespeare's usual mode, which
is to ingratiate himself with his audience (in contrast with Marlowe or Jonson's more
pugnacious attitudes[3]). While he often adopts a tone of self-deprecation to effect a
partnership between actor and audience, Shakespeare ordinarily stresses the need for
co-operation. The Chorus in *Henry V* repeatedly asks the audience to 'piece out' the
actors' 'imperfections' with their 'thoughts'. His voice epitomises Shakespeare's usual
mode of genial apology: 'But pardon, gentles all, / The flat unraised spirits that hath
dar'd / On this unworthy scaffold to bring forth / So great an object' (*H5*, 1 Chorus
5–8).[4] Rosalind is similarly coy in her epilogue: she tells the audience she 'cannot
insinuate with you in the behalf of a good play' (*AYLI* Epilogue 8–9). Her playful tone
is matched in their different ways by Puck at the end of *A Midsummer Night's Dream*:
'Gentles, do not reprehend. / If you pardon, we will mend' (5.1.429–30), and Feste,
who sings us to the end of *Twelfth Night* with a promise: 'we'll strive to please you
every day' (5.1.408). The contrast between such endings and the last lines of Pandarus'

---

[1] Or so Shakespeare's most recent biographer contends: see Jones, *Life*, pp. 143–5.

[2] Among the main combatants were Dekker and Marston, whose *Satiromastix* appeared in early 1601 and
attacked Jonson, who responded with *Poetaster* soon afterwards. Bednarz contends that far from being
Marston's friend, Shakespeare satirised him in his portrayal of the scurrilous Thersites.

[3] As illustrated, for example, by the Prologues to *Tamburlaine* or *Volpone* or the Induction to *Bartholomew
Fair*.

[4] See Berger, pp. 122–5, for a comparison of the *H5* Chorus speeches and the *Tro.* Prologue, which he
describes as 'brusque, impersonal and indifferent' (p. 125).

epilogue could hardly be more pronounced:

> Till then I'll sweat and seek about for eases,
> And at that time bequeath you my diseases.

The tone is compatible with the kinds of grotesque physicality and cheerful disdain prominent among writers like Marston or Chapman, though its cheekiness distinguishes it from their sensationalism or the contempt one sometimes senses behind the satiric flourishes of Ben Jonson. But again, such a tone is not necessarily a mark of specific Inns of Court provenance, and was indeed a feature of both the public stage and the more exclusive up-market performances held at the so-called 'private' theatres where the boys' companies, in Hamlet's words, 'carr[ied] it away' (2.2.360).[1]

It is possible that the play's abrasiveness contributed to what seems to have been its failure to achieve much success with its original audiences. There are no records of actual performance and the blurb-writer's claim in 1609 would not have carried much weight if the play had still been in the repertory. At the same time, it is important to stress that the intellectual demands of the play, its refusal to pander to expectation, its ethical uncertainties, and its unsentimental portrayal of aggression and sexual desire are not in themselves reason to assume that a Globe audience would not have appreciated it. That audience was varied in its make-up, but like film audiences today, often sophisticated in its judgements. Still, what audience is likely to enjoy being addressed as bawds and pimps or being bequeathed diseases by a syphilitic old voyeur?

THE PLAY AND THE EARL

While Pandarus' epilogue, with its references to 'Winchester geese' and the like, has a topical flavour, the play has frequently attracted much more elaborate theories about its topicality. According to Ernst Honigmann, the reason why the play was never performed at the Globe was that during a preliminary run, perhaps at Cambridge, the players suddenly realised that their dazzling new play could easily be read as a commentary on recent and dangerous events concerning the famous Robert Devereux, second Earl of Essex, who was executed for treason on 25 February 1601. Once they saw the implications, they pulled the play from their repertoire.[2] The theory seems unlikely, since, given the Earl's fame and his already well-established association with Achilles, Shakespeare would almost certainly have recognised the connections earlier, if there were any. Still, the possibility remains of some link between the play and one of the most talked about events of the time.

---

[1] Hamlet refers to theatres like Blackfriars and Paul's, where the boys' companies performed in the early years of the seventeenth century; these were not really 'private' – they were simply less public than the large outdoor amphitheatres like the Globe, charging more for admission and thereby assuring a more status-conscious and elitist crowd.

[2] Honigmann, *Myriad-Minded*, pp. 116–17. He goes on to suggest that the players' self-censorship explains the apparent absence of the play from the public stage and the long delay in publication: the players, whom the epistle calls the 'grand possessors', were reluctant to allow the play into circulation for fear of reprisals. But as suggested above, the evidence for no public performance is unreliable, and there were often delays in publication. Half of Shakespeare's plays were never published in quarto form, and James Roberts, who 'entered' the play in 1603, probably never intended to publish it. See Blayney.

Those modern commentators who have sought to associate Essex's dashing career and tragic fall with *Troilus and Cressida* have mostly concentrated on the figure of Achilles. Essex's career, and especially his relationship with the Queen, had been tumultuous. Like Achilles in the play, he frequently sulked instead of taking decisive action, sometimes even feigning illness (cf. 2.3.68–77) because of imagined or real slights from the Queen; and, again like Achilles, he was repeatedly urged by his friends to emerge from his retreat. Despite his sullen withdrawal, the Queen made him Earl Marshal in 1597, but their relations remained volatile. In March 1599, he was sent to suppress the Irish rebels (his hoped-for triumph is alluded to in the Chorus to Act 5 of *Henry V*)[1] but in September, fame turned to infamy when the god-like hero returned in disgrace from Ireland; a little more than a year later, he staged an abortive coup against the Queen's closest advisors and indeed the monarch herself. Shakespeare's company was involved since they were commissioned to stage a production of *Richard II* on the eve of the rebellion (7 February 1601); since that play dramatises a successful attempt to dethrone a monarch, the production was presumably meant as an allegory of a victorious deposition. The players were exonerated, but Shakespeare's old patron, the Earl of Southampton, was imprisoned and Essex beheaded. The times were dangerous.

The association between Achilles and Essex, its negative as well as its more positive aspects, was well established by the time Shakespeare began *Troilus and Cressida*, going back, as Honigmann points out, at least to 1594.[2] In 1598, George Chapman published a translation of seven books of *The Iliad*, dedicated to '*THE MOST HONORED now living Instance of the Achilleian vertues eternized by divine HOMERE, the Earle of ESSEXE* '. In his epistle, Chapman praises the 'unmatched vertues' of Essex's 'royall humanitie' and urges him to persevere 'in godlike pursute of Eternitie', i.e. the kind of enduring fame that Homer gave to Achilles and that Chapman modestly hopes, in his translation, to secure for his patron (and no doubt himself). Since Shakespeare had praised Essex in the *Henry V* Chorus and since his treatment of Achilles is largely negative (he even ironically shifts Chapman's epithet 'god-like' to the ineffectual Agamemnon (1.3.31)), allegorisers have sometimes sought to link the portrayal of Achilles with the opposing faction, led by Sir Robert Cecil. But this leads to highly tenuous allegorical identifications, such as Cecil with Ulysses, and his father, the great Lord Burghley (who had died in 1598), with 'that stale old mouse-eaten dry cheese, Nestor' (5.4.8).

As Hillebrand remarks, 'in reading political allegory into the play one risks confusing fancy with scholarship'. Nevertheless, he adds, 'at certain moments in the play it is easy to be haunted by the memory of Essex'.[3] In a sharp-witted pursuit of that ghost, Eric Mallin links the play's political echoes to a contradiction in Elizabethan courtly culture

---

[1] In the Chorus' 'loving' but 'lower' likelihood, Essex is compared with the triumphant Henry, and envisioned as *perhaps* ('in good time he may') returning victorious from Ireland to be welcomed by shouting crowds. The slight ambivalence in the comparison is continued in 'Much more, and much more cause, / Did they this Harry.' See Gary Taylor, 'Introduction' to *H5* (Oxford Shakespeare), 1984, pp. 4–5, 7.

[2] *Myriad-Minded*, p. 115.

[3] Variorum, p. 380.

between a nostalgic ideal of aristocratic chivalry, constructed by and around figures like Essex and idealised in the memory of Sir Philip Sidney, and the naked self-interest and rapacity that this ideal sought to mask.[1] The Essex faction stood opposed to crafty politicians such as Cecil, whose careful manoeuvrings may be glanced at in the play when Ulysses reports Achilles' disdain for 'bed-work' and 'mapp'ry' (1.3.198–211); Cecil's mind was subtle though his deformed body, lacking the aristocratic graces and chivalric bearing associated with the largely illusory neo-feudal order of Essex, drew nothing but scorn. The aristocratic hauteur of the Essex faction was compounded by the sense that the 'old order' was slipping away (the Cecil family were regarded as upstarts) and the 'politicians' had gained the upper hand.[2] Add to this the humiliation of being ruled by a woman (an aging one at that!), and both the nostalgia and the fury surrounding Essex are understandable.

Why then did Shakespeare write a play that was bound to make spectators think of recent political events, all of which are portrayed in a harsh, unflattering light? Honigmann's argument that the connection between the play's events and recent politics was at first 'unappreciated' by Shakespeare and his company does address the basic uncertainty: either Shakespeare realised the possible allegorical connections or he did not. If he did not, which, as I said, strains credibility, then Honigmann's scenario offers a perceptive explanation. But it strikes me as more likely that the playwright knew what he was about, and that he was to some extent testing the relative autonomy of the players in the entertainment marketplace. Even the exoneration of the players for their ill-fated performance of *Richard II* can be read in that way. They indeed claimed that they were only doing business, offering a service for hire. If challenged over *Troilus and Cressida*, they could similarly respond that the play is patently *not* about Essex and any resemblance purely coincidental. They could, in other words, pursue their own interests, laying claim to a kind of incipient artistic autonomy. As Heather James persuasively argues, Shakespeare, in choosing as his subject the ancient and complex 'matter of Troy', was entering territory he knew to be politically fraught, an area open to a variety of unorthodox opinions. He may, then, have been 'test[ing] the political issues raised by the [Essex] rebellion', such as the liberty of the subject and even some limited freedom of speech, and offering, as James proposes, a 'critique' of the increased surveillance and restrictiveness felt in the wake of Essex's fall.[3]

Whether the play would be any different were it not for Essex is impossible to determine – its connection with him is entirely circumstantial. But there is no doubt that Shakespeare shows himself to be profoundly sceptical about the extravagant claims

[1] Mallin, pp. 36 ff., especially pp. 59–61. Though he goes farther into allegory than I would be willing to follow him, Mallin offers a penetrating analysis of the kinds of cultural conflict that Shakespeare was responding to, and commenting on, in *Tro.*

[2] For a description of Cecil, who was hunchbacked and a dwarf, see G. P. V. Akrigg, *Jacobean Pageant Or The Court of King James I*, 1962, pp. 104–7. Cecil was often mocked for his appearance which, however, did not interfere with his reputed success with ladies; according to one report, graffiti on his grave included the following: 'Here lies Robert Cicil / Compos'd of back and Pisle.'

[3] James, especially pp. 112–18; quotation, p. 116. See also Norbrook, who shows how the Homeric past was exploited in Renaissance debates about sovereignty and political legitimacy.

of chivalric honour, and critical of the destructiveness of aristocratic 'emulation' (the word, which combines ideas of imitation, envy, and rivalry, recurs frequently in the play). He is as well acutely aware of the debilitating power, and the attendant dangers, of what the politician Ulysses calls the 'providence that's in a watchful state' – the 'mystery' in the 'soul of state' with which 'relation / Durst never meddle' (3.3.197– 203). Ulysses uses theological language but his real subject is political surveillance, about which, he warns, one should not ever dare to speak. Responsive as always to contradictory currents in the contemporary world, Shakespeare reveals a deep suspicion of the idealist propaganda so often used as a cover for political manipulation.

Symmetrical structures

PLOT
Recent criticism and recent performance have tended to highlight discontinuity and fragmentation, generic ambiguity, deep-rooted scepticism, and tonal bitterness, but structural parallels abound and provide a balanced ground for the more conspicuous asymmetries.

The play is organised around a fundamental, and highly traditional, polarity – love and war. Almost its very first words announce the double theme in self-consciously balanced terms: 'Why', asks Troilus, 'should I war without the walls of Troy / That find such cruel battle here within?' (1.1.2–3). The Prologue, though it curiously omits any mention of Troilus and Cressida themselves, has already described how the war has been generated by 'wanton Paris' sleeping with the 'ravished Helen, Menelaus' queen' (9–10), so the collocation between love and war is wholly appropriate. As the language of both Troilus and the Prologue suggests, these opposites, like other polarities throughout the play, can easily collapse into deep and ironic relatedness. War and lechery, to use Thersites' phrase, are but two aspects of unholy desire.

There are two plots, one devoted primarily to war, the other to love, just as there are two distinct groups of characters, Greeks and Trojans, and two contrasting locales, the Greek tents and the more luxurious mansions of Troy. But these seeming contrasts dovetail with and mirror each other. The war plot concerns the dissension in the Greek camp, Hector's challenge, and the various manipulative efforts to lure Achilles back into battle. Love is not absent from this series of events, however, since Hector's challenge is based on the chivalric idea that the knight should prove the worth of his lady, and Achilles' refusal to fight is linked to his love for Trojan Polyxena. The second plot concerns the lovers of the title, whose desires must overcome the obstacles of distance, secrecy, bashfulness, and uncertainty, and whose one blissful night together occupies the very centre of the play. But of course the war intervenes – indeed it is built into the fabric of their relationship. What the Prologue calls the 'chance of war' leads them to fail each other in profound ways, and the early stages of their romance are treated with complex irony, but nevertheless Shakespeare is here ringing variations on a plot sequence that he had used many times before in both comedy and tragedy.

Each plot has its symmetries. The lovers are introduced to us in the two opening scenes which, in parallel, present first Troilus' unsatisfied love for Cressida and then

Cressida's more circumspect, but finally declared, love for Troilus. Troilus, teased along by Pandarus, complains about the difficulty of achieving Cressida, while Cressida, in scene 2, wittily parries the various offensive moves that Pandarus makes on Troilus' behalf. The later rivalry between Diomedes and Troilus, with the two of them appearing together in a series of tense and aggressive scenes (4.4.108–38, 5.2.4–105, 5.4.15–19, 5.6.6–11), reconfigures the parallelism: Diomedes' brutal courtship and no doubt equally brutal sexual manners are set in stark contrast to Troilus' rather delicate and nervous love-making. The war plot begins with Achilles' pride which is soon mimicked by that of Ajax, and the dissension in the ranks that sparks the debate about 'degree' in 1.3 is later mirrored by the deliberate scorn directed towards Achilles by his military inferiors, which in turn leads to the philosophical discussion of 'reflection' between Ulysses and Achilles in 3.3.

The Greek generals face a crisis of rule (Achilles' refusal to be governed) which they seek to resolve through the invocation of a crucial political virtue – the necessity for order and proper hierarchy, what Ulysses calls 'degree' (1.3.78–130). But abstract argument is not the province only of the Greeks. It invades the couches of Troy as well. The Greek debate is matched by the Trojan argument (in 2.2) about what constitutes value. Confronting a similar dilemma, the Trojans are deeply divided over whether to keep Helen or send her back in accordance with the ordered and hierarchical 'law / Of nature' (2.2.176–7). Even the lovers on their way to bed are prone to abstract reflection on their passion – they seem less comfortable gazing into each other's eyes than discussing the 'monstrosity in love' where 'the will is infinite and the execution confined . . . the desire is boundless and the act a slave to limit' (3.2.69–71).

The two plots intertwine, though they don't exactly culminate, on the battlefield. Troilus meets his rival, Diomedes, but the results are indecisive. Achilles kills Hector, thus paving the way for eventual Greek victory, but again ironic anti-climax rather than honourable closure characterises the action. Achilles, of course, has rebuffed all the Greek blandishments and refuses to fight. Hector, in parallel, will not listen to his counsellors, Andromache, Cassandra, and Priam, and refuses *not* to fight (5.3). Achilles finally goes to battle, but only because of rage at the death, at Hector's hands, of his beloved friend Patroclus. Confronting his great rival in what promises to be a climactic duel, Achilles quickly wearies (he is out of shape) and nothing happens. Achilles withdraws – but he returns with his Myrmidon goons and, in a spectacular scene vividly staged in most modern productions, murders the defenceless Hector. The battle, and the two plots, end with a mourning Troilus, enraged at both the death of Hector and the loss of Cressida, vowing revenge and hissing at Pandarus – who has appeared incongruously on the battlefield and whose self-pity and diseases bring the play to its inconclusive conclusion.

PARALLEL CHARACTERS
Helen and Cressida
Another way that Shakespeare gives shape to his play is through the many pairings of parallel characters. Helen and Cressida are a case in point: both are tokens of war; they each change sides, Helen the Greek is given to a Trojan, Cressida the Trojan is

traded to the Greeks. Each takes a new lover in her new environment, though exactly how willingly is not clear. Each is an object of desire, and, precisely because of her desirability, each becomes a 'theme of honour and renown' – an incentive to battle. Helen of course is far more worldly, and, in many productions, little else but a vamp. But she is more sensitive and weary than she may at first appear. Her sexuality is more overt than Cressida's – perhaps she is what the younger woman is frightened of becoming. The two are brought into painfully deft relation when, in the midst of his mission to fetch Cressida from Troy and Troilus, Diomedes comments bitterly to Paris that Helen is the occasion for 'a hell of pain and world of charge' (4.1.58).

Hector–Achilles–Ajax

Hector and Achilles are the leading warriors of their respective armies, but Hector's commitment to honour and his determination to fight, while at times foolhardy and vain, contrast with the cowardice and brutality of Achilles, who, when he cannot best his rival sets his Myrmidon dogs on him. Hector is also paired with Ajax, who is himself a surrogate for, and burlesque of, Achilles. Ajax is mostly a fool, but he manages to hold his own against his powerful cousin when the two meet in the 'friendly' jousting match in 4.5. And the fact that they are cousins, who embrace as such after their tournament, accentuates the likeness of the two sides. When Hector emphasises the impossibility of separating out the 'commixtion' of Greek and Trojan sinews or drops of blood in Ajax (4.5.124–35), we are made aware that making such a distinction is impossible not only in Ajax, but in the intermingled blood and desire that underpin the whole conflict, which is in many respects a civil war.

Troilus and Diomedes

Troilus of course is paired, mostly through contrast, with Diomedes. They are rivals for Cressida, though Diomedes is hardly a conventional lover. He is brutally exact, unyielding, harsh, cynical, where Troilus is naïve and even sweet, fuzzy around the edges, soft, manipulable, and romantic. In 4.4, Troilus meekly hands Cressida over to his rival with the promise that if he behaves chivalrously to her, Diomedes will be spared the wrath of Troilus' sword (for all his amorous lassitude Troilus is a powerful warrior). Diomedes pointedly ignores him and speaks directly, and with mocking courtesy, to the lady. To Troilus' ensuing bluster, he replies, with that combination of sarcastic politeness, arrogant bluntness, and precise intelligence that is his hallmark:

> O be not moved, Prince Troilus.
> Let me be privileged by my place and message
> To be a speaker free; when I am hence
> I'll answer to my lust. And know you, lord,
> I'll nothing do on charge: to her own worth
> She shall be prized, but that you say be't so,
> I speak it in my spirit and honour, no.
> (128–34)

Poor Troilus hardly knows how to respond and, though he turns back to Cressida, he seems already defeated.

There is, though, another side to Troilus: to Ulysses he is as 'Manly as Hector, but more dangerous', and, when aroused, 'more vindicative than jealous love', that is, a serious fighter as well as a man of honour – 'matchless firm of word' (4.5.97–107). Ulysses' description, coming late in the play, might seem to contradict much of what we've seen of Troilus, but its point is to offer us a different view, preliminary to the final act, when we see Troilus in action, rising towards, if not quite achieving, genuine heroism. He criticises Hector's 'vice of mercy' (5.3.37), and on the battlefield does 'Mad and fantastic execution' (5.5.38); though he at first loses his horse to Diomedes he later successfully takes him and Ajax on simultaneously. Diomedes may gloat over his victory in their initial skirmish, sending Troilus' horse to Cressida in a gesture of cynical chivalry (5.5.1–5), but their rivalry is left unfinished. Diomedes wins the sexual duel hands down, but in the field neither really outweighs the other.

Pandarus and Thersites

Of the various paired figures, perhaps the most striking are the two commentators, Trojan Pandarus and Greek Thersites. Each is a voyeur and a cynic, though Pandarus has a maudlin romantic streak as well, which keeps him from being as sharp-eyed and devastatingly reductive as his Greek counterpart. Pandarus has moments when he seems to really care about his young friends, while Thersites remains bitterly detached and critical throughout. This distance confers on Thersites a kind of spurious authority, so that he has often been taken, especially in modern productions, as the play's spokesman. He is not. As with Pandarus in his epilogue, his is one voice among many, contributing to, but not drowning out, the play's multi-vocal resonances.

Pandarus has a more active role in the plot. He figures prominently in the two opening scenes, but then disappears till Act 3, where he plays a crucial role in arranging and commenting on the lovers' tryst and, in Act 4, teasing them the morning after. As the news of the exchange arrives, he is left to lament their enforced separation. He is eager, fussy, and meddling, but he seems genuinely delighted by the amorous success of his charges, even if, at the same time, he is living vicariously through them. And while he seems to care more for Troilus than for Cressida, his own flesh and blood ('. . . would thou hadst ne'er been born!' he says to Cressida when he hears about the exchange, 'I knew thou wouldst be his death' – 4.2.83–4), his feelings and behaviour are in tune with the male-dominant values of his society. A garrulous gossip, he has trouble keeping a secret, but in the scene with Paris and Helen (3.1) he does his best to hold out, and he proves himself a good singer of bawdy songs. Not privy to what Troilus has witnessed in the Greek camp, he is no doubt confused by Troilus' vicious rejection in 5.3 and again at the end. His epilogue registers his and the play's descent from romantic hope to diseased dejection.

Pandarus and Thersites tend to dominate different parts of the play, the former looming large in Acts 1, 3, and 4, the latter commanding Acts 2 and 5 (the final act is the only one where both have a major voice, though that of Thersites is more clamorous). Thersites first appears at the beginning of 2.1, and his voice echoes through that act; he arrives immediately following the pompous deliberations of the Greek debate, debunking the 'botchy core' at the centre of their pretensions (2.1.5). He is wittily reductive and brilliantly intelligent, howling at stupidity but powerless to do anything about the folly he sees all around him. A splendid mimic, a master of insult, and a lover of disease, his method is either to burlesque, as he does when he imitates the absurd pride of Ajax in 3.3, or to reduce both desire and idealism to a mere itch: 'I would thou didst itch from head to foot and I had the scratching of thee: I would make thee the loathsomest scab in Greece' (2.1.22–4). His target at that moment is Ajax, but the line could be a motto for his attitude generally. In 2.2, Troilus and the Trojans speak grandly of Helen as a 'theme of honour and renown' (199) but a moment later Thersites reminds us that 'all the argument is a whore and a cuckold' (2.3.64).[1] The diseased or excrescent body is Thersites' ground zero, and animals, especially disagreeable ones, provide him with many of his most vivid comparisons: Agamemnon 'has not so much brain as earwax' and Menelaus is 'both ox and ass' while Thersites himself would rather be 'the louse of a lazar' than Menelaus (5.1.48–59). His outrageous invective is often hilarious, so the fact that he both makes us laugh and helps us see straight aligns our sensibilities with his. Like the clowns and fools in plays as diverse as *As You Like It*, *Twelfth Night*, and *King Lear*, his voice is a crucial corrective to the benign or cruel delusions of the main characters. His verbal inventiveness, corrosive scepticism, and special relationship with the audience have frequently given him pride of place – especially when a top actor such as Simon Russell Beale (in 1990) plays the part. Beale's Thersites was part 'dung-beetle voyeur' (Wardle, *Independent on Sunday*, 6 May), part failed idealist himself, a man who got a sexual charge out of watching the murder of Hector but who was saddened, even nonplussed, by the betrayal of Cressida.[2] He was given full command of the stage in Act 5, a stand-in for the audience even in places where the script has him offstage. This type of choice tends to unbalance the play, since as I've said and as Beale himself has insisted, Thersites is only one voice.[3] The multi-perspectival focus needs to be maintained. But Thersites' dominance in Act 5 – the coward of strong words taking the centre just when the stage resounds with the clang of action – is real and deliberate, as he circles through the camp and battlefield, delivering himself of the most inventive invective in all of Shakespeare. The play moves towards tragedy but, partly because of Thersites, never gets there. Hector is dead, but Thersites survives. And his voice, like that of Pandarus, who is given the last, mocking and irreverent, word, is never silenced.

---

[1] This telling phrase, which does not truly sum up the play, has nevertheless been seized on by a number of productions as a kind of motto, and given a prominent place in the programme (in 1976 at the RSC, for example, it was emblazoned in red on the cover).

[2] See Beale, p. 173.

[3] *Ibid.*, p. 162.

Figure 2. Simon Russell Beale as Thersites in Sam Mendes' RSC
production of 1990.

As Frank Kermode remarks, *Troilus and Cressida* 'will not yield a single ethical sense'.[1]
This is revealed not only through the parallelism between various characters, but in
the balanced way most of them are conceived as individuals. While their venality and
selfishness come under the searchlight, they are rescued by their yearning for something
better than they are able to achieve. Troilus and Cressida are trapped in themselves but
eager for self-transcendence, Ulysses is scheming and manipulative, but aware of the
need for broader political values, Achilles is part thug and part philosopher, Hector
is noble and heroic as well as self-deluding, Pandarus has a fussy, endearing warmth
to match his cynicism, Helen is indolent and vain but she and Paris share what may
be the only successful relationship in the play and she shows herself aware of the cost

[1] Kermode, p. 179.

as well as the pleasure of love. Even Ajax, mostly buffoon, has a gracious side, as he shows in 4.5 when he welcomes his noble cousin Hector to the camp. Thersites alone seems to be conceived in one vein only – his perceptions are bitter and frequently accurate, and his language is astonishingly resourceful, helping to shape our reactions to everything we witness. His very single-mindedness gives him power, which is why theatrical production and critical analysis have often yielded to the temptation to see the action in his way. But the play makes clear that there is more in circulation than 'wars and lechery'. There are wars, and there is lechery, plenty of both, but there is also love, courage, value. Abstractions like love and courage, honour and magnanimity, are easy to debunk, but they express a kind of need that the play very carefully marks. The warriors, philosophers, and lovers that inhabit the play's world struggle with that need and we have to respect them for it, even as we are deeply, inevitably, aware of how far they fall short.

LOOKING AND LOVING

In 4.5, two Trojan visitors arrive at the Greek camp. Cressida, a victim of the war and its exchanges, is kissed and fondled, and then dismissed, by the Greek generals; immediately after, Hector is greeted with chivalric pride and pomp, but in the embraces that follow the tournament with Ajax, there is more than a hint of aggressive, rivalrous, homoerotic attraction, parallel to, though gendered differently from, the precise erotic observation accorded Cressida. Ulysses claims to read Cressida like an open book: 'There's language in her eye' and she 'unclasp[s] the tables of [her] thoughts / To every ticklish reader' (55–61). Later, Achilles confronts a similarly legible Hector: 'Now Hector I have fed mine eyes on thee, / I have with exact view perused thee, Hector, / And quoted joint by joint', and Hector responds: 'O, like a book of sport thou'lt read me o'er . . . Why dost thou so oppress me with thine eye?' (231–3, 239–41). The parallels in the scene as a whole dramatise an interplay between what Eve Sedgwick has called 'homosocial' rivalry and 'mimetic' heterosexual desire, and the looking relations (i.e. the power differential between observer and observed) that characterise them. The central love story turns on a triangle of desire which leads to Troilus' need to encounter Diomedes in battle and wrest his love-token from him.[1]

These various issues are epitomised in 5.2, a richly and carefully structured scene of multiple observation; Shakespeare had used this strategy of layered observation and split perspective before, in *Love's Labour's Lost*, 4.3, for example, and in the Mousetrap scene in *Hamlet*, but never to such devastating effect. The scene is all about watching; in it, at the centre, Diomedes accosts the hesitant, half-willing Cressida, demanding sexual favour and impatient with what he regards as her teasing. They are watched by an increasingly distraught Troilus who himself is observed and cautioned by his Greek companion, Ulysses. At the edges of the scene hovers the ubiquitous Thersites, commenting sourly on the spectacle of betrayal and lust before him. And, of course, we the audience form the outer circle of this web of observation. The fracturing of point

---

[1] On homosociality, see Sedgwick, *passim*, on 'mimetic desire', Girard, pp. 196–201, and on looking relations in the play, Hodgdon.

Figure 3. Henry Fuseli's 1804 impression of the observation scene (5.2) makes the lust of Diomedes and the sexual availability of Cressida unmistakable, while a helpless and distraught Troilus hovers voyeuristically in the background.

of view becomes itself a theatrical metaphor for the breakdown of fidelity – Cressida's, of course, but Troilus' too, since he observes but never intervenes, even though he has promised Cressida that he will bribe the Grecian sentinels. Indeed, this free visit to the Greek camp (for the tournament) gives him a perfect opportunity which he never seeks to capitalise on. His interest, it seems, is stirred as much by rivalry with Diomedes as by love for Cressida. Why else, when the three are together onstage in 4.4 and again in 5.2, would the focus of Troilus' most intense energy be his rival, not his beloved? Inasmuch as this is the case, it connects to the strong sense of homoeroticism in the battle scenes, in the rivalry especially between Hector and Achilles, and in the relationship between Achilles and Patroclus, which seems, surprisingly, the most heartfelt and compassionate in the whole play.

The action throughout has been suffused with looking. 1.2 begins with a movement over the stage and Cressida's question 'Who were those went by?', implying that Queen Hecuba (who never otherwise appears in the play) and Helen may have passed in view of the audience. Even if they haven't, Cressida's question introduces the theme, and the stage action, of observation. Later in the same scene, in a sequence in many ways parallel to that in 5.2, Cressida and Pandarus stand aside, observing and commenting on the warriors returning from the field like spectators at a play.[1] 'What sneaking fellow comes yonder?' asks Cressida (192), knowing full well that it is Troilus, but trying to get a rise out of her uncle. Her question resonates with the later scene (5.2), where Troilus does indeed sneak, and where the looking relations are reversed; Troilus at that point has become the observer.[2] In 1.3, the theatrical aspect of observation, implied throughout, is made explicit when Ulysses describes to the assembled generals the mimetic antics of Patroclus, played for the voyeuristic amusement of Achilles; that sequence is in turn paralleled by Thersites' enactment of the absurd pride of Ajax before the same audience at the end of 3.3. The chivalric combat between Ajax and Hector in 4.5 is another obvious example of a spectacle performed for onstage observers, and most of the battle sequence in the final act is watched, and ridiculed, by Thersites. Even the most intimate moments in the play seem 'staged': Pandarus, the play's most genial voyeur, watches the love scene between Troilus and Cressida (3.2) and parts of both the 'morning after' and the departure scenes (4.2 and 4.4).

Hence the elaborate framing in 5.2 is part of a larger meta-theatrical pattern. The viewpoint is multiplied and broken up, but at the same time we are aware of the careful parallelism. The process is analogous to the rhetoric in the scene, and elsewhere in the play, engaging our sense of symmetry and architectural form, but at the same time leading us into ethical or metaphysical puzzlement. This doubleness comes to a climax in Troilus' great speech of bifurcation:

> If beauty have a soul this is not she,
> If souls guide vows, if vows be sanctimonies,
> If sanctimony be the gods' delight,
> If there be rule in unity itself,
> This is not she. O madness of discourse
> That cause sets up with and against itself –
> Bifold authority, where reason can revolt
> Without perdition, and loss assume all reason
> Without revolt! This is and is not Cressid.
>   (137–45)

---

[1] For a detailed analysis of the way several productions have positioned Cressida and frequently robbed her of the power of her observing eye in this scene, see Hodgdon.

[2] As Laura Mulvey and others have suggested, the observer typically has power over the observed, and that power often derives from or confers a sense of deeper subjectivity.

The rhetorical balance of the speech accompanies, indeed seems inseparable from, what Troilus himself recognises as the 'madness' of his thought processes.[1] He observes himself, aware of the split ('Bifold') authority of his thinking: his reason can rebel against the evidence of his senses without loss, and the very collapse of logical thought can assume the appearance of reason without apparent contradiction. His conclusion ('This is and is not Cressid') is irrational, but derives from a structured sequence of reasoning. The world has ceased to make sense, the 'rule in unity' whereby one thing can only be one, not two, is dissolved, and yet of course it hasn't – as Thersites is quick to remind us: 'Will 'a swagger himself out on's own eyes?' (135). Despite Troilus' insistence on fragmentation ('The fractions of her faith, orts of her love, / The fragments, scraps, the bits and greasy relics / Of her o'er-eaten faith' (157–59)), the stubborn wholeness of things remains.

This, of course, does not cancel out the metaphysical questioning. Rather, it sets it into dynamic relationship with a sense of pragmatic reality, just as the collapse into relativism of the Trojan debate about value in 2.2 and the attendant capitulation of Hector does not erase the desirability of clear ethical principles, and just as the discussion between Hector and Achilles in 3.3 concerning the rule that virtue be communicated and reflected does not preclude the actual existence of intrinsic virtue. In general, the play offers a dialectical viewpoint; its symmetries paradoxically support a sense that patterns cannot hold, while its courting of fragmentation and uncertainty nevertheless sustains a perception of value.

Interpreting the language

Troilus' speech, just quoted, with its unsettling combination of abstract speculation and greasy concreteness, exemplifies both the brilliant originality of the play's language and the interpretive difficulties it poses. Readers, actors, and audiences have to struggle a little to unlock its secrets. Whether because of unusual vocabulary, tortuous syntax, rarefied abstraction, or unusual, even perverse, metaphor, almost every line seems to demand careful attention. The difficulty arises partly out of the play's self-consciousness about the act of interpreting itself. Shakespeare, as it were, made a choice to confront his inherited narrative in a way that highlighted its status as a much-repeated story, a series of events that can be subjected to varied interpretation. In the course of the play, he frequently broaches the topic of interpretation either directly, as when Achilles and Ulysses discuss 'speculation' (3.3.109 ff.), or, as we have just seen, by dramatising recurrent acts of watching and judging. At the same time, he impedes his audience's ability to interpret by eliminating generic stability and by creating a language that sets obstacles in our way. He thus deprives us of important means of suiting meaning to expectation.

Shakespeare's way with language is endlessly inventive, but in this play he makes up words with more verve than usual, often in difficult contexts. In Agamemnon's initial

---

[1] See Commentary notes to these lines.

speech (1.3.1–30), for example, there are four neologisms and three other words that appear nowhere else in the canon.[1] There are five other words that turn up in only one other Shakespearean text. Three of the twelve unusual words in this one speech begin with the prefix un–, a characteristic of the language throughout the play, and one that has the cumulative effect of undermining and inverting positive statement.[2] The text also shows a penchant for invented adjectives ending in –ive and nouns in –ure: of the former we get not only 'tortive', 'protractive', and 'persistive' in Agamemnon's speech but also 'corresponsive' (Prologue 18), 'dumb-discoursive' (4.4.89), 'unrespective' (2.2.71), and 'unplausive' (3.3.43) – the latter two combining the un– prefix with the –ive suffix; examples of –ure words include 'insisture' (1.3.87), 'fixure' (1.3.101), 'soilure' (4.1.57, F only), 'rejoindure' (4.4.35), and 'embrasure' (4.4.36). Even 'exposure' (1.3.196) and 'rapture' (3.2.111) are used in new ways. Such vocabulary lends an abstract air to the language and frequently creates eddies in the smooth flow of our understanding. This seems a deliberate strategy of impediment, which, like generic uncertainty, character inconsistency, and epistemological scepticism, tends to throw the audience off balance.

If we move from single words to larger verbal units, we can observe a similar tendency to abstraction, often combined with a contrasting concreteness of imagery. Let us take a look at a few representative passages. Here is Nestor on Hector's challenge:

> Yet in the trial much opinion dwells,
> For here the Trojans taste our dear'st repute
> With their fin'st palate; and trust to me, Ulysses,
> Our imputation shall be oddly poised
> In this vile action.   (1.3.338–42)

He is discussing how Greek prowess will be judged, how the 'trial' will generate 'opinion'.[3] The initial metaphor, 'dwells', is misleading since Nestor implies the complete opposite – that opinion does not dwell anywhere; rather, it is constantly moving. He goes on to declare, using one of the play's most characteristic images, that their reputation will be 'taste[d]' with a 'fin[e] palate', and notes how their 'imputation' (the value conferred on them by others' judgements) will hang in the balance despite the relative insignificance of the 'action'. Some of the play's most crucial issues, circling around the concepts of reputation, opinion, reflection, and value, are at stake in this passage but the writer has not made clarity a priority. Indeed, the linkage to concrete images, which should make for clarity, actually obscures it: Nestor does not mean that the Trojans will savour Greek reputation, he means they will judge it on the basis of their own skill in combat; and while putting 'imputation' in a balance is moderately clear, the word 'oddly', which suggests lack of balance, undoes the meaning of 'poised'.

---

[1] Lancashire, p. 731; the invented words are: conflux, tortive, protractive, and persistive, the other three unique words are unbodied, abashed, and unmingled.

[2] There are at least twenty such unusual usages, including, besides 'unbodied', 'unread', and 'unmingled' in Agamemnon's first speech, 'unpractised' (1.1.12), 'untimbered' (1.3.43), 'unrespective' (2.2.71), 'unfamed' (2.2.159), 'untent' (2.3.152), 'unsecret' (3.2.106), 'unplausive' (3.3.43), and 'uncomprehensive' (3.3.199).

[3] On 'Opinion' and its connections to ideas of truth and judgements of value, see Kermode.

When Troilus finally reaches what he expects will be his haven of love, he too wades boldly into abstraction: 'This is the monstrosity in love, lady, that the will is infinite and the execution confined, that the desire is boundless and the act a slave to limit' (3.2.69–71). Here, as so often in the play (and this is a feature it shares with *Hamlet*), the urge to generalise hollows out the present moment. We might expect such abstraction when philosophical issues are being debated – degree, value, epistemological truth – but as love talk it has a peculiar ring. So too Cressida when she is considering the dangers of love: 'That she belov'd knows nought that knows not this: / Men prize the thing ungained more than it is . . . Achievement is command, ungained beseech' (1.2.248–53). She bypasses Troilus as an individual and what *he* might be like, considering him strictly as a particular instance of a general class – men. Later, when Achilles feels himself slighted or ignored, he imitates Agamemnon in the face of the Greek army's frustrating lack of success: he immediately generalises, avoiding his particular responsibility:

> for men, like butterflies,
> Show not their mealy wings but to the summer,
> And not a man for being simply man
> Hath any honour, but honour for those honours
> That are without him   (3.3.78–82)

Individual experience in the play leads inexorably to general propositions. Troilus' pain when he witnesses Cressida's betrayal becomes an indictment of all women, Thersites sees nothing but war and lechery, the lovers and Pandarus become symbols of their future literary roles (3.2.153–82), and specific characters obsessively generalise their personal situations. Ulysses does this more than anyone, with his elaborate philosophical justifications for strategic actions. He also displays a corresponding fondness for what we might paradoxically call the abstract metaphor: 'venerable Nestor, hatched in silver, / Should, with a bond of air strong as the axle-tree / On which heaven rides, knit all the Greekish ears / To his experienced tongue' (1.3.65–8). Modern style manuals, following the advice of writers like George Orwell, will tell you that a successful metaphor should conjure up a strong visual image; in Ulysses' formulation, Nestor's speech ('bond of air'), first compared with the axis of heaven and then depicted as somehow knitting his tongue to Greekish ears, refuses us that insight or pleasure.

When Ulysses describes Achilles' swollen pride, he opens up for us a way of understanding the play's marked tendency towards inflated language:

> Possessed he is with greatness
> And speaks not to himself but with a pride
> That quarrels at self-breath; imagined worth
> Holds in his blood such swoll'n and hot discourse
> That 'twixt his mental and his active parts
> Kingdomed Achilles in commotion rages
> And batters down himself.   (2.3.154–60)

What is both remarkable and characteristic about this speech is that it locates Achilles' opinion of his own value in his physical body. The passage concerns inflated self-conceit, and it registers such mental and bodily swelling as a disease of blood, breath, and, by extension, language. Frank Kermode, in tracing the history of the word 'opinion', its synonyms and uses in the play, notes that the 'imagination' of 'worth' has its roots in the sensory and he links this to the play's persistent language of tasting, seeing, and disease.[1] Renaissance rhetorical theory frequently deployed bodily images to distinguish between genuine copiousness and swollen, puffed-up grandiloquence – which was a mere 'simulacrum' of the real thing.[2] Achilles' pride, then, is a sort of false speech, a 'swollen discourse' derived from an inflated imagination of worth, and its consequence is physical self-destructiveness – the man's 'kingdom' is embroiled in civil war.[3] The process is essentially the same as that Ulysses describes during the Greek council where appetite, 'an universal wolf', at last eats up itself (1.3.120–4); in both cases inflation of value and self-opinion cause disease, though in this passage the emphasis on language links self-destruction to inflated rhetoric, a disease that afflicts almost every character in the play – ironically including Ulysses himself.[4]

Bloating, as Patricia Parker demonstrates, is a feature of the play's bodies as well as its language: Priam's 'waist most fathomless' (2.2.30), Achilles' 'great bulk' and 'portly size' (4.4.127, 4.5.162), Ajax's 'spacious and dilated parts' (2.3.233), even Helen's 'contaminated carrion weight' (4.1.72).[5] Indeed, there is a marked rhythm of inflation and deflation discernible not only in the language, but in the action (with its tendency towards anti-climax), and in the pervasive ascription of values (high and low pricing). The expectation that affects the 'skittish spirits' of both warriors and lovers (as well as the audience) is extended and dilated, but then deflated in an enervated exhalation. The epic promise of the Prologue is quickly reduced to the theatrical here and now,[6] just as the Homeric grandeur of the heroes is contracted to the *performance* of greatness by both the actors and the characters themselves. Thersites' catalogue of diseases in his curse on Patroclus is a paradigm of the whole process: 'the rotten diseases of the south, the guts-griping, ruptures, catarrhs, loads o'gravel in the back, lethargies, cold palsies, raw eyes, dirt-rotten livers, wheezing lungs, bladders full of imposthume, sciaticas, lime-kilns i'th'palm, incurable bone-ache, and the rivelled fee-simple of the tetter, take and take again such preposterous discoveries' (5.1.17–22). It is a brilliantly amplified example of rhetorical copiousness, but it pushes to extreme lengths the idea of the invaded and inflated body that underlies action, pride, and discourse. And it leads to immediate deflation: 'thou idle immaterial skein of sleave-silk, thou green sarcenet flap for a sore eye, thou tassel of a prodigal's purse . . . Ah, how the poor world is pestered with such waterflies, diminutives of nature' (28–31); 'gall' and 'finch egg' in the

---

[1] Kermode, especially pp. 172–5.

[2] Parker, pp. 220–1.

[3] Shakespeare is here putting his own spin on traditional images, not only linking language and the swollen body to rhetorical theory, but also employing the standard association between individual and commonwealth in a unique way; by contrast, he employs the image more conventionally in *JC* 2.1.67–9: '. . . the state of a man / Like to a little kingdom, suffers then / The nature of an insurrection'.

[4] See Parker, pp. 220–8.

[5] *Ibid.*, pp. 222–5.

[6] Berger, pp. 124–5.

next lines continue the reductive insults – everything is made tiny and insignificant.[1] The inflated language of heroes and heroines actually reduces them, making them smaller, more suited to the edgy, satirical portrayal of epic tradition that the play offers.

If the language is often inflated and the characters accordingly diminished, it and they can also be deeply thoughtful and inventive. Ulysses can be brilliant in his analysis of trouble and his suggestions for remedy. Even the thug Achilles is precise and acute in his philosophical speculation. Agamemnon, for all his prolixity, can spin an apt metaphor: 'checks and disasters / Grow in the veins of actions highest reared, / As knots, by the conflux of meeting sap, / Infects the sound pine and diverts his grain / Tortive and errant, from his course of growth' (1.3.5–9). The unusual words add a dimension to the tense ductility of the image, its precise evocation of natural courses, and its rich suggestion for the play as a whole of valued processes gone awry. So too, Troilus can be eloquent in both expectation ('Th'imaginary relish is so sweet / That it enchants my sense' (3.2.16–17)), and disappointment:

> Injurious time now with a robber's haste
> Crams his rich thiev'ry up he knows not how:
> As many farewells as be stars in heaven,
> With distinct breath and consigned kisses to them,
> He fumbles up into a loose adieu,
> And scants us with a single famished kiss
> Distasted with the salt of broken tears. (4.4.41–7)

Sensuous self-regard (expressed in the characteristic language of taste) melds paradoxically with an intense if also slightly superficial longing for transcendence.

In many ways the language of the play resembles that of the Sonnets.[2] The pervasive sense of self-division and intense scrutiny of personal motive characteristic of the 'I' of the Sonnets carries over into the play, as do the obsession with time and decay, with betrayal, with sexual disaffection. There is a similar ambivalence about aristocratic hauteur, a similar yearning for and cynicism about fidelity, a similar nostalgia for the loss of beauty and truth. None of the characters in the play achieves anything like the brilliant and bitter introspection that the sonnet-speaker masters – they are, rather, like the figures upon whom he bends his searching gaze. But the combination of a blissful rhetoric of sensuality and a salty rhetoric of disillusion *is* like the Sonnets,[3] as is the way the abstract is enmeshed in the concrete, the philosophical in the unsatisfied body. In both texts Shakespeare found a way to speak a profoundly dislocated doubleness that is at the same time strangely hopeful and fully grown-up.

[1] A softer, but still characteristic, example of the tendency to diminish is Paris' use of the diminutive form 'Nell' (3.1.45, 119) to address Helen of Troy.
[2] There is the further, perhaps coincidental, parallel that the Sonnets and *Tro.* were printed by the same publisher in the same year.
[3] Jones, in *Sonnets*, pp. 101–2, cites Rosalie Colie on this aspect of the Sonnets' language.

Cressida

As prescribed by the ancient narrative, Cressida betrays Troilus. This is the primary fact of her literary existence, the role she had always played since she was invented in the twelfth century by Benoît de Ste Maure.[1] Shakespeare, as was his habit, developed the story in his own way, though he stuck to the main points of it fairly closely. His treatment of Cressida, while she has a relatively small role and is only one of the play's six or seven major characters, has been the subject of much of the recent criticism of the play, and certainly no other single character has received the kind of attention that she has. There are at least two reasons for this. One is the rise of feminist criticism and the other is her enigmatic nature. Though George Bernard Shaw declared in 1884 that she was 'Shakespeare's first real woman', for many years after that she was typically dismissed as nothing but a wanton and flirt, her character supposedly epitomised by Ulysses' vindictive description of her in 4.5: 'her wanton spirits look out / At every joint and motive of her body' (56–7). His portrayal has resonated with critics and directors through most of the stage and critical history of the play, frequently being taken as Shakespeare's final word on the subject of his heroine, instead of a reflection of both the dramatic situation and Ulysses' character (just as the same character's famous speech on degree used to be taken out of context as a statement of Shakespeare's belief in hierarchical order). But feminist criticism of the play has been successful in rescuing her from such reductiveness – so successful that there is now a danger of erring on the other side and discharging her of any responsibility.

What, or who, is Cressida? Troilus himself certainly has no idea:

> Tell me Apollo, for thy Daphne's love,
> What Cressid is, what Pandar, and what we:
> Her bed is India, there she lies a pearl
> $\qquad$ (1.1.92–4)

He constructs a metaphor to describe her, a conventional one to be sure, but with a self-regarding edge: as Gayle Greene remarks, his 'too-precise naming of her "bed" as his goal . . . impugns his lofty idealism'.[2] She has a more realistic, but also more divided, sense of herself. It is difficult to catch her exactly, since Shakespeare has conferred on her a kind of opacity consistent with an only partially knowable subjectivity. As with Hamlet, we sense a mystery at the heart of her character, difficult if not impossible to pluck out. It emerges initially in her opening scene, first in her banter with Pandarus, where, not unlike some of Shakespeare's more obviously innocent heroines (such as Portia or Beatrice), she uses her bawdy wit to cover her true feelings, and then in her self-presenting soliloquy after Pandarus' departure:

---

[1] See the Appendix on sources; though her name goes back to Chryseis in *The Iliad*, the story of her love for and betrayal of Troilus seems to have originated with Benoît (who calls her Briseida, a name that derives from Briseis in *The Iliad*).

[2] Greene, p. 138.

But more in Troilus thousandfold I see
Than in the glass of Pandar's praise may be.
Yet hold I off. Women are angels, wooing:
Things won are done, joy's soul lies in the doing;
That she beloved knows nought that knows not this:
Men prize the thing ungained more than it is;
That she was never yet that ever knew
Love got so sweet as when desire did sue.
Therefore this maxim out of love I teach:
Achievement is command, ungained beseech.

(1.2.244–53)

For these sentiments, Cressida has been both castigated as manipulative and praised as properly cautious.[1] She recognises that in the world she inhabits, where women have little room to manoeuvre and where both her situation and her status render her vulnerable, she has to be careful. Like Prince Hal, she explains herself to the audience. But unlike him, she lacks the power to follow through on the strategy she outlines.

Her father, a traitor, has gone over to the enemy, leaving her under the guardianship of a seedy and untrustworthy uncle. She is being wooed by a prince when she herself is a commoner, the daughter of a priest. Whatever we may think of Polonius' warnings to Ophelia, there is clearly room for caution when a prince woos a woman beneath his station, and marriage is therefore unlikely (and Cressida is much lower on the social scale than Ophelia). In fact Troilus never mentions marriage; he seems not even to consider it a possibility – if he did, why would he not proclaim his intentions when the exchange is announced? Any power Cressida might have, therefore, resides in her ability to extend the wooing, to keep Troilus uncertain. That there is some ethical complexity in this is part of the point. At the same time, her attitude as expressed in the soliloquy is not an indication of previous sexual experience, as has sometimes been claimed; it isn't even especially radical advice. Playing hard to get is fairly conventional wisdom, so much so that three of the lines – 247, 249, 253 – are marked as gnomic quotations in Q, the last in F as well, where it is also, as in Q, italicised.

One difficulty the speech raises is, why does Cressida abandon her position? The next time we see her is on the night of the assignation, to which she has presumably agreed, though we hear nothing of that. And, facing Troilus for the first time, she is clearly torn. Again, this scene has been variously interpreted, but feminist critics have typically seized on Cressida's speech of self-division as definitive:

I have a kind of self resides with you,
But an unkind self that itself will leave
To be another's fool. I would be gone.
Where is my wit? I know not what I speak.[2]

(3.2.128–31)

---

[1] On the negative side stands, for one, Alice Walker, for whom Cressida 'is cheap stuff' and Troilus' 'infatuation' comic and absurd (pp. xii–xiii); feminist critics such as H. Adams, p. 77, Burns, pp. 110–11, Greene, p. 139, etc., see her hesitation much more positively.

[2] This speech is quoted in virtually all feminist readings of the play. For examples, see H. Adams, p. 80, Adelman, p. 48, Burns, p. 120, Greene, p. 140, and Tylee, p. 65.

She has just decided to take her leave, an idea that shocks Troilus, and this is her explanation. What does it mean? Consistent with her view in the soliloquy, she thinks that the part of her that she has given, is giving, to Troilus is 'unkind' (the word has the force of 'unnatural' as well as 'cruel'), because it is abandoning the other ('truer'?) part of her to be the mere plaything of 'another'. Her wit, which she has relied on before and will again, has temporarily deserted her. Like Hamlet, she has a kind of nostalgia for wholeness, but even more than he, she finds herself in a play-world pervaded by breakage and fragmentation. Love has divided her, but, despite her misgivings, there is no turning back.

There is another, contradictory way of interpreting her skittish behaviour: if Thersites were present, he would no doubt hiss, as he does in 5.2, 'Now she sharpens, well said, whetstone!' (74). She declares her love and then backtracks, casting some doubt on her sincerity; she even dangles before Troilus the interpretive possibility that she is leading him on: 'Perchance my lord I show more craft than love / And fell so roundly to a large confession / To angle for your thoughts' (3.2.133–5). Perhaps her wit has returned to help her avoid being pinned down. No doubt because she is in conflict, it is difficult to make out where she actually stands. The point is, precisely, her split, opaque self.

The same interpretive difficulty attends her behaviour with the Greek generals in 4.5. It is noteworthy that she says nothing in the early part of the sequence, being simply handed from one man to another. Only when she is addressed directly does she say anything, and that is to parry Menelaus' attempted kiss. She is more biting with Ulysses, telling him to 'beg then' (48), and, in Juliet Stevenson's performance, snapping her fingers and 'gesturing imperiously toward the ground'[1]. Her wit, which she felt had deserted her in 3.2, comes to her rescue here, but it is scant defence, and she bends towards Diomedes, perhaps for protection. Perhaps.

Her move to Diomedes is indeed the crux. Why does she do it? The answers have been various: (1) She is a mere wanton – but this flattens the character and ignores a mass of evidence to the contrary. (2) The literary tradition demands it. This is a complex issue, which I will deal with at length in the following section; it is certainly true that Shakespeare, though he often ignores what the literary tradition demanded (witness the dark, and wholly new, ending of *King Lear*),[2] here pointedly and self-consciously follows it. But he also excavates and adds layers to the inherited tradition. Cressida is more than a simple legacy. (3) She is in a terribly vulnerable situation and, given the evidence of her sexualised reception in the Greek camp, needs protection. While it is certainly true that she is vulnerable, for her to capitulate so quickly to Diomedes on that ground alone undermines her previous protestations of love and implies superficiality. Perhaps, it has been suggested, she is deeply frightened by Diomedes who exudes an aura of menace. (4) Troilus, with his callous and callow acceptance of the exchange after he has had his way with her, along with the suspicions about her fidelity that he cannot help but

---

[1] Rutter, p. 131.
[2] While in some earlier versions of the story, Cordelia later commits suicide, she always outlives her father. Shakespeare's version introduces her murder as well as the mortal pain of her bereaved father.

Figure 4. Cressida is closely surrounded by the Greek warriors, as Nestor takes her arm and prepares to kiss her, and Achilles in the foreground looks eager to 'take that winter' from her lips (4.5.23). This drawing, one of many done by John Gilbert for Howard Staunton's edition of Shakespeare (1858–60), may be compared to figure 10 , which shows a modern stage version of the same scene.

reiterate, provokes her to it. His initial response is devastatingly laconic and spineless: 'Is it so concluded?' is all he says (4.2.66). This interpretation, adopted by some recent productions, doesn't exactly exonerate her but it can deliver powerful dramatic results. When, at the end of Trevor Nunn's National Theatre production (1999), Cressida was left alone onstage as the gates and walls of the set banged shut around her, the awful sense of her being shut out, isolated in no man's land, derived directly from her sense of having been abandoned by Troilus. This had emerged especially strongly when his strident demands in 4.4 that she 'be true' drove her to sudden fury (a veil was lifted and she saw him as utterly different from how she had imagined him). The final and unscripted tableau made Troilus' failure and Cressida's solitude physically immediate.

But despite such strong theatrical moments, we may have to admit frankly that Cressida does indeed fail Troilus; yes, he fails her, perhaps even more glaringly. But this cannot excuse her entirely, cannot, that is, if we wish to grant her both autonomy and dignity as a fully represented person, instead of seeing her as a mere victim – of Troilus, of men, of patriarchy. She succumbs – to her weakness, her needs, her new situation; the point is that, like Macbeth, she succumbs, knowing full well that she shouldn't. This doesn't make her a whore, a casualty, or a beacon of feminist hope, it makes her a complex character with some tragic dimension:

> Troilus, farewell, one eye yet looks on thee,
> But with my heart the other eye doth see.
> Ah, poor our sex, this fault in us I find:
> The error of our eye directs our mind.
> (5.2.106–9)

This speech, recalling the earlier one quoted above, delineates her split self, now imaged as eyes (with a pun on 'I') looking in different directions. The image links to the theme, rhetoric, and action of looking, already discussed (see above, pp. 19–22). Anticipating Troilus' bifurcated vision ('This is and is not Cressid'), which results from his observation of her parallel sense of division, she briefly turns her gaze on herself and to some extent reclaims the agency she has lost by being a mere spectacle. But she evokes her agency only to deny it. Like Othello at his end, she seeks to evade responsibility for her choice, blaming it on the demands of her heart (but was her heart not engaged with Troilus?), and then trails off into misogynist cliché as a further explanation. What this seems to indicate is that she doesn't really know *why* she has done what she has done, but she recognises it as irrevocable, and can foresee, with startling clarity, the pain it will entail: speaking frankly to Diomedes, she says of the sleeve that Troilus had given her as a pledge, ''Twas one's that loved me better than you will. / But now you have it, take it' (89–90).

She makes one more, enigmatic, appearance, this time as a text. At the end of the following scene (5.3), Troilus tears up the letter she has written him, perhaps after her encounter with Diomedes. We are never told what the letter says, but her final appearance is one in which she is literally read, as she was metaphorically by the Greek generals, when Ulysses accused her of 'unclasp[ing] the tables of [her] thoughts / To every ticklish reader' (4.5.60–1). Both readings, like all such in the play, are limited: she remains both constantly read, and unreadable. Her inscribed, hidden, and inconsistent self provides her with theatrical weight and a pained, intimate personhood. She is unfaithful, and in being so, she both exemplifies the crisis of fidelity that the play constantly exposes and establishes herself as something of a tragic figure. But the play being the sort of mixed thing it is, hers is not the only story, nor is it even the dominant one. Her tragedy then is muted, partial. It remains a motif, set into a wider design that dramatises a range of infidelities and breakage, a kind of gesture towards tragedy rather than the thing itself. In being so, it is aligned with a feature of the play already alluded to, but to which I now want to turn more directly – its literary self-consciousness and the relation between that and its concern with fractured identities.

Literary identity

Cressida, of course, is not the only character in the play with a literary past. All the main characters are so burdened. Achilles and Hector, the mighty antagonists of Homer's *Iliad*; Ulysses, crafty hero of *The Odyssey*; Agamemnon, leader of men; Menelaus, the world's most famous cuckold; Helen, the unfaithful, or ravished, wife whose face, in Marlowe's unforgettable words, 'launched a thousand ships'; Nestor, fount of geriatric wisdom; Cassandra, doomed prophetess – all of these derive from ancient sources and were well known to Shakespeare's contemporaries. Troilus and Pandarus too, while of more recent lineage,[1] were famously identified with their roles: the word 'pander' had entered the language by the sixteenth century and Shakespeare makes fun of Troilus' well-known fidelity by giving his name to Petruchio's spaniel, that most fawningly faithful of dogs (*Shr.* 4.1.150). Of the major figures in the play, only Thersites may seem relatively free of his past – perhaps that is why he is suddenly revealed as a bastard in Act 5 – but even his biting ferocity derives ultimately from *The Iliad*: 'A man of tongue whose ravenlike voice a tuneles jarring kept . . . The filthiest Greeke that came to Troy, he had a goggle eye; / Starcke-lame he was of eyther foote . . .'[2] And he was frequently cited in rhetorical handbooks as an emblem of detraction.[3]

While Shakespeare typically reworked familiar material, as in the history plays he produced during the previous decade, in this play he obtrudes the mythic past self-consciously into the action and characterisation. This has first of all a satiric effect, though the debunking of heroism and idealistic love which he indulges is not his own invention. It was already established as common practice, part of a dualistic way of reconstructing the literary past in the period. While the Trojans had traditionally been seen as ancestors of the British (Brut, one of Aeneas' descendants, was the legendary founder of Great Britain), this myth did not prevent them from being the target of criticism and satiric attack.[4] What Shakespeare uniquely does, however, is to make his characters' literariness, their belatedness, part of the subject matter of his play. It is as if the characters were aware of their literary past, and mired in it. They are in a sense victims of their future fame. The most painful, and contrived, example of this occurs ironically just at the moment of sexual truth, when Troilus and Cressida are preparing to go off to consummate their relationship:

---

[1] For a full account of their origins see the Appendix on sources; Chaucer, of course, though not the main source for the play as a whole, is the most important precursor for the love story, giving Shakespeare many of the essentials of the love plot, and ideas of character for the three principals. See Donaldson.

[2] Chapman, *Seven Books*, pp. 531–2; also Bullough, p. 120.

[3] Kimbrough, pp. 38–9, makes clear that Thersites had a citational existence independent of Homer as a 'walking, talking figure of speech'.

[4] George Peele's 'Tale of Troy' (1589) for example, even though generally sympathetic to the Trojans, castigates them for 'ryot, rape, and vaine credulitie' (Peele, line 410).

TROILUS   True swains in love shall in the world to come
               Approve their truth by Troilus: when their rhymes,
               Full of protest, of oath and big compare,
               Want similes, truth tired with iteration –
               . . .
               Yet after all comparisons of truth,
               As truth's authentic author to be cited,
               'As true as Troilus' shall crown up the verse
               And sanctify the numbers.
CRESSIDA   Prophet may you be!
               If I be false or swerve a hair from truth,
               When time is old and hath forgot itself
               . . .
                      let memory
               From false to false among false maids in love
               Upbraid my falsehood
               . . .
               Yea, let them say to stick the heart of falsehood,
               'As false as Cressid'.

PANDARUS Go to, a bargain made . . . let all constant men be Troiluses, all false women Cressids,
      and all brokers-between panders.   (3.2.153–82)

This curious exchange, which Heather James calls 'trope-plighting', gestures forward to the 'notorious', emblematic identity that each of these characters will eventually come to inhabit, and marks a problem for both the characters and the writer.[1] The characters are constrained by the literary identities that have been conferred upon them by tradition; this is most evident in the treatment of Cressida in the passage, since her falseness has not been an issue in anything that leads up to this moment. As Linda Charnes puts it, Cressida's awareness of her own textual future 'casts every present moment as a past moment'.[2] In order to emphasise the pre-established pattern, Shakespeare has to put in a conditional ('If I be false . . .'), and wrench the whole scene off its psychologically realistic moorings. The effect of this for the writer is to emphasise *his* belatedness, the fact that he has, simply, come after. The play thematises its own distrustful reproduction of the sources it relies on, and, in Barbara Bowen's formulation, harbours 'the suspicion that the present is a diminished and distorted version of the past'.[3] Immediately following the departure of the lovers, Pandarus, who has enjoined them to 'press [their bed] to death' turns to the audience and breaks the frame of the fiction: 'And Cupid grant all tongue-tied maidens here / Bed, chamber,

---

[1] James, p. 106. Linda Charnes uses the term 'notorious identity' to describe the dilemma of the characters caught in the web of literary citation; in a strong and influential reading, she opposes such fixed identity to the struggle for subjectivity that the characters also evince, as they try to escape the web in which they are enmeshed. In doing so, she builds on the brilliant essay by Elizabeth Freund. This same issue has also been perceptively treated by Barbara Bowen and by James, who refers to the characters' 'scandalous reproducibility' (p. 97).

[2] Charnes, p. 79.

[3] Bowen, p. 143.

pander, to provide this gear' (188–9). This is a most unusual moment. The actor himself becomes a kind of pander, offering all kinds of 'gear' to the spectator. Rarely in Shakespeare does a character involved in the middle of the action drop his fictional identity to address the audience directly as actor speaking to spectators.[1] The device is common enough in epilogues, prologues, and the like, while speakers of soliloquies and asides routinely address the audience directly – but they typically speak as characters. Meta-theatrical allusions are of course sprinkled liberally throughout the canon, but this moment is subtly different. It frames and distances the fiction, reminding the audience of their presence and their role, and in so doing, it highlights the problem of literary identity by linking it to theatrically constructed personhood more generally. It is as if the fictionality of the characters is doubled – not only are they in a play, but even within their play-reality they are ciphers, signs of a literary tradition.

A kind of theatrical recursiveness is in play at such moments. Another example occurs earlier, when Ulysses describes Achilles, applauding from his 'pressed bed' (1.3.163 – a phrase that links his description to Pandarus' admonitions to Troilus and Cressida),[2] the theatrical antics of Patroclus mimicking the serious business of the august generals. The passage is complexly layered. Patroclus acts the part of the 'strutting player whose conceit / Lies in his hamstring' (154–5), putting on both the 'topless deputation' (153) of Agamemnon and Nestor's 'faint defects of age' (173) much to the amusement of the lolling Achilles. But all we get is Ulysses' report, not the thing itself (which in any case would only be acting), so that Patroclus' parodic representation of the Greek generals is at two removes. Ulysses decries such 'imitation' (151) but at the same time indulges in it, through his verbal account and in offering his own impersonation of Patroclus by, in some productions at least, adding a little actorly 'strutting'. His is an imitation of an imitation, acted out in front of the generals of whom it is supposed to be a (faulty) representation. Patroclus is a coarse actor, but can theatrical representation ever measure up? We are left with the suspicion that imitation is all that is available to these heroes – they are but 'poor players', shadows of their former selves.

This kind of dilemma is a familiar one for the post-modern world, and is one of the sources of the play's present appeal. While the characters would like to be, in Troilus' phrase, 'authentic authors' of themselves, their implicit sense of their literary entrapment precludes such autonomy. The post-modern self, we are often told, is similarly burdened by a sense of delusory autonomy and actual entrapment. When Troilus declares 'But, alas, / I am as true as truth's simplicity' (3.2.149–51), he may believe, or hope, that he is stating a truth about himself, but he is actually citing himself as a sign, as he does again on the brink of Cressida's departure: 'Alas it is my vice, my fault . . . I with great truth catch mere simplicity' (4.4.101–3). On a psychological level, to be an 'authentic author' of his truth, as Troilus believes he is, would be to be a free

---

[1] One parallel is Petruchio's comment at the end of his soliloquy on taming Kate: 'He that knows better how to tame a shrew, / Now let him speak' (*Shr.* 4.1.210–11). Even more than Petruchio, Pandarus here seems briefly to become the actor speaking through the character but at the same time independently – like Prospero in his epilogue to *Temp.*

[2] Bowen, pp. 134–5.

agent, writing his own destiny, but in declaring himself to be a figure of citation, he is haunted by a sense of being unfree.

For all the tenuousness and fragility of the characters' citational identity, there is another side to the play's representation of personhood. Elizabeth Freund underlines the 'powerful sense of [Cressida's] sincere scruples' – i.e. her authenticity as a person – accompanying the 'rhetoric of citation' that renders her helpless. Linda Charnes suggests that the characters' 'secret' (and fleeting) subjectivity is actually produced by the deconstructive strategies of the play.[1] Both critics seem to be trying to account for the powerful sense of personhood that accompanies the characters' rhetorical constructedness. The theatrical presence of the characters offsets their rhetorical, spectral unreality. The actor, as in any play, gives flesh to the role; but here the emphasis on the literary and belated lends special significance to the actorly. In one way, the characters remain at a distance, part of a set of inherited narratives. But even while the actors are impersonating these absent figures, we feel their present, immediate reality as persons. This engages the participation of the audience in a special way. Our sense of the characters' belatedness contributes to a heightened awareness of 'personation' – the process by which dramatic characters are constructed and at the same time given authentic life – but this is combined with the pleasure of theatrical identification.[2] In this manner, the dilemmas of literary identity are set in dialectical tension with the pleasure of theatrical presence. The strongest example of this in the play is once again the great scene in which Troilus witnesses Cressida's betrayal. The characters are acting out their mythic roles and the whole episode could hardly be more elaborately framed, more meta-theatrical; but Troilus' pained fascination and his sense of personal and cosmic chaos, along with Cressida's deep sense of self-division, are powerfully present.

Scepticism and speculation

KNOWING BY (PARTIAL) REFLECTION

How does personal identity relate to being seen and judged? Is there such a thing as intrinsic virtue, or is virtue simply an effect of external assessment, and hence subject to public whim? Such questions lie behind the action (as they do behind that of *Coriolanus*), and become explicit topics for philosophical investigation when, as part of his strategy of manipulation, Ulysses tries to teach Achilles a lesson in 'reflection'. His approach to the problem is characteristically wily and displays his talent for what I earlier called 'abstract metaphor':

> A strange fellow here
> Writes me that man, how dearly ever parted,
> How much in having, or without or in,

---

[1] Freund, p. 23, and Charnes, pp. 91–102.
[2] I have discussed this process fully in relation to 'participation' in the first chapter of Dawson and Yachnin, especially pp. 22–9.

> Cannot make boast to have that which he hath,
> Nor feels not what he owes, but by reflection –
> As when his virtues, aiming upon others
> Heat them, and they retort that heat again
> To the first givers.   (3.3.98–102)

Ulysses suggests that the actual 'parts' of people exist only insofar as they are reflected by knowers. The word 'parted' adds to the problem, since, while in this passage its dominant meaning is 'endowed with virtues' or 'parts', the term echoes the play's insistent language of fragments and separation, and evokes as well the walking shadows of theatrical parts and their tendency to dissolve presence in representation.[1] Heroes can only *act out* their 'parts', but in doing so are in danger of reducing those parts (virtues) to mere performance; this makes them subject to the kind of caricature typified by Patroclus' mocking imitations of the Greek generals (1.3.150–85). But Ulysses' scepticism exists in tension with a notion of intrinsic value; his phrasing suggests that the existence of someone's 'parts' is indeed actual, however inaccessible they might be in themselves. Ulysses doesn't say that his hypothetical man has no 'parts' but rather that, without 'reflection', he cannot experience, nor even claim to have, what he actually has.[2] This is a germane paradox in the play, one accentuated by its being deployed at this moment as a manipulative strategy (Ulysses is playing a part). As when Troilus rejects Hector's measured idealist argument for surrendering Helen with the sceptical, 'What's aught but as 'tis valued?' (2.2.52), Ulysses' tactics expose the political interest involved not only in constructions of value themselves, but even in the sceptical philosophical basis of those judgements. But, while the play stresses the difficulty of judgement and the uncertainty of knowledge, and recognises the ways in which political desire can colour all philosophical position-taking, it does not empty out knowledge, honour, or virtue as categories.

In modern productions, Achilles is often played as a leather-clad thug, so that the earnest philosophising he engages in here seems weirdly jarring and out of place. But it is an important part of who he is. He responds:

> This is not strange, Ulysses:
> The beauty that is borne here in the face
> The bearer knows not, but commends itself
> To others' eyes; nor doth the eye itself,
> That most pure spirit of sense, behold itself,
> Not going from itself, but eye to eye opposed,
> Salutes each other with each other's form,
> For speculation turns not to itself
> Till it hath travelled and is mirrored there
> Where it may see itself. This is not strange at all.
>   (3.3.102–11)

---

[1] See Bowen, pp. 107–8.
[2] Many commentators have taken Ulysses' words as an indication of total scepticism, but as Ellis-Fermor (pp. 66–7) pointed out long ago, that is not precisely the position he is taking.

And yet it is rather strange – strange at least to have Homeric heroes carrying on
such a debate in the middle of an already densely written play. But the discussion is
also deeply characteristic. It fits with the speculative tendency towards generalisation
and abstraction that we noted in the language, it anchors the stress on seeing and
watching in both language and action, and it reminds the audience of the creative and
frustratingly disabling aspects of seeing – our gaze may fashion the onstage persons but
we cannot see ourselves.[1] Despite their abstract quality, then, these reflections reflect
directly on the action of the play, where the heroic gestures of the warriors are being
subjected to parodic scrutiny. The discussion follows fast on Achilles' sudden loss of
reputation, which has been engineered by Ulysses and consciously acted out by his
fellow warriors. It is as though the play itself is pausing to take account of what it is
engaged in dramatising. If the characters are struggling with the burden of being heroes,
they need to think about reputation – which is, after all, the basis for their being in the
story. If their very presence depends on how they are regarded, by each other and by the
audience, Achilles' speculation is but an extension of his particular circumstances into
the realm of abstract thought. He reminds us that his storied existence is dependent
on stage representations – he is a person created by author and audience.

In his response, Ulysses quickly tries to turn the argument to his own strategic
advantage:

> I do not strain at the position –
> It is familiar – but at the author's drift,
> Who in his circumstance expressly proves
> That no man is the lord of anything,
> Though in and of him there be much consisting,
> Till he communicate his parts to others;
> Nor doth he of himself know them for aught
> Till he behold them formed in the applause
> Where they're extended, who, like an arch, reverb'rate
> The voice again, or like a gate of steel
> Fronting the sun, receives and renders back
> His figure and his heat.   (112–23)

The first part of the speech repeats what he has said before; the second half turns
to the crucial problem of self-knowledge: the only way one *knows* one's 'parts' is by
seeing them *formed* by the applause of others. The similes he then adduces, as Bowen
remarks, are odd.[2] Both the arch and the gate of steel render back attenuated versions of
what they reflect; arches are certainly not exact echo-sounders and steel is imperfectly
reflective as a source of either heat or light. Of course reflection is always only a replica,
not the thing itself, but these particular similes stress the inadequacy of representation
(the replica inevitably fails the original) even as the passage as a whole suggests that

---

[1] The debate may seem to mirror the kind of thing indulged in by the young men of the Inns of Court
(Elton, p. 70, regards the discussion as 'commonplace', full of 'expatiated clichés'), but Bowen, pp. 101–6,
shows convincingly that Shakespeare is defamiliarising a traditional idea for radical purposes.
[2] Bowen, pp. 108–9.

representation is the only pathway to knowledge. This squares with Achilles' remarks about how the eye (punning on the 'I') inevitably fails to see itself. And yet, as distinct from the debilitating relativism of post-modernism, the implication is not that there is no such thing as truth, but rather that, though truth is perspectival, it is no less real for it. The play in this sense remains early modern, despite the way it touches on matters that have become more visible to us with the development of post-modern theories such as deconstruction.

The whole passage is a meditation on Renaissance scepticism, and no doubt owes something to Montaigne, who was familiar to Shakespeare even before Florio's translation of 1603.[1] Montaigne stresses the relativism of knowing, but frequently reverts to standards of both truth and value that seem incompatible with full-scale classical scepticism. Ulysses certainly implies that virtues and values can be inherent – the difficulty is one of knowing. The play never surrenders the human need for some kind of value – its scepticism is, in Graham Bradshaw's words, 'radical' but not 'terminal';[2] it does not adopt the easy relativist position of reducing value and truth to mere words. That kind of reductiveness, while it has been embraced by a number of recent critics, is not what the play's questioning of value is about.

VALUING

Troilus' famous question, already quoted, 'What's aught but as 'tis valued?', is really a statement of strategic relativism, propounding a sceptical attitude in the realm of ethics analogous to the epistemological scepticism just discussed. Troilus is essentially saying that value, like knowledge and 'truth' and even selfhood, is a matter of 'reflection' and spectatorship.[3] The subject is Helen, whose 'value' has little to do with her intrinsic merit as a person, and everything to do with how she is regarded by Greeks and Trojans. Is she worth continuing to fight for? That is the issue being debated, and Hector claims that 'she is not worth what she doth cost / The keeping' (2.2.51–2); Troilus' position is that her value depends on how her worth is construed by others. Greeks and Trojans *make* her worthy by fighting for her, by turning her into a 'theme of honour and renown' (199). If, Troilus argues, we stop fighting for her, we not only reduce her 'price', we also impugn our own honour for having fought on her behalf in the first place. Like Cressida, Helen is 'a pearl' with a high exchange value: her 'price' says Troilus recalling Marlowe, but giving the transaction an explicitly economic turn, 'hath launched above a thousand ships' (82).

Troilus' relativism wins the day, but Hector has the better argument. He tries to lift the debate out of the marketplace frame that surrounds all acts of evaluation in the play:[4]

---

[1] See Bradshaw, pp. 38–9, 154–6. Shakespeare may, of course, have read the text in French or have seen Florio's translation in manuscript, but, as Bradshaw points out, this kind of sceptical outlook is habitual with Shakespeare and noticeable in his work before there is clear evidence of his having read Montaigne.

[2] Bradshaw, p. 154.

[3] 'Imputation' is another word for getting at the same set of ideas; see 1.3.341 and n.; see also Kermode on 'opinion'.

[4] Lars Engle suggests the prevalence of the language and strategies of the marketplace and demonstrates the centrality of the act of exchange.

But value dwells not in particular will;
It holds his estimate and dignity
As well wherein 'tis precious of itself
As in the prizer. 'Tis mad idolatry
To make the service greater than the god,
And the will dotes that is inclineable
To what infectiously itself affects,
Without some image of th'affected merit.
                            (53–60)

His point is that the value of something does not derive solely from its value to the 'prizer', but, at least to some extent, is to be found in the thing itself. A will that chooses only on the basis of blind desire, 'without some image' of the merit of what is desired, is said to 'dote', i.e. to lack any rational basis for action. Hector, in other words, insists on intrinsic value. But he runs into problems trying to hold to this position. Note his phrasing: value exists in the thing itself *as well as* in the 'prizer'; the desiring person needs some *image* of the merit of what he or she desires. Surely this image is affected by, even the product of, desire; furthermore, images are representations, and the whole play, as we have seen in the discussion of reflection, consistently destabilises the relations between representation and truth.

Hector seems here to be edging towards Troilus' position without fully realising it. Later, he compounds the problem by shifting his ground away from the concept of intrinsic merit to natural and human law. Nature, he says, craves that 'All dues be rendered to their owners', and what greater debt than wife to husband? He backs this up with an appeal to human legislation that is designed to 'curb those raging appetites that are / Most disobedient and refractory' (173–82). Since human (or 'positive') law was recognised by some theorists to be notoriously arbitrary, and even natural law difficult to distinguish from custom, Hector is on slippery ground here.[1] The position he is adopting parallels that of Troilus, since law is a matter of custom, and one way of interpreting Troilus' position is that value is a long-term effect of collective acts of valuing. Troilus puts his view in overtly relativistic terms, but the play as a whole, in refusing to take sides, suggests the possibility of a more moderate interpretation: that value is located in the field of communal work and systems of belief rather than in the marketplace, where value can rise and fall in a moment. By the end of the debate, Hector's confusion is apparent: 'Hector's opinion / Is this in way of truth', he says, but then, in an abrupt reversal that exemplifies Ulysses' point that 'truth' is a matter of reflection, he accepts Troilus' argument that the wife of Menelaus is a 'theme of honour', a wellspring of Trojan 'dignities', and agrees to 'keep Helen still' (188–93). His blatant inconsistency has shocked many commentators, but it is of a piece with the

---

[1] This issue was the subject of a good deal of Renaissance debate and comes up frequently in Montaigne: e.g. 'men call that barbarisme which is not common to them . . . we have no other ayme of truth and reason, than the example and *Idea* of the opinions and customes of the countrie we live in' ('Of the cannibals', p. 163). Montaigne's influential scepticism certainly affected Shakespeare in multiple ways, most importantly as a 'constellation' of ideas delineating human limitation: *'a man were better bend towards doubt, than encline towards certaintie, in matters of difficult triall'* ('Of the lame or crippel', pp. 934–5); 'Mans eye cannot perceive things, but by the formes of his knowledge' ('An apologie of Raymond Sebond,' p. 480). I am indebted to an unpublished paper by William M. Hamlin for these references.

CRY TROJANS CRY
ACT·II·SC·II·

Figure 5. Cassandra bursts in on the Trojan council scene with her warnings of disaster (2.2). Byam Shaw produced this and several other bold images for a lavishly illustrated edition of 1902 in Art Nouveau style.

widespread instability of character and value typical of the play. Moreover, Hector has already sent off his chivalric challenge to the Greeks (in 1.3), which implies that his concern with honour has all along outweighed his philosophical scruples.

The arguments about the value of Helen are further ironised by the brief view we get of her. She appears only once, with Paris and Pandarus, though we might catch a glimpse of her at the beginning of 1.2 if a production were to lean that way. Her mythic beauty and desirability are deflated exactly as the chivalric glory and martial prowess of the warriors are. But as so often with this play, that is not the whole story. Though she has usually been condemned as a lazy sensualist, a piece of erotic fluff, and the role has often been performed that way, Shakespeare not only gives her theatrical weight, but hints at a depth of feeling too often left unexplored. In performance, she has emerged naked out of a steam room with Paris before being wrapped in a sarong, appeared in a pink gown lounging by a piano and pulling on a cigarette-holder, and been unwrapped by Paris like a gigantic golden valentine.[1] Her one scene has been a boon for designers eager for spectacle and flash, and can be as sexy as it is amusing. And at least occasionally Helen can add something more. Sally Dexter's performance in the Mendes production of 1990 was not short on sex – she was all over Pandarus, and embraced him on 'this love will undo us all' (3.1.94). But at the same time she spoke the line prophetically, suddenly aware of the dark side of love, and turned away for her thrice-repeated 'Cupid, Cupid, Cupid . . .', creating a moment of self-awareness for herself, for Troilus, Cressida, and Diomedes, and for the play as a whole.[2] Pandarus' naughty song that followed also had a dark edge. In such a context, Paris' romantic line, 'Sweet, above thought I love thee,' which ends the scene, can take on a poignancy that might remind an audience that values are not just words, that the struggle to claim value is neither entirely foolhardy nor inevitably futile.

JUDGING HECTOR

Though he is in many ways the most admirable character in the play and has often been regarded as its moral centre, Hector is certainly not without flaws. He pays no attention to the pleas of his wife and sister when they try to dissuade him from battle, and is insensitive to the pain in his father's reluctant blessing (5.3). And his death, while it is the result of despicable cowardice on Achilles' part, results at least partly from Hector's own cupidity. It is a chilling sequence. Having subdued and then extended courtesy to Achilles, Hector pursues a Greek in fine armour, kills him offstage and returns with his prize: 'Most putrefièd core, so fair without, / Thy goodly armour thus hath cost thy life' (5.9.1–2). While many commentators have taken this literally and imagined an already putrefied corpse encased in golden arms, Hector means only that the body will decompose while the armour stays fresh. Either way, of course, it is an especially apt symbol for the play's satire on hollow ideals, and a sour prelude to Hector's death – he is then ambushed and given no chance. Has his desire for the Greek's armour put him in a vulnerable position? While it hasn't done so directly, the incident works to diminish the potential for tragic feeling by reducing Hector's stature.

His last day begins with foreboding – Andromache's dreams and Cassandra's warnings (5.3.6–25, 80–90) are the stuff of tragic destiny. But his death is horrific and ignominious rather than tragic. Though it is followed by a deeply felt sense of loss and an encomium, both of which are typical features of Shakespearean tragedy, Troilus'

---

[1] In productions for, respectively, the RSC (1996, dir. Ian Judge), the Old Vic (1956, dir. Tyrone Guthrie) and the RSC (1990, dir. Sam Mendes); details derived from *Sketch*, 25 April 1956; Paul Taylor, *Independent*, 27 July 1996; R. V. Holdsworth, *TLS*, 4 May 1990; and Rutter, p. 119.

[2] Martin Hoyle, *Financial Times*, 28 April 1990.

wild rage and Pandarus' satiric epilogue introduce contrasting tones incompatible with tragic finality. Though critics and textual scholars have often argued that Shakespeare first designed the play as a tragedy and then changed his mind,[1] this strikes me as highly unlikely. Throughout the battle, Hector's heroism is juxtaposed with the bitter, sometimes comic, commentary of Thersites, the overblown antics of Ajax, the nasty rivalry of Troilus and Diomedes, the utterly unheroic cruelty of Achilles; no single tone is allowed to dominate, so that the shift at the very end is in keeping with what has come before. Hector's partial tragedy is, like that of Cressida, an element or motif, part of a larger pattern woven of multiple and differently coloured strands.

Neither a spokesman for, nor as an exemplar of, value, does Hector emerge as singular or pure. He is a model in the play for the 'judgemental dilemmas'[2] that it recurrently poses for us. As with Hector, so with most of the other characters: we are encouraged to evaluate, but the criteria for evaluation are constantly being undermined. Even a figure as ridiculous as Ajax is presented in a mixed way: his contradictory attributes are spelled out by Alexander at the beginning (1.2.17–26), and though he frequently makes a fool of himself (as in 2.3.130 ff.), his behaviour in the tournament scene with Hector is far more dignified than absurd. Our judgement of Troilus and Cressida is similarly vexed. Their relationship is both romantic and mercantile: for Troilus, Cressida, is a 'pearl' (as he says also of Helen in 2.2), and he is a 'merchant' dependent on a leaky vessel – Pandarus himself, 'our convoy and our bark' (1.1.94–8). For Cressida, as we have already seen, love is a risky 'enterprise' dependent on the manipulation of perceived value.[3] Later, in their evening love scene, Cressida chaffs Troilus, and lovers generally, for 'swearing' more than they are able to 'perform', while at the same time holding a certain amount in 'reserve', and not spending it – 'vowing more than the perfection of ten and discharging less than the tenth part of one' (3.2.72–5).[4] The arithmetic recalls Hector's struggle in the debate scene to quantify Helen's destructive potential: 'Let Helen go. / Since the first sword was drawn about this question / Every tithe soul 'mongst many thousand dismes / Hath been as dear as Helen' (2.2.17–20). Honour, love, worth, and value all are in danger of collapsing into accounting. And yet they don't – not quite. Judging Hector, like judging the others, is a model for a necessary but painfully flawed process: the play both impels us to judge the characters on ethical grounds and simultaneously promotes scepticism towards not only the criteria for judgement, but even the act itself.

INVOKING DEGREE

The same modified deployment of scepticism is called for when considering the dominant political value explored by the play – what Ulysses in a famous and often-cited

---

[1] See Honigmann, 'Date and revision' and especially *Myriad-Minded*, for the most developed example; Gary Taylor and others have argued for two separate versions of the play designed for two different venues. See Textual Analysis, pp. 241–2, for a full discussion.

[2] Bradshaw, pp. 139–40.

[3] Engle, pp. 152–3, points to the market terminology in Troilus' and Cressida's first act soliloquies (1.1.93–8; 1.2.242–53).

[4] See notes on these lines, and compare Sonnet 129.

speech calls 'degree' (1.3.83–124). His defence of degree used to be seen as the paradig-matic expression of what was called the 'Elizabethan world picture',[1] and Ulysses him-self was often regarded as the play's spokesman.[2] That view was effectively exploded once critics and producers began taking a closer look at both Ulysses' use of his doc-trine and the doctrine itself. He offers his defence of ordered hierarchy in order to explain the disarray of the Greek war effort – the insubordination and effrontery of Achilles, the imitative pride of Ajax, and the general rise of 'emulation' (envious rivalry) and factionalism. At the opening of the scene, Agamemnon had proposed a different explanation: their project has failed in the 'promised largeness' because the fate that attends all great actions inevitably burdens them with 'checks and disasters'. Adversity, he says, should be understood as 'the protractive trials of great Jove', designed to test a man's constancy and mettle (3–23). At one level, the argument is absurd, since not *all* actions fail to achieve their goal[3] – the Greeks after all end up winning the war, and Achilles succeeds in destroying Hector as he planned. The second point, that obstacles can be morally strengthening, is a truism consistent with Stoic and Christian doctrine. Agamemnon's appeal to it hides the real issue – that he himself has failed to provide the necessary leadership to rule the army. That is the burden of Ulysses' remarks, though he is careful to lay the blame not at Agamemnon's feet but at those of his recalcitrant subordinates.

Ulysses describes an ideal whereby a smoothly functioning political order is united under a monarch-like head who directs the action of the whole body. He draws elaborate analogies with the natural world; the planets, for example, are necessarily subordinated to the sun:

> The heavens themselves, the planets and this centre
> Observe degree, priority, and place,
> Insisture, course, proportion, season, form,
> Office, and custom in all line of order.
> And therefore is the glorious planet Sol
> In noble eminence enthroned and sphered
> Amidst the other   (1.3.85–91)

Without the harmony provided by degree, 'the bounded waters / Should lift their bosoms higher than the shores / And make a sop of all this solid globe' (111–13). So too the human world depends on ordered, hierarchical relationships: without degree, 'the rude son should strike his father dead' (115), and social institutions of all sorts would be endangered. '. . . communities, / Degrees in schools and brotherhoods in cities, / Peaceful commerce from dividable shores, / The primogenity and due of birth' only 'stand in authentic place' because of the benignly enabling action of 'degree' (103–8).

---

[1] The classic statement of this view is that of E. M. W. Tillyard in *The Elizabethan World Picture* (1943).
[2] As he is, for example, by Alice Walker in her introduction to the New Shakespeare edition of the play.
[3] Bradshaw, pp. 148–9.

This ideal is shadowed somewhat by the fact that Ulysses' position is ideologically motivated, with clear-cut political designs: Agamemnon should crack down on Achilles and the other rebels, and assert his waning authority. Moreover, Ulysses has no intention of actually trying to put his doctrine into effect, probably because he realises that to do so would be futile. Instead he devises, at the end of the scene, a manipulative scheme to trick Achilles back into the war, improvising on the opportunity provided by Hector's challenge. This contrivance, however, does not really impugn Ulysses' philosophical position and render his idea of order invalid. It registers the political difficulty of imposing harmonious order, and it certainly undermines the possibility of absolute principles as a basis for governance, but it does not invalidate the effort to describe, and even act on, *limited* ideals. Despite the obviously strategic thrust of his commentary, then, one has to admit that Ulysses has a point. The Greeks are in disarray, and some orderly structure needs to be established and maintained. Hence the claim for the play's subversiveness that has sometimes been made (i.e. that it is a scathing critique of the dominant Elizabethan ideology of order)[1] has to be tempered by an awareness that what Ulysses is trying to do in an imperfect and all-too-human situation is to persuade his fellow aristocrats 'to act for the common good rather than remaining locked in their own egos'.[2]

In exploring these issues, Shakespeare was contributing to an ongoing cultural debate. As David Norbrook has persuasively shown, the question of the rhetorical uses of political doctrine, and the specific relation of such questions to the Homeric past, was 'much invoked in sixteenth-century discussions of political order'.[3] In Book II of *The Iliad*, Agamemnon and Odysseus (i.e. Ulysses) co-operate in an elaborate and deceptive scheme to rally the troops and bring them back under the umbrella of command.[4] In a grand speech to the assembled army, Agamemnon proposes a plan that is the precise opposite of what he actually wants: because dissension has protracted and undermined the war-effort, he says, the Greeks should retreat and return home. When the soldiers respond eagerly and rush to their ships, Odysseus beats them back, invoking hierarchy.[5] Much to the delight of the men, he thrashes Thersites as a scapegoat (since this is the only section of the poem where Thersites appears, it seems that Shakespeare must have paid some attention to it) and, along with Nestor, stirs up the troops for battle. Agamemnon then takes the lead once more, proposing peace with Achilles and even blaming himself for their quarrel, an admission that supports his goal of inciting his

---

[1] Ellis-Fermor was one of the first and is still one of the most persuasive of critics to have made this claim, and she has been followed by many since.

[2] Norbrook, p. 159.

[3] *Ibid.*, p. 144. I am indebted to Norbrook's excellent article for much of the analysis in this paragraph. For a painstakingly thorough presentation of the classical, medieval, and Renaissance backgrounds to this speech (marred somewhat by an untenable view that the author of the passage is not Shakespeare), see Baldwin's discussion in Variorum, pp. 397–410.

[4] Since Book II was one of Chapman's *Seven Books of the Iliad* published in 1598, there is little doubt that Shakespeare was familiar with it. See Appendix: Sources of the play, pp. 253–61.

[5] Chapman's translation of the key lines is as follows: 'The rule of many is absurd: one Lord must leade the ring / Of far-resounding government – one king whome Saturn's sonne [Zeus] / Hath given a scepter and sound lawes to beare dominion' (*Seven Books*, II.198–200).

men to renew the fight. The whole episode, while deeply manipulative in the way it upholds and justifies monarchical authority, was cited in support of *both* sides of the Renaissance debate about legitimacy and power. As Norbrook shows, 'there was a well-established cluster of arguments around Odysseus, natural analogies and rhetoric . . . [and] natural analogies could be used to argue on both sides of the case [i.e. both in favour of, and against, monarchy]' (p. 146); this interest was particularly high in the Inns of Court milieu of the 1590s.

Furthermore, Ulysses' degree speech itself is full of rhetorical ironies that add to its complexity. Not the least of these is its insistent use of *gradatio* (derived from *gradus* – degree, or a step on a ladder), the standard term for the technique of building step by step to a climax:

> Force should be right, or rather, right and wrong,
> Between whose endless jar justice resides,
> Should lose their names, and so should justice too;
> Then everything include itself in power,
> Power into will, will into appetite,
> And appetite, an universal wolf,
> So doubly seconded with will and power
> Must make perforce an universal prey
> And last eat up himself.   (1.3.116–24)

Ulysses himself draws attention to the ambiguity in his insistent use of *gradatio* by calling degree 'the ladder of ['to' in F] all high designs' (102);[1] the image of climbing a ladder to get to the top, which he goes on to develop, undermines his central point that degree and high place are fixed and immutable:

>   The general's disdained
> By him one step below, he by the next,
> That next by him beneath – so every step,
> Exampled by the first pace that is sick
> Of his superior, grows to an envious fever
> Of pale and bloodless emulation
>   (130–5)

Far from an image of harmony, this part of the speech evokes a picture of a crowd of unruly aspirants trying to jostle each other off the rungs of an unstable scaffold. Lars Engle argues that the speech alludes indirectly to a rising 'ethic of competition', which he associates with the passage from 'idealized feudalism to early modern capitalism', and the shift of social life 'toward being seen as a market of opportunity' rather than an unchanging hierarchy.[2] Indeed, he suggests, Ulysses is much more concerned about social mobility than about anarchy. Ulysses' clever deployment of rhetoric in favour of a traditional principle does not quite succeed in hiding the strain of a social fabric threatened by internal tensions.

---

[1] See Baldwin in Variorum, pp. 408–9, and Norbrook, p. 157.
[2] Engle, p. 155.

Shakespeare, then, places Ulysses' invocation of degree in a composite space: while it is in part a critique of the frankly political uses of rhetoric, it is also an expression of a genuine need for stable political order, made even more urgent in a society where an ethic of competition is in contest with, and gradually replacing, an ethic of hierarchical harmony. There is a built-in awareness that absolute values are suspect and impossible to support, but as I said above, this does not mean that values of some kind cannot or should not play a role in politics. There is even a subtext suggesting that the theatre, an institution very much connected to the emerging ethic of competition (in both a market and an artistic sense), might have a role to play in bringing debates about political order into the public sphere. As both Norbrook and Heather James in different ways suggest,[1] publicly staging this kind of debate meant broadening what had been mainly academic argument, making it available to a wider spectrum of citizens. In scenes such as this one, where Ulysses addresses the claims of both hierarchy and individual mobility, Shakespeare's theatre can thus be seen as making a kind of bid for itself as a legitimate forum for political debate, and perhaps, as a consequence of extending the range of public discourse, even a voice for broader social liberty.

The play in performance

1601–1960

Troilus and Cressida does not seem to have made a hit when it was first written. After a few early performances, it disappeared from the stage till Dryden rewrote it in 1679, and his version was only occasionally revived.[2] In the 1790s, the great classical actor John Philip Kemble planned a new staging; he prepared a rearranged version that began with the Greek council scene, emphasised the heroic manliness of the heroes on both sides, especially the Greeks, and subordinated love to war in the plotting; he even cast many of the parts (he himself would play Ulysses, and his younger brother Charles, Troilus), but in the end decided that it was unplayable.[3] Finally, in 1898 something like Shakespeare's play was presented in Germany, but only about a third of the text survived the cutting, which was done to accommodate an elaborate 'Ye Olde Globe' atmosphere that almost smothered what remained of the play. Thersites, however, survived and became a contemptuous 'censor of the world', the voice of Shakespeare 'in his bad moments'[4] – a role he has frequently adopted since. The first English production, as much a recital as a dramatic performance, was in 1907, under the auspices of Charles

[1] Norbrook, pp. 158–9, and James, pp. 116–18.
[2] See above, pp. 1–2 and n.
[3] Kemble developed his text (which is in the Folger Library) from Bell's acting edition put together by Francis Gentleman in 1774. Kemble's version removes much of the inflated speech and satirical bite (both Thersites and Pandarus have their roles drastically reduced), while the stature of the military figures is augmented. Kemble seems loath to undermine the dignity of most of his characters. A major change occurs in Act 5, where Achilles meets Hector in single combat, without the aid of the Myrmidons, and defeats him cleanly. The lovers too are allowed to suffer more straightforwardly; both their delight and anguish are presented with a minimum of satirical commentary. See Newlin for a full account.
[4] Franz Held, quoted in Variorum, p. 512.

Fry, who played Thersites. Hence, for just over three hundred years Shakespeare's
Troilus and Cressida was absent from the English stage, one of the longest such gaps
for any of his plays.[1] And the *Times* suggested that Fry was unwise to try to close the
gap, declaring that the play 'is better left unacted and read in the study by people who
need a corrective to romanticism'.[2] Such relatively elitist views echo the sentiments of
the play's first critic, the writer of the quarto epistle, for whom the play's absence from
the stage was a sign of its worth.[3]

In 1912, William Poel staged an amateur production at King's Hall in Covent Garden,
a space associated, appropriately enough, with boxing.[4] Despite its inauspicious location and unknown actors, the production proved decisive. Poel was an influential figure
who emphasised the importance of early modern styles of production (simple staging,
Elizabethan costumes, quick verse-speaking) and who began the process of undermining the tired conventions of nineteenth-century pictorial scenography as they impinged
on Shakespearean production. His *Troilus* introduced Edith Evans to the English stage;
Evans played Cressida as 'amoral, that was all',[5] a 'sexually experienced' court lady who,
while Troilus pressed her for oaths of fidelity, was 'manifestly preoccupied with pinning
on her hat'.[6] The play also featured a woman, Elspeth Keith, as Thersites. By playing
him as a clown with a Scottish brogue, she greatly reduced his venom. While much of
the production was comic, the accent at the end was on the tragic note: the epilogue
disappeared and Troilus was lit in a bluish light as he knelt in grief over Hector's
corpse; the final sound was a muffled wail from Cassandra with drums beating in the
distance.[7]

Perhaps the sense of impending war was an impetus behind Poel's choice of the play.
It certainly was in 1938, when Michael Macowan directed a modern-dress production
for the London Mask company at London's Westminster Theatre. Opening night was
21 September, 'the eve of Mr Chamberlain [the British Prime Minister]'s second visit
to Germany in the cause of peace',[8] with its dangerous message of 'appeasement'.
Macowan dressed the Trojans in British khaki and the Greek generals in blue uniforms
that reminded some of Germany or the Balkans;[9] Troilus was a young officer, Cressida
and Helen 'cocktail party lovelies'; Hector's challenge was conveyed to the Greeks over

[1] Only *3H6* seems to have been absent from the stage for longer, though bits of it were played in conjunction
with *2H6* or *R3*; *Tit.*, like *Tro.*, was adapted during the Restoration but in a version (by Edward Ravenscroft)
closer to the original than Dryden's *Troilus*.
[2] *Times*, 3 June 1907, quoted in Variorum, p. 505. The *Daily Chronicle* was similarly dour: 'It has the
unpardonable fault of being dull. Worse, it is cynical and in bad taste' (3 June 1907), quoted in Kimberly,
p. 39.
[3] See above, pp. 7–8.
[4] The opening was on December 10, and the play was remounted the following May for two performances
at Stratford. Kimberly mentions the venue's connection with boxing.
[5] Evans, quoted in Kimberly, p. 54.
[6] Marion O'Connor, *William Poel and the English Stage Society*, 1987, p. 97. This bit of business no doubt
came naturally to the young actress, who began her working life as a milliner.
[7] *Morning Post*, 14 May 1913.
[8] *Times*, 25 September 1938.
[9] Gordon Crosse in his diary (Vol. XVII in the Birmingham Public Library) notes the German connection,
and the *ILN* saw Ulysses and Nestor as 'Balkan statesmen of our own time' (8 October 1938).

Figure 6. Elspeth Keith struts and jeers as Thersites, a jester figure with a Scottish brogue, in William Poel's 1912 version. Poel's productions were influential in the early twentieth-century trend towards using Elizabethan styles of costume and staging.

the wireless and, in a move that was to have long-term influence, Thersites became a highly perceptive though 'dingy' war correspondent.[1] The descriptions of scene locations in the programme hint at the contemporary look: 'Troy: a hotel terrace' for the opening scene, or 'A room in Helen's flat' (3.1). The setting allowed Ruth Lodge to give a contemporary and sympathetic spin to Cressida, who emerged as 'a woman of some mind and merit', maybe even 'a theorist of free love'.[2] The director called the play a 'tragedy of disillusion' that 'questions the heroic conception of war [and] the romantic conception of love'; Thersites became the mouthpiece for Shakespeare's own 'bitterness and torment of spirit' (programme note). In the event, however, the war plot far outweighed that of the lovers, Troilus' loss a minor casualty in a much larger catastrophe. This choice was no doubt inevitable given the time and place, but was also

[1] Desmond McCarthy, *New Statesman and Nation*, 1 October 1938.
[2] Ivor Brown, *Observer*, 25 September 1938.

Figure 7. An elegant Pandarus (Paul Rogers) plays the white grand piano while Helen (Wendy Hiller), gorgeous in a 'shocking pink' evening gown, flirts provocatively with a smitten Paris, in Tyrone Guthrie's Old Vic production (1956), which was set on the eve of the First World War.

characteristic of most productions before 1980. As Barbara Bowen suggests, it was only with the rise of feminism and the consequent recuperation of Cressida that the love plot began to regain the kind of priority it once had in the hands of an adapter like Dryden, and still retained early in the twentieth century.[1]

While there were important productions at the Old Vic in 1923 and at Stratford in 1936 (both, like Poel's, in Elizabethan costume), the version of the play that established it as a regular on English-speaking stages was that of Tyrone Guthrie in 1956, at the Old Vic.[2] Guthrie set his revival in the period just prior to the First World War. Braided uniforms, plush chairs, and gorgeous side curtains provided a resplendent look, but a cannon in the back draped with flags (during 2.2) was a menacing reminder of the reality of war. In the programme, Guthrie spoke of the 'confused and unreasonable' grounds of war, and claimed that the Trojans are undermined by 'frivolity', the Greeks

---

[1] Bowen, p. 49.
[2] The 1923 Old Vic production (*Tro.* was the last in a multi-year presentation of the complete cycle of Folio plays) was directed by Robert Atkins, that in 1936 by Ben Iden Payne. There were also two other Stratford productions, in 1948 (Anthony Quayle) and 1954 (Glen Byam Shaw), both of which ended with a vision of a defeated Troilus who, in the latter, was left alone on stage with 'drawn sword amid the deepening gloom' (Harold Hobson, *Sunday Times*, 18 July 1954).

by 'faction'. The production was designed to generate that meaning. The initial image (the Prologue was cut) was Pandarus as 'an elderly exquisite' in top hat, gloves, and morning suit, just back from Ascot. Cressida's riding costume and Helen's 'shocking pink' evening dress as she perched provocatively on a grand piano dragging at a cigarette holder epitomised the thoughtless luxury of Trojan life.[1] The Trojan warriors were 'glass-smashing officers' – even Troilus, whose speech of expectation, 'I am giddy . . .' was induced partly by alcohol.[2] The monocled Greeks had a heel-clicking Prussian air, though Achilles lounged in a dressing-gown, and there were hints of 'sado-masochism' in his relation with Patroclus.[3] Once again, Thersites set the tone and became the main spokesman. As in 1938, he was a war correspondent, this time with a camera capturing the folly on film, as if to emphasise the play's interest in the simulacrum, its engagement with issues of representation and literary reproduction.[4]

During the 1960s and '70s, the play came into its own as an anti-war play. And since that time it has become a standard in the repertoire, performed almost as often as *Hamlet* or *As You Like It* in theatres in England and North America. If Guthrie and Macowan emphasised the folly of war and the failure of statesmen to measure its seriousness, later productions have highlighted its savagery, its passion, its corrosive destruction of values. Design has once more led the way. The trend has been to move away from a single identifiable period or place, with costumes often combining traces of the primitive and hints of the nineteenth or twentieth centuries. Set designers have striven to find ways of expressing the play's depiction of disintegration, as with the huge decaying stone mask behind the horizontal bars in Anthony Ward's design in 1990 or Ralph Koltai's crumbling Crimean mansion with 'rickety balustrades' (RSC 1985), in which a wrecked Pandarus 'obsessively play[ed] the piano throughout the final battle sequences while the set collapsed around him'.[5]

PERFORMING POLITICS

Again and again, directors have alluded to contemporary wars, so much so that productions were sometimes criticised if they did *not* make the linkage clear. During the 1960s and '70s especially, productions sounded strong political notes, usually of an anti-war kind, often with direct reference to the parallels between the Vietnam and Trojan Wars;[6] other productions went in for anti-imperialism (e.g. 'dark-skinned' Trojans beset by Greeks 'represented as white French or American' colonists in parachute gear),[7] or interventions in contemporary politics (in 1963, Michael Langham dressed

---

[1] John C. Trewin, *ILN*, 14 April 1956. Guthrie borrowed the idea of the piano from Helen's 'flat' in Macowan's production.

[2] Kenneth Tynan, *Observer*, 8 April 1956.

[3] *Times*, 4 April 1956, *Daily Telegraph*, 4 April 1956, and Tynan, 8 April 1956.

[4] See above, pp. 32–5, on literary identity.

[5] Quotations from Michael Billington, *Guardian*, 27 June 1985, and Roger Warren, *SQ* 37.1 (1986), 118.

[6] Commenting on his production in 1968, Barton stresses the parallel on the grounds that both sides 'are inexorably committed' (quoted in Bowen, p. 43).

[7] Leiter, p. 750, describing Alf Solberg's Stockholm production of 1967.

his Myrmidons in the outfits of the Ku Klux Klan).[1] Dryden was the first, but certainly not the last, to redesign the thrust of the play to suit his own time and ideological interests. His stress on the public good outweighing both private values and personal desires served his faith in a reasoned public order under the benevolent gaze of a legitimate monarch. The final speech of his play, in marked contrast to Pandarus' Epilogue in the original, makes his political point clear: Ulysses, the wise spokesman throughout, hails the rightful king, Agamemnon, for triumphing over his 'factious Nobles' who had urged 'publique good . . . for private ends'. He concludes by warning the audience (the Civil War and Interregnum were only a generation in the past, the Glorious Revolution of 1688 a few years in the future): 'Then, since from homebred Factions ruine springs, / Let subjects learn obedience to their Kings.'

Where Dryden urged an optimistic politics, recent adapters and directors have tended towards pessimism and distrust; and where Dryden supplied a splendid battle, modern productions have typically adopted Thersites' attitudes towards war and highlighted his suspicion about its motivations and his cynicism about the ways in which it is actually waged. The remarkable rise in the importance of Thersites, who for Dryden was a mainly comic figure, is a measure of how the play's political and moral attitudes are typically interpreted. This trend originated with Michael Macowan, who not only made Thersites into a truth-telling, left-leaning war correspondent but added to his clout by giving him the Prologue to speak.[2] In 1964, Roger Planchon produced the play in a working-class district of Lyons in France. His Thersites was the only Greek character who wasn't a fool or a knave – he was played with 'brooding seriousness' while Ulysses was a demagogue whose speech on degree was a 'partisan harangue'.[3] Planchon's was a committed theatre in the manner of Brecht and his version, built on a design that was constantly shifting shape, was meant to enlist Shakespeare as a leftish social critic. Accordingly, he 'sought to reveal the discontinuities of the text by showing the backside of the military and amorous virtues', and the dynamic setting aptly mirrored the 'disorder, treachery, and fragmentation' of the play's world.[4]

The first modern performance of *Troilus and Cressida* was, as I noted, in Germany. While it was entirely apolitical, there have been several important German-language productions that have taken a political stance. Otto Falckenberg directed two versions (both staged in Munich), one in 1925, the second in 1936. In both, Thersites, as so often, loomed large. In 1936 he became, according to *The Times* 'almost a figure of tragedy'.[5] There were echoes of Nazi voices as heard on the radios of the period and, perhaps inevitably, political resonances developed even though the director's stated aims were primarily aesthetic. Two years later in Zurich, Oskar Wälterlin brought those political meanings centre stage as a warning to Switzerland to arm itself against war.

[1] Bowen, p. 49, reporting on a production at Stratford, Ontario.
[2] Apfelbaum, p. 30, notes this and says that Macowan was probably the first director to assign the Prologue to a specific character. Since then, Thersites has often had the honours (RSC 1981, 1996, 1998) though Pandarus too has sometimes become the play's unofficial spokesman (RSC 1990).
[3] Leiter, p. 757, and Kennedy, p. 215.
[4] Kennedy, p. 215.
[5] Quoted in Hortmann, p. 108.

Like Macowan's, this production coincided with Chamberlain's fateful visit to Munich in September 1938; in it, as one critic wrote, Ajax's 'suicidal war propaganda' was a reminder that his breed 'lives just across the border, he is Hitler, Goering, Goebbels'. In an even more pointed reference, one of the actors wore a Mussolini mask.[1] That same year, Picasso's great anti-Fascist and anti-war painting, *Guernica*, was on view for the first time in London, so that a theatregoer could see the painting in the afternoon and Macowan's meditation on the disillusions of war in the evening – different media and different venues, but in every case a protest and a warning. An anti-war version of the play in Dresden in 1962 (directed by Hannes Fischer) used an enlarged reproduction of *Guernica* as an emblem on the stage curtain. That version, even more than usual, was dominated by Thersites, whose message was ambivalently aligned with the 'official' East German policy of peace, while at the same time the audience could quite easily construe the strutting of the various warmongers as a deliberate satire on the state functionaries who controlled their lives.

To politicise the play in the kind of ways just outlined is to simplify it, but also to give it bite and appeal. The theatre is, and must be, in some way partisan. And it would certainly be wrong to think of the play as non-political. Part of its original impetus was political, and the play investigates at great depth the values and motives that drive political decisions. But it does so with a kind of passionate objectivity, rather than with an overt agenda. In order for productions to catch the complex balance of the play, it might be necessary to give Ulysses more weight than he frequently gets these days, without falling into the old mode of seeing him as the play's spokesman, and, like Dryden, giving him the last word.

THE 1960S: THE EROTICS OF WAR

While the play's political horizons were being expanded in the 1960s, there arose as well an interest in the passion of battle, the stirring effects of blood, the deep male bonding and concomitant ambivalence towards women. The text itself satirises forms of chivalry that were already outmoded in Shakespeare's time – Hector's challenge, Aeneas' courtly language, Troilus' courtly love. Positioning them as he does, Shakespeare reduces their charge – what looks like chivalry turns out to be mere posturing. Since the modern world offers little in the way of chivalry, outmoded or otherwise, this is a feature of the text that is hard for modern producers to register. The emphasis on male bonding might have been an attempt to catch both the energy and the satire associated with chivalry in the play, though it was no doubt more a response to the text's stress on the intimate physicality of bodies, and to the widening cultural awareness in the 1960s and '70s of the subterranean relations between sex and violence.[2] Of the various directors who have taken the play in this direction, none is more important than John Barton, who was responsible for three productions between 1960 and 1976, all for the Royal Shakespeare Company.

---

[1] Hortmann, p. 168, quoting Curt Riess.
[2] Films such as *Bonnie and Clyde* (1967) could be cited as evidence of this growing awareness.

Figure 8. Achilles (Patrick Allen) and his Myrmidons menace the unarmed Hector (Derek Godfrey), as he
crouches in the middle of the octagonal sandpit that formed the main scenic element of Barton and Hall's
1960 production at the RSC. The abstract backdrop, with its scraps of ancient design reminiscent of Lascaux,
can be seen in the background.

   In the first of these, Barton and Peter Hall, together with designer Leslie Hurry, set
the action in an octagonal sandpit with a reddish, restlessly abstract cloth behind. The
fury of the fighting warriors in Act 5 gained power from such a setting, especially the
murderous ritual of Achilles' brutal and cowardly attack on Hector, who had been played
throughout as magnanimous and heroic. As the battle heated up, smoke wreathed,
drums beat, occasional flashes of glancing metal broke through the gloom. The climax
came when the Myrmidons surrounded Hector and downed him with 'three concerted
spear thrusts' before Achilles stepped in to deliver the final blow.[1] The stage image of
the furrow cut by his body as it was dragged through the white sand spoke eloquently
of the emptiness and sterility of war. In such a context, the lovers and their plight could
hardly compete.
   Barton next tackled the play in 1968. In that version he initiated a trend that has
become almost irresistible to producers ever since. This was to bring into full view the
homoerotic undercurrents of the play, most prominently in the depiction of Achilles
and Patroclus, though nearly all the actors appeared semi-nude. The set was simple,

[1] Kimberly, p. 128.

Figure 9. Male flesh and male violence are on dramatic display as Achilles (Alan Howard) and Hector (Patrick Stewart) clash during their 'beaked dance of metallic-crested birds' (R. Bryden, *Observer*, 11 August), a climactic scene from Barton's erotically charged 1968 production for the RSC.

with movable pieces against a black backdrop; the design took its inspiration from Attic friezes and amphorae, giving one reviewer a sense of an early tribal Mediterranean world.[1] Another commented that the 'bareness of the set is equalled by the bareness of the actors'[2] who were clad, if that's the right word, in an array of leather straps, codpieces, and plumed helmets. For their combat, Ajax and Hector sported only tiny loincloths, their buttocks glowing with strain and sweat, their heads and faces covered by bird-like helmet–masks.[3] This was followed by a striking *coup de théâtre*: as the Greek warriors and their Trojan visitors prepared for their feast, Helen's litter was carried onstage, galvanising Menelaus with expectation, but when its veil was parted there was Achilles in a blond wig and almost naked, beckoning Hector 'to mount him'.[4] Again Thersites played a major role – himself appearing almost naked despite his diseased body, and amusing himself and the audience with a codpiece shaped like a mask with a long leering tongue–phallus. In a script-bending move, he was present at the end for

[1] Ronald Bryden, *Observer*, 11 August 1968.
[2] Bertram A. Young, *Financial Times*, 9 August 1968.
[3] Barton had his warrior–actors on a weight-lifting regimen throughout the rehearsal period (Apfelbaum, p. 35).
[4] Of the many descriptions of this moment, Carol Rutter's (quotation, p. 122) is the most vivid.

Pandarus' epilogue to drive home the message of decay.[1] The hapless lovers were again upstaged, their love merely another version of war, just as the warriors turned war into eros. As a whole, the production countered the popular anti-war motto of the time, 'Make love not war,' by stressing, as the text had always done, the connection between the two.

Barton had indeed seized on a crucial element: the play is rife with homoerotic tension. Men fight other men, but the hatred they generate is charged with intimate bodily feeling. The central moment in the play for this kind of tension is the encounter between Hector and Achilles in 4.5.[2] While the scenes between the warriors have per-haps too often featured leather codpieces and oiled thighs, they have also registered Shakespeare's interest in the ambivalent bonds that tie opponents to each other. In Sam Mendes' production (1990), Achilles and Patroclus stood on upstage ladders gazing down at Hector with frank but disdainful desire; Achilles then descended, circling his prey and finally twisting Hector's hand ('Thy hand upon that match', 270). In Trevor Nunn's production (National, 1999), a rather naïve Hector was drawn in spite of himself into an edgy erotic dance. At the same time, the relationship between Pa-troclus and Achilles was given an unusual emotional depth. Patroclus was small and boyish, Achilles indolent and ominous, with black-lined eyes and a pony-tail. There was a revealing moment when Patroclus reacted with surprised dismay upon hearing of Achilles' love for Polyxena.[3] Later, upon the news of his young friend's death at Hector's hands, Achilles scraped black war-paint over his face: 'thou boy-queller' thus made powerful emotional sense and led directly to Achilles' despicable but somehow understandable murder of his rival.

Such readings of particular moments extend the range of the play's eroticism, opening up textual features that might have remained obscure. We begin to notice, for example, that the fervently heterosexual Troilus is as fixated on Diomedes as he is on the loss of Cressida, that Pandarus, while enjoying the erotic energy of the young lovers, and that of Paris and Helen when he cavorts with them in 3.1, nonetheless tends to bend erotically more towards Troilus than he does towards anyone else. In recent performances, he has often been played with a strongly homoerotic flair. Indeed the insistent maleness of the world, especially of the Greek camp, the love relationship between Achilles and Patroclus (which does not preclude Achilles' affair with Polyxena), the potentially homoerotic obsessions of Thersites – all these suggest a world in which eroticism is 'boundless', even though, as Troilus laments, the 'act [is] a slave to limit' (3.2.71).

THE 1970S AND '80S: SCENIC ECLECTICISM, EROTIC UNCERTAINTY
In 1976, when Barton directed the play again, this time with Barry Kyle, his approach was more multivalent, less fiercely, and perhaps less effectively, theatrical, but more

---

[1] This move was repeated in 1976 (RSC), and has appeared occasionally since – as in 1999 (National Theatre) where Cressida too was brought back onstage.

[2] See above, p. 19.

[3] In 1990, Paterson Joseph similarly registered a 'moving . . . pain at Achilles' comments on Polyxena' (Holland, p. 73).

nuanced. One result of this was a reduction in Thersites' role; another was a new emphasis on the plight of the women, almost forgotten in 1968 (though there was still plenty of male flesh on view). A single stage image spoke eloquently of this shift: Helen was attached to Paris by a golden chain, a glittering sign of her subjection.[1] But Cressida, despite efforts to give her depth in the early parts, was disrobed by Diomedes in front of the Greek generals to reveal a courtesan's outfit that proclaimed what she 'really' was – an 'assured sexual specialist'[2] who got a kick out of the kissing game. Hence the male bonding was played out through the humiliation of Cressida.[3] This has been until quite recently a standard way of playing the crucial sequence when Cressida first arrives in the Greek camp. As with Hector's arrival a bit later, multi-levelled and aggressive eroticism is on view. In many productions a deep ambivalence emerges: critique of machismo and sexual exploitation is yoked with a perhaps not fully intended sense of Cressida's own complicity in the treatment she receives.

The scene can even become a ground of disagreement between actor and director, as it did in the Stratford production of 1985, when the attempt to make a statement about male sexual brutality ended up reproducing some of the attitudes it apparently sought to dislodge. Juliet Stevenson played Cressida, in a production directed by Howard Davies. Like Shaw, she saw Cressida as a 'real woman', rather than a literary fantasy, and sought ways to play her sympathetically. Her performance clashed to some extent with Davies' view of the character, or at least with his idea of the semi-conspiratorial relations between Troilus, Pandarus, and Cressida.[4] Gendered conflict in the rehearsal room imitated that on the stage, but in the end, despite Stevenson's skill in discovering both the vulnerability and witty strength of the character, the old view of Cressida at least partially prevailed. Appearing in her nightgown in 4.2 (the morning after), she was hurried off to the Greek camp without being given a chance to change, though a distraught Troilus threw his greatcoat over her for protection. This meant that the kissing scene was played in that same nightgown (the coat slipping off after her arrival to a chorus of approving Greek sighs). While emphasising her vulnerability, the costume also made her a beguiling sexual object. Stevenson, however, played against this; in the words of Carol Rutter, she discovered 'a Cressida who neither solicited the generals nor surrendered to them'; despite the atmosphere of gang rape, she managed to 'rout' her accosters, especially Ulysses, who reacted with the sexualised 'sour grapes' of someone whose manhood has been called into question, 'trashing' Cressida as a 'daughter of the game'.[5] But, what happened in Cressida's next (and final) appearance in the betrayal scene tended to undo some of the complexity created by the interaction with the Greek

[1] Bowen, p. 53. Adducing other moments (Cressida in 5.2 with a courtesan's mask on the back of her head, Thersites at the end clutching a life-size female doll), Bowen comments: 'Barton was suggesting that Cressida's self-division . . . is inevitable in a world that turns women into icons.'

[2] Irving Wardle, quoted in Rutter, p. 129.

[3] Such treatments are an essential background to the revolutionary attempt of Juliet Stevenson, in Howard Davies' production of 1985, to present a very different Cressida, as outlined in the next paragraph.

[4] See Tylee, p. 72.

[5] Rutter, p. 131, and Michael Billington (for the 'sour grapes' quotation), *Guardian*, 27 June 1985.

Figure 10. Juliet Stevenson's strong-minded Cressida confronts the Greek generals in her nightgown, Troilus' coat temporarily offering a modicum of provocative protection; despite her vulnerability, Stevenson's Cressida gained the edge in the encounter (Howard Davies directed for the RSC, 1985).

generals. Stevenson 'entered looking like a blowsy Carmen, hair down and bunched to dangle over one ear, peasant blouse lowered'. Where had this costume, so out of tune with Stevenson's performance, come from? 'Certainly nothing . . . had suggested that [Stevenson's] Cressida kept anything like that gypsy get-up in her wardrobe.'[1] And so, as Rutter persuasively argues, costume design prevailed over the subtlest of performances to proclaim Ulysses' view as valid after all.

The play has often attracted directors with a penchant for the extreme and bizarre: audiences have been confronted with dead horses and barbed-wire fences, a cosmic battle between spacemen and Martians, Achilles with a green feather boa, Nestor completely blind, a red net thrown over the helpless Hector as the Myrmidons moved ritualistically towards their prey, Ajax caught in a privy (literalising an Elizabethan joke on his name as 'A Jakes'). Terry Hands in 1981 (RSC, Aldwych) took a wildly eclectic, spectacularly sexualised approach, reducing value to decadence and consistency to jumble. The Greeks were moronic, strutting soldiers out of the First World War, while the Trojans belonged to a completely different, vaguely medieval era. Nestor slobbered on an orange during Ulysses' degree speech, Helen was groped by all kinds of men,

---

[1] Rutter, p. 130.

Figure 11. Pandarus (Peter Lühr) and Cressida (Sunnyi Melles) celebrate the delights of anticipated love (1.2) in Dieter Dorn's splendid Munich production of 1986; the strings of beads on Cressida's face and neck, her high metal necklace, Pandarus' beaded cap and the energetic and colourful 'action' painting on the backdrop illustrate the mix of archaic and post-modern styles that characterised this production.

Cressida was unwrapped in front of the Greeks by Diomedes (exactly as she had been in 1976) and revealed as a willing prey, and, in a final shocking image, Pandarus was splayed over barbed wire. Perhaps such strategies are an indication of a kind of bewilderment, an uncertainty about how to do justice to the play's subtle demands. Whether we encounter the loosely Homeric look, some identifiable period, or a mix of the historical and symbolic, as with Koltai's decayed mansion and crumbling staircase

(RSC 1985), the vagaries of setting are no doubt a response to the mixed messages that the play itself delivers. Lately, a trend that seems more precisely in tune with the play's deliberate inconsistencies has emerged – designing a strangely atemporal and atopic theatrical space that combines elements of ancient Greece and modern killing fields.

One of the strongest of the latter kind of production was that of Dieter Dorn in Munich in 1986. He and designer Jürgen Rose put together a scenography that combined modern abstract elements, such as action painting, with a variety of tribal and culturally distinct modes, such as native American headbands for some of the warriors, whose bare chests were crossed by straps or, in the case of Troilus, numerous strings of beads. Pandarus and Cressida had robes reminiscent of African or Mexican weaving and Cressida's face was etched into segments by thin strings of beadwork. Kabuki-like movement marked some of the scenes, while 'ritual gestures around a bowl of water (for the Greeks) and a bowl of fire (for the Trojans)' added to the exotic but strongly embodied effect. The overall impression, writes Wilhelm Hortmann, 'was of something archaic and passionate, of eruptive ferocity barely restrained'. Dorn used an almost complete text, a choice that sought to respond to the play's multi-sidedness by blending philosophical exploration with the exotic feel. Sunnyi Melles' Cressida typified the approach, catching the contradictory shades of the character: Hortmann describes her as 'a creature of the moment, both helpless prey to conflicting impulses and playful coquette', who gained and then abruptly lost power; but she was also an 'abused victim', both 'willing' and 'tragic' in her betrayal, mixing lies and truth in a manner that was (appropriately) hard to read.[1]

THE 1990S — CRESSIDA AND TROILUS

By the end of the twentieth century, with major wars, hot or cold, no longer threatening Western Europe, the play remained no less popular, but it became even more eclectic and multi-dimensional. It was given four major British productions in the 1990s, three at the RSC and one at the National, which made it the single most frequently performed Shakespeare play of the decade at those venues. All of these productions put Cressida at or near the centre and they all featured eclectic design, though two them, in 1990 and 1998, went for a distinctly twentieth-century feel while the other two, in 1995 and 1999, sought to evoke the ancient and tribal.[2]

Anthony Ward's set in 1990 was abstract, with a trio of wide metal ladders standing near the back of the Swan stage and a gigantic, partially crumbling mask behind and slightly to the side. There was also a round trap in the centre of the stage floor, that served as a pool for Pandarus and Cressida to dip their toes in as they awaited the arrival of the Trojan warriors in 1.2 and then for the returning soldiers to wash or groom themselves; later, Patroclus' body was laid on a grille over the 'pool' and Hector

---

[1] Hortmann, pp. 325–6, and Michael Merschmeier in *Theater Heute* 27.5 (1986), 10.
[2] The RSC productions (1990, 1995, 1998) were directed and designed by, respectively, Sam Mendes and Anthony Ward, Ian Judge and John Gunter, and Michael Boyd and Tom Piper, that at the National (1999) was directed by Trevor Nunn and designed by Rob Howell.

Figure 12. Pandarus (Norman Rodway) dips his toes while bantering with Cressida (Amanda Root) by the little pool that formed an important scenic element in Sam Mendes' RSC production of 1990 (designed by Anthony Ward).

ritually slaughtered in the same place. As smoke swirled, their bodies each cast ominous shadows from the lighting beneath so that Achilles' entrance to bear off his friend/lover was visually linked to his later appearance with his Myrmidons, to consummate the ritual murder. The costumes were mixed. Some of the Greeks wore greatcoats and nineteenth-century cravats with armour beneath, Agamemnon had an old cardigan over his breastplate. Thersites scuttled about in a greasy raincoat and dusty pinstripes, with a leather helmet and a clown's bauble; Achilles, his hair greased and shiny, sat menacingly at the entrance to his tent munching popcorn, clad in a black string vest; Helen and Cressida sported ancient-looking bracelets and necklaces along with high heels and contemporary-looking gowns. Coffee mugs, a radio, and desk lamps jostled against the swords and armour of ancient battle all to the tune of insistent drumming and droning pipes. Mendes' idea was to mix past and present, to sound as many notes as possible, and once again the effort paid off for Cressida (Amanda Root), who together with Troilus and Pandarus struck one reviewer as pathetically eager and innocent – 'casualties rather than instances of the folly and futility of war'.[3] In her scenes with

3 Roger V. Holdsworth, *TLS*, 4 May 1990.

Troilus, she seemed to be playing against her awareness of the precariousness of her situation. Thrust before the sex-starved Greeks, she was awakened from a dream that she knew was too good to be true, and, grateful to Diomedes for rescuing her, she turned to him for protection.[1] But the star of the show was Simon Russell Beale's Thersites, variously described as a 'dung beetle voyeur', a 'hilarious scuttling sado-masochist', and a twisted, thwarted idealist whose deformities keep him from being the warrior he would like to be.[2] Beale played him as an insider with an upper-class accent – he really did 'serve here voluntary' (2.1.86), but at the same time he 'oozed physical exclusion and emotional resentment'.[3] A poignant moment that brought Cressida and Thersites together occurred at the end of the betrayal scene, after her departure with her new man, when Thersites picked up the scarf that Cressida had thrown seductively on the floor as she gave in to Diomedes, sniffed it and spoke 'Lechery, lechery . . . (5.2.191), not with disgust but with sadness ('O the pity of it, Iago' as Othello says).[4]

In contrast, the 1996 production went back to the bare flesh, leather jockstraps and camp eroticism of the 1960s and 70s, this time with a post-modern air of tired 'iteration' – sex and war, like everything else, having become nothing but performance. Thersites, fittingly, spoke the Prologue with cynical disbelief ('And *that's* the quarrel?' was spoken with an 'interrogative lilt'), Paris and Helen emerged naked out of a steam bath, Achilles was besotted with his blond beauty Patroclus but still 'flash[ed] his nakedness at Hector' when they met in 4.5, and Pandarus was a desperate old queen with heavy make-up and long black wig, whose final disease carried with it the dark resonances of AIDS.[5] Within this context, Philip Voss's serious, well-spoken Ulysses seemed out of place. His marginalisation can perhaps be seen as a sign of how this character, once the centre of the play's ideological, even moral, meaning, has been sidetracked and hamstrung in recent productions. It is now almost impossible to play Ulysses 'straight' since that is likely to clash with the overall concept, and yet to caricature his role is to diminish him. It is a dilemma that any serious modern production has to face up to.

As Cressida, Victoria Hamilton was ardent and earnest with Troilus, aware of the precariousness of her situation, but also 'fascinated by the carnal', allowing her gaze to linger on Diomedes when she first met him.[6] She remained onstage for Ulysses'

[1] Wardle, *Independent on Sunday*, 6 May 1990, and Charles Spencer, *Daily Telegraph*, 28 April 1990.
[2] Wardle, *Independent on Sunday*, 6 May 1990; Paul Taylor, *Independent*, 30 April 1990; and Beale himself in *Players of Shakespeare 3*. Beale describes how the complexity of the character narrowed somewhat during the run, becoming more and more a performer, when he'd started with the idea that Thersites' cynicism derives from his own physical weakness and inability to fight. His anger at Achilles came from his contempt at Patroclus' weakness and Achilles' self-debasement in loving him. See fig. 2 (p. 18).
[3] Holland, p. 73.
[4] Peter Holland saw the moment a little differently from some other reviewers; for him, Beale's Thersites was not so much saddened as amazed, unable to make anything of the lovers' passion – it was 'simply beyond his comprehension' (p. 73).
[5] Robert Smallwood, *S.Sur.* 50 (1996), 211–13.
[6] Nicholas de Jongh, *Evening Standard*, 25 July 1996; Paul Taylor, *Independent*, 27 July 1996; and Rutter, p. 130.

withering attack on her, taken aback by his description of her as a 'daughter of the game' and crushed by the chorus of his colleagues who turned their cry of 'The Trojan's trumpet' to 'The Trojan strumpet'.[1] Later, giving in to Diomedes, she refused to be dishonest with herself, projecting a mix of 'anguished reluctance' and 'clear-eyed pragmatism'.[2] One phrase in the betrayal scene seemed to encapsulate her whole trajectory: 'Troilus farewell . . .' (5.2.106) began with a tremulous, pained cry on his name, and then shifted abruptly to a curt, matter-of-fact 'farewell'.[3]

The next two productions followed fast upon one another, one opening in November 1998, the other the following March. Michael Boyd's strangely mixed version for the RSC featured a design that spoke of 'O'Casey's Ireland . . . with a dash of Lorca's Spain'[4] and touches too of the Balkans in the nineties. The set was a bullet-pocked room, perhaps a chapel, with a large icon of the Virgin at the back; in 3.1, black-shawled vota-resses chanted, but the statue started moving and showing signs of unseemly sexual plea-sure, explained by Paris suddenly rolling out from under her skirts while she metamor-phosed into Helen. There were other liberties – Patroclus was played by a woman (was she Polyxena in drag?) whom Ulysses, with an ambiguous gesture, instructed Diomedes to shoot in order to win Achilles back to the fray (the significance of the gesture only be-came clear in retrospect); Achilles had no Myrmidons, but simply shot Hector and then cut out his heart.[5] Once again Thersites was a war correspondent, an especially leering and clownish one who persisted in photographing all the most distasteful moments (the kissing scene, for example, which was, as so often, a kind of gang-rape, here presided over by Cressida's father).[6] Pandarus' epilogue was moved back to the end of 5.3 (a move no doubt prompted by the textual puzzle)[7] so that Troilus' reiterated threat 'I reck not though I end my life today' (from 5.6.26) ended the play as Cressida appeared like a ghost behind him. Earlier Cressida was sweet and unassuming, dressed in a dowdy print frock, driven to frenzy when forced to go (she tore her clothes from her small valise and threw them about, Troilus rather meekly helping to gather them up); but when accosted in the Greek camp, she was beaten down, forced into a cruel insistent dance that reduced her to an automaton, surrendering to Diomedes.[8]

Trevor Nunn's version for the National took the same approach to Cressida, even including the dance in 4.5, but moved her even more emphatically into the

---

[1] Rutter, p. 130–1. For the question of whether Cressida remains on stage during Ulysses' speech see note to 4.5.53 SD, and for the possible pun on strumpet, see 4.5.64 n.

[2] Taylor, *Independent*, 27 July 1996.

[3] Billington, *Guardian*, 25 July 1996, and Taylor, 27 July 1996.

[4] *Time Out*, 6–12 November 1998.

[5] Much of the compression (the part of Nestor was also cut) was due to the fact that the production was designed for touring, so there was a lot of doubling and eliminating of roles – as in the Elizabethan theatre.

[6] The stage direction at the beginning of the scene calls for the presence of Calchas, but he is nowhere acknowledged, nor does he speak. See note to 4.5.0 SD.2.

[7] See Textual Analysis, pp. 240–2. Apfelbaum discusses this problem at length though he does not cover this production.

[8] Details in this paragraph are derived from Robert Smallwood, *S.Sur.* 53 (2000), 260, promptbook and production photos, and Spencer, *Daily Telegraph*, 9 November 1998.

centre.[1] To do so he rearranged the text, opening with the second part of 1.2 where she and Pandarus observe the homecoming warriors. The bantering beginning of 1.2 and its thoughtful ending were delayed till after the Greek council scene (1.3) and Troilus' scene with Pandarus (1.1), so that the various emphases and parallels that Shakespeare is at pains to set up in the first act were reconfigured to put the stress on Cressida – while other characters and issues were made less salient (1.3 was also broken into two separate pieces – as it was by Kemble two hundred years earlier). The production took pains to differentiate Greeks and Trojans much more emphatically than Shakespeare does; the Greeks were vaguely Homeric, with brush helmets and leather breastplates, the Trojans exotic and Middle Eastern, Priam a cross between a despotic pasha and an Old Testament prophet. There were bowls of flame on tripods, and all the Trojans wore white, the men in loosely flowing gowns, Cressida in a fitted dress. To add to the contrast, all the Trojans (except, unaccountably, Pandarus) were black while the Greeks were all white. This made the production visually effective, especially when a very blonde Helen appeared in the midst of her totally black (except again for Pandarus) entourage, or when Cressida and then Hector appeared in the Greek camp, both of them forced unwillingly into an unfamiliar and demeaning erotic dance. But it missed a crucial point – the two sides are not that different. That Ajax and Hector are cousins is a paradigm of the relations between the warring parties, so that the oppositions between them are to a large degree constructed in order to validate the conflict – each side 'others' the other.

Sophie Okenedo, as Cressida, carried the weight of the interpretation. A great deal hinged on Troilus' reaction to the exchange; his shallowness, possessiveness and self-pity suddenly broke in on her – his insistence that she 'be true' showed her that he just didn't get it. Then her treatment in the Greek camp (4.5) forced her into Diomedes' cynical arms: on her entry, she tried to ward off Agamemnon's at first courteous and, when she refused, violently aggressive, kiss. His line of attack was of course imitated by his subordinates following their leader, so that her wit with Menelaus came off as self-protective, as did the desperate little dance that followed. At the end, in an unscripted entry, she appeared with Pandarus who tried to reconcile the maddened Troilus to her; she hung on him, but he thrust her viciously aside ('ignominy and shame / Pursue thy life . . .' being delivered to her more than Pandarus) and stormed off. While the leprous and scabrous Thersites hovered at the back, she stood rigid while Pandarus delivered himself of his epilogue and exited, followed by Thersites. The six great doors of the set then clanged shut and part of the upper wall descended to enclose her, a stricken and lonely victim of lust and war.

Of all the characters who have lost ground with the promotion of Cressida, Thersites, and Pandarus to the centre of the play, Troilus, even more than Ulysses, is the most important. No longer either admirable as a young soldier nor pitiable as a jilted lover, he is more likely nowadays to be scorned for letting down Cressida and blamed for

---

[1] I have relied mostly on my own notes for my discussion of this production, supplemented by Robert Smallwood's very full account in his review in *S.Sur.* 53 (2000), 257–9.

her betrayal. His strength and valour in war, acknowledged by Greek and Trojan alike, now appear at best like mindless violence, at worst like a mere delusion. There is no question that Shakespeare treats him ironically – his self-absorption in the first scene is a mark of this – but he also gives a kind of youthful grace to his hero (if that is the right word – at least Troilus has a better claim to the title than any other character). To his enemies he is, in Ulysses' words, 'Manly as Hector, but more dangerous . . . more vindicative than jealous love' (4.5.104–7). The simile is of course prophetic, since Troilus' jealous love leads him to unprecedented feats of blood, 'Mad and fantastic execution' (5.5.38). But Ulysses, in this crucial speech that Shakespeare may have added in revision, touches on a characteristic that any actor playing the part has to pay attention to – Troilus' mercilessness when 'provoked' (4.5.99). In 5.3 he accosts his more controlled older brother, scolding him for his 'vice of mercy' (37). The phrase is revealing: Troilus throws himself into battle as he does into love, with a kind of admirable folly. He is impetuous, 'not yet mature', as Ulysses is careful to say (4.5.97). But he is also, fatally, superficial. He has some of Romeo's ardour and courage but too much as well of Bertram's aristocratic narcissism. It is hard to make him count in a production that, like most these days, has other agendas. And it is easy to fault him. But if Cressida gets all the sympathy in what happens, then the play is slackened, its tensions unduly eased.

Like most of the productions surveyed, Nunn's was powerful but one-sided, not able finally to sound the many, and often discordant, notes of this frustrating but rewarding play. He went for a particular line or 'concept', one that inevitably sprang from the cultural currents of the day. Cressida, as I pointed out earlier, has emerged in the wake of feminism as a major, perhaps the main, character in the play, even though her role is a small one, especially in comparison to those of Ulysses or Troilus. This represents a distortion, no less so than the distortions produced by earlier productions where the lovers were submerged in the machismo of the war plot. But it is an entirely understandable one. All performances interpret, they all do what they can with the multivalent opportunities that the script provides. That's why it is important to see and understand a wide variety of productions – they each can cast a beam on a different facet of the play.

STAGING THE STAGING

A pervasive motif of *Troilus and Cressida* is the way the characters watch each other like spectators at a play. This feature naturally lends itself to experimental representation on the stage – indeed it underlies much of the elaborate scene-making just discussed. When Cressida and Pandarus observe from a distance the return of the Trojan warriors in the second scene, they establish a pattern that persists throughout. Cressida, like several of Shakespeare's comic heroines (Portia and Rosalind are good examples), is given an early scene in which her wit is displayed and her power enhanced. In her case, her power is tied explicitly to the act of watching. As Barbara Hodgdon has argued, Cressida is given a certain mastery over her own gaze, as opposed to that of the men, and she could even be said to call certain of the warriors, most pointedly Troilus, on to the stage.[1] At the same time the tone is playful, with Pandarus patently trying to impress and Cressida protesting in mock resistance.

The scene is a paradigm of the theatrical process itself and exemplifies how what is crucial in the play is presented to us in a double way – it is at one and the same time emphatic and mediated. It illustrates the dynamic of watcher and watched on-stage, with the audience as an extended part of the circle of observation. The action makes the heroes subject to the eyes of Pandarus and Cressida, whose act of 'reflection' (to use Ulysses' term) establishes them as 'heroes' or 'sneaking fellows' within the fiction itself – just as our watching establishes all of them as actors. The same issue comes up when Ulysses describes the theatrical mimicry of Patroclus, when Thersites imitates Ajax, when Cressida and Hector arrive among the 'merry Greeks', and when Troilus watches Cressida become 'not Cressid'. In every case the theatrical representation is in itself highlighted and remarked, and any production has to find a way to build that awareness into its own staging. This does *not* mean that the pain the characters feel, the amorous or martial dilemmas they struggle with, are any the less real for being so framed. But they are somewhat removed, so that as an audience we are exposed both to the raw emotions and to the frame that they are in. This enables the kind of critique, alternately savage and satirical, that the play mounts, but it does not cancel out the characters' feelings nor eliminate our emotional responses to them.

The play's concern with watching and performance culminates in the split-level sequence which enacts Cressida's betrayal and Troilus' reaction to it (5.2). One key here is Thersites, the ultimate voyeur and gossip ('They say he keeps a Trojan drab' (5.1.87) he says of Diomedes before following him to Calchas' tent). Even more than Pandarus, Thersites embodies the play's concern with watching and sneaking. His observation of, and observations on, the battle throughout the last act diminish it to 'wars and lechery', a motto endorsed by the programme of many a one-sidedly cynical production, 'Nothing else holds fashion' (5.2.192). His attendance at Cressida's betrayal turns it emphatically into a pageant, something rehearsed. In one sense, this belittles it, but in another sense the act of reflection focuses the intricate feelings by shining a spotlight upon them. The staging requires different spaces, perhaps slightly raised, for the watchers/commentators to speak from, with Diomedes and Cressida somewhere in the centre. The trick here is to mirror the first watching scene, with Troilus and Ulysses (as in the Barton–Kyle version in 1976), or perhaps Thersites, occupying the same platform as Cressida and Pandarus had occupied earlier. And now there's an extra layer, two sets of onstage watchers, a fact that the spatial layout will somehow register. Within this self-conscious frame there are vibrant human feelings being acted out: Troilus' pain and ontological anxiety, Cressida's self-division, Diomedes' impatient lust, Thersites' own voyeuristic desire.[2] That is the way the play works: Cressida is

---

[1] Hodgdon, pp. 262–72.
[2] Actors have occasionally given his repeated, 'now, now, now . . .' (5.2.64) an almost orgasmic frisson.

a theatrical spectacle but she is also painfully present. She, like Troilus, like Ulysses, like Thersites, is a creature of representation, but she, like them, is no less real for all that. Her presence, like theirs, to some degree escapes the theatrical prison-house of the space she inhabits. And finding a suitable style for that paradoxical mix of distance and proximity, scepticism and intensity, is the challenge that the play poses to directors, actors and, ultimately, audiences.

NOTE ON THE TEXT

The textual history of *Troilus and Cressida* is particularly knotty. There are two early editions, the quarto of 1609 (Q) and the Folio of 1623 (F). While these two are independent of each other (that is, the later edition is not simply a reprint of the earlier but was printed with reference to a different manuscript), their precise relation is difficult, even impossible, to determine. There are some 5,000 differences between the two texts, of which about 500 are substantive (i.e. different words, added words or lines etc.). Shakespeare seems to have made revisions at different stages of writing, copying, and performing the play and many of these revisions have apparently made their way into only one text, and not the other. This presents a number of problems to the editor. In the case of each variant, I, as editor, have had to determine as best I could which text offers the revised reading. The present text thus derives from a huge number of individual decisions – based on careful consideration of the best available evidence, but still fallible. For reasons discussed in the Textual Analysis (pp. 236–51), in which I provide a thorough account of the textual puzzles and suggest some tentative solutions, I have decided to base the present text on Q, which I believe contains a greater number of 'superior' readings. Where variants are more or less 'indifferent' (i.e. where they don't make much difference), I typically follow Q. An example is at 1.3.298, where Q reads 'my withered brawns' and F 'this withered brawn' (spelling modernised). But because the textual situation is so complex, I have felt free to draw from both texts, selecting readings from F that I consider to be superior to those offered by Q. Because these judgements are necessarily subjective, readers interested in this aspect of the play are encouraged to pay close attention to the collation (the small print below the play text on each page), which records all substantive variants between the two texts; this will allow them to assess the choices I have made.

The citations in the collation always begin with the reading that I have adopted for this text, followed by the source of that reading. When the adopted reading is from Q, the collation will then follow with the F reading (in original spelling) if that is different, and vice versa. If the adopted reading is an emendation from another source, then the rejected readings will follow in chronological order. Occasionally, editorial emendations that have been frequently adopted by subsequent editors, and are thus well established, are included in the collation even if I have not adopted them.

Reading the collation requires some practice. Here are some examples of entries that may serve as a brief guide.

Collation for 1.2.6

6 chid] Q; chides F

This means that in line 6 of Act 1, scene 2, my text follows the Q reading, 'chid', where F prints 'chides'.

Collation for 1.2.33

33 SD] F *(after 31); not in* Q

This indicates (1) that the stage direction (SD) following line 33 comes from F, but in this text it is placed not after line 31 as it is in F, but after line 33; and (2) that the stage direction does not occur at all in Q.

Collation for 1.3.31

thy godlike] *Theobald;* the godlike Q; thy godly F

Here the present text follows an emendation first made by the eighteenth-century editor Lewis Theobald who combined the Q and F readings recorded here. (The names of editors and commentators cited in the collation are explained in the List of Abbreviations, pp. ix–xvi.)

Collation for 2.2.51–2

51-2 Brother . . . keeping] *Theobald (substituting* holding *for* keeping*); as prose* Q; Brother . . . worth / What . . . holding F

Verse lineation is frequently noted in the collation. In this complex example, the entry indicates that my text follows Theobald's lineation, while Q prints the passage as prose and F places the line-break differently (after 'worth'); the collation also reveals that Theobald follows F in reading 'holding' for Q's 'keeping' whereas I follow Q (as recorded in the following collation note for 52).

In the case of obvious misprints, there is no collation. Nor do I collate punctuation differences unless they significantly alter the meaning of a line. When one text has 'est' and the other ''st' at the end of a verb form (e.g. 'seemest' and 'seem'st'), this edition does not provide a collation, and typically the elided form is chosen unless the metre requires otherwise. Similarly, variants such as 'th'haue' and 'they'aue' (modernised to 'they've'), 'haue't' and 'ha't', or 'ne'er' and 'neuer' are not collated. (Since the language of Pandarus and Thersites is characteristically colloquial, I usually choose the elided form in their speeches when the early texts vary, collating when necessary.) There is some small evidence of proof-reading having been done on the F text, because of the resetting of the first page (explained in the Textual Analysis, p. 245), and again in parts of 3.1. These are collated as 'corr.' (corrected) and 'uncorr.' (uncorrected).

The language, spelling, and punctuation of this edition have been modernised. Hence the collation does not record modernisation of words such as: 'lose' for 'loose' (1.3.118;

3.2.33); 'corpse' for 'coarse' or 'course' (2.3.27); 'got' for 'gat' (2.3.224); 'yon' for 'yond' (4.5.220); 'good night' for 'God night' (5.1.64); 'woo' for 'woe', or 'ay' for 'I' (both of which occur frequently), etc. Similarly, when 'and' in the original text means 'an' (i.e. 'if'), this edition prints 'an' without collation; so too when 'a' means 'he', it is printed as ''a'. Compound words are also silently modernised: thus 'any thing' becomes 'anything', 'some thing' 'something'. With some words that have been treated by previous editors as emendations, the collation records the change as a modernisation, as, for example (at 1.3.2) 'jaundice] Q (Iaundies), F' or (at 1.3.157) 'scaffoldage] Q (scoaffollage), F (Scaffolage)'. For words that are now archaic, the modern equivalent appears if it does not disturb the metre or rhyme, and the change is collated (e.g. 'porcupine' for 'porpentin(e)' at 2.1.21). Proper names have also been modernised and regularised, and are printed in roman though in the early texts they are generally in italic. Thus 'Troylus' is spelled 'Troilus' throughout, 'Aiax' 'Ajax', etc. Shortened forms such as 'Cressid' and 'Diomed' are used when they so appear in the early texts. Other classical names are spelled according to modern conventions. For words ending in –ed, this edition prints 'èd' when the syllable is sounded, and 'ed' when it is unsounded. Where there is ambiguity, the 'e' is elided (e.g. 'dogg'd' (1.3.364), 'belov'd' (4.5.292)). Modernisation, while obviously helpful to today's readers, can occasionally result in suppression of a potential play on words available to Elizabethan readers and playgoers. Where it appears to me that there is some kind of alternative or submerged meaning produced by the looseness of early modern spelling, I have pointed that out in the Commentary – e.g. at 1.3.208 and 3.3.110.

Stage directions pose another problem. Stage directions inside square brackets ([]) are editorial additions to the early texts, inserted in order to help the reader imagine the stage action. This is a tricky enterprise, since, as varying stage interpretations constantly remind us, the same text can yield very different stage enactments. When stage action seems ambiguous, it is often best to indicate that in the Commentary, a practice I have frequently followed, sometimes omitting stage directions where other editors have seen fit to include them. In printing stage directions, I have placed square brackets around anything that appears in *neither* Q nor F. I have done so not only because of the complex relationship between Q and F, but also because, as explained in the Textual Analysis (pp. 242–4), the F text, though not my copy text, bears the marks of some theatrical revision. The square brackets, then, alert the reader to my additions to either or both of the early texts. All such changes and additions to original stage directions are collated, as are all differences in stage directions between Q and F.

The punctuation in this edition, while modernised, is somewhat lighter than in most previous editions. I have tried to catch something of the flavour of Elizabethan punctuation by omitting commas where they might appear in modern discourse (after a vocative for instance), and by using more colons and dashes, and fewer full stops. In doing this I have tried to keep performance always in mind, punctuating for the voice more than for the eye. Since the text contains a lot of complicated syntax, it is not always possible to achieve the lightness one would like. The important thing, in reading the text, is to try to get the breath and the voice around the words, using the punctuation as a guide but not a straitjacket.

Because of the complexities of the textual situation, I have included all the passages that occur in F only, even though some of them were probably cut by Shakespeare during the preparation of the manuscript behind Q, with three exceptions: one short passage after 1.3.355, the phrase 'They call him Troilus' in F at 4.5.96 (which occurs again twelve lines later), and the passage after 5.3.111 that is repeated at 5.11.32–4. The reasons for these omissions are explained in the Textual Analysis, pp. 240–2.

Troilus and Cressida

A NEVER WRITER TO AN EVER READER: NEWS

Eternal reader, you have here a new play, never staled with the stage, never clapper-clawed with the palms of the vulgar, and yet passing full of the palm comical – for it is a birth of your brain that never undertook anything comical vainly. And were but the vain names of comedies changed for the titles of commodities, or of plays for pleas, you should see all those grand censors that   5
now style them such vanities, flock to them for the main grace of their gravities – especially this author's comedies that are so framed to the life that they serve for the most common commentaries of all the actions of our lives, showing such a dexterity and power of wit that the most displeased with plays are pleased with his comedies.   10

And all such dull and heavy-witted worldlings as were never capable of the wit of a comedy, coming by report of them to his representations, have found that wit there that they never found in themselves, and have parted better witted than

---

This prefatory epistle appears only in the 1609 Quarto (second state). I discuss its relevance for the play's early performance and publication history in the Introduction (pp. 7–8) and in the Textual Analysis (pp. 234–5). Its author is unknown.

1–3 never . . . palm comical never made stale by being performed onstage, never foolishly applauded by vulgar, popular audiences, yet graced with comic excellence ('palm' = laurel bestowed on the victorious). Since this is a publisher's blurb, the claim that the play was never performed publicly is suspect, just as the statement that the play is 'new' (1) is false (see Introduction, pp. 6–8).

3 your that (i.e. Shakespeare's). 'Your' is frequently used in this kind of general way in colloquial English even today.

4 vainly in vain.

4–5 And . . . pleas The language here is that of business and law, the common currency of the intended purchasers of the volume.

4 vain unprofitable.

5 commodities objects with commercial value.

5 pleas lawsuits.

5 grand censors self-important critics (those allied with the city or Church authorities who opposed the theatre).

6 style . . . vanities call them 'vanities' – i.e. worthless pursuits (as in the biblical phrase 'all is vanity').

6 gravities seriousness (in contrast to 'vanities').

7 framed . . . life realistic, lifelike. Note that the author here seems to be thinking of the 'life' of the stage which he had previously denigrated, since that is where the mimetic exactitude of Shakespeare's plays is most evident.

11 worldlings those devoted to pleasure.

12 representations performances. Again, the author seems to contradict himself, now praising the stage instead of scorning it.

they came, feeling an edge of wit set upon them more than ever they dreamed
they had brain to grind it on. So much and such savoured salt of wit is in his   15
comedies that they seem (for their height of pleasure) to be born in that sea that
brought forth Venus. Amongst all there is none more witty than this. And had I
time I would comment upon it, though I know it needs not, for so much as will
make you think your testern well bestowed, but for so much worth as even poor
I know to be stuffed in it. It deserves such a labour as well as the best comedy   20
in Terence or Plautus. And believe this, that when he is gone, and his comedies
out of sale, you will scramble for them and set up a new English Inquisition.
Take this for a warning and, at the peril of your pleasure's loss, and judgement's,
refuse not, nor like this the less for not being sullied with the smoky breath of
the multitude. But thank fortune for the scape it hath made amongst you, since   25
by the grand possessors' wills I believe you should have prayed for them rather
than been prayed. And so I leave all such to be prayed for – for the states of their
wits' healths – that will not praise it. *Vale.*

14–15 feeling . . . it on finding that their wits have been sharpened more than they could have imagined
(the image is of a blade ('wit') on a whetstone ('brain')).

17 Venus Goddess of love, who was born from the sea (as depicted, for example, in Botticelli's famous
painting).

17–20 And . . . stuffed in it If I had time, I would offer commentary (though I know there is no need)
showing the value that even a poor fellow like myself might find in it, enough to make you think your sixpence
('testern' – the cost of the book) well spent.

21 Terence or Plautus Latin comic playwrights, known to all Elizabethan schoolboys, and considered
the very pattern of comic writing.

21 he Shakespeare.

22 Inquisition Search, with a joking reference to the Spanish Inquisition, the notorious ecclesiastical
office whose mission was to root out heresy. Muir sees an allusion to an attempt on Archbishop Whitgift's
part in 1584 to set up an ecclesiastical commission to seek out unlawfully printed books and other 'puritan'
abuses.

24–5 sullied . . . multitude another scornful allusion to the 'vulgar' audience at public stage performances. The author's ambivalence about the stage is one of the most salient features of this preface.

25 scape escape – i.e. the publication of the play which has thus been made available for the reader's
delectation.

26–7 by the grand . . . been prayed i.e. I think that (if the owners of the play (see next n.) had had their
way) you would have been begging them to release it rather than now being begged to buy your own copy.

26 grand possessors owners of the play – presumably the players who no doubt owned the MS. It used
to be thought that acting companies would oppose publication because it would make the text available to
whatever troupe might want to stage it, but recent theatre historians have undermined this view (see Blayney,
pp. 385–7, 416–17 and Knutson, pp. 469–70). Just why in this case the possessors of the MS. on which the
quarto is based should have opposed publication is not clear.

26 prayed Continuing the play on words, the author now ironically uses 'pray' in the religious sense,
implying that those who 'will not praise' *Troilus and Cressida* are in danger of losing not their souls but their
wit.

28 Vale Farewell (Latin).

LIST OF CHARACTERS

PROLOGUE

The Trojans

PRIAM, *King of Troy*
HECTOR
PARIS, *Helen's lover*
DEIPHOBUS } *Priam's sons*
HELENUS, *a priest*
TROILUS
MARGARELON, *a bastard son of Priam*
AENEAS } *Trojan commanders*
ANTENOR
CALCHAS, *Cressida's father, a Trojan priest, who has defected to the Greeks*
CASSANDRA, *Priam's daughter, a prophetess*
ANDROMACHE, *Hector's wife*
CRESSIDA, *Calchas' daughter*
PANDARUS, *a lord, Cressida's uncle*
ALEXANDER, *servant to Cressida*
A BOY, *servant to Troilus*
MAN, *servant to Troilus*
SERVANT *to* Paris
Soldiers, musicians, and attendants

The Greeks

AGAMEMNON, *the Greek general*
MENELAUS, *Agamemnon's brother and Helen's husband*
NESTOR
ULYSSES
ACHILLES
AJAX } *Greek commanders*
DIOMEDES
PATROCLUS
THERSITES, *a bitter, cynical fool*
HELEN, *Menelaus' wife, living with Paris in Troy*
SERVANT *to Diomedes*

75

A MYRMIDON
Other servants, soldiers, Myrmidons, attendants, trumpeter

Notes

There is no *dramatis personae* in Q or F. Rowe was the first to provide one, though it was incomplete; lists in modern editions derive from Malone.

PROLOGUE First included as a character by Walker.

PARIS Called upon to judge a beauty contest among the gods, the Paris of mythology was rewarded by the winner, Aphrodite (Venus), with the gift of the most beautiful woman in the world – Helen.

MARGARELON This is the spelling in Q, F though recent editors (Oxford, Bevington²) have preferred 'Margareton' as in Benoit, Lydgate ('Margariton'), and Caxton. Since the error is just as likely to have been Shakespeare's as the compositors', I have followed Q, F.

ANTENOR He speaks not a word in the whole play, though he appears in several scenes, most crucially when he is exchanged for Cressida (4.3 and 4.4).

CASSANDRA In Greek mythology, she offended Apollo by resisting his advances; as a result, though she could accurately foresee the future, she was condemned never to be believed.

CRESSIDA Often called 'Cressid' as well; the name derives from Chryseis, Agamemnon's mistress in *The Iliad*, but her story is medieval in origin.

PANDARUS As with Cressida, he appears in Homer, but his real origin is medieval. The common word 'pander' derives from his name, a fact that Shakespeare occasionally alludes to in the play.

MENELAUS The ancient world's most famous cuckold, he has lost Helen to Paris and the Trojan War is the result.

ULYSSES The clever and wily hero of *The Odyssey*, he is the shrewdest of the Greeks in the play.

ACHILLES The most famous of the Greek warriors, the wrathful hero of *The Iliad*.

AJAX In the play and its medieval sources, though not in Greek mythology, he is identified as the son of Hesione, Priam's sister. He is thus a first cousin of his Trojan opponents, Hector, Troilus, and their brothers.

DIOMEDES Much more frequently called 'Diomed' in the play.

THERSITES Throughout 2.1 and 2.3, he is called a 'fool' (i.e. a licensed commentator, one who can freely speak his mind – though Ajax beats him for it); at 2.3.82, we are told that Ajax's fury derives from the fact that Achilles has 'inveigled' Ajax's 'fool' (i.e. Thersites) from him. He is often depicted as deformed or diseased.

HELEN Though known as 'Helen of Troy' she was a Greek, carried to Troy by Paris, and the unwitting cause of the Trojan War.

TROILUS AND CRESSIDA

Prologue

[*Enter the* PROLOGUE *in armour*]

PROLOGUE In Troy there lies the scene: from isles of Greece
    The princes orgulous, their high blood chafed,
    Have to the port of Athens sent their ships,
    Fraught with the ministers and instruments
    Of cruel war. Sixty and nine that wore   5
    Their crownets regal from th'Athenian bay
    Put forth toward Phrygia, and their vow is made
    To ransack Troy, within whose strong immures
    The ravished Helen, Menelaus' queen,
    With wanton Paris sleeps – and that's the quarrel.   10
    To Tenedos they come,
    And the deep-drawing barks do there disgorge
    Their warlike freightage; now on Dardan plains
    The fresh and yet unbruisèd Greeks do pitch

Prologue 0–31] F; *not in* Q   0 SD] *Walker (after Collier*[3]*);* PROLOGUE. *Spoken by one in* Armour / Singer; *not in* F
1 SH] *Walker; not in* F   8 immures] F2; *emures* F   12 barks] F2; *Barke* F   13 freightage] F *(frautage)*

Prologue

0 SD The Prologue, though it appears only in F, was probably written for an early performance (see 23 n.). It certainly suggests a performance of some kind and would thus contradict the claims of those who think the play was never acted. In recent productions it has been spoken by a variety of characters, most often Thersites or Pandarus; strangely, the speech contains no reference to Troilus and Cressida.

2 **orgulous** proud. The word occurs in Caxton, but was already archaic in 1600.

2 **high blood** aristocratic valour.

2 **chafed** heated, brought to the boiling point (cf. modern 'chafing-dish').

3–7 **Have . . . Phrygia** The details here (the 'port of Athens', 'Sixty and nine') are taken from Caxton, but the high heroic tone, tinged with irony, is Shakespeare's own.

4 **Fraught** Loaded, weighed down.

6 **crownets** coronets, small crowns.

7 **Phrygia** An area in Asia minor, now Turkey, where Troy was thought to have been located.

8 **immures** walls.

9 **ravished** stolen, abducted. The word has a sexual connotation but does not necessarily imply a lack of consent on Helen's part.

11 **Tenedos** An island off the coast near Troy.

12 **deep-drawing barks** boats ('barks') that because of their size and weight 'draw', i.e. displace, a great depth of water (*OED* Draw *v* 13). Cf. 2.3.249.

12 **disgorge** empty out.

13 **warlike freightage** i.e. the Greek troops.

13 **Dardan** Trojan; the word derives from 'Dardanus', son of Zeus and grandfather of Tros, founder of Troy, as described in *The Iliad* xx.200 ff. (Chapman, *Iliads*).

14 **yet unbruisèd** not yet wounded. This is the first of many instances in the play of words beginning with the prefix 'un–' (e.g. 'unpractised', 1.1.12; 'ungracious', 1.1.83; 'ungained', 1.2.249;

Their brave pavilions. Priam's six-gated city,   15
Dardan and Timbria, Helias, Chetas, Troien,
And Antenorides with massy staples
And corresponsive and fulfilling bolts
Spar up the sons of Troy.
Now expectation, tickling skittish spirits   20
On one and other side, Trojan and Greek,
Sets all on hazard. And hither am I come,
A prologue armed, but not in confidence
Of author's pen or actor's voice, but suited
In like conditions as our argument,   25
To tell you, fair beholders, that our play
Leaps o'er the vaunt and firstlings of those broils,
Beginning in the middle, starting thence away,
To what may be digested in a play.
Like, or find fault, do as your pleasures are,   30
Now good or bad, 'tis but the chance of war.   [*Exit*]

---

17 Antenorides] *Theobald;* Antenonidus F   **19** Spar] *Pope*² (Sperre; *conj. Theobald*); Stirre F   **31** SD] *Walker (subst.);*
not in F

'unbodied', 1.3.16, etc.); many of these are Shake-spearean coinages.

15 brave splendid. The word, together with the chivalric associations of 'pavilions' (large tents), creates a sense of grandeur offset by the venality of the Greek heroes when they appear.

16–17 Dardan . . . Antenorides The names of the six gates of Troy (taken from Caxton).

17–18 massy . . . bolts huge metal braces into which fit correspondingly huge bolts.

19 Spar up Enclose and secure (*OED* v^1 3). Theobald's suggestion for F's 'Stirre' puts the emphasis where the rest of the sentence would seem to require – on the protective strength of the city's gates. Compare 'There sparred up in gates, / The valiant Thaebane . . . a following fight awaites' (William Warner, *Albion's England*, 2.12.50 (1589), cited in *OED*). Technically, the verb should be singular, since the subject is 'city' (15), but the naming of the six gates makes the grammatical slippage understandable; some editors, notably Palmer, have regarded 'sons of Troy' as the subject of the sentence and envisaged them 'stirring up' the city. But such a reading not only makes the grammar awkward but misses the emphasis on protection.

20 expectation The feeling of anticipation on both sides is personified, and imagined to be flirtatiously toying with ('tickling') the lively ('skittish') spirits of the soldiers. Bevington² notes that 'tickle' occurs frequently in the play, usually with teasingly sexual implications – see, for example,

1.2.119, 3.1.104, 5.2.56 and 176.

22 Sets . . . hazard Puts everything at risk, as in a game of chance (*OED* Hazard *sb* 1, 3).

23 armed The Prologue wears armour appropriate to the occasion. There is probably a satirical allusion here to Jonson's play, *Poetaster* (1601), which also features an armed prologue. If so, this would suggest that the Prologue, though not printed till 1623, was written for an early performance, since only then would the allusion have had much bite. See Introduction, p. 6.

23–4 not . . . voice without much confidence in either play or performance – a comment in the self-deprecating style of Shakespeare's prologues (e.g. *H5*) and epilogues (e.g. *AYLI*). See Introduction, p. 9.

24–5 suited . . . argument dressed in a way suitable to our theme.

27 vaunt beginning (cf. 'vanguard'). 'Vaunt and firstlings' is deliberately and sonorously redundant, the first of many such doublets in the play. There may also be a hint of 'vaunt' in the sense of 'boast', the kind of thing that warriors do before combat.

28 Beginning . . . middle Epic poems also typically begin *in medias res* – a further instance of the ironically heightened rhetoric of this speech.

29 digested suitably contained in; the term introduces the pervasive strain of eating and cooking images in the play.

31 War, like theatrical success, was notoriously and proverbially (Dent c223) chancy.

[1.1] *Enter* PANDARUS *and* TROILUS

TROILUS Call here my varlet – I'll unarm again.
　　　　Why should I war without the walls of Troy
　　　　That find such cruel battle here within?
　　　　Each Trojan that is master of his heart,
　　　　Let him to field. Troilus, alas, hath none.　　　　　　5
PANDARUS Will this gear ne'er be mended?
TROILUS The Greeks are strong and skilful to their strength,
　　　　Fierce to their skill and to their fierceness valiant,
　　　　But I am weaker than a woman's tear,
　　　　Tamer than sleep, fonder than ignorance,　　　　　10
　　　　Less valiant than the virgin in the night,
　　　　And skilless as unpractised infancy.
PANDARUS Well, I have told you enough of this. For my part, I'll not
　　　　meddle nor make no farther: he that will have a cake out of the
　　　　wheat must tarry the grinding.　　　　　　　　　　15
TROILUS Have I not tarried?
PANDARUS Ay, the grinding, but you must tarry the bolting.
TROILUS Have I not tarried?
PANDARUS Ay, the bolting, but you must tarry the leavening.
TROILUS Still have I tarried.　　　　　　　　　　　　　20

Act 1, Scene 1   1.1] F *(Actus Primus. Scœna Prima.); not in* Q   15 must] Q; must needes F   19 leavening] Q; leau'ning
F *(first setting);* leau'ing F *(second setting)*

Act 1, Scene 1

1 Call ... varlet Troilus, coming onstage
armed but with no taste for battle, directs an
offstage attendant to call his personal servant ('varlet').

2–3 The image of love as an internal battle is
a common one and marks Troilus out as in some
respects a traditional courtly lover. The language
announces the persistent linking of love and war in
the play as a whole.

5 none Troilus has no heart, having given it to
Cressida.

6 gear business.

7, 8 to Either (1) in proportion to, or (2) in addition to. Troilus here employs an intricate rhetorical
figure, a form of reduplication in which verbal ideas
are repeated in an alternating way. He follows this
with extended parallelism in the next four lines, in
which he elaborates the antitheses of the same ideas
(strength / weakness, fierceness / tameness, etc.) as

they apply to him. All of this indicates the self-
consciousness with which he suffers the pangs of
love.

12 unpractised inexperienced.

13–14 not ... farther have nothing more to do
with. A proverbial phrase (Dent M852) repeated at
77.

15 tarry await.

17 bolting sifting. That these baking terms
have a sexual reference seems clear from Justini-
ano's remarks in Dekker and Webster's *Westward
Ho* (1604): 'Why should I long to eate of Bakers
bread onely, when theres so much Sifting, and
bolting, and grynding in euery corner of the
Citty; men and women are borne, and come
running into the world faster than coaches doe
into Cheap-side vvpon *Symon* and *Iudes* day'
(2.1.169–73, in *The Dramatic Works of Thomas
Dekker*, ed. Fredson Bowers, Cambridge, 1955,
vol. 2).

PANDARUS Ay, to the leavening; but here's yet in the word hereafter
the kneading, the making of the cake, the heating of the oven, and
the baking; nay, you must stay the cooling too or you may chance
burn your lips.

TROILUS Patience herself, what goddess e'er she be,   25
    Doth lesser blench at suff'rance than I do:
    At Priam's royal table do I sit
    And when fair Cressid comes into my thoughts –
    So traitor! 'When she comes!' When is she thence?

PANDARUS Well, she looked yesternight fairer than ever I saw her look,   30
or any woman else.

TROILUS I was about to tell thee – when my heart,
    As wedgèd with a sigh, would rive in twain
    Lest Hector or my father should perceive me,
    I have, as when the sun doth light a storm,   35
    Buried this sigh in wrinkle of a smile.
    But sorrow that is couched in seeming gladness
    Is like that mirth fate turns to sudden sadness.

PANDARUS An her hair were not somewhat darker than Helen's –
well go to, there were no more comparison between the women;   40
but for my part she is my kinswoman, I would not, as they term
it, praise her, but I would somebody had heard her talk yesterday
as I did. I will not dispraise your sister Cassandra's wit but –

---

21 hereafter] Q, F; 'hereafter' *Dyce*   22 heating of] F *(second setting)*; heating Q, F *(first setting)*   23 you may] F; yea
may Q   24 burn] Q; to burne F   26 suff'rance] Q *(suffrance)*; sufferance F   29 So traitor . . . thence?] *Rowe² (subst.)*;
So traitor then she comes when she is thence. Q; So (traitor) then she comes, when she is thence. F   30–1] Q; Well: /
She . . . looke, / Or . . . else.   F   35 a storm] *Rowe*; a scorne Q; a-scorne F; askance *Oxford*   42 praise her] Q; praise
it F

21 **the word** i.e. 'tarry' which implies that after
the leavening must come the kneading, etc. Many
editors follow Dyce in assuming that 'word' refers
to 'hereafter' (21), but 'tarry' seems the likelier possibility.
26 **blench** blanch, flinch. Though Troilus means
that Patience is less able to endure painful waiting
than he is, he actually says the opposite.
29 Troilus calls himself a traitor for even entertaining the possibility that Cressida might sometimes be absent from his thoughts. Although some
editors follow Q, F here, Rowe's emendation makes
excellent sense. If the emendation were rejected,
the line would read, 'So, traitor, then she comes
when she is thence', and Troilus would be be-
rating himself for sometimes forgetting Cressida

(since she can only come into his thoughts (28) if
she is absent from them).
33 **wedgèd** split (as with a wedge).
33 **rive** break.
35 **a storm** Although Q, F's 'a-scorne' has been
defended, notably by Evans who understands it
to mean 'in mockery', Rowe's emendation fits the
context well, especially in the light of the interplay between sorrow and 'seeming gladness' in 37–
8. A graphic misreading is also possible. In both
Lear and *Oth.*, 'scorn' and 'storm' are (possibly)
confused. The quarto of *Lear* (at 3.1.10), in lines
not in F, reads 'outscorne' but many editors have
emended to 'outstorm' and Q1 of *Oth.* has 'scorne
of fortunes' at 1.3.249 while F reads 'storme'.
39 **An** If (as frequently in the play).

TROILUS O Pandarus! I tell thee Pandarus,
       When I do tell thee there my hopes lie drowned   45
       Reply not in how many fathoms deep
       They lie indrenched. I tell thee I am mad
       In Cressid's love, thou answer'st she is fair,
       Pour'st in the open ulcer of my heart
       Her eyes, her hair, her cheek, her gait, her voice,   50
       Handlest in thy discourse – O that her hand,
       In whose comparison all whites are ink
       Writing their own reproach, to whose soft seizure
       The cygnet's down is harsh and spirit of sense
       Hard as the palm of ploughman – this thou tell'st me,   55
       As true thou tell'st me, when I say I love her.
       But saying thus, instead of oil and balm
       Thou lay'st in every gash that love hath given me
       The knife that made it.
PANDARUS I speak no more than truth.   60
TROILUS Thou dost not speak so much.
PANDARUS Faith, I'll not meddle in it – let her be as she is; if she be
    fair 'tis the better for her; an she be not, she has the mends in her
    own hands.
TROILUS Good Pandarus, how now Pandarus!   65
PANDARUS I have had my labour for my travail, ill-thought on of her
    and ill-thought on of you, gone between and between, but small
    thanks for my labour.
TROILUS What, art thou angry Pandarus, what, with me?
PANDARUS Because she's kin to me, therefore she's not so fair as Helen;   70
    an she were not kin to me she would be as fair o'Friday as Helen

---

51 discourse – . . . hand,] *Capell (subst.);* discourse: . . . hand Q; discourse. . . . hand F   **62** in it] Q; in't F   **67** on of you] F; of you Q   **71** not kin] F *(second setting);* kin Q, F *(first setting)*   **71** o'Friday] Q *(a Friday);* on Friday F

49 ulcer Troilus' image is characteristically excessive. It fits with the strain of disease imagery in the play generally and hints at a dark undertone to the love theme.

51 Again Troilus interrupts himself (as in 29), this time losing track of the grammar of his sentence. 'Handlest' (= treat of, discuss) suggests Cressida's white hand to him, and he follows that vein for the next four lines.

53–4 to whose . . . harsh in comparison to whose soft grasp ('seizure'), the down of a baby swan ('cygnet') seems rough.

54 spirit of sense the most delicate touch. In

Elizabethan physiology, each sense had its own 'spirit' or vapour that flowed through the body, conveying sensation to the brain. See 3.3.106 n.

63 mends remedy (*OED* Mend *sb* 2).

65 Perhaps Pandarus has turned as if to go, prompting Troilus' remonstration.

66 my . . . travail my labour ('travail', with a pun on the 'travel' involved in going between) has been the only reward I have received.

67 gone between The standard action of the pander, or 'go-between'.

71–2 an she . . . Sunday if she weren't related to me, I would say that she is as lovely on an ordinary

is on Sunday. But what care I? I care not an she were a blackamoor,
'tis all one to me –

TROILUS Say I she is not fair?

PANDARUS I do not care whether you do or no. She's a fool to stay be-   75
hind her father – let her to the Greeks and so I'll tell her the next
time I see her; for my part, I'll meddle nor make no more i'th'matter.

TROILUS Pandarus –

PANDARUS Not I.

TROILUS Sweet Pandarus –   80

PANDARUS Pray you speak no more to me; I will leave all as I found
it and there an end.   *Exit*

Sound alarum

TROILUS Peace, you ungracious clamours, peace, rude sounds!
Fools on both sides, Helen must needs be fair
When with your blood you daily paint her thus.   85
I cannot fight upon this argument,
It is too starved a subject for my sword.
But Pandarus – O gods how do you plague me!
I cannot come to Cressid but by Pandar
And he's as tetchy to be wooed to woo   90
As she is stubborn, chaste against all suit.
Tell me Apollo, for thy Daphne's love,
What Cressid is, what Pandar, and what we:
Her bed is India, there she lies, a pearl;
Between our Ilium and where she resides   95
Let it be called the wild and wand'ring flood,
Ourself the merchant and this sailing Pandar

---

72 what care] F; what Q   75 SH] Q, F *(first setting, subst.); Troy.* F *(second setting)*   82 SD *Exit*] Q; *Exit Pand.* F   91 stubborn, chaste] Q, F; stubborn-chaste *Theobald*   95 resides] F *(recides);* reides Q

weekday (or perhaps 'on a day of abstinence') as Helen is when she's dressed up in her Sunday best.

72 blackamoor black African. Elizabethans regarded pale skin as an element of ideal female beauty. Cf. 1.2.81 n.

75–6 stay behind her father remain in Troy after her father (Calchas) has left.

82 SD *alarum* call to battle (usually with trumpet and drum).

86 argument theme, cause.

87 starved narrow, unfulfilling. The word alludes to the pervasive language of eating, weight, inflation, stuffing, etc. (see Parker, p. 225).

90 tetchy touchy.

92 Apollo wooed the nymph Daphne, who refused his advances and finally escaped his pursuit

by being changed into a laurel tree (Ovid, Book 1).

94 While India is a traditional source of exotic wealth (compare *Oth.* 5.2.347–8 where Othello compares himself to a 'base Indian' who 'threw a pearl away / Richer than all his tribe'), Troilus' explicit comparison with Cressida's *bed* is indecorous and 'impugns his . . . idealism' (Greene, p. 138). See also 2.2.81–2 n.

95 Ilium The ancient name for Troy, frequently used also to denote the palace; here, though, the reference is more to the city itself, as Cressida's bed is imagined to be far-off India.

97–8 Troilus compares himself to a merchant ship and Pandarus to a 'bark' or smaller ship, acting as a 'convoy' or escort (*OED* Convoy *sb* 3, 7b; *OED* dates the first specifically nautical use of the noun

Our doubtful hope, our convoy and our bark.

Alarum. Enter AENEAS

AENEAS How now, Prince Troilus! Wherefore not afield?
TROILUS Because not there; this woman's answer sorts,   100
    For womanish it is to be from thence.
    What news, Aeneas, from the field today?
AENEAS That Paris is returnèd home and hurt.
TROILUS By whom, Aeneas?
AENEAS Troilus, by Menelaus.   105
TROILUS Let Paris bleed – 'tis but a scar to scorn,
    Paris is gored with Menelaus' horn.

Alarum

AENEAS Hark what good sport is out of town today!
TROILUS Better at home if 'would I might' were 'may'.
    But to the sport abroad – are you bound thither?   110
AENEAS In all swift haste.
TROILUS Come, go we then together.

Exeunt

[1.2] *Enter* CRESSIDA *and her man* [ALEXANDER]

CRESSIDA Who were those went by?
ALEXANDER   Queen Hecuba and Helen.

99] Q; *two lines (Troylus? / Wherefore) F   109 'would . . . might' . . .'may'] Theobald (subst.); would . . . might
. . . may Q, F   Act 1, Scene 2 1.2] Capell (subst.); not in Q, F   0 SD ALEXANDER] Theobald; not in Q, F
1 SH ALEXANDER] Malone (subst.); Man Q, F (throughout scene)*

in 1636, but this seems to be an earlier instance).
The image of the lover as a boat tossed by wind and
wave is another of Troilus' clichés adapted from the
courtly love tradition.
    100 woman's answer referring to the proverb,
'Because is woman's reason' (Dent B179).
    100 sorts is fitting.
    106 scar wound.
    107 horn The reference is to the cuckold's
horns, the classic mark of masculine sexual shame,
resulting from a wife's infidelity. Similar jokes re-
cur throughout.
    108, 110 sport Aeneas is referring to the athletic
challenge of battle, but Troilus puns on 'sport' in
the sense of 'sexual play'.

Act 1, Scene 2
    0 SD Editors often place Cressida, Alexander, and
later Pandarus on the upper stage for this scene. Although this would give them a vantage point from

which they can review the procession of heroes
later on, it seems unnecessarily restrictive. For one
thing, the first 150 lines of the scene do not require
any such expedient. The Elizabethan upper stage,
which offered no visible access to the main level,
was a relatively small area and was rarely used for
scenes of this length. Exceptions, such as the 'bal-
cony scene' in *Rom.* (2.2) or the castle scene in *R2*
(3.3) typically have a split focus, with much of the
action on the main platform. Modern productions,
with more flexible stage spaces, often find a com-
promise solution, perhaps a slightly raised platform
at the back to which Pandarus and Cressida can
move at 151–2 (see n.). The scene simply requires us to imagine Cressida and the others standing somewhere outdoors, but within the Trojan
citadel.
    1 Hecuba and Helen As in a few modern
productions this reference could mean that they
are briefly visible to the audience, though Hecuba

CRESSIDA And whither go they?

ALEXANDER   Up to the eastern tower,
Whose height commands as subject all the vale,
To see the battle. Hector, whose patience
Is as a virtue fixed, today was moved: 5
He chid Andromache and struck his armourer
And, like as there were husbandry in war,
Before the sun rose he was harnessed light
And to the field goes he, where every flower
Did as a prophet weep what it foresaw   10
In Hector's wrath.

CRESSIDA   What was his cause of anger?

ALEXANDER The noise goes, this: there is among the Greeks
A lord of Trojan blood, nephew to Hector,
They call him Ajax.

CRESSIDA   Good, and what of him?

ALEXANDER They say he is a very man *per se* and stands alone.   15

CRESSIDA So do all men, unless they are drunk, sick, or have no legs.

ALEXANDER This man, lady, hath robbed many beasts of their particular additions: he is as valiant as the lion, churlish as the bear, slow
as the elephant, a man into whom nature hath so crowded humours
that his valour is crushed into folly, his folly sauced with discretion.   20
There is no man hath a virtue that he hath not a glimpse of, nor any
man an attaint but he carries some stain of it. He is melancholy

---

6 chid] Q; chides F   12] Q; *two lines* (this; / There) F   15] Q, F; *as verse* (se, / And) *Capell*   16 they] F; the Q
20 sauced] Q, F; farced *Theobald;* forced *Cam.*

---

never again appears in the play. This is the first
of many instances where characters watch and
comment upon one another (see Introduction,
pp. 19–22).

3 The tower is compared to a king who controls
those beneath him.

3 vale valley.

5 fixed constant, steadfast.

5 moved agitated, angry.

7 like as as if.

7 husbandry thrift, good management. There
is an implied comparison to a careful farmer who
goes early to the 'field' (9).

8 harnessed light Either (1) lightly armed, or
(2) quickly dressed in armour.

9–11 where . . . wrath In Alexander's rather
strained conceit, the dew on the flowers is interpreted as tears that foretell the suffering Hector
will inflict on the Greeks.

12 noise rumour.

13 nephew According to the tradition Shakespeare follows in the rest of the play, Ajax is
actually Hector's cousin, son of Priam's sister,
Hesione, the 'old aunt' referred to in 2.2.77.

15 *per se* in himself; i.e. one of a kind, in a class
by himself.

17–25 Alexander's hybrid, even contradictory,
assessment of Ajax links to the general difficulties
of evaluation posed by the mixed and inconsistent
status of many of the play's characters. See Introduction, pp. 38–41.

18 additions qualities, attributes.

19 humours contradictory inclinations.

20 valour . . . discretion his valour is mixed
with (literally, squeezed into) folly and his folly
flavoured with discretion. The metaphor is from
cookery.

22 attaint fault.

22 stain tinge, blot. In both sound and meaning,
'stain' echoes 'attaint'.

without cause and merry against the hair; he hath the joints of everything, but everything so out of joint that he is a gouty Briareus,
many hands and no use, or purblind Argus, all eyes and no   25
sight.

CRESSIDA But how should this man that makes me smile make Hector
     angry?

ALEXANDER They say he yesterday coped Hector in the battle and
     struck him down, the disdain and shame whereof hath ever since   30
     kept Hector fasting and waking.

CRESSIDA Who comes here?

ALEXANDER Madam, your uncle Pandarus.

Enter PANDARUS

CRESSIDA Hector's a gallant man.

ALEXANDER As may be in the world, lady.   35

PANDARUS What's that, what's that?

CRESSIDA Good morrow, uncle Pandarus.

PANDARUS Good morrow, cousin Cressid, what do you talk of? Good
     morrow, Alexander. How do you, cousin? When were you at Ilium?

CRESSIDA This morning, uncle.   40

PANDARUS What were you talking of when I came? Was Hector armed
     and gone ere ye came to Ilium? Helen was not up, was she?

CRESSIDA Hector was gone but Helen was not up.

PANDARUS Even so. Hector was stirring early.

CRESSIDA That were we talking of, and of his anger.   45

PANDARUS Was he angry?

CRESSIDA So he says here.

PANDARUS True, he was so – I know the cause too: he'll lay about him
     today I can tell them that [*He dismisses Alexander*], and there's
     Troilus will not come far behind him, let them take heed of Troilus,   50

---

25 purblind] Q; purblinded F   30 disdain] Q; disdaind F   33 SD] F *(after 31)*; *not in* Q   42 ye] F2; yea Q, F   49 SD]
This edn.; *not in* Q, F; *Exit Alexander / Palmer*

23 against the hair contrary to the prevailing
mood (i.e. when there is no good reason).

23 joints pieces, bits (used especially of parts of
the body).

24–6 Briareus . . . sight In mythology, Briareus
was a giant with a hundred hands and Argus,
the guardian of Io, had a hundred eyes. Ajax
has, as it were, their extraordinary parts, but his
many hands are wracked by gout, and his eyes
are blind. This is the first of many descriptions of

the various Homeric heroes that mock their heroic
pretensions.

29 coped encountered, fought with.

34 Cressida no doubt wants her comment to be
overheard by the approaching Pandarus.

38 cousin relative, here niece.

39 Ilium The royal palace. See 1.1.95 n.

48 lay about do some damage with his sword.

49 SD Since Alexander does not speak for
the rest of the scene, and the banter between

I can tell them that too.

CRESSIDA What, is he angry too?

PANDARUS Who, Troilus? Troilus is the better man of the two.

CRESSIDA O Jupiter! There's no comparison.

PANDARUS What, not between Troilus and Hector? Do you know a   55
man if you see him?

CRESSIDA Ay, if I ever saw him before and knew him.

PANDARUS Well, I say Troilus is Troilus.

CRESSIDA Then you say as I say, for I am sure he is not Hector.

PANDARUS No, nor Hector is not Troilus in some degrees.   60

CRESSIDA 'Tis just to each of them: he is himself.

PANDARUS Himself? Alas, poor Troilus! I would he were.

CRESSIDA So he is.

PANDARUS Condition I had gone barefoot to India.

CRESSIDA He is not Hector.   65

PANDARUS Himself? No, he's not himself – would 'a were himself!
Well the gods are above, time must friend or end; well, Troilus,
well, I would my heart were in her body. No, Hector is not a better
man than Troilus.

CRESSIDA Excuse me –   70

PANDARUS He is elder –

CRESSIDA Pardon me, pardon me –

PANDARUS Th'other's not come to't – you shall tell me another tale

---

53] Q; *as verse* (*Troylus? / Troylus*) F   59] Q; *as verse* (say, / For*)* F   60 nor] Q; not F   61 just to . . . them: he] *Rowe*
(*subst.*)*;* iust, to . . . them he Q, F   62 Himself? Alas] F (*subst.*)*;* Himselfe, alas Q   66 Himself? No,] *Rowe*² (*subst.*)*;*
Himselfe? no? Q, F

Pandarus and Cressida implies his absence, it is reasonable to have him exit somewhere here, probably as a result of a gesture from Pandarus, who has private matters to discuss with his niece. Note too that the F stage direction at 241 indicates that Pandarus exits alone, and Cressida is clearly alone onstage for her soliloquy at the end of the scene; hence Alexander must exit somewhere before Pandarus.

57 In keeping with her witty evasiveness throughout this scene, Cressida deliberately misunderstands Pandarus and adds the first of a long series of bawdy puns ('knew' = had intercourse with).

62 Here Pandarus deliberately misinterprets Cressida: Troilus is not 'himself' because he is unwell, alienated from himself because of unfulfilled love.

64 Condition i.e. On the condition that. The impossible condition proves that Troilus is not 'himself'. Emilia uses a similar turn of phrase: 'I

know a lady in Venice would have walk'd barefoot to Palestine for a touch of his nether lip' (*Oth.* 4.3.38–9).

65 Cressida persists, once again avoiding the obvious implications of Pandarus' line of thinking. As Palmer points out, the play with identity here takes on much more serious implications later, culminating in Troilus' tortured declaration, 'This is and is not Cressid' (5.2.145).

66 'a he (as frequently in the play).

67 time . . . end time will tell. Like 'the gods are above', the phrase is proverbial, though Pandarus adds his own flavour to it (see Dent H348, M874, and T308.2). Pandarus relies on such traditional 'wisdom' more than any other character in the play.

70 Excuse me An expression of polite disbelief, as with 'Pardon me' (72).

73, 74 come to't reached full maturity, with a sexual innuendo.

when th'other's come to't; Hector shall not have his wit this year.

CRESSIDA He shall not need it if he have his own.   75

PANDARUS Nor his qualities –

CRESSIDA No matter.

PANDARUS Nor his beauty.

CRESSIDA 'Twould not become him, his own's better.

PANDARUS You have no judgement, niece. Helen herself swore th'other   80
day that Troilus, for a brown favour – for so 'tis I must confess –
not brown neither –

CRESSIDA No, but brown.

PANDARUS Faith, to say truth, brown and not brown.

CRESSIDA To say the truth, true and not true.   85

PANDARUS She praised his complexion above Paris'.

CRESSIDA Why Paris hath colour enough.

PANDARUS So he has.

CRESSIDA Then Troilus should have too much: if she praised him
above, his complexion is higher than his; he having colour enough   90
and the other higher is too flaming a praise for a good complexion.
I had as lief Helen's golden tongue had commended Troilus for a
copper nose.

PANDARUS I swear to you I think Helen loves him better than Paris.

CRESSIDA Then she's a merry Greek indeed.   95

PANDARUS Nay, I am sure she does: she came to him th'other day into
the compassed window – and you know he has not past three or
four hairs on his chin –

CRESSIDA Indeed a tapster's arithmetic may soon bring his particulars
therein to a total.   100

PANDARUS Why he is very young and yet will he within three pound
lift as much as his brother Hector.

CRESSIDA Is he so young a man and so old a lifter?

74 wit] *Rowe;* will Q, F   102 lift] F; liste Q   103 he so] Q; he is so F

74 **wit** understanding. Rowe's emendation makes
better sense than Q, F's 'will' (i.e. desire), and has
been generally adopted. The fact that Q is the only
authoritative source for this part of the text adds
weight to the emendation.

74 **this year** Used indefinitely, to mean 'for a
long time'.

81 **a brown favour** someone with a dark complexion. Cf. 1.1.72 n.

86 **above** above that of.

90 **his . . . his** Troilus' . . . Paris'.

90 **he** Paris.

92 **had as lief** would just as soon.

93 **copper** red from too much drinking.

95 **merry Greek** someone of loose morals, a
wanton. The phrase is proverbial (Dent M901), but
the wit here resides in the fact that Helen really is
a Greek. See 4.4.55.

97 **compassed window** curved bay window.

99 **tapster's arithmetic** Tapsters served drinks
in taverns and needed only the simplest arithmetic
to keep track of what they sold.

103 **so old a lifter** such a practised thief; Cressida puns on the slang and literal senses of 'lifter'.

PANDARUS But to prove to you that Helen loves him, she came and
    puts me her white hand to his cloven chin –   105
CRESSIDA Juno have mercy! How came it cloven?
PANDARUS Why you know 'tis dimpled; I think his smiling becomes
    him better than any man in all Phrygia.
CRESSIDA O, he smiles valiantly.
PANDARUS Does he not?   110
CRESSIDA O yes, an 'twere a cloud in autumn.
PANDARUS Why go to then, but to prove to you that Helen loves
    Troilus –
CRESSIDA Troilus will stand to the proof if you'll prove it so.
PANDARUS Troilus? Why he esteems her no more than I esteem an   115
    addle egg.
CRESSIDA If you love an addle egg as well as you love an idle head,
    you would eat chickens i'the shell.
PANDARUS I cannot choose but laugh to think how she tickled his chin –
    indeed she has a marvellous white hand I must needs confess –   120
CRESSIDA Without the rack.
PANDARUS And she takes upon her to spy a white hair on his chin –
CRESSIDA Alas, poor chin! Many a wart is richer.
PANDARUS But there was such laughing! Queen Hecuba laughed that
    her eyes ran o'er –   125
CRESSIDA With millstones.
PANDARUS And Cassandra laughed –

---

107 dimpled; I] *Pope (subst.);* dimpled, / I Q, F   114] Q; *as verse (*thee / Proofe*)* F   114 the] F2; thee Q, F

105 puts me puts ('me' is an old dative form, by Elizabethan times a colloquial remnant, often used narratively to draw attention to the speaker himself; see Abbott 220).

105 cloven cleft or dimpled; Pandarus does not mean 'split in two', but Cressida (106) deliberately misinterprets.

111 cloud in autumn An obscure remark, since smiles are not normally compared to clouds. Perhaps Cressida means that Troilus' smiling promises rain, as storm clouds do in autumn; or that he tries to put his best face forward, hiding his fear in the face of approaching winter, like a sunlit cloud (hence 'smiles valiantly' (109)); or that he does not smile any more than a cloud in autumn does, i.e. not at all.

114 stand . . . proof successfully meet the test, with a deliberately bawdy pun on 'stand'.

116 addle egg An egg that has germinated and contains an embryonic (and often dead) chick.

121 Without the rack Without being tortured on the rack (a mechanism by which the bodies of prisoners were horribly stretched in order to extort confessions). Cressida teases Pandarus about one of his habitual turns of phrase, 'I must needs confess . . .'

126 With millstones Those too hard-hearted to shed tears were proverbially said to weep millstones (Dent M967). Cressida's comment seems to be directed at the fact that there is nothing funny about Pandarus' story. An alert audience might also note that the women, Hecuba and Cassandra, described as laughing so hard at Troilus' witticism, are archetypes of 'royal grief' and 'prophetic gloom' respectively (Thomas E. McAlindon, 'Language, style, and meaning in *Troilus and Cressida*', *PMLA* 84.1 (1969), p. 38).

CRESSIDA But there was a more temperate fire under the pot of her
    eyes – did her eyes run o'er too?

PANDARUS And Hector laughed.   130

CRESSIDA At what was all this laughing?

PANDARUS Marry, at the white hair that Helen spied on Troilus' chin.

CRESSIDA An't had been a green hair, I should have laughed too.

PANDARUS They laughed not so much at the hair as at his pretty answer.

CRESSIDA What was his answer?   135

PANDARUS Quoth she, 'Here's but two and fifty hairs on your chin and
    one of them is white.'

CRESSIDA This is her question.

PANDARUS That's true, make no question of that. 'Two and fifty hairs',
    quoth he, 'and one white – that white hair is my father and all   140
    the rest are his sons.' 'Jupiter!' quoth she, 'which of these hairs is
    Paris my husband?' 'The forked one', quoth he, 'pluck't out and
    give it him.' But there was such laughing, and Helen so blushed
    and Paris so chafed and all the rest so laughed, that it passed.

CRESSIDA So let it now, for it has been a great while going by.   145

PANDARUS Well, cousin, I told you a thing yesterday – think on't.

CRESSIDA So I do.

PANDARUS I'll be sworn 'tis true, he will weep you an 'twere a man
    born in April.

CRESSIDA And I'll spring up in his tears an 'twere a nettle against May.   150

Sound a retreat

PANDARUS Hark, they are coming from the field. Shall we stand up

---

128 was a] Q; was F   136–43 'Here's ... white.' ... 'Two ... hairs', ... 'and ... sons.' 'Jupiter!' ... 'pluck't ...
him.'] *Capell (subst.); no quotation marks in* Q, F   145–6] Q; So ... now, / For ... by. / Well Cozen, / I ... on't. F
145 it has] Q; is has F   147 do] Q; does F   150 SD] *as in Capell; after 149* Q, F

128–9 there . . . eyes i.e. there was not enough
heat to make Cassandra's eyes boil over – another
cooking metaphor, this time rather grotesque.

132 Marry A mild oath (deriving originally from
'By Mary the Virgin'), here with the force of 'Why'.

139 two and fifty Traditionally, Priam had fifty
sons. Editors have worried that perhaps Shakespeare got his tradition or his arithmetic wrong,
and some have offered the ingenious but unnecessary explanation that the 'forked' hair represents
two. There are many examples of Shakespeare's in-
difference to this kind of detail.

142 forked Suggesting the horns of the cuckold (see 1.1.107 n.), and hence hinting that Helen
might continue her pattern of betrayal by cuckold-
ing Paris.

144 passed surpassed description (*OED* Pass *v*

19b – though Cressida in the next line deliberately
takes it in the ordinary sense of 'passed by').

146 thing i.e. Troilus' love for her.

148–9 he . . . April he weeps over you as though
he were born in the rainiest month of the year.

150 Cressida promises nettles instead of the
proverbial May flowers as a consequence of Troilus'
April tears (Dent s411).

150 SD *retreat* Trumpet signal for the forces to
retire.

151–2 up here See 1.2.0 SD n. Editors interpret this phrase to indicate the upper stage, but, as
in modern stage usage, 'up' may merely indicate
somewhere at the back of the stage. As Pandarus'
next speech indicates, the two observers move
quickly (and surely only a short distance) to an
'excellent place'. In most modern productions, the

here and see them as they pass toward Ilium, good niece? Do,
sweet niece Cressida.

CRESSIDA At your pleasure.

PANDARUS Here, here, here's an excellent place, here we may see most   155
bravely. I'll tell you them all by their names as they pass by, but
mark Troilus above the rest.

Enter AENEAS [*and passes over the stage*]

CRESSIDA Speak not so loud.

PANDARUS That's Aeneas, is not that a brave man? He's one of the flowers of Troy, I can tell you, but mark Troilus, you shall see anon.   160

CRESSIDA Who's that?

Enter ANTENOR [*and passes over the stage*]

PANDARUS That's Antenor. He has a shrewd wit, I can tell you, and he's
a man good enough, he's one o'the soundest judgements in Troy
whosoever, and a proper man of person. When comes Troilus? I'll
show you Troilus anon – if he see me, you shall see him nod at me.   165

CRESSIDA Will he give you the nod?

PANDARUS You shall see.

CRESSIDA If he do, the rich shall have more.

Enter HECTOR [*and passes over the stage*]

PANDARUS That's Hector, that, that, look you that, there's a fellow!
Go thy way Hector! There's a brave man, niece. O brave Hector!   170
Look how he looks: there's a countenance, is't not a brave man?

CRESSIDA O, a brave man.

157 SD *and . . . stage*] Rowe (subst.); not in Q, F; so too SDs at *161, 168, 180, 185, 192*   160 can tell] Q; can F   163 a
man] F; man Q   163 judgements] Q; iudgement F   165 him] Q; him him F   172 a brave] Q; braue F

two observers take up their station on some sort of a
raised platform or dais. In 1990 at the Swan (RSC)
they occupied a side gallery in the auditorium.
  156 **bravely** excellently.
  157 SD What follows is a processional scene,
where the almost ritual formality of the return from
battle, one hero on the heels of another, is placed
in counterpoint to the informal banter of the observers; audience interest is focused as much on the
exact status of Cressida's feelings for Troilus as it
is on the warriors as they are introduced to us.
Modern productions are divided as to whether the
warriors should see Cressida and Pandarus or remain oblivious to their presence. Some productions
cut the warriors altogether, leaving uncle and niece

to gaze out at the audience, sometimes with the aid
of binoculars (Old Vic 1956, RSC 1985). Exactly
when the various figures, especially Helenus, Antenor, and Troilus, enter (after or before they are
mentioned) has been debated – see Hodgdon. Except at 180 (Paris' entrance) I have followed Q, F
throughout.
  159 **brave** admirable, impressive (as in 170–2,
182, 194, and 196).
  162 **shrewd** sharp.
  164 **proper . . . person** a handsome man.
  166 **give you the nod** (1) nod to you, (2) call
you fool ('noddy').
  168 **the rich . . . more** he (Pandarus) that already has much (folly) will have even more.

PANDARUS Is 'a not? It does a man's heart good, look you what hacks
   are on his helmet, look you yonder, do you see? Look you there,
   there's no jesting, there's laying on, take't off who will, as they   175
   say; there be hacks!
CRESSIDA Be those with swords?
PANDARUS Swords, anything, he cares not an the devil come to him,
   it's all one; by God's lid, it does one's heart good. Yonder comes
   Paris, yonder comes Paris.   180

   Enter PARIS [*and passes over the stage*]

   Look ye yonder, niece, is't not a gallant man too, is't not? Why
   this is brave now. Who said he came hurt home today? He's not
   hurt – why this will do Helen's heart good now, ha! Would I could
   see Troilus now! You shall see Troilus anon.
CRESSIDA Who's that?   185

   Enter HELENUS [*and passes over the stage*]

PANDARUS That's Helenus. I marvel where Troilus is. That's Helenus.
   I think he went not forth today. That's Helenus.
CRESSIDA Can Helenus fight, uncle?
PANDARUS Helenus? No – yes, he'll fight indifferent well. I marvel
   where Troilus is – hark, do you not hear the people cry 'Troilus'?   190
   Helenus is a priest.
CRESSIDA What sneaking fellow comes yonder?

   Enter TROILUS [*and passes over the stage*]

PANDARUS Where? Yonder? – that's Deiphobus. 'Tis Troilus! There's
   a man, niece. Hem! Brave Troilus, the prince of chivalry!
CRESSIDA Peace, for shame, peace!   195
PANDARUS Mark him, note him, O brave Troilus! Look well upon

173 man's] F *(subst.)*; man Q   175 there's laying] Q; laying F   175 take't off who will] F3; takt off, who will Q; tak't
off, who ill F   180 SD] *as in Capell; after 177* Q, F   184 shall see] Q; shall F   189 indifferent well] F2; indifferent, well
Q, F   190 'Troilus'] *Dyce; Troylus* Q, F   196 note] Q; not F

173 **hacks** hack marks, dents.
175 **laying on** dealing of blows.
175 **take't off who will** no matter what one may say to the contrary. There may also be a sly sexual suggestiveness in this and the previous phrase. Pandarus often seems as interested in the sexual prowess of the warriors as in the military (compare 'good enough' (163))
179 **God's lid** God's eyelid (a harmless oath).
186, 189 **marvel** wonder.
187 **he** Troilus.
189 **indifferent** moderately.
192 **sneaking** shifty.
194 **Hem!** Probably an attempt to get Troilus' attention.
195 Cressida is embarrassed at the fuss Pandarus is making.

him niece: look you how his sword is bloodied and his helm
more hacked than Hector's, and how he looks and how he goes.
O admirable youth, he ne'er saw three and twenty. Go thy way
Troilus, go thy way! Had I a sister were a grace or a daughter a   200
goddess, he should take his choice. O admirable man! Paris? Paris
is dirt to him, and I warrant Helen to change would give an eye
to boot.

Enter common soldiers [and pass over the stage]

CRESSIDA Here comes more.

PANDARUS Asses, fools, dolts – chaff and bran, chaff and bran! Porridge   205
after meat! I could live and die i'th'eyes of Troilus. Ne'er look,
ne'er look, the eagles are gone: crows and daws, crows and daws!
I had rather be such a man as Troilus than Agamemnon and all
Greece.

CRESSIDA There is amongst the Greeks Achilles, a better man than   210
Troilus.

PANDARUS Achilles? A drayman, a porter, a very camel!

CRESSIDA Well well.

PANDARUS 'Well well?' Why, have you any discretion, have you any
eyes? Do you know what a man is? Is not birth, beauty, good shape,   215
discourse, manhood, learning, gentleness, virtue, youth, liberality,
and such like, the spice and salt that season a man?

CRESSIDA Ay, a minced man, and then to be baked with no date in the
pie, for then the man's date is out.

202 an eye] Q; money F   203 SD *Enter . . . stage*] *Capell (subst.); Enter common Souldiers* F; *not in* Q   204 comes] Q;
come F   206 i'th'eyes] F; in the eyes Q   210 amongst] Q; among F   214 'Well well?'] *Staunton (subst.);* Well, well, Q,
F *(subst.)*   217 such like] Q; so forth F   217 season] Q; seasons F   219 date is] Q; dates F

198 goes walks.

200 grace One of the three graces – Greek
goddesses who, in Spenser's words, 'on men all
gracious gifts bestow / Which decke the body or
adorn the mynde' (*Faerie Queene*, VI.10.23.1–2).

202 change exchange (i.e. Paris for Troilus).

202 an eye The first significant variant that
points to a different MS. behind most of F (printing of F from Q broke off at 1.2.198). See Textual
Analysis, pp. 245–6.

203 to boot in addition.

205 chaff and bran husks, the worthless part
of grain.

205 porridge a thick soup. Seeing other soldiers
after Troilus is like having the soup after the main
course.

207 daws jackdaws (insignificant in comparison

to eagles), and, figuratively, mere fools.

212 drayman one who drives a brewer's
cart.

212 very camel mere beast of burden. Cf.
2.1.47.

216 discourse conversational skill.

216 gentleness gentility, breeding.

218 minced made up entirely of bits and pieces,
as in a mince pie, with an added suggestion of
something lacking in the way of male prowess. See
218–19 n.

218–19 date . . . out Continuing the cookery
metaphors, Cressida puns on 'date', insinuating
that Troilus may be sexually deficient, lacking a
date (= penis (see Williams, *Glossary*)), and concluding that he is behind-hand, or 'out' of date,
and thus no fit match for her.

PANDARUS You are such a woman – a man knows not at what ward   220
    you lie.

CRESSIDA Upon my back to defend my belly, upon my wit to defend
    my wiles, upon my secrecy to defend mine honesty, my mask to
    defend my beauty, and you to defend all these; and at all these
    wards I lie, at a thousand watches.   225

PANDARUS Say one of your watches.

CRESSIDA Nay, I'll watch you for that, and that's one of the chiefest of
    them too. If I cannot ward what I would not have hit, I can watch
    you for telling how I took the blow, unless it swell past hiding and
    then it's past watching.   230

Enter [Troilus'] BOY

PANDARUS You are such another!

BOY Sir, my lord would instantly speak with you.

PANDARUS Where?

BOY At your own house, there he unarms him.

PANDARUS Good boy, tell him I come.   235

                                              [Exit Boy]

    I doubt he be hurt. Fare ye well, good niece.

CRESSIDA Adieu, uncle.

PANDARUS I'll be with you, niece, by and by.

---

220 such a] Q; such another F   220 a man] Q; one F   225 lie, at] Q; lie at, at F   228 too] F; two Q   230 SD] *as in* F;
after 231 Q   230 SD *Troilus'*] Capell; *not in* Q, F   234 there . . . him] Q; *not in* F   235 SD] Capell; *not in* Q, F   238 I'll
be] F; I wilbe Q

220 **ward** posture of defence in fencing (*OED*
sb 8); possibly, Pandarus also plays on 'ward',
a subdivision of a parish, implying that it is
not known where Cressida lies (i.e. lives, lies
down), with no doubt a teasing sexual suggestion.
222 **Upon . . . belly** An odd, perhaps ironic,
way for Cressida to defend her chastity, but her remark might help explain her behaviour later, when
she arrives in the Greek camp.
223 **secrecy . . . honesty** Cressida equivocates:
both her silence and her sense of independent selfhood ('secrecy') will allow her to retain a reputation
for chastity (one meaning of 'honesty'), if not the
thing itself.
223 **mask** veil worn to protect the face from the
sun.
224 **you . . . these** The tone is playful, since
Cressida knows that Pandarus is unlikely to defend
her belly or her honesty.

225–30 This passage, continuing from 'ward'
as 'defensive posture' (220), plays on the phrase
'watch and ward', meaning to guard or watch over
(*OED* Watch *v* 6b).
225 **watches** ways of looking out for oneself.
Pandarus' response (226) adds the meanings: sen-
tries, times of guard, and divisions of the night
(as in 'night watches'), with a sly innuendo that
Cressida may divide her night among several
watches (i.e. men).
227 **watch you for that** Cressida hints that she
will have to keep an eye on *him* if it comes to ward-
ing off men in the night.
228–30 **If I . . . watching** If I cannot protect
what I would not want a man to 'hit' (sexually),
I can 'watch' you so you won't gossip about it, unless I 'swell past hiding' (become visibly pregnant),
and then it is beyond keeping secret.
231 You are quite a woman!
236 **doubt he be** fear he might be.

CRESSIDA To bring, uncle?

PANDARUS Ay, a token from Troilus.   240

CRESSIDA By the same token, you are a bawd.

Exit Pandarus

Words, vows, gifts, tears, and love's full sacrifice
He offers in another's enterprise,
But more in Troilus thousandfold I see
Than in the glass of Pandar's praise may be.   245
Yet hold I off. Women are angels, wooing:
Things won are done, joy's soul lies in the doing;
That she belov'd knows nought that knows not this:
Men prize the thing ungained more than it is;
That she was never yet that ever knew   250
Love got so sweet as when desire did sue.
Therefore this maxim out of love I teach:
Achievement is command, ungained beseech.
Then though my heart's content firm love doth bear,
Nothing of that shall from mine eyes appear.   *Exit*   255

---

239 bring, uncle?] *Hudson;* bring vncle: Q; bring Vnkle. F   241 SD] F *(subst.); not in* Q   247, 249] F; *quotation marks at left margin* Q   249 prize] F; price Q   253] *italicized and with quotation marks* Q, F   254 Then] Q; That F   254 content] Q; Contents F

239 To bring Editors have had trouble with Cressida's 'enigmatic rejoinder' (Evans). After 'be with you' the phrase 'to bring' was often used as an intensive, connoting a vague threat of some kind (Variorum). Here it probably carries a bawdy suggestion as well (sex is what is being threatened). Pandarus takes the phrase literally, but he may, as frequently in the scene, be deliberately misinterpreting Cressida's apparent meaning.

241 bawd procurer. Often spoken playfully, this accusation was suddenly deadly serious in Juliet Stevenson's performance (RSC 1985), suggesting something of her fears for the future (Roger Warren review in *SQ* 37.1 (1986), 117).

242 love's full sacrifice whatever 'the lover can offer to his mistress in the way of selfless devotion' (Bevington[2]).

246 wooing during courtship, while being wooed.

247 (1) The joy of pursuit ('doing') falters once the prize is won; (2) The joy of sex ('doing') vanishes once love-making is over. The

second sense is sharply registered in Sonnet 129. The quotation marks in the left margin in Q (for this line and 249) are an indication of aphoristic speech.

248 That she Any woman who is.

249 Men value an object that is as yet ungained more than it is really worth. This idea links to the persistent questioning of *value* in the play (and made explicit in Q's spelling of 'prize' as 'price'). See Introduction, pp. 38–41.

250 she woman.

251 Love got The achievement of love.

252 Cressida's 'maxim' introduces an important element into her rather sententious speech: that withholding love confers power on the woman, which is lost once she surrenders (the man's 'achievement' gives him 'command'). This of course helps to explain Cressida's witty defensive manoeuvres during the preceding exchange with her uncle. The gnomic quality of the line is indicated in both Q and F by italics and quotation marks.

254 my heart's content Either (1) my heart's capacity, or (2) my heart's full satisfaction.

[1.3] *Sennet. Enter* AGAMEMNON, NESTOR, ULYSSES, DIOMEDES,
MENELAUS, *with others*

AGAMEMNON Princes,
　　　What grief hath set the jaundice on your cheeks?
　　　The ample proposition that hope makes
　　　In all designs begun on earth below
　　　Fails in the promised largeness: checks and disasters　　　　　5
　　　Grow in the veins of actions highest reared,
　　　As knots, by the conflux of meeting sap,
　　　Infects the sound pine and diverts his grain,
　　　Tortive and errant, from his course of growth.
　　　Nor, princes, is it matter new to us　　　　　　　　　　　　10
　　　That we come short of our suppose so far
　　　That after seven years' siege yet Troy walls stand,
　　　Sith every action that hath gone before
　　　Whereof we have record, trial did draw
　　　Bias and thwart, not answering the aim　　　　　　　　　　15
　　　And that unbodied figure of the thought
　　　That gave't surmisèd shape. Why then, you princes,

Act 1, Scene 3　1.3] *Capell (subst.); not in* Q, F　0 SD.1 *Sennet*] F; *not in* Q　1–2] F; *as one line* Q　2 the] F; these Q
2 jaundice] Q *(*Iaundies*)*, F　2 on] F; ore Q　8 Infects] Q; Infect F　13 every] F; euer Q

Act 1, Scene 3
　0 SD.1 *Sennet* Processional trumpet notes.
　0 SD.1 DIOMEDES Although he says nothing,
Diomedes' watchful presence in this scene can
add an ominous note – as in Trevor Nunn's 1999
National Theatre production.
　1–54 Agamemnon and Nestor's speeches are full
of windy rhetoric and circumlocution, with simple
ideas weighed down by abstraction and tortured expression. Their political discourse is analogous to
Troilus' excessively self-conscious language of love.
But they also express important political positions.
Many performances have, all too easily, delighted
in mocking the rhetorical pretensions of the various Greek speakers, even including Ulysses. See
Introduction, pp. 23, 43–5.
　1 **Princes** Kings. Agamemnon uses a formal title to address the leaders of the Greek army, many
of whom are monarchs of the territories they command.
　2 **jaundice** yellowish skin and wanness – signs
of melancholy.
　3–5 **The . . . largeness** The rich plans and pro-
posals which hope inspires in all earthly endeavours
always fail to achieve the expected fulfilment.

　5–9 **checks . . . growth** obstacles ('checks') and
disasters plague the greatest actions, as knots, developing where the sap flows together, infect the
healthy pine, twisting the grain of the wood from
its normal 'course of growth'.
　7 **conflux** flowing together (earliest citation in
OED – the first of many Latinate coinages in this
scene; see nn. to 9, 20, 21, 87, 99, 101, 111, 196).
　8 **Infects . . . diverts** Shakespeare frequently
uses the singular form of the verb with a plural
subject, here probably as a result of the proximity
of the singular 'sap'.
　9 **Tortive and errant** Twisted and straying.
'Tortive' is Shakespeare's coinage (*OED*).
　11 **suppose** expectations.
　13 **Sith** Since.
　13 **action** great enterprise.
　14 **record** Accented on the second syllable.
　14 **trial** being put to the test (a personified abstraction, subject of the verb 'did draw'; the object
of 'draw' is 'action' in the previous line).
　15 **Bias and thwart** Off-centre and crosswise.
　15–17 **not . . . shape** not commensurate with
the original goal and abstract idea that gave the
action its imagined shape.

Do you with cheeks abashed behold our works
And call them shames, which are indeed nought else
But the protractive trials of great Jove   20
To find persistive constancy in men,
The fineness of which metal is not found
In Fortune's love? For then the bold and coward,
The wise and fool, the artist and unread,
The hard and soft, seem all affined and kin;   25
But in the wind and tempest of her frown,
Distinction, with a broad and powerful fan
Puffing at all, winnows the light away,
And what hath mass or matter by itself
Lies rich in virtue and unmingled.   30

NESTOR With due observance of thy god-like seat,
Great Agamemnon, Nestor shall apply
Thy latest words. In the reproof of chance
Lies the true proof of men: the sea being smooth,
How many shallow bauble boats dare sail   35
Upon her patient breast, making their way
With those of nobler bulk.
But let the ruffian Boreas once enrage
The gentle Thetis, and anon behold
The strong-ribbed bark through liquid mountains cut,   40
Bounding between the two moist elements
Like Perseus' horse. Where's then the saucy boat

---

19 call them shames] Q; thinke them shame F   27 broad] Q; lowd F   31 thy god-like] *Theobald;* the godlike Q; thy godly F   33] Q; *two lines (*words. / In*)* F   36 patient] F; ancient Q

20 **protractive** protracted (earliest citation in *OED*).

21 **persistive** persevering (earliest citation in *OED*).

22 **metal** constancy, with a pun on mettle = strength of character. The image is from metallurgy: trials *refine* human character, while 'Fortune's love' (23) does not.

23 **then** i.e. when Fortune smiles.

25 **affined** related.

26 **her** Fortune's.

27–30 Distinction (= discrimination, another personified abstraction) winnows away the light chaff with its 'fan', leaving the rich and heavy grain of virtue undiluted on the threshing floor. 'Distinction' also carries a suggestion of noble status and renown – cf. 3.2.24 n.

31 **observance of** deference to.

31 **god-like seat** throne, position as commander.

34 **proof** test.

35 **bauble boats** literally, toy boats, here used figuratively.

38 **Boreas** The north wind.

39 **Thetis** A sea-nymph, mother of Achilles, here representing the sea.

40 **bark** ship.

41 **two moist elements** i.e. water and air (as distinct from the two dry ones, fire and earth).

42 **Perseus' horse** Pegasus, the winged horse. Shakespeare was not alone in misassigning Bellerophon's horse to Perseus. The error goes back to ancient times, and appears in Boccaccio, Rabelais, Spenser, Rubens etc. See 4.5.186 n. and Variorum, which cites T. W. Baldwin, 'Perseus purloins Pegasus', *PQ* 20 (1941), 361–70.

42 **saucy** impudent, upstart.

Whose weak untimbered sides but even now
Co-rivalled greatness? Either to harbour fled
Or made a toast for Neptune. Even so   45
Doth valour's show and valour's worth divide
In storms of fortune; for in her ray and brightness
The herd hath more annoyance by the breese
Than by the tiger; but when the splitting wind
Makes flexible the knees of knotted oaks   50
And flies flee under shade, why then the thing of courage,
As roused with rage, with rage doth sympathise,
And with an accent tuned in self-same key
Retires to chiding fortune.

ULYSSES   Agamemnon,
Thou great commander, nerve and bone of Greece,   55
Heart of our numbers, soul and only spirit
In whom the tempers and the minds of all
Should be shut up, hear what Ulysses speaks.
Besides th'applause and approbation
The which [*To Agamemnon*] most mighty for thy place and
        sway,   60
And thou [*To Nestor*] most reverend for thy stretched-out
        life,
I give to both your speeches, which were such

47] Q; *two lines* (Fortune. / For) F   51] Q; *two lines* (then / The) F   51 flee] *Capell;* fled Q, F   54 Retires] Q, F
(*subst.*); Returns *Pope;* Replies *Hanmer;* Retorts *Hudson* (*conj. Dyce*)   55 nerve] F; nerues Q   59 th'] Q; the F
60 SD] *Rowe* (*subst.*); *not in* Q, F   61 SD] *Rowe* (*subst.*); *not in* Q, F   61 thy] F; the Q

---

44 **Co-rivalled** Competed with.

45 **toast** a tasty morsel (literally, a bit of toasted bread floating in liquor).

45 **Neptune** The god of the sea.

48 **breese** gadfly.

52 **As roused . . . sympathise** Having been roused by the rage of the storm, the 'thing of courage' (51) responds sympathetically with rage of its own.

54 **Retires** Returns, responds (?). Different emendations have been suggested, Dyce's 're-torts' being the most popular, but the agreement of Q and F in a part of the play where the two texts are quite independent suggests that 'Retires' appeared in both MSS. The general sense is clear enough even if it is not possi-

ble to recover exactly what Shakespeare had in mind.

54–69 The rhetoric of Ulysses' preliminary speech is so excessively balanced and deferential that it seems slightly mocking of the venerable leaders to whom it is addressed.

57 **tempers** temperaments, dispositions.

58 **shut up** embodied.

62–8 **which . . . tongue** Once again the elaborate rhetoric obscures the meaning. Ulysses declares that Agamemnon's speech should be etched in brass and Nestor's should forge a 'bond of air' (66), paradoxically as strong as the very axis ('axle-tree') of the universe, that would bind the Greeks to him and to each other. It is hard to escape the implication that the bond of air is just that – air.

As Agamemnon and the hand of Greece
Should hold up high in brass, and such again
As venerable Nestor, hatched in silver,   65
Should, with a bond of air strong as the axle-tree
On which heaven rides, knit all the Greekish ears
To his experienced tongue, yet let it please both
Thou great, and wise, to hear Ulysses speak.

AGAMEMNON Speak, prince of Ithaca, and be't of less expect   70
That matter needless, of importless burden,
Divide thy lips, than we are confident
When rank Thersites opes his mastic jaws
We shall hear music, wit, and oracle.

ULYSSES Troy, yet upon his basis, had been down   75
And the great Hector's sword had lacked a master,
But for these instances:
The specialty of rule hath been neglected,
And look how many Grecian tents do stand

---

63 As . . . the] Q, F; As, Agamemnon, all the *Deighton;* As, Agamemnon, every *Oxford*   67 On . . . rides] Q; In which the Heauens ride F   67 all the Greekish] Q; all Greekes F   70–4] F; *not in* Q   75 SH] F; *not in* Q   75 basis] F; bases Q

63 As . . . Greece The curious syntax has led to various emendations, but it seems best to read 'and' = 'who is', so that Ulysses states that Agamemnon, as the representative 'hand' of Greece, should engrave his speech for all to read. At the beginning of his speech, Ulysses calls Agamemnon the 'nerve and bone' (55) of Greece, and this appears to be an extension of that kind of metaphor. To turn 'Agamemnon' into a vocative, as in Oxford (and Deighton earlier), distorts the parallelism of the speech, since 'Nestor' (65) is certainly not a vocative.

65 hatched in silver white-haired (literally, 'hatched' = engraved, or inlaid *OED* Hatch v^2 1, 2).

70–4 Agamemnon's speech does not appear in Q; its omission there may be accidental or it could represent a deliberate cut. It is difficult to imagine Shakespeare *adding* these excessively tortuous lines, even though they are not out of character with the style of the scene as a whole.

70 of less expect less likely.

71 of importless burden without significant meaning.

73 rank corrupt, foul.

73 mastic related to 'mastix' = a scourge, perhaps recalling a character in Sidney's *Arcadia* of that name, described as 'one of the repiningest fellowes in the world, and that beheld no body but with a mind of mislike' (cited in White and Variorum); cf. also the titles of the satirical plays, *Satiromastix*, written by Dekker in 1602 as an attack on Ben Jonson, and *Histriomastix* by Marston, both linked to skirmishes in the so-called War of the Theatres (see Introduction, p. 9, and Bednarz). No doubt Shakespeare is thinking too of 'masticate', hence biting, a fitting epithet for Thersites' jaws. Since 'mastic' is a gummy vegetative resin used by Elizabethans to ease decaying teeth, it is possible also that, by association, mastic here = decayed, rotten.

75 basis foundation.

78–138 Ulysses' speech on degree, the most famous in the play, has many roots and has been much discussed. See Introduction, pp. 42–6, and Variorum pp. 389–410.

78 specialty of rule proper exercise of, and obedience to, authority.

79–80 i.e. there are as many fruitless ('hollow') factions in the Greek camp as there are tents. Editors have sometimes omitted the first 'Hollow'

Hollow upon this plain, so many hollow factions.   80
When that the general is not like the hive
To whom the foragers shall all repair,
What honey is expected? Degree being vizarded,
Th'unworthiest shows as fairly in the mask.
The heavens themselves, the planets and this centre   85
Observe degree, priority, and place,
Insisture, course, proportion, season, form,
Office, and custom in all line of order.
And therefore is the glorious planet Sol
In noble eminence enthroned and sphered   90
Amidst the other, whose med'cinable eye
Corrects the influence of evil planets
And posts like the commandment of a king
Sans check to good and bad; but when the planets
In evil mixture to disorder wander,   95
What plagues and what portents, what mutiny,
What raging of the sea, shaking of earth,
Commotion in the winds, frights, changes, horrors,

---

87 Insisture] F; In sisture Q; Infixture *Oxford*   92 influence . . . planets] Q; ill Aspects of Planets euill F

partly because of the metre and partly because it
suggests empty tents. But the tents are figuratively,
rather than literally, hollow. The doubling of the
word is an intensifier.

82 foragers worker bees. The analogy between
the bee-hive and the well-ordered state was traditional: compare *H5* 1.2.187 ff. and Milton's
Paradise Lost, 1.768–75.

83 Degree (1) Rank, or (2) The principle according to which elements are ordered hierarchically. Here and in 104 the first meaning predomi-
nates, whereas the second is primary in 101, 108,
109, 126, and 128, and is indeed the theme of the
whole speech.

83 vizarded masked (and hence not observed).

84 Th'unworthiest . . . mask Understood after this line is a phrase like 'as the worthiest'.

85 this centre the earth (considered the centre
of the universe in the Ptolemaic system).

87 Insisture Either (1) steady continuance of
motion, or (2) a 'moment of (apparent) stasis when
a planet, as viewed from the earth, seems to pause
before reversing its former motion' (Palmer). *OED*
gives only this instance of the word, which Shakespeare may simply have invented, though he could
have derived it from Cicero (Variorum). This is the

first of several apparently coined words in the play
ending in '–ure'.

88 Office Proper function, duty.

89 Sol The sun (regarded as a planet in Ptolemaic cosmology).

90 sphered placed on a sphere. Each planet was
thought to occupy a place on its own transparent,
revolving sphere.

91 other other planets.

91 med'cinable eye healing eye (of the sun).

92 the influence . . . planets This is a salient
example of a variant that is impossible to adjudi-
cate conclusively (see Textual Analysis, pp. 239–40,
for a discussion of this feature of the texts). To
this editor's ears, Q is clear and straightforward,
while F's 'the ill Aspects of Planets euill' sounds
slightly awkward and redundant; but at the same
time F's reading has the advantage of extending
the logic of the metaphor of the sun's medicinal
eye ('Aspects' = glances, the baleful looks cast by
evil planets).

92 influence a 'streaming' from the planets 'of
an etherial fluid acting upon the character and destiny of men' (*OED sb* 2).

93 posts hastens.

94 Sans check Without interruption.

Divert and crack, rend and deracinate,
The unity and married calm of states   100
Quite from their fixure! O, when degree is shaked,
Which is the ladder of all high designs,
The enterprise is sick. How could communities,
Degrees in schools and brotherhoods in cities,
Peaceful commerce from dividable shores,   105
The primogenity and due of birth,
Prerogative of age, crowns, sceptres, laurels,
But by degree stand in authentic place?
Take but degree away, untune that string,
And hark what discord follows: each thing meets   110
In mere oppugnancy; the bounded waters
Should lift their bosoms higher than the shores
And make a sop of all this solid globe;
Strength should be lord of imbecility,
And the rude son should strike his father dead;   115
Force should be right, or rather, right and wrong,

---

102 of] Q; to F   106 primogenity] Q *(primogenitie);* primogenitiue F; primogeniture *Rowe*   110 meets] F; melts Q

99 deracinate uproot (another Shakespearean invention, first used in *H5* 5.2.47).

100 married unified, harmonious.

101 fixure fixed and stable position. (Possibly a Shakespearean coinage, though *OED* cites Drayton's *Barons' Wars*, published in 1603, as earlier. Since the play was probably written and performed in 1601, perhaps Drayton saw a performance and remembered the word.)

102 The metaphor of the ladder puns on the literal meaning of 'degree' (a step or rung), and in doing so invites us to imagine an upward (and downward) movement that threatens the abstract and fixed sense of 'degree' that Ulysses is advocating. See 128–35 and nn.

104 Degrees in schools Academic ranks or steps.

104 brotherhoods trade guilds.

105 dividable *OED* defines the word as 'having the function of dividing' (*a* 2), the only recorded use in that sense, but 'shores' do not strictly speaking divide; rather they mark a boundary between land and water. The word's main force is rhetorical – it rolls off Ulysses' eloquent tongue with an orotund sound but only a vague meaning.

106 primogenity right of inheritance for the first-born male. The word is not recorded else-

where and, until recently, Rowe's emendation to the standard 'primogeniture' was widely adopted. But, given Shakespeare's habit of inventing words, Q's 'primogenitie' probably represents what he wrote. F's 'primogenitiue', which occurs elsewhere only as an adjective and then only in the nineteenth century, is probably a misreading of MS., perhaps abetted by 'prerogative' at the beginning of the next line.

108 authentic place their appropriate places within an authoritative, hierarchically ordered system.

111 mere oppugnancy absolute conflict (another instance of an apparently invented word).

112 Should Would (as in the following six lines as well).

113 make a sop of drown ('sop' = a bit of bread soaked in liquor).

114 The strong would rule over the weak ('imbecility'); thus, might rather than right would determine precedence.

116–17 Force ... resides In the eternal struggle ('endless jar') between good and evil, justice is to be found, as Capell remarked, 'as a power to hinder right being trampl'd on' (*Notes* (1780), cited in Variorum). Commentators have seen a parallel with the Aristotelian idea that virtue follows a 'middle

Between whose endless jar justice resides,
Should lose their names, and so should justice too;
Then everything include itself in power,
Power into will, will into appetite,   120
And appetite, an universal wolf,
So doubly seconded with will and power
Must make perforce an universal prey
And last eat up himself.
Great Agamemnon,   125
This chaos, when degree is suffocate,
Follows the choking;
And this neglection of degree it is
That by a pace goes backward with a purpose
It hath to climb. The general's disdained   130
By him one step below, he by the next,
That next by him beneath – so every step,
Exampled by the first pace that is sick
Of his superior, grows to an envious fever
Of pale and bloodless emulation;   135

117] F *(in parentheses); in italics and parentheses* Q   118 their] Q; her F   119 include] Q; includes F   124–5] Q, F; *as one line* / Rowe²   128 it is] Q; is it F   129 with] Q; in F

way' between two vicious extremes, but this aligns
'right' with a vice, which is contrary to the sense.
The idea, rather, is that justice consists in adjudicating between opposing claims, one of which is
right and the other wrong. Q italicises the line to
emphasise its aphoristic quality.
  118 i.e. would become indistinguishable, as
would justice (which, as 117 says, consists in sorting out right from wrong).
  119–24 The distinction between 'power', 'will',
and 'appetite' in these lines is imprecise but this
does not interfere with the force of the image
('will' = rampant egotism, 'appetite' = lust,
whether for power or self-gratification). The general point is that brute power in both the state and
the individual, if it is unchecked by 'degree', leads
to an abandonment to wolfish desire.
  119 include itself would be included.
  121–4 And appetite . . . himself The idea of
vicious human appetite preying on itself is echoed
by Albany's denunciation of Goneril in *Lear*
4.2.48–50: 'It will come, / Humanity must perforce prey on itself, / Like monsters of the deep',
though Albany looks to the heavens to punish,
while Ulysses looks to political action to reinstate

degree. See also Agamemnon's comment on the
self-consuming nature of pride (2.3.141–3).
  124–5 While most editors have followed Rowe,
it is possible that the Q, F lineation (followed here)
might reflect theatrical practice, where an incomplete verse line could indicate a pause: thus Ulysses
pauses after 'himself' to let his point sink in, and
then follows his address to Agamemnon with another measured break.
  126 suffocate choked.
  128–30 And . . . climb The neglect of degree
proceeds step by step down the hierarchical ladder
even as those at various levels seek to climb up.
  132 step (1) rung (of the ladder); (2) step taken
by the person on the rung.
  133 first pace initial step taken by the person
just above who is in turn 'sick / Of his superior'.
  135 emulation envious rivalry. The word includes as well the idea of imitation – catching
the 'fever' of 'emulation' by imitating others. This
sense is central to the action of both plots – the
Troilus–Cressida–Diomedes triangle as well as the
struggles in the Greek camp. It was also a prominent feature of the lives of high-ranking Elizabethan courtiers (see Introduction, pp. 11–13).

And 'tis this fever that keeps Troy on foot,
Not her own sinews. To end a tale of length,
Troy in our weakness stands, not in her strength.
NESTOR Most wisely hath Ulysses here discovered
    The fever whereof all our power is sick.   140
AGAMEMNON The nature of the sickness found, Ulysses,
    What is the remedy?
ULYSSES The great Achilles, whom opinion crowns
    The sinew and the forehand of our host,
    Having his ear full of his airy fame,   145
    Grows dainty of his worth and in his tent
    Lies mocking our designs; with him Patroclus
    Upon a lazy bed the livelong day
    Breaks scurril jests,
    And with ridiculous and silly action –   150
    Which, slanderer, he imitation calls –
    He pageants us: sometime, great Agamemnon,
    Thy topless deputation he puts on,
    And like a strutting player, whose conceit
    Lies in his hamstring and doth think it rich   155
    To hear the wooden dialogue and sound
    'Twixt his stretched footing and the scaffoldage –

---

138 stands] Q; liues F   150 silly] Q; aukward F   157 scaffoldage] Q (scoaffollage), F (Scaffolage)

It is 'pale and bloodless' through association with 'envious fever' in the previous line, envy being traditionally associated with pallor. See also 2.2.212, 2.3.65, 3.3.156, and 4.5.123.

138 stands Another uncertain variant. All the talk of sickness and fever might have suggested F's 'liues', though the sense so far has been that the Greeks, not the Trojans, are sick; moreover, 'stands' contrasts more vividly with 'weakness'.

144 forehand foremost.

145 airy The word suggests that fame is both evanescent and dependent on mere words.

146 dainty of over-concerned about.

149 scurril scurrilous, abusive.

150 silly Most editors prefer F's 'aukward', but Ulysses' point is not the style of Patroclus' jests, but their mocking and trivialising nature ('silly' carrying the sense of 'insignificant'). To the charge that 'ridiculous and silly' is redundant, one can point to dozens of examples of such doublings in this

play and Shakespeare generally, such as 'pale and bloodless' (135).

152 pageants mimics, as in a show.

153 topless deputation supreme position. 'Topless' (without a top or rival) recalls, not without irony given the context, Marlowe's famous lines about Helen of Troy, whose beauty 'launched a thousand ships / And burnt the topless towers of Ilium' (*Doctor Faustus*, 5.1.90–1 ('A' text)). 'Deputation' derives from 'depute' in the original sense of 'appoint' (*OED* Depute *v* 1).

154 conceit intellect (with a glance at the modern meaning).

155 Lies . . . hamstring Consists in the ability to 'strut' (compare the 'poor player' described at *Mac.* 5.5.23–5).

156–7 wooden . . . scaffoldage sonorous echo of his great strides upon the stage. The image is doubly theatrical since it imagines the interplay between actor's foot and wooden stage as itself a kind of melodramatic dialogue.

Such to-be-pitied and o'er-wrested seeming
He acts thy greatness in; and when he speaks
'Tis like a chime a-mending, with terms unsquared,   160
Which, from the tongue of roaring Typhon dropped,
Would seem hyperboles. At this fusty stuff
The large Achilles, on his pressed bed lolling,
From his deep chest laughs out a loud applause,
Cries 'Excellent! 'Tis Agamemnon right;   165
Now play me Nestor: hem, and stroke thy beard
As he being dressed to some oration.'
That's done as near as the extremest ends
Of parallels, as like as Vulcan and his wife;
Yet god Achilles still cries 'Excellent!   170
'Tis Nestor right. Now play him me, Patroclus,
Arming to answer in a night alarm.'
And then, forsooth, the faint defects of age
Must be the scene of mirth, to cough and spit
And with a palsy fumbling on his gorget   175
Shake in and out the rivet; and at this sport
Sir Valour dies, cries 'O enough, Patroclus,
Or give me ribs of steel! I shall split all
In pleasure of my spleen.' And in this fashion
All our abilities, gifts, natures, shapes,   180

---

158 o'er-wrested] Q *(ore-rested)*, F   160 unsquared] F; vnsquare Q   162 seem] Q; seemes F   165–7, 170–2, 177–9] *marked as quotation, Hanmer; not marked in* Q, F   165 right] Q; just F   166 hem] Q; hum F

158 o'er-wrested seeming strained performing style.

160 a-mending being repaired (and hence out of tune).

160 terms unsquared inappropriate expressions ('unsquared' is a term from carpentry or masonry).

161 Typhon A mythological monster with a hundred heads, identified as the father of the winds, and associated with volcanoes, especially Mt Etna in Sicily. Patroclus' bombast would seem exaggerated even coming from such a monster.

162 fusty stale.

163 pressed weighed down (emphasising Achilles' great size), with an apparent allusion to sexual activity; see 3.2.187 where 'press' is used in a specifically sexual sense.

166 hem clear your throat.

167 dressed to addressed to, ready to begin.

168–9 That's done . . . wife Patroclus' performance is as much like Nestor as Vulcan (the bandy-legged blacksmith of the gods) is like his wife, Venus, i.e. the exact opposite.

172 Arming himself in response to a night alert.

175 palsy palsied, unsteady.

175 gorget piece of armour covering the throat (French *gorge*, throat).

176 rivet metal fastener for armour.

177 Sir Valour Achilles. Shakespeare's characters often use such titled abstractions, usually, as here, with a sarcastic bite – cf. 'my dear Lady Disdain' and 'my Lady Tongue' (*Ado* 1.1.118 and 2.1.275), 'Sir Oracle' (*MV* 1.1.93), 'Sir John Paunch' (*1H4* 2.2.66).

177 dies dies laughing.

179 spleen Supposed to be the physiological seat of both mirth and fits of temper, peevishness or melancholy.

              Severals and generals of grace exact,
              Achievements, plots, orders, preventions,
              Excitements to the field, or speech for truce,
              Success or loss, what is or is not, serves
              As stuff for these two to make paradoxes.   185
NESTOR   And in the imitation of these twain,
              Who as Ulysses says opinion crowns
              With an imperial voice, many are infect:
              Ajax is grown self-willed and bears his head
              In such a rein, in full as proud a place,   190
              As broad Achilles, keeps his tent like him,
              Makes factious feasts, rails on our state of war
              Bold as an oracle, and sets Thersites,
              A slave whose gall coins slanders like a mint,
              To match us in comparisons with dirt,   195
              To weaken and discredit our exposure
              How rank soever rounded in with danger.
ULYSSES They tax our policy and call it cowardice,
              Count wisdom as no member of the war,
              Forestall prescience, and esteem no act   200
              But that of hand; the still and mental parts
              That do contrive how many hands shall strike
              When fitness calls them on, and know by measure
              Of their observant toil the enemy's weight –
              Why this hath not a finger's dignity;   205

191 keeps] Q; and keepes F   196 and] F; our Q   203 calls] Q; call F

181 Both our particular ('Severals') and our general qualities of merit.
   182 preventions precautions.
   183 Excitements Exhortations.
   185 paradoxes absurdities masquerading as true
imitations.
   187 opinion fame. As Kermode shows, this is
an important word in the play.
   188 imperial absolutely authoritative.
   188 infect infected.
   189–90 bears . . . rein holds his head like a
horse haughtily disdaining the rein; in the theatre,
the word might be heard as 'reign', so that Ajax's
pretensions to 'imperial' rule would predominate.
   191 broad large, over-proud.
   192 factious faction-inducing.
   192 rails on denounces.
   194 gall bitterness, rancour (like 'spleen' (179),

a term which suggests the physiological basis of
feeling as understood by early modern medical
theory).
   196 exposure exposed military position (this
and *Mac.* 2.3.127 are the earliest *OED* citations).
   197 No matter how thickly ('rank') we are surrounded by dangers.
   198 tax our policy criticise our strategy.
   200 Forestall prescience Obstruct or undermine (through their criticism) tactical planning.
   200–1 no act . . . hand nothing but hand-to-
hand combat.
   203 fitness appropriate time.
   203–4 know . . . weight assess through careful
observation the numbers and strength of the enemy.
   205 finger's dignity the worth of a finger in
relation to the body as a whole.

They call this bed-work, mapp'ry, closet-war,
So that the ram that batters down the wall,
For the great swing and rudeness of his poise,
They place before his hand that made the engine
Or those that with the fineness of their souls   210
By reason guide his execution.
NESTOR Let this be granted, and Achilles' horse
    Makes many Thetis' sons.
                            Tucket
AGAMEMNON What trumpet? Look, Menelaus.
MENELAUS From Troy.   215

                Enter AENEAS [*with trumpeter*]

AGAMEMNON What would you 'fore our tent?
AENEAS Is this great Agamemnon's tent, I pray you?
AGAMEMNON Even this.
AENEAS May one that is a herald and a prince
    Do a fair message to his kingly ears?   220
AGAMEMNON With surety stronger than Achilles' arm
    'Fore all the Greekish heads which with one voice
    Call Agamemnon head and general.
AENEAS Fair leave and large security. How may

---

208 swing] F; swinge Q   213 SD] F; *not in* Q   215 SD *Enter* AENEAS] F; *not in* Q   215 SD *with trumpeter*] Sisson (subst.);
not in Q, F   220 ears] F; eyes Q   222 heads] Q, F; host *Muir, conj. Kinnear;* lords *Palmer*

206 bed-work, mapp'ry, closet-war mere intellectual exercise of the sort done while lying
down, poring over maps, or musing in the study
('closet'). 'Bed-work' might also carry a sexual suggestion continued in 'ram' and 'swing' in the next
two lines.
    207 ram battering-ram.
    208 swing forcible motion (*OED sb²* 6). Q's
'swinge' may be a spelling variant or a different
word meaning 'impetus' (*OED sb¹* 3), but the two
words are so close that it seems preferable to use
the modern form.
    208 rudeness . . . poise violence of its weight.
    209 place before value more than.
    209 engine military machine (here the battering
ram).
    211 his execution its operation.
    213 Is equal to several Achilles (the son of the
nymph Thetis).
    213 SD *Tucket* A series of military notes on a

trumpet.
    222 heads The word seems unsatisfactory and
has caused editors trouble. Eye-skip to 'head' in
the following line (or mistaken repetition there of
'head' here) might be responsible for an error in Q,
F (but see Textual Analysis, pp. 245–50, for a discussion of the independence of the two texts).
However, suggested emendations such as 'host' and
'lords' do not fit comfortably into the grammar of
the sentence ('host' would require 'Calls' as verb
and 'which' is awkward, though not impossible,
with 'lords'). The ambiguous reference of the
whole phrase adds to the confusion. Does ''Fore
all the Greekish heads' refer to *Achilles* before (either 'superior to' or 'leading') the Greek army, or to
Agamemnon as he speaks now, before his lieutenant-
generals, who are also 'heads' of their own divisions? The line is awkward, whether emended or
not.
    224 security assurance.

A stranger to those most imperial looks   225
Know them from eyes of other mortals?
AGAMEMNON   How?
AENEAS Ay,
    I ask that I might waken reverence,
    And bid the cheek be ready with a blush
    Modest as morning when she coldly eyes   230
    The youthful Phoebus.
    Which is that god in office guiding men,
    Which is the high and mighty Agamemnon?
AGAMEMNON This Trojan scorns us, or the men of Troy
    Are ceremonious courtiers.   235
AENEAS Courtiers as free, as debonair, unarmed,
    As bending angels: that's their fame in peace.
    But when they would seem soldiers, they have galls,
    Good arms, strong joints, true swords, and – great Jove's
        accord –
    Nothing so full of heart. But peace, Aeneas,   240
    Peace, Trojan, lay thy finger on thy lips!
    The worthiness of praise distains his worth
    If that the praised himself bring the praise forth;
    But what the repining enemy commends,
    That breath fame blows; that praise, sole pure, transcends.   245

227–8] *Malone; as one line* Q, F   229 bid] Q; on F   230–1] F; *as one line* Q   237 fame] F; *same* Q   239 and – great
Jove's accord –] Q *(and great Ioues accord); and Ioues accord* F; *and, Jove's accord, Theobald*   243 that the] Q; *that
he* F

225 those . . . looks Agamemnon's kingly looks.
Aeneas' question is teasing, but with an aggressive
edge.
227–33 Aeneas adopts a tone which straddles the
line between courteous flattery and ironic mockery,
as Agamemnon's following comment indicates.
229 the cheek Aeneas' own.
236 debonair gentle, gracious.
236 unarmed i.e. while they are unarmed.
237 bending bowing, submissive to God.
237 fame reputation.
238 galls spirit, courage. Editors usually gloss
as 'spirit to resent injury', following *OED* Gall *sb*[1]
3b which cites *Oth.* 4.3.92–3: 'we have galls; and
though we have some grace, / Yet have we some
revenge'. But Aeneas means simply that the Trojans are spirited and ready for battle when called

for, just as they are 'debonair' in courtly situations.
239 great Jove's accord with Jove's consent, by
God's permission.
240 Nothing . . . heart Nothing is so full of
lively courage.
242 distains his worth loses (literally, stains,
sullies) its value.
243 If the person praised does the praising himself. Compare 2.3.142–3. See also Proverbs 27.2
('Let another man praise thee, and not thine owne
mouth'), and Dent M476 and P547.
244 repining grudging.
245 Fame broadcasts such laudatory words
('That breath'); such praise, the only pure kind,
transcends all other acclaim. The image is of Fame
with her trumpet, spreading the commendations of
the 'repining enemy'.

AGAMEMNON Sir, you of Troy, call you yourself Aeneas?

AENEAS Ay, Greek, that is my name.

AGAMEMNON What's your affair I pray you?

AENEAS Sir, pardon, 'tis for Agamemnon's ears.

AGAMEMNON He hears naught privately that comes from Troy.   250

AENEAS Nor I from Troy come not to whisper with him;
    I bring a trumpet to awake his ear,
    To set his sense on the attentive bent,
    And then to speak.

AGAMEMNON   Speak frankly as the wind,
    It is not Agamemnon's sleeping hour.   255
    That thou shalt know, Trojan, he is awake,
    He tells thee so himself.

AENEAS   Trumpet, blow loud,
    Send thy brass voice through all these lazy tents
    And every Greek of mettle let him know
    What Troy means fairly shall be spoke aloud.   260

               Sound trumpet

    We have, great Agamemnon, here in Troy
    A prince called Hector – Priam is his father –
    Who in this dull and long-continued truce
    Is resty grown; he bade me take a trumpet
    And to this purpose speak: kings, princes, lords,   265
    If there be one among the fair'st of Greece
    That holds his honour higher than his ease,
    That seeks his praise more than he fears his peril,
    That knows his valour and knows not his fear,
    That loves his mistress more than in confession   270
    With truant vows to her own lips he loves,

---

248 affair] F; affaires Q   250] Q; *two lines* (priuatly / That) F   251 whisper with] Q; whisper F   253 sense on the] F; seat on that Q   257 loud] F; alowd Q   260 SD] Q; *The trumpets sound* F   263 this] F; his Q   264 resty] Q; rusty F   266 among] Q; among'st F   268 That seeks] F; And feeds Q

254–7 At this point in Sam Mendes' 1990 production (RSC), Agamemnon picked up a battered nameplate from a table crowded with papers, lamps, and radio, and waved it at Aeneas in exasperated proof of his doubtful identity. In Michael Macowan's 1938 production in modern dress, Hector's challenge (261 ff.) was delivered over the 'wireless'.

259 mettle spirit.

263 truce While here the truce is said to be long-lasting, in the first two scenes war is being vigorously waged. This kind of inconsistency does not seem to have bothered Shakespeare or his audience. See 3.1.116–17 n.

264 resty (1) restive, (2) indolent, sluggish.

270–3 That loves . . . hers That loves his lady more sincerely than can be indicated by untrustworthy ('truant') vows, and dares to prove her beauty and value in chivalric combat rather than in her embraces; 'arms' (273) brings the military and sexual senses deftly together in a minor verbal

And dare avow her beauty and her worth
In other arms than hers, to him this challenge:
Hector in view of Trojans and of Greeks
Shall make it good or do his best to do it,   275
He hath a lady wiser, fairer, truer,
Than ever Greek did couple in his arms,
And will tomorrow with his trumpet call
Midway between your tents and walls of Troy
To rouse a Grecian that is true in love.   280
If any come, Hector shall honour him;
If none, he'll say in Troy when he retires
The Grecian dames are sunburnt and not worth
The splinter of a lance. Even so much.
AGAMEMNON This shall be told our lovers, Lord Aeneas.   285
If none of them have soul in such a kind,
We left them all at home; but we are soldiers,
And may that soldier a mere recreant prove
That means not, hath not, or is not in love.
If then one is, or hath, or means to be,   290
That one meets Hector; if none else, I am he.
NESTOR Tell him of Nestor, one that was a man
When Hector's grandsire sucked; he is old now
But if there be not in our Grecian host
One noble man that hath one spark of fire   295
To answer for his love, tell him from me
I'll hide my silver beard in a gold beaver

---

277 couple] Q; compasse F   290 hath, or] F; hath a Q   291 I am] Q; Ile be F   294 host] Q; mould F   295 One noble . . . one spark] F; A noble . . . no spark Q

instance of the thematic linkage that characterises the whole play.
   277 couple Although the primary meaning is 'embrace', with sexual overtones, the word also has heraldic implications, which are continued in 'arms' in the same phrase. There is also, perhaps, a glance (as Walker suggests) at the 'chivalric convention of a knight's displaying some symbol of his mistress about his armour' (as later in the play with Cressida's sleeve (5.2.64 ff., 5.4.3–21)). The play on 'couple' and 'arms' here continues that in 273.
   283 sunburnt dark (a feature that would make them ugly according to Elizabethan notions of female beauty). Hector proclaims his

love to be 'fairer' (276) than the Greek ladies in two senses – lighter skinned and more beautiful.
   284 splinter splintering. Aeneas suggests that the Greeks' unwillingness to meet Hector's challenge would indicate that they regard the beauty of their mistresses as not worth defending.
   288 recreant someone who breaks faith. In this case, any soldier who is not also a lover breaks the chivalric code which links loyalty in battle to truth in love.
   297 beaver hinged face-guard on a helmet. The 'gold' of the helmet replacing the silver hair suggests, in keeping with the passage as a whole, a return to golden-haired youth.

And in my vambrace put my withered brawns,
And, meeting him, tell him that my lady
Was fairer than his grandam and as chaste   300
As may be in the world; his youth in flood,
I'll prove this truth with my three drops of blood.
AENEAS Now heavens forbid such scarcity of youth!
ULYSSES Amen.
AGAMEMNON Fair Lord Aeneas, let me touch your hand;   305
To our pavilion shall I lead you first.
Achilles shall have word of this intent,
So shall each lord of Greece from tent to tent.
Yourself shall feast with us before you go,
And find the welcome of a noble foe.   310

Exeunt [all but] Ulysses and Nestor

ULYSSES Nestor!
NESTOR What says Ulysses?
ULYSSES I have a young conception in my brain:
Be you my time to bring it to some shape.
NESTOR What is't?   315
ULYSSES This 'tis:
Blunt wedges rive hard knots; the seeded pride
That hath to this maturity blown up
In rank Achilles must or now be cropped
Or, shedding, breed a nursery of like evil   320
To overbulk us all.

---

298 vambrace] Q, F *(F: Vantbrace)*   298 my withered brawns] Q; this wither'd brawne F   299 tell] Q; will tell F   302
prove] Q; pawne F   303 forbid] F; for-fend Q   303 youth] F; men Q   305 SH] F; *speech continued (305–10) to Ulysses*
Q   305] *as in Pope; part of previous line* Q; Faire . . . Aeneas, / Let . . . hand: F   306 first] F; sir Q   310 SD] Capell;
Exeunt. / Manet Vlysses, and Nestor. F; *not in* Q   316 This 'tis:] F; *not in* Q

298 **vambrace** armour to cover the arms. F's
'Vantbrace' is an alternate spelling.
298 **brawns** arms (literally, muscles, as in modern 'brawny').
301 **his . . . flood** even though he is in the full
tide of youth.
307 **this intent** Hector's challenge.
311 Ulysses, hanging back from the others, calls
softly to the departing Nestor.
313–14 Nestor, whose long time in the world is
continually emphasised, is here paradoxically associated with the period of pregnancy. As Father
Time, he will bring Ulysses' conception to full
term. Metaphorical linking of the two senses of
'conception' was common.

317 **Blunt . . . knots** To cut through ('rive') the
toughest knots in the wood, a blunt wedge is better than a sharp blade. A twist on the proverb: 'A
knotty piece of timber must have sharp wedges'
(Dent P289).
317–21 **the seeded pride . . . all** Achilles'
pride, planted ('seeded') sometime in the past,
has now grown ('blown up') to maturity, and
must be cut ('cropped') or, if it is allowed
to shed its seeds, it will 'breed' a whole
new crop and overwhelm ('overbulk') us all.
Achilles is like, in Hamlet's phrase, 'an un-
weeded garden / That grows to seed', possessed by things 'rank and gross' (*Ham.* 1.2.135–
6).

NESTOR Well, and how?

ULYSSES This challenge that the gallant Hector sends,
　　　　However it is spread in general name,
　　　　Relates in purpose only to Achilles. 325

NESTOR True, the purpose is perspicuous as substance
　　　　Whose grossness little characters sum up,
　　　　And in the publication make no strain
　　　　But that Achilles, were his brain as barren
　　　　As banks of Libya – though Apollo knows 330
　　　　'Tis dry enough – will with great speed of judgement,
　　　　Ay with celerity, find Hector's purpose
　　　　Pointing on him.

ULYSSES And wake him to the answer, think you?

NESTOR Yes, 'tis most meet. Who may you else oppose 335
　　　　That can from Hector bring his honour off
　　　　If not Achilles? Though't be a sportful combat,
　　　　Yet in the trial much opinion dwells,
　　　　For here the Trojans taste our dear'st repute
　　　　With their fin'st palate; and trust to me, Ulysses, 340
　　　　Our imputation shall be oddly poised
　　　　In this vile action; for the success,
　　　　Although particular, shall give a scantling
　　　　Of good or bad unto the general.
　　　　And in such indexes, although small pricks 345

---

326 True, the] Q; The F　326 as] Q; even as F　329 were] F; weare Q　332–3] F; *as one line* Q　335 Yes] F; Why Q　336 his honour] F; those honours Q　338 the] Q; this F　342 vile] Q *(*vilde*)*; wilde F

324 spread ... name offered to all (the Greeks).

326–7 perspicuous ... up as obvious as great wealth, the mass ('grossness') of which can be summed up in a few small written numbers ('characters'), as in an account book.

328 in the publication i.e. when the challenge is proclaimed publicly.

328 make no strain have no doubt.

330 Libya Covering most of north Africa, Libya was connected in the Elizabethan imagination with sand and desert.

332 celerity speed.

338 opinion reputation (i.e. the credit of each side rides on the outcome).

339 taste ... repute put our finest reputation to the test – with a play on 'taste' in the usual sense of 'savour'; the latter idea is continued in the next line, where the fine 'palate' of the Trojans refers to their skill in combat. One of the many refer-

ences to highly refined tasting in the play. Compare 3.2.18–19 where the image refers to the delights of love.

341 imputation reputation. 'Nestor, like Ulysses in 3.3, sees men's repute as subject to change, and only maintained by continual effort' (Palmer).

341 poised weighed, set in balance.

342 vile relatively insignificant. F's 'wilde' may simply be a misprint for Q's 'vilde'.

342 success outcome.

343 particular pertaining to the individual. Throughout this speech, Nestor explores the relation between particular and general, or part and whole, with reference especially to one man, Achilles, as a representative of all the Greeks.

343 scantling pattern, specimen.

345–8 And ... large The 'scantling', still with reference to the warrior who will represent the

To their subsequent volumes, there is seen
The baby figure of the giant mass
Of things to come at large. It is supposed
He that meets Hector issues from our choice,
And choice, being mutual act of all our souls,   350
Makes merit her election and doth boil
As 'twere from forth us all a man distilled
Out of our virtues, who, miscarrying,
What heart receives from hence a conquering part
To steel a strong opinion to themselves?   355
ULYSSES Give pardon to my speech: therefore 'tis meet
Achilles meet not Hector; let us like merchants
First show foul wares and think perchance they'll sell:
If not,
The lustre of the better shall exceed   360
By showing the worse first. Do not consent
That ever Hector and Achilles meet;
For both our honour and our shame in this
Are dogg'd with two strange followers.
NESTOR I see them not with my old eyes – what are they?   365
ULYSSES What glory our Achilles shares from Hector,

354 receives from hence a] Q; from hence receyues the F   355 themselves?] Q; themselues, / Which entertain'd, Limbes
are in his instruments, / In no lesse working, then are Swords and Bowes / Directiue by the Limbes. F; themselues . . .
Limbes are his instruments . . . Limbes. F2   356–60] Capell; same lineation (except 359–60 make one line) Q; Giue . . .
speech: / Therefore . . . Hector: / Let . . . Wares, / And . . . not, / The . . . shew, F   358 First show foul wares] Q;
shew our fowlest Wares F   360–1 shall . . . first] Q; yet to shew / Shall shew the better F   363–4] F; as prose Q

Greeks, now becomes an 'index', or table of contents, that indicates what will follow in the volume
as a whole, the small part being a figure for the
much larger whole.
   351 Makes . . . election Makes a selection on
the basis of merit.
   351 boil distil by boiling.
   353 miscarrying if he should miscarry.
   354–5 What heart could derive from that (i.e. the
miscarrying just referred to) the kind of courage
needed to conquer in the war at large? In F
only, Nestor follows up his question with two
and a half extraordinarily obscure lines, whose
syntactical relation to the rest of the speech is
very loose (see collation). These were, I am convinced, cut in the MS. behind Q and I omit them
here. The Q text also shows signs of revision in
Ulysses' response (356–61 and n.), suggesting that
Shakespeare, perhaps while making a fair copy,

reworked this section (see Textual Analysis, pp.
238–9). In the F-only lines, Nestor completes his
thought in a pedantic and unnecessary way, explaining how, if their designated hero should win,
the Greeks would be able to 'entertain' a 'strong
opinion' of their own prowess, and this confidence
would in turn make their limbs its ('his') instruments, in the same way that their limbs direct their
weapons.
   356–61 Evidence of revision is once again apparent in these lines (see 354–5 n.), and once again it
is Q that probably provides the revised reading. F's
awkward repetition of 'better' and 'shew' in 360–1
is eliminated.
   360 shall exceed will be enhanced.
   364 strange followers undesirable consequences. (Whether Achilles wins or loses, the results will be equally bad for the Greeks – as Ulysses
then goes on to explain.)

Were he not proud, we all should share with him.
But he already is too insolent,
And it were better parch in Afric sun
Than in the pride and salt scorn of his eyes   370
Should he 'scape Hector fair; if he were foiled
Why then we do our main opinion crush
In taint of our best man. No, make a lott'ry
And by device let blockish Ajax draw
The sort to fight with Hector; among ourselves   375
Give him allowance for the better man,
For that will physic the great Myrmidon,
Who broils in loud applause, and make him fall
His crest that prouder than blue Iris bends.
If the dull brainless Ajax come safe off,   380
We'll dress him up in voices; if he fail,
Yet go we under our opinion still
That we have better men. But hit or miss,
Our project's life this shape of sense assumes:
Ajax employed plucks down Achilles' plumes.   385
NESTOR Now Ulysses, I begin to relish thy advice
And I will give a taste thereof forthwith
To Agamemnon – go we to him straight.
Two curs shall tame each other, pride alone
Must tar the mastiffs on as 'twere a bone.   390

Exeunt

---

367 share] Q; weare F   369 it] Q; we F   372 do] Q; did F   376 for the better] Q; as the worthier F   386 Now Ulysses]
Q, F; Ulysses, / Now *Steevens*   387 thereof] Q; of it F   390 tar] F *(tarre); arre* Q   390 a bone] Q; their bone F

370 salt corrosive.

372 main opinion general reputation.

375 sort lot.

376 Give him allowance for Acknowledge him
to be.

377 physic cure, purge.

377 great Myrmidon Achilles (the leader of
this warlike Thessalian clan).

378 broils in is overheated by (and hence in
need of 'physic'), with a glance at the culinary
metaphors prominent in many parts of the play.

378 fall let fall, bow.

379 crest (1) head feathers (as of a bird), (2)
plumes on helmet, and hence (3) pride. See 385.

379 Iris Juno's messenger and goddess of the
rainbow (hence 'bends' = arches). But since she
was not especially associated with undue pride, the

comparison seems inapposite.

381 dress . . . voices cover him with praise.
Shakespeare frequently associates clothing with in-
sincerity, as in Hamlet's reminder that 'a man might
play' at grief by donning an 'inky cloak' and 'suits
of solemn black', though he himself 'has that within
which passes show' (1.2.77–86).

382 go . . . opinion we maintain our reputation.

390 tar incite, provoke. Q's 'arre' may not be a
simple error, since the word was used in Shakespeare's time to mean to snarl or growl like a dog
(*OED* Arr *v*[2]). But since 'arre' does not include the
sense of provocation, which is central to the meaning here, and since Shakespeare twice uses 'tarre'
or 'tarre on' in that sense (*John* 4.1.116–17, where
the reference is also to fighting dogs, and *Ham.*
2.2.353), this seems the likelier reading.

[2.1] *Enter* AJAX *and* THERSITES

AJAX Thersites!

THERSITES Agamemnon, how if he had boils – full, all over, generally?

AJAX Thersites!

THERSITES And those boils did run – say so – did not the general run
    then, were not that a botchy core?   5

AJAX Dog!

THERSITES Then would come some matter from him, I see none now.

AJAX Thou bitch-wolf's son, canst thou not hear? Feel then.

Strikes him

THERSITES The plague of Greece upon thee, thou mongrel, beef-witted
    lord.   10

AJAX Speak then, thou whinid'st leaven, speak! I will beat thee into
    handsomeness.

THERSITES I shall sooner rail thee into wit and holiness, but I think thy
    horse will sooner con an oration than thou learn a prayer without
    book. Thou canst strike, canst thou? – a red murrain o'thy jade's   15
    tricks.

AJAX Toadstool, learn me the proclamation.

Act 2, Scene 1 2.1] *Rowe (subst.); not in* Q, F   **4–5** run then] Q; run F   **7** Then] Q; Then there F   **8** SD] F; *not in*
Q   **11** thou] Q; you F   **11** whinid'st] F; vnsalted Q; vinewed'st *Knight*   **14** an oration] F; an oration without booke Q
14 a prayer] F; prayer Q   **15** o'thy] F3; ath thy Q; o'th thy F

Act 2, Scene 1

0 SD Ajax and Thersites probably enter by different doors. Thersites, meditating on the corruption of the Greek leaders, whom we have just seen
in conclave, pays no attention to Ajax, though he
presumably hears him yelling. As this scene began in the RSC production of 1990, Simon Russell
Beale's Thersites was setting up Ajax's dinner
into which he 'slowly and deliberately drooled'
(Holland, p. 73).

2 boils hard, swollen, and suppurating sores.

2 generally with a pun on Agamemnon as the
general of the army, continued in 4.

5 botchy core decayed, ulcerous centre (both in
general, and specifically of a boil), with puns on
Latin *cor* 'heart', and French *cor[p]s*, 'body'. See
5.1.5–6 and 5.9.1 and nn.

7 matter something substantial, i.e. pus, since
no 'matter' (= 'reasoned argument') currently flows
from him.

9 beef-witted cow-brained. There is probably a reference to the folk-belief that eating too
much beef made one stupid (the idea may have
arisen among the peasantry who saw their lords

work their way through vast quantities while
they themselves had to settle for brown bread).
Steevens noted a parallel in *TN*, where Sir Andrew remarks: 'I am a great eater of beef, and
I believe that does harm to my wit' (1.3.85–
6).

11 whinid'st mouldiest. Editors usually adopt
the form 'vinewed'st' after Knight, though *OED*
lists 'finewed' as the primary form, and 'vinewed'
and 'whinid' among many variants. Q's 'vnsalted' is
a much milder insult, especially since 'leaven' does
not strictly require salt, though bread without salt
is tasteless enough.

11 leaven A fermenting culture added to dough
to make certain kinds of bread, such as modern
sour-dough. But Ajax may very well be thinking
here simply of the dough itself.

12 handsomeness decency, courteousness.

13 rail berate.

14 con learn by heart.

15 red murrain bloody plague.

15–16 jade's tricks violent outbursts of a bad
tempered horse.

17 learn me (1) tell me; (2) find out for me.

THERSITES Dost thou think I have no sense thou strik'st me thus?

AJAX The proclamation!

THERSITES Thou art proclaimed fool I think.   20

AJAX Do not, porcupine, do not, my fingers itch –

THERSITES I would thou didst itch from head to foot and I had the
scratching of thee: I would make thee the loathsomest scab in
Greece. When thou art forth in the incursions, thou strik'st as
slow as another.   25

AJAX I say, the proclamation!

THERSITES Thou grumblest and railest every hour on Achilles,
and thou art as full of envy at his greatness as Cerberus is at
Proserpina's beauty – ay, that thou bark'st at him.

AJAX Mistress Thersites –   30

THERSITES Thou shouldst strike him.

AJAX Cobloaf!

THERSITES He would pun thee into shivers with his fist as a sailor
breaks a biscuit.

AJAX [*Beating him*] You whoreson cur –   35

THERSITES Do, do –

AJAX Thou stool for a witch.

THERSITES Ay do, do, thou sodden-witted lord, thou hast no more
brain than I have in mine elbows: an asinico may tutor thee. Thou
scurvy valiant ass, thou art here but to thrash Trojans, and thou   40

20 fool] Q; a foole F   21 porcupine] Q *(Porpentin)*, F (Porpentine)   24–5 When . . . another] Q; *not in* F   24 strik'st]
Q *(strikest)*   33–5] F; *as one speech of Thersites* Q   35 SD] *Pope; not in* Q, F   37] Q, F; *assigned to Thersites / Walker*
39–40 elbows: . . . thee. Thou . . . ass, . . . Trojans,] F; elbowes, . . . thee, you . . . asse, . . . Troyans, Q   39 asinico] Q,
F; assinego *Pope*   39–40 Thou scurvy] F; you scuruy Q

18 sense feeling.

21 porcupine a small animal with sharp quills
(and thus an appropriate epithet for Thersites).

24 incursions battles.

28 Cerberus Three-headed dog who guards the
gates of the underworld. According to one tradition, anyone who wished to marry Proserpina (see
29 n.) had to fight him.

29 Proserpina Queen of the underworld, kept
there by its god Pluto six months a year and allowed to visit earth the rest of the time, bringing
spring and regeneration with her.

30 Mistress Perhaps a jibe at Thersites'
shrewish tongue, or a reference to effeminacy, cowardice, or even homosexuality.

31 him Achilles.

32 Cobloaf A small round loaf; Ajax's mind
seems to be running on bread (see 11 and n.) as
well as animals. The aptness of this epithet is not
apparent – perhaps a reference to Thersites' deformities or to his small size? In general, Ajax's

insults are no match for those of his opponent, so
he resorts to blows.

33 pun pound.

33 shivers bits, fragments.

37 stool privy. Walker and others, including
Evans, assign this speech to Thersites, mainly
because of the common Elizabethan pun on
'Ajax' = 'a jakes' (privy). But, as Palmer remarks,
Shakespeare is usually more obvious with such
puns; and further, since F clears up the other
speech heading problems in this passage, the
agreement of Q and F creates a strong likelihood that they got it right. If Ajax is the
speaker, the implied joke about 'jakes' turns
back on him because he is too stupid to recognise it. And Thersites' alliterative 'sodden-witted'
(38) sounds like a mocking retort to Ajax's
insult.

39 asinico little ass (Spanish).

40 scurvy valiant contemptibly valiant (because
his valour manifests itself in beating a weakling like

art bought and sold among those of any wit like a barbarian slave.
If thou use to beat me I will begin at thy heel and tell what thou
art by inches, thou thing of no bowels, thou.

AJAX You dog!

THERSITES You scurvy lord!   45

AJAX [*Beating him*] You cur!

THERSITES Mars his idiot, do rudeness, do camel, do do!

Enter ACHILLES *and* PATROCLUS

ACHILLES Why how now, Ajax, wherefore do ye thus?
    How now, Thersites, what's the matter, man?

THERSITES You see him there, do you?   50

ACHILLES Ay, what's the matter?

THERSITES Nay look upon him.

ACHILLES So I do – what's the matter?

THERSITES Nay but regard him well.

ACHILLES Well, why so I do.   55

THERSITES But yet you look not well upon him, for whosomever you
    take him to be, he is Ajax.

ACHILLES I know that, fool.

THERSITES Ay, but that fool knows not himself.

AJAX Therefore I beat thee.   60

THERSITES Lo, lo, lo, lo, what modicums of wit he utters: his evasions
    have ears thus long. I have bobbed his brain more than he has beat
    my bones. I will buy nine sparrows for a penny, and his pia mater

---

46 SD] *Rowe; not in* Q, F   47 SD] F; *not in* Q   48 ye thus] Q; you this F   53 So I do] Q; I do so F   56 whosomever]
Q *(who some euer)*, F; whosoever F3   63 I] F; It Q

Thersites or because in general he is all brawn and
no brain).
  41 bought and sold traded back and forth,
hence manipulated or exploited.
  42 use continue.
  43 bowels sympathy; another instance of the or-
gan thought to be the seat of a feeling being used
to represent the feeling itself, cf. 'spleen' and 'gall'
in 1.3.179, 194, 238.
  47 Mars his idiot The god of war's fool. Thersites is deliberately goading Ajax, inviting his blows
('do . . . do . . . do!'), and continuing his attack on
Ajax's brainlessness. The possessive form 'Mars
his' (modern 'Mars's') was common in early modern English, especially with proper names.
  60 Perhaps one of Ajax's 'evasions' (61) and if

so, certainly a lame one. He no doubt means that
he beat Thersites because he does not like being
called a fool, but his response unwittingly suggests that he agrees with Thersites' assessment of
him as someone who does not recognise his own
folly.
  61 modicums little bits.
  61 evasions attempts to avoid a verbal thrust.
  62 ears thus long ears as long as those of an
ass (cf. 'asinico' (39)), indicated by an appropriate gesture – a good example of a stage direction
embedded in the dialogue.
  62 bobbed thumped.
  63 pia mater brain (literally, a membrane covering the brain). The phrase occurs with the same
general meaning in *LLL* 4.2.69 and *TN* 1.5.115.

is not worth the ninth part of a sparrow. This lord, Achilles, Ajax,
who wears his wit in his belly and his guts in his head, I'll tell you   65
what I say of him.

ACHILLES What?

THERSITES I say, this Ajax –

        [*Ajax threatens to beat him and Achilles intervenes*]

ACHILLES Nay good Ajax.

THERSITES Has not so much wit –   70

ACHILLES [*To Ajax*] Nay I must hold you.

THERSITES As will stop the eye of Helen's needle, for whom he comes
to fight.

ACHILLES Peace, fool.

THERSITES I would have peace and quietness, but the fool will not –   75
he there, that he, look you there.

AJAX O thou damned cur, I shall –

ACHILLES Will you set your wit to a fool's?

THERSITES No I warrant you, the fool's will shame it.

PATROCLUS Good words, Thersites.   80

ACHILLES What's the quarrel?

AJAX I bade the vile owl go learn me the tenor of the proclamation,
and he rails upon me.

THERSITES I serve thee not.

AJAX Well go to, go to.   85

THERSITES I serve here voluntary.

ACHILLES Your last service was sufferance – 'twas not voluntary; no
man is beaten voluntary. Ajax was here the voluntary and you as
under an impress.

THERSITES E'en so; a great deal of your wit too lies in your sinews,   90
or else there be liars. Hector shall have a great catch if he knock
out either of your brains: 'a were as good crack a fusty nut with
no kernel.

ACHILLES What, with me too, Thersites?

65 I'll] F; I Q   68 SD] *Rowe (subst., after 67); placed here Dyce; not in* Q, F   70 wit –] F2; wit. Q, F   71 SD] *Collier*[3];
not in Q, F   79 the fool's] Q *(the fooles);* for a fooles F   82 the vile] Q; thee vile F; thee, vile F4   82 tenor] Q; tenure F
91–2 if he knock out] F; and knocke at Q

74 Spoken to Thersites, who deflects the insult
towards Ajax.
  80 **Good words** Speak gently.
  87 **sufferance** (1) imposed, (2) painful.
  88–9 **as . . . impress** (1) pressed into service,
drafted, (2) marked, imprinted.
  90–3 Thersites, like a terrier nipping at a pair
of mastiffs, now turns his corrosive wit against
Achilles.
  92 **fusty** mouldy.

THERSITES There's Ulysses and old Nestor, whose wit was mouldy ere   95
    your grandsires had nails on their toes, yoke you like draught-oxen
    and make you plough up the wars.

ACHILLES What, what?

THERSITES Yes good sooth: to, Achilles! to, Ajax! to –

AJAX I shall cut out your tongue.   100

THERSITES 'Tis no matter, I shall speak as much as thou afterwards.

PATROCLUS No more words Thersites, peace!

THERSITES I will hold my peace when Achilles' brach bids me, shall I?

ACHILLES There's for you Patroclus.

THERSITES I will see you hanged like clotpolls ere I come any more   105
    to your tents. I will keep where there is wit stirring and leave the
    faction of fools.   *Exit*

PATROCLUS A good riddance.

ACHILLES Marry this, sir, is proclaimed through all our host:
    That Hector by the fifth hour of the sun   110
    Will with a trumpet 'twixt our tents and Troy
    Tomorrow morning call some knight to arms
    That hath a stomach, and such a one that dare
    Maintain – I know not what – 'tis trash. Farewell.

AJAX Farewell – who shall answer him?   115

ACHILLES I know not, 'tis put to lottery; otherwise he knew his man.
                           [Exeunt Achilles and Patroclus]

AJAX O, meaning you! I will go learn more of it.   *Exit*

---

96 your] *Theobald;* their Q, F   96 on their toes] F; *not in* Q   97 wars] Q; warre F   101 as much] Q, F; as much
wit *Capell*   102 Thersites, peace!] Q; *Thersites.* F   103 brach] *Rowe;* brooch Q, F (*subst.*)   110 fifth] F; first Q   114
Maintain –] *Hanmer;* Maintaine Q, F   116] *This edn; as verse (*otherwise, / He) Q, F   116 SD] *Capell (subst.); not in*
Q, F   117 SD] F; *not in* Q

96–7 yoke . . . wars i.e. make you do the dirty
work of war.

99 to . . . to . . . to Thersites, continuing his
comparison of Achilles and Ajax to oxen, here
imagines a farmer calling to them.

101 as much Capell's addition of 'wit' after this
phrase has appealed to many subsequent editors,
but seems quite unnecessary. Thersites has a habit
of elision (as at 18, 20, 39) and his meaning is clear
enough – that Ajax's words are empty of wit, mere
noise.

103 brach bitch. The word carries with it something of the connotation of 'masculine whore', another of Thersites' terms for Patroclus (5.1.17). Q
and F's 'brooch' is inappropriate (though it could
simply be an odd spelling derived from MS.), while

Rowe's emendation involves only a slight graphic
change and makes excellent sense.

105 clotpolls blockheads.

113 stomach (1) will, desire, appetite; (2) boldness, courage.

116 'tis put to lottery it will be settled by drawing lots (according to the plan devised by Ulysses
and Nestor in 1.3.373–85).

116 SD Capell recognised that Achilles and
Patroclus depart at 116, leaving Ajax onstage for
the last line (F's *Exit* at 117 is thus correct,
though most editors emend to *Exeunt*). But the
dialogue suggests that Achilles turns to go at
114, and Ajax's question at 115 is a parting shot.
Achilles perhaps tosses back his answer over his
shoulder.

[2.2] Enter PRIAM, HECTOR, TROILUS, PARIS, and HELENUS

PRIAM After so many hours, lives, speeches spent,
       Thus once again says Nestor from the Greeks:
       'Deliver Helen, and all damage else,
       As honour, loss of time, travail, expense,
       Wounds, friends, and what else dear that is consumed   5
       In hot digestion of this cormorant war,
       Shall be struck off.' Hector, what say you to't?
HECTOR Though no man lesser fears the Greeks than I
       As far as toucheth my particular,
       Yet, dread Priam,   10
       There is no lady of more softer bowels,
       More spongy to suck in the sense of fear,
       More ready to cry out 'Who knows what follows?'
       Than Hector is. The wound of peace is surety,
       Surety secure, but modest doubt is called   15
       The beacon of the wise, the tent that searches
       To th'bottom of the worst. Let Helen go.
       Since the first sword was drawn about this question
       Every tithe soul 'mongst many thousand dismes
       Hath been as dear as Helen, I mean of ours;   20
       If we have lost so many tenths of ours

Act 2, Scene 2   2.2] *Rowe (subst.); not in* Q, F   3–7 'Deliver . . . off.'] *Capell (subst.);* Deliuer . . . off, Q, F *(subst.)*
9–10] *Collier; as one line* Q, F   9 toucheth] Q; touches F   13 'Who . . . follows?'] *Pope (subst.);* who . . . followes Q, F
14–15 surety, / Surety] F; surely / Surely Q   17 worst] Q, F; wound *Hanmer*

Act 2, Scene 2
  0 SD The entrance of the Trojan council is undoubtedly a formal one, designed as parallel to that
of the Greeks at the beginning of 1.3. The debate
that follows is focused not on order and 'degree',
but on another crucial theme: the question of value
and how it is assigned to human actions (see Introduction, pp. 38–41). Productions have typically
treated this scene with more dignity than its Greek
counterpart.
  4 travail labour.
  6 cormorant voracious (the cormorant, a large
sea bird, was said to have a ravenous appetite). The
idea that the war 'digests' honour, friends, etc. fits
with the recurrent images of eating and consuming
in the play.
  9 As far as I am concerned personally.
  11 more softer bowels greater compassion (see
2.1.43 and n.). The double comparative is often

used for added emphasis by Shakespeare and his
contemporaries (Abbott 11).
  14 The . . . surety Overconfidence endangers
peace.
  16 tent surgical probe.
  17 worst Hanmer suggested 'wound' here to fit
with 'tent' in the previous line, but Q and F agree
on 'worst' and most editors comply.
  19–20 As so often in the play, the phrasing is
obscure, though the meaning is reasonably clear:
'we have lost thousands and they are all as dear as
Helen'. 'Tithe' and 'disme' both mean 'tenth',
so that literally Hector says that a tenth of the
tenths we've lost are 'dear', but as Deighton suggested, Hector apparently means that thousands of
'dismes' (picking up on 'tithe soul' and meaning
simply 'souls') have been taken by the war as a
kind of 'tithe' (a payment of 10 per cent of one's
goods, required for the support of the Church).

To guard a thing not ours, nor worth to us
(Had it our name) the value of one ten,
What merit's in that reason which denies
The yielding of her up?
TROILUS   Fie, fie, my brother,   25
Weigh you the worth and honour of a king
So great as our dread father in a scale
Of common ounces? Will you with counters sum
The past-proportion of his infinite,
And buckle in a waist most fathomless   30
With spans and inches so diminutive
As fears and reasons? Fie, for godly shame.
HELENUS No marvel, though you bite so sharp at reasons,
You are so empty of them. Should not our father
Bear the great sway of his affairs with reasons   35
Because your speech hath none that tell him so?
TROILUS You are for dreams and slumbers, brother priest,
You fur your gloves with reason. Here are your reasons:
You know an enemy intends you harm,

---

27 father] F; fathers Q   29 past-proportion] *Johnson*; past proportion Q, F; vast proportion *Rowe*   30 waist] Q, F
(waste)   33 sharp at] F; sharp of Q   35 reasons] F; reason Q   36 tell] Q; tels F

---

23 Had . . . name Even if she were one of us, a
Trojan.

23 one ten a single 'tithe' (in the sense suggested
by 19–20).

24 reason argument. The term introduces a network of complicated word-play on various meanings of 'reason' over the next twenty-five lines; see
35 n.

28 counters metal tokens, worth nothing in
themselves.

29 past-proportion immeasurability, literally
'beyond comparison' (Johnson's hyphen makes the
phrase into a compound noun and clarifies the
meaning).

29 his infinite Priam's incomparable value.

30 buckle confine.

30 fathomless without bound. The bizarre image of Priam's inflated 'waist' is supplemented, especially in performance, by the auditory echo with
'waste', pointing to the very issue at stake in the
Trojan debate.

31 spans hand-breadths (standard measures of
9 inches).

35 reasons The choice between Q's 'reason' and
F's 'reasons' would seem minor but raises a number of problems and offers another example of the
difficulty of adjudicating between readings in this
text, and indeed, the inevitable losses that ensue
simply because one must make a choice. Q's 'reason' makes sense: Helenus would be referring to
the rational faculty which makes considered judgements. Furthermore, as Palmer points out, there is
an interplay between singular and plural in this sequence (compare 38, which has slightly more force
if reason remains in the singular here). 'Reasons',
on the other hand, goes back to the sense in which
Hector uses the word in 24, i.e. 'arguments'; the
common meaning of 'ground or motive for taking
an action' is also in play in the plural usage. I take
Helenus to be speaking of such grounds and arguments, even though it is true that the general
sense is also present. Also, the phrase 'hath none
that tell' in the next line supports the plural form
better than the singular.

38–50 Here are . . . deject Troilus, accelerat-
ing the play on 'reason(s)', mockingly turns his
brother's supposed allegiance to rational thought
into mere self-interest – enlightened perhaps, but
also cowardly.

38 fur your gloves keep yourself comfortable, with reference to the soft luxury of fur-lined
gloves.

You know a sword employed is perilous,   40
And reason flies the object of all harm:
Who marvels then, when Helenus beholds
A Grecian and his sword, if he do set
The very wings of reason to his heels
And fly like chidden Mercury from Jove,   45
Or like a star disorbed? Nay, if we talk of reason
Let's shut our gates and sleep: manhood and honour
Should have hare hearts would they but fat their thoughts
With this crammed reason. Reason and respect
Make livers pale and lustihood deject.   50

HECTOR Brother, she is not worth what she doth cost
The keeping.

TROILUS   What's aught but as 'tis valued?

HECTOR But value dwells not in particular will;
It holds his estimate and dignity
As well wherein 'tis precious of itself   55
As in the prizer. 'Tis mad idolatry
To make the service greater than the god,
And the will dotes that is inclineable

45–6] Q; *lines reversed* F   47 Let's] F; Sets Q   48 hare] Q; hard F   50 Make] Q; Makes F   51–2 Brother . . . keeping]
Theobald (substituting holding *for* keeping); *as prose* Q; Brother . . . worth / What . . . holding F   52 keeping] Q; holding
F   56 mad] Q; made F   58 inclineable] F; attributiue Q

41 the . . . harm whatever presents itself as
harmful.

45 Mercury The messenger of the gods, typically represented with wings on his heels, and often
reprimanded ('chidden') by the imperious Jove.

46 disorbed unsphered, knocked out of orbit
(hence, a shooting star). The term recalls Ulysses'
speech on degree (1.3.83–103).

48 hare timid (like a hare's).

49 crammed The image is from the practice
of overfeeding fowls. Honourable men would turn
cowardly, their 'livers' (the seat of valour (50))
would become bloodless and soft, if they were
force-fed with reason.

49 respect cautious circumspection.

50 lustihood deject (make) manly strength
downcast.

52 keeping F's 'holding' makes equally good
sense, but the Q reading is supported by its re-
currence in 81 and 149.

52 What's . . . valued i.e. the worth of anything
derives from the value ascribed to it by individual or community. Troilus' famous question echoes
through the whole play, undermining, although he
does not recognise it, the foundation on which he
wishes to build his love affair with Cressida, and

casting doubt on the reasons for going to war, maintaining reputation, being constant in love, etc. See
Introduction, pp. 38–41.

53–60 Hector, more of a philosophical idealist than Troilus, argues for inherent value in the
thing itself, rather than allowing relativism to transform value into mere preference on the part of the
'prizer' (56).

54 his its.

56 in the prizer in the opinion of him who
prizes, or values.

56–7 'Tis . . . god Perhaps a jibe at the forms
of Catholic worship, so often castigated as idola-
trous by the Protestant reformers of the sixteenth
century. There may also be an allusion to Matthew
23.19: 'Ye fooles and blinde, whether it is greater,
the offring, or the altar which sanctifieth the
offring'.

58–60 Any person's will that leans towards ('is
inclineable / To') what it desires ('affects') without
some image of the 'merit' of what is 'affected' (60)
may be said to 'dote' (like an old fool doting on a
young beloved).

58 inclineable Q's 'attributiue' (= attributes
value to) is possible but more obscure, and might
therefore have led to revision.

To what infectiously itself affects,
Without some image of th'affected merit.   60
TROILUS I take today a wife, and my election
Is led on in the conduct of my will,
My will enkindled by mine eyes and ears,
Two traded pilots 'twixt the dangerous shores
Of will and judgement: how may I avoid,   65
Although my will distaste what it elected,
The wife I chose? There can be no evasion
To blench from this and to stand firm by honour.
We turn not back the silks upon the merchant
When we have soiled them, nor the remainder viands   70
We do not throw in unrespective sieve
Because we now are full. It was thought meet
Paris should do some vengeance on the Greeks;
Your breath with full consent bellied his sails;

---

64 shores] F; shore Q   67 chose] F; choose Q   70 soiled] Q; spoyl'd F   71 sieve] Q (siue); same F; place F2; sink
Delius; sewer *Oxford (conj. Schmidt)*   74 with] Q; of F

59 infectiously i.e. the will infects itself because it is fixated on its own desires (first recorded example in *OED*).

61 I . . . wife Ostensibly, Troilus is constructing a hypothetical case as part of his argument, not talking about his own situation, but his feelings for Cressida perhaps influence the example he chooses to illustrate his point (though he nowhere mentions the possibility of marrying her).

61–5 my election . . . judgement Though he alludes skilfully to traditional Aristotelian psychology, Troilus is somewhat confused. He argues that one's choice ('election') is 'led on' by will, when the orthodox view is that the will chooses what reason ('judgement', 65) presents to it as a good. Part of the confusion arises from the slippage in the meaning of 'will' from 'desire' (62, 63) to 'the mental faculty that effects choice' (65); and part derives from the image of the senses ('eyes and ears') as experienced 'pilots' plying between the 'shores' of reason and will. In the traditional scheme, the senses provide data to the reason, which judges, and then the will puts such judgements into effect. Perhaps Troilus regards will and judgement as 'dangerous' because they have the power to distrust the evidence provided to them by the senses and hence shipwreck desire. Shakespeare treats the whole matter comically in

MND: 'The will of man is by his reason sway'd; / And reason says you are the worthier maid' (2.2.115–16).

66 Although Even if.
66 distaste (come to) dislike.
67 evasion contrived argument.
68 blench shrink, turn away.
70 viands food.

71 unrespective indiscriminate, thrown together (a transferred modifier, properly applied to the 'viands', not to the receptacle into which they are tossed).

71 sieve basket for scraps. F's 'same' seems a simple misreading, one that is inexplicable if the annotator had Q before him (see Textual Analysis, pp. 247–8); F2's 'place' is a weak attempt to improve on 'same'. Other emendations derive from an apparent inability on the part of editors to imagine a receptacle to hold scraps (which might then be fed to the pigs); they see the refuse being thrown directly into the 'sink' (= common sewer).

74 bellied filled. A similar idea occurs in *Temp.*, Epilogue 11–12, 'Gentle breath of yours my sails / Must fill'; and, with an added image of pregnancy, in *MND* (2.1.128–9), 'we have laugh'd to see the sails conceive / And grow big-bellied with the wanton wind'.

The seas and winds, old wranglers, took a truce   75
And did him service; he touched the ports desired
And for an old aunt whom the Greeks held captive
He brought a Grecian queen, whose youth and freshness
Wrinkles Apollo's and makes stale the morning.
Why keep we her? The Grecians keep our aunt.   80
Is she worth keeping? Why, she is a pearl
Whose price hath launched above a thousand ships
And turned crowned kings to merchants.
If you'll avouch 'twas wisdom Paris went
(As you must needs for you all cried 'Go, go'),   85
If you'll confess he brought home worthy prize
(As you must needs for you all clapped your hands
And cried 'Inestimable!'), why do you now
The issue of your proper wisdoms rate,
And do a deed that never Fortune did: 90
Beggar the estimation which you prized
Richer than sea and land? O theft most base,
That we have stol'n what we do fear to keep;
But thieves unworthy of a thing so stol'n,
That in their country did them that disgrace   95
We fear to warrant in our native place.

CASSANDRA [*Within*] Cry, Trojans, cry!

PRIAM   What noise, what shriek is this?

---

79 stale] F; pale Q   85 'Go, go'] *Pope (subst.);* go, go Q, F *(subst.)*   86 he] F; be Q   86 worthy] Q; Noble F   88
'Inestimable!'] *Hanmer (subst.);* inestimable Q, F   90 never Fortune] Q; Fortune neuer F   97, 99 SDS] *Theobald; not in*
Q, F

---

75 wranglers opponents.

77 for in retaliation for.

77 old aunt Hesione, Priam's sister, who had been rescued from a sea monster by Hercules and given to a Greek leader, Telamon; as we learn in 4.5.120, she is Ajax's mother.

78–9 whose . . . morning i.e. Helen makes the radiant youth of the sun-god, Apollo, appear wrinkled, and the freshness of the morning seem stale.

81–2 she is . . . ships The lines echo Faustus' famous cry on being presented with Helen of Troy: 'Was this the face that launched a thousand ships / And burnt the topless towers of Ilium?' ('A' text, 5.1.90–1; Marlowe was himself borrowing from classical and contemporary sources). But the differences are also telling: Troilus' image is mercantile – it is Helen's *price*, not her beauty, which launches the ships (compare his description of Cressida 1.1.93–8). There is also an ironic allusion

to the 'perle of great price' in Matthew 13.46.

84 avouch affirm.

89 issue result.

89 rate berate, criticise.

90 And act much more inconstantly than Fortune ever would.

91 Beggar the estimation Reduce the value.

94–6 We are unworthy thieves because here at home we are afraid to stand behind, or ratify ('warrant', 96), the action that disgraced the Greeks in their own land.

97 SD The dialogue suggests that Cassandra does not enter until line 100, though both Q and F have her enter here. As in 4.4, the offstage voice intruding on the present action is deeply unsettling. Here the suppressed tension of the council is exploded by the only Trojan who sees the situation whole. But Cassandra's gift of prophecy has been cursed: in the play, as in the myth, no one will believe her.

TROILUS 'Tis our mad sister, I do know her voice.
CASSANDRA [*Within*] Cry, Trojans!
HECTOR It is Cassandra.   100

Enter CASSANDRA *raving, with her hair about her ears*

CASSANDRA Cry, Trojans, cry, lend me ten thousand eyes
        And I will fill them with prophetic tears.
HECTOR Peace, sister, peace.
CASSANDRA Virgins and boys, mid-age and wrinkled eld,
        Soft infancy that nothing canst but cry,   105
        Add to my clamours: let us pay betimes
        A moiety of that mass of moan to come.
        Cry, Trojans, cry, practise your eyes with tears!
        Troy must not be, nor goodly Ilium stand   –
        Our firebrand brother Paris burns us all.   110
        Cry, Trojans, cry, a Helen and a woe!
        Cry, cry! Troy burns – or else let Helen go!   *Exit*
HECTOR Now youthful Troilus, do not these high strains
        Of divination in our sister work
        Some touches of remorse, or is your blood   115
        So madly hot that no discourse of reason,
        Nor fear of bad success in a bad cause
        Can qualify the same?
TROILUS   Why brother Hector,
        We may not think the justness of each act
        Such and no other than event doth form it,   120
        Nor once deject the courage of our minds

100 SD] *Evans (placed as in Theobald); Enter Cassandra raving* Q *(after 96); Enter Cassandra with her haire about her eares* F *(after 96)*   104 eld] *Collier (conj. Theobald);* elders Q; old F   105 canst] Q; can F   106 clamours] Q; clamour F

100 SD Combining Q and F, this direction gives a vivid sense of the depiction of madness on the Elizabethan stage, at least as it applies to women characters. Loosened hair and hysteria characterise figures as different as Ophelia, Lady Macbeth, and Isabella in Kyd's *The Spanish Tragedy*. Of course, Cassandra is not mad, but caught in the grip of what Othello calls 'prophetic fury' (*Oth.* 3.4.72).

104 eld F's 'old' is an easy misreading of 'eld', so that Theobald's conjecture fits nicely. Q's 'elders' may be compositorial, or a first, unmetrical, attempt on Shakespeare's part.

105 canst can do.
106 betimes early.
107 moiety part.

108 practise employ, put to use (*OED v* 7).
110 firebrand Hecuba, when she was pregnant with Paris, dreamed that she would give birth to a firebrand that would burn Troy (*Aeneid*, VII.320, X.704).
117 success outcome.
118 qualify moderate, cool.
119–20 Here Troilus extends the position he has been developing in the debate. 'Justness' inheres in an action, regardless of the outcome ('event'), because, as he goes on to suggest in 123–5, one engages one's honour in choosing to perform it and sticking by that choice. The initial valuation, that is, commits one to a particular course of action which it would be dishonourable to abandon.
120 event the outcome.

Because Cassandra's mad; her brain-sick raptures
Cannot distaste the goodness of a quarrel,
Which hath our several honours all engaged
To make it gracious. For my private part,   125
I am no more touched than all Priam's sons,
And Jove forbid there should be done amongst us
Such things as might offend the weakest spleen
To fight for and maintain.

PARIS Else might the world convince of levity   130
As well my undertakings as your counsels.
But I attest the gods, your full consent
Gave wings to my propension and cut off
All fears attending on so dire a project.
For what alas can these my single arms,   135
What propugnation is in one man's valour
To stand the push and enmity of those
This quarrel would excite? Yet I protest
Were I alone to pass the difficulties,
And had as ample power as I have will,   140
Paris should ne'er retract what he hath done
Nor faint in the pursuit.

PRIAM   Paris, you speak
Like one besotted on your sweet delights:
You have the honey still but these the gall;
So to be valiant is no praise at all.   145

PARIS Sir I propose not merely to myself
The pleasures such a beauty brings with it,
But I would have the soil of her fair rape

123 **distaste** sour, make distasteful.

125 **gracious** honourable, right (according to the code by which their 'honours' are all 'engaged,' or bound (124)).

126 **touched** affected (i.e. we are all equally involved).

128 **spleen** temperament, spirit. The word normally refers to fits of temper (see 1.3.179), but here slides over to a more generalised meaning. Troilus' point is that even the most scrupulous Trojan should be able to support the motion to retain Helen.

130 **convince** convict.

132 **attest** call to witness.

133 **propension** inclination, desire (as with 'propugnation' (136), and 'propend' (190), Shakespeare's sole use of the word).

136 **propugnation** defence.

137 **stand the push** withstand the attack.

139 **pass the difficulties** experience the challenge (of such a 'quarrel').

142 **faint** slacken.

143 **besotted on** intoxicated by.

144 **gall** Originally, bile, but extended to mean simply a very bitter substance; used frequently by Shakespeare, as Palmer notes, as an antonym for sweetness.

148 **soil . . . rape** This contradictory phrase epitomises the whole debate; it manifests a paradoxical awareness of both the guilt of the abduction ('rape') and the honour that presumably accompanied it (see 72–80). An alternative, less likely, way of interpreting 'fair rape' would be to read 'fair' as a kind of substantive, so that the phrase would mean 'the abduction of the fair one'.

Wiped off in honourable keeping her.
What treason were it to the ransacked queen,   150
Disgrace to your great worths and shame to me,
Now to deliver her possession up
On terms of base compulsion! Can it be
That so degenerate a strain as this
Should once set footing in your generous bosoms?   155
There's not the meanest spirit on our party
Without a heart to dare or sword to draw
When Helen is defended, nor none so noble
Whose life were ill bestowed or death unfamed
Where Helen is the subject. Then I say,   160
Well may we fight for her whom we know well
The world's large spaces cannot parallel.
HECTOR Paris and Troilus, you have both said well,
And on the cause and question now in hand
Have glossed, but superficially – not much   165
Unlike young men whom Aristotle thought
Unfit to hear moral philosophy.
The reasons you allege do more conduce
To the hot passion of distempered blood
Than to make up a free determination   170
'Twixt right and wrong, for pleasure and revenge
Have ears more deaf than adders to the voice
Of any true decision. Nature craves
All dues be rendered to their owners: now,
What nearer debt in all humanity   175
Than wife is to the husband? If this law

---

150 **were it** it would be.
150 **ransacked** carried off as plunder.
152 **her possession** the possession of her.
153 **terms . . . compulsion** terms that force us to stoop or debase ourselves.
154 **strain** streak, tendency.
155 **generous** noble (opposite to 'degenerate' in the previous line).
156 **meanest** lowliest.
156 **party** side.
165 **glossed** commented (as on a text), sometimes with a suggestion of specious reasoning. Most editors follow Q and F in reading 'gloz'd', but modernised spelling requires 'glossed', as Oxford recognises.
166 **Aristotle** An obvious anachronism, since

Aristotle lived several centuries after the Trojan War. This is the kind of error that Shakespeare neither notices nor cares about. As a writer, he simply makes use of what he needs for the dramatic tenor of the scene. Palmer (Appendix 3) argues that this allusion to Aristotle's *Ethics* is not an isolated one, but that many of the debates about morality and politics in the play go back to that source.
168 **conduce** tend.
170 **determination** judgement.
172 **more . . . adders** The adder, a small poisonous snake, was thought to be able to stop its ears; its deafness was proverbial (Dent A32 and Psalm 58.4–5).
173 **Nature** Natural law (which underpins human morality).

Of nature be corrupted through affection,
And that great minds, of partial indulgence
To their benumbèd wills, resist the same,
There is a law in each well-ordered nation   180
To curb those raging appetites that are
Most disobedient and refractory.
If Helen then be wife to Sparta's king,
As it is known she is, these moral laws
Of nature and of nations speak aloud   185
To have her back returned. Thus to persist
In doing wrong extenuates not wrong,
But makes it much more heavy. Hector's opinion
Is this in way of truth; yet ne'ertheless,
My sprightly brethren, I propend to you   190
In resolution to keep Helen still,
For 'tis a cause that hath no mean dependence
Upon our joint and several dignities.
TROILUS Why there you touched the life of our design!
Were it not glory that we more affected   195
Than the performance of our heaving spleens,
I would not wish a drop of Trojan blood
Spent more in her defence. But, worthy Hector,
She is a theme of honour and renown,
A spur to valiant and magnanimous deeds,   200
Whose present courage may beat down our foes
And fame in time to come canonise us.
For I presume brave Hector would not lose

---

185 nations] Q; Nation F

177 **affection** passion.

178–9 And if wise men, out of a selfish ('partial') tendency to indulge their desensitised ('benumbèd') wills, resist this same law of nature.

180 The law of nations referred to here derives from and upholds the 'law of nature' referred to in 176–7, though the two were typically distinguished in sixteenth-century political and ethical theory.

182 **refractory** stubborn.

190 **propend** incline, yield. Hector's unexpected reversal, coming as it does on the heels of a strong argument rooted in orthodox thinking about moral law, is a prime example of the inconsistency that characterises the world of the play and its inhabitants. See Introduction, pp. 3, 39–40.

192–3 For our honour, both collective and individual ('joint and several'), depends in no small measure upon our commitment 'to keep Helen still'.

195–6 If we did not seek honour more than the mere acting out of spiteful resentment.

199–202 Here is the heart of Troilus' argument: Helen in herself may be worthless, but she has been and remains a motive, a pretext for magnanimous action and the possibility of eternal glory. As such she is worth the 'cost' of 'keeping' her (51–2).

202 **canonise** memorialise, set down in the calendar of (secular) saints (accented on second syllable).

So rich advantage of a promised glory
As smiles upon the forehead of this action   205
For the wide world's revenue.

HECTOR   I am yours,
You valiant offspring of great Priamus.
I have a roisting challenge sent amongst
The dull and factious nobles of the Greeks
Will strike amazement to their drowsy spirits.   210
I was advertised their great general slept
Whilst emulation in the army crept:
This I presume will wake him.

                                            Exeunt

[2.3] *Enter* THERSITES *alone*

THERSITES How now, Thersites? What, lost in the labyrinth of thy
    fury? Shall the elephant Ajax carry it thus? He beats me and
    I rail at him: O worthy satisfaction! Would it were otherwise –
    that I could beat him, whilst he railed at me. 'Sfoot, I'll learn
    to conjure and raise devils but I'll see some issue of my spiteful   5
    execrations. Then there's Achilles, a rare engineer. If Troy be not
    taken till these two undermine it, the walls will stand till they fall

---

210 strike] F; shrike Q   **Act 2, Scene 3** 2.3] *Capell (subst.); not in* Q, F   0 SD *alone*] Q, F *(solus)*   1 SH] *Hanmer; not in* Q, F

206 revenue wealth (accented on second syllable).
    208 roisting rousing.
    209 factious split by faction.
    210 strike F's reading is blander than Q's
'shrike' (= shriek) but better fits Hector's style
and tone. 'Shriek' would seem more appropriate
to Cassandra, though it could be a kind of imag-
istic recall of her presence. Honigmann argues cogently that 'shrike' is Shakespearean and not simply
a misreading (*Stability*, pp. 88–9); if so, it looks as
though 'strike' is a revision.
    211 advertised informed (accented on second
syllable).
    211 general Probably Achilles, though it could
refer to Agamemnon, who is the only Greek normally called 'general', and whose lax regime has allowed emulation to creep (212) through the Greek
ranks.

212 emulation envious infighting; see 1.3.135
n.
    213 The scene ends abruptly, the debate fore-
closed, and Priam and Helenus silenced.

Act 2, Scene 3
    2 carry it have the upper hand. Thersites is still
smarting from his encounter with Ajax in 2.1.
    4 'Sfoot An oath, 'by God's foot'.
    5 conjure . . . devils Another possible allusion
to Marlowe's *Doctor Faustus*, which features such
conjuration, as does Robert Greene's *Friar Bacon
and Friar Bungay*.
    5 issue result.
    6 execrations curses.
    6 engineer (1) plotter, (2) contriver of military
devices (alluded to in the next sentence). Many editions follow F in printing 'enginer' but *OED* gives
'engineer' as the standard modern form.

of themselves. O thou great thunder-darter of Olympus, forget that
thou art Jove the king of gods, and Mercury, lose all the serpentine
craft of thy caduceus, if ye take not that little little less than little   10
wit from them that they have, which short-armed ignorance itself
knows is so abundant scarce it will not in circumvention deliver a
fly from a spider without drawing their massy irons and cutting the
web. After this, the vengeance on the whole camp! Or rather the
Neapolitan bone-ache, for that methinks is the curse depending   15
on those that war for a placket. I have said my prayers and devil
Envy say 'Amen'. What ho, my Lord Achilles!

PATROCLUS [*Appearing at the entrance of the tent*] Who's there?
Thersites? – Good Thersites, come in and rail. [*Goes back inside
the tent*]   20

THERSITES If I could've remembered a gilt counterfeit, thou wouldst
not have slipped out of my contemplation, but it is no matter: thyself upon thyself. The common curse of mankind,
folly and ignorance, be thine in great revenue, heaven bless
thee from a tutor, and discipline come not near thee. Let thy   25

---

10 ye] Q; thou F   13 their] Q; the F   15 Neapolitan] Q (Neopolitan); not in F   15 depending] Q; dependant F
17 'Amen'] Hanmer (subst.); Amen Q, F   18 SD] This edn; not in Q; Enter Patroclus F (after 17); Within / anon.
conj. Cam.; Enter Patroclus at the door to the tent / Oxford   19–20 SD] This edn; not in Q, F; Patroclus disappears
briefly / Bevington²   21 could've] This edn; could a Q; could have F   21 wouldst] F; couldst Q

8 O thou . . . Perhaps Thersites kneels at this
point when he begins his 'prayer'. This would then
motivate Patroclus' later question, 'wast thou in
prayer?' (but see 30 n.).

10 caduceus Mercury's wand, entwined by two
serpents. Both the serpents and Mercury himself
were famed for their 'craft' or cunning.

11 short-armed lacking in reach.

12–14 it . . . web they are so deficient in good
sense ('wit') that they will draw their huge swords
('massy irons') to free a fly from a spider's web.

15 Neapolitan bone-ache Syphilis (also called
the 'French disease', reflecting the tendency to
blame such troubles on foreigners).

15–16 depending on hanging over.

16 placket slit in a petticoat, used derisively and
with a strong sexual overtone to mean 'woman', and
particularly, 'vagina' (see Williams, *Glossary*).

17 Envy Probably a reference to the personified
figures of the seven deadly sins (of which Envy is
one) in the morality plays and in *Doctor Faustus*.
Note that Thersites is aware of the source of his
venom within himself, and the theatrical allusion
suggests that he is also alert to his own histrionic
streak.

18–20 SDs Q has no directions for Patroclus

here, while F has him entering after 17 and remaining onstage through Thersites' next speech.
F's arrangement has struck a number of editors as
dramatically awkward. Although Thersites is not
averse to cursing Patroclus and others to their faces,
it seems uncharacteristic for them to stand pas-
sively by while Thersites rails on at such length.
'Who's there? Thersites?' suggests that Patroclus
looks out to see who is calling, and then ducks
back into the tent (that there was some kind of
tent-like structure onstage is suggested by 3.3.37
SD.2 (see n.) and ensuing dialogue). Another possibility could be that Patroclus does not appear at
all until after 28, but speaks 18–19 from 'within'.

21–22 If . . . contemplation If I were in the
habit of remembering glittering falsehood, you
would not have 'slipped' my mind (with a pun on
'slip' = a counterfeit coin).

23 thyself upon thyself Having cursed the others, Thersites now calls down the ultimate (and
paradoxical) plague on Patroclus – that he, the very
prince of counterfeit, simply be himself.

24 revenue abundance.

24–25 heaven . . . near thee may heaven grant
you freedom from a tutor and his discipline (so that
your folly remains intact).

blood be thy direction till thy death; then, if she that lays thee
out says thou art a fair corpse, I'll be sworn and sworn upon't she
never shrouded any but lazars. Amen.

[Enter PATROCLUS]

Where's Achilles?
PATROCLUS What, art thou devout, wast thou in prayer?   30
THERSITES Ay, the heavens hear me!
PATROCLUS Amen.
ACHILLES [*Within*] Who's there?
PATROCLUS Thersites, my lord.

[Enter ACHILLES]

ACHILLES Where, where, O where? Art thou come? Why, my cheese,   35
    my digestion, why hast thou not served thyself in to my table so
    many meals? Come, what's Agamemnon?
THERSITES Thy commander, Achilles. Then tell me, Patroclus, what's
    Achilles?
PATROCLUS Thy lord, Thersites. Then tell me, I pray thee, what's   40
    Thersites?
THERSITES Thy knower, Patroclus. Then tell me, Patroclus, what art
    thou?
PATROCLUS Thou must tell that knowest.
ACHILLES O tell, tell.   45
THERSITES I'll decline the whole question: Agamemnon commands
    Achilles, Achilles is my lord, I am Patroclus' knower, and Patroclus
    is a fool.
PATROCLUS You rascal!
THERSITES Peace, fool, I have not done.   50
ACHILLES He is a privileged man. Proceed, Thersites.
THERSITES Agamemnon is a fool, Achilles is a fool, Thersites is a fool,
    and as aforesaid Patroclus is a fool.

---

27 thou art] F; thou art not Q   28 SD] *Walker (conj. Cam.); not in* Q; *after 17* F   30 in] Q; *in a* F   32] Q; *not in* F
33 SD] *Palmer; Enter Achilles* Q, F *(on preceding line)*   34 SD] Q *(after 32)*, F *(after 31)*   35 Where, where, O where?]
Q; *Where, where,* F   41 Thersites] Q; *thy selfe* F   44 must] Q; *maist* F   49–53] F; *not in* Q

26 blood lust, desire.
28 lazars lepers.
30 Patroclus could have caught a glimpse of
Thersites on his knees at line 17, but is probably
just reacting to Thersites' concluding 'Amen' (28).
35 cheese Traditionally eaten at the end of a
meal as an aid to digestion.

42 Thy knower One who knows you.
46 decline take each point in order (a technical
term in grammar – one declines a noun by system-
atically listing its various forms).
51 privileged man licensed fool (and hence allowed to take liberties, as, for example, Lear's Fool
does).

ACHILLES Derive this, come.

THERSITES Agamemnon is a fool to offer to command Achilles,   55
Achilles is a fool to be commanded of Agamemnon, Thersites
is a fool to serve such a fool, and Patroclus is a fool positive.

PATROCLUS Why am I a fool?

THERSITES Make that demand to the creator. It suffices me thou art.
Look you, who comes here?   60

Enter AGAMEMNON, ULYSSES, NESTOR,
DIOMEDES, *and* AJAX

ACHILLES Patroclus, I'll speak with nobody. Come in with me,
Thersites.   *Exit*

THERSITES [*Aside*] Here is such patchery, such juggling, and such knav-
ery: all the argument is a whore and a cuckold – a good quarrel
to draw emulous factions and bleed to death upon. Now the dry   65
serpigo on the subject, and war and lechery confound all! [*Exit*]

AGAMEMNON Where is Achilles?

PATROCLUS Within his tent, but ill disposed my lord.

AGAMEMNON Let it be known to him that we are here.
He shent our messengers and we lay by   70

---

56 of Agamemnon] F; *not in* Q   57 Patroclus] F; *this* Patroclus Q   59 to the creator] F; *of the Prouer* Q   60 SD
DIOMEDES, *and* AJAX] *Capell; Diomed, Aiax & Calcas* Q, F (*after 58*)   61 Patroclus] F; *Come* Patroclus Q   62 SD]
F; *not in* Q   63 SD] *This edn; not in* Q, F   64 whore and a cuckold] Q; *Cuckold and a Whore* F   65 emulous] Q;
emulations, F   65–6 Now . . . all] F; *not in* Q   66 SD] *Theobald; not in* Q, F   70 shent] *Theobald;* sate Q; sent F; *faced*
Oxford

54 Derive Explain the source of (another quasi-grammatical term, applied specifically to the etymology of words).

60 SD Although Calchas is given an entry here in both Q and F, he has no words to speak and nothing to identify him to an audience. He would thus simply look like an extra. Perhaps Shakespeare originally intended to introduce the business of the exchange at this point and then postponed it till after the love tryst in 3.2.

63 patchery folly, roguery (from 'patch' = a fool or jester).

63 juggling cheating or hypocrisy, with an added suggestion of lechery (see Williams, *Glossary*).

65 emulous factions rival parties motivated by envious competition. A crucial phrase for the world of the play, and one that has been seized on by a number of critics seeking to relate the play's characters and theme to the cut-throat world of the late Elizabethan court (see 1.3.135 n. and Introduction, pp. 11–12).

66 serpigo a skin disease.

70 shent abused. Theobald's emendation makes good sense and is supported by four other occurrences of 'shent' in Shakespeare, though all the others are in the passive voice. Q's 'sate' (= 'ignored') has been defended by Hulme (*Explorations*, p. 260) and adopted by Palmer, though the evidence is scanty and unconvincing; *Textual Companion* argues that 'sate' and F's 'sent' are both misreadings of MS. 'facd', meaning 'faced down' or 'bullied' and so Oxford prints 'faced'. Although such misreadings are possible, there seems no reason to assume a single MS. source. If, as suggested in the Textual Analysis, pp. 245–51, F and Q derive from different manuscripts, variants such as this one may derive from MS. differences. My guess is that there is some kind of revision at work, though in which direction is impossible to tell. Whatever stands behind Q's 'sate' seems irretrievable; 'sent' could easily be a typographical error (as Bevington[2] suggests (LN)) or a misreading of 'shent' (abetted by the

Our appertainings visiting of him;
Let him be told so, lest perchance he think
We dare not move the question of our place
Or know not what we are.

PATROCLUS I shall say so to him.   [*Exit*]   75

ULYSSES We saw him at the opening of his tent:
He is not sick.

AJAX Yes, lion-sick, sick of proud heart; you may call it melancholy
if you will favour the man but, by my head, 'tis pride. But why,
why? Let him show us the cause. A word, my lord.   80
[*Takes Agamemnon aside*]

NESTOR What moves Ajax thus to bay at him?

ULYSSES Achilles hath inveigled his fool from him.

NESTOR Who, Thersites?

ULYSSES He.

NESTOR Then will Ajax lack matter, if he have lost his argument.   85

ULYSSES No, you see he is his argument that has his argument –
Achilles.

NESTOR All the better: their fraction is more our wish than their
faction. But it was a strong composure a fool could disunite.

ULYSSES The amity that wisdom knits not, folly may easily untie.   90
Here comes Patroclus.

Enter PATROCLUS

NESTOR No Achilles with him.

---

71 appertainings] Q; appertainments F   72 told so, lest] Q; told of, so F   75 say so] Q; so say F   75 SD] *Rowe²; not in* Q, F   79 if you will] Q; if will F   79 'tis] Q; it is F   80 the cause] F; a cause Q   80 A ... lord] F; *not in* Q   80 SD] *Capell (subst.); not in* Q, F   89 composure] Q; counsell that F   91 SD] F; *not in* Q

semantic connection with 'messengers'), by either compositor or scribe. Strictly speaking, then, Theobald's emendation applies to F only, and it is as such that I have adopted it.

71 **appertainings . . . him** prerogatives of rank to visit him.

73 **move . . . place** insist on our authority.

78 **lion-sick** sick with pride.

81 **bay** howl, bark (the sounds made by hounds in pursuit of prey).

85 'Matter' and 'argument' are debating terms of the sort bandied about by witty undergraduates and young Inns of Court men. 'Argument' carries its ordinary modern meaning, but also means 'theme' or 'subject matter', with specific reference in the

present case to Thersites himself, who has been 'lost' to Ajax.

86 **he** i.e. Achilles. Ulysses says that Ajax has new matter for his 'argument': having lost Thersites, he now has Achilles, who 'has his [Ajax's] argument' (i.e. Thersites).

88 **fraction** conflict, quarrel.

89 **faction** joining together to form an opposing party.

89 **composure** alliance (the sentence is ironic); another –ure word that Shakespeare seems to have been the first to use in this sense (*OED* does not list this meaning, though it states that 'composure' was used in various senses of 'composition', one of which is 'a mutual agreement' (*sb* 22)).

ULYSSES The elephant hath joints but none for courtesy: his legs are
    legs for necessity not for flexure.

PATROCLUS Achilles bids me say he is much sorry   95
    If anything more than your sport and pleasure
    Did move your greatness and this noble state
    To call upon him; he hopes it is no other
    But for your health and your digestion sake,
    An after-dinner's breath.

AGAMEMNON   Hear you Patroclus.   100
    We are too well acquainted with these answers,
    But his evasion wing'd thus swift with scorn
    Cannot outfly our apprehensions.
    Much attribute he hath, and much the reason
    Why we ascribe it to him, yet all his virtues   105
    Not virtuously on his own part beheld
    Do in our eyes begin to lose their gloss,
    Yea, like fair fruit in an unwholesome dish,
    Are like to rot untasted. Go and tell him
    We come to speak with him, and you shall not sin   110
    If you do say we think him over-proud
    And under-honest, in self-assumption greater
    Than in the note of judgement; and worthier than himself
    Here tend the savage strangeness he puts on,
    Disguise the holy strength of their command,   115
    And underwrite in an observing kind

93–4] *Malone; as verse* (courtesie, / His*) Q, F (*subst.*)   93 his legs] Q; His legge F   94 flexure] Q; flight F   100] after-dinner's] *Rowe;* after dinners Q, F (*subst.*)   106 on] Q; of F   108 like] Q; and like F   110 come] Q; came F   114 tend] Q; tends F

93–4 There is probably a reference here to a proverb cited by Erasmus (*Adages*) that compares the proud man to an elephant, presumably because of the popular belief that elephants had no knee joints and hence could not bend or kneel (see Variorum and Dent, *PLED*, E108.11).

94 **flexure** bending, curtseying.

97 **noble state** distinguished group of councillors.

103 **outfly our apprehensions** escape our understanding (with a play on 'apprehension' = 'arrest' or 'capture' as part of the bird image).

106 If he does not regard (and hence conduct) himself in a virtuous manner.

108–9 **fair . . . untasted** The image connects with the common strain of tasting in the play, as well as with the recurrent notion of a rotten interior

under a fair exterior. But its tenor is slightly different in that it suggests that Achilles' genuine virtue is being contaminated by the external postures he has adopted.

112 **self-assumption** what he assumes himself to be worth; this is the first of several such compounds in this scene (see 150, 156, 222), which is dominantly concerned with what constitutes the worth of the 'self'.

113 **Than . . . judgement** Than judicious observers judge him to be.

113–14 **worthier . . . on** worthier men than he are here waiting upon ('tend') the outrageous aloofness ('savage strangeness') he has chosen to affect.

116 **underwrite . . . kind** submit to in a deferential way.

His humorous predominance, yea watch
His pettish lines, his ebbs, his flows, as if
The passage and whole carriage of this action
Rode on his tide. Go tell him this, and add   120
That if he overhold his price so much
We'll none of him, but let him, like an engine
Not portable, lie under this report:
'Bring action hither, this cannot go to war';
A stirring dwarf we do allowance give   125
Before a sleeping giant. Tell him so.

PATROCLUS I shall, and bring his answer presently.   [*Exit*]

AGAMEMNON In second voice we'll not be satisfied –
We come to speak with him. Ulysses, enter you.

                                                          Exit Ulysses

AJAX What is he more than another?   130

AGAMEMNON No more than what he thinks he is.

AJAX Is he so much? Do you not think he thinks himself a better man
than I am?

AGAMEMNON No question.

AJAX Will you subscribe his thought and say he is?   135

AGAMEMNON No, noble Ajax, you are as strong, as valiant, as wise, no
less noble, much more gentle, and altogether more tractable.

118–19] F; His course, and time, his ebbs and flowes, and if / The passage, and whole streame of his commencement, Q
118 lines] F; lunes *Hanmer*   123 report:] *Hanmer*; report. Q, F   124 'Bring . . . war'] *Theobald*; Bring . . . warre Q, F
127 SD] *Rowe; not in* Q, F   129 enter you] F; entertaine Q   129 SD] F; *not in* Q

117 **humorous predominance** capricious assumption of superiority. The image is based on
'humour' theory – the predominance of one or another bodily fluid, in this case blood.

118–19 Again we are faced with what seems like
a clear instance of Shakespearean revision. Both Q
and F make sense as they stand, but for me F is
superior (and hence, I assume, the revised version)
because it avoids the awkward metaphor of a stream
riding upon a tide and because the exact meaning
of Q's 'commencement' is obscure in the context.
Some editors, notably Palmer, have preferred Q on
the basis of the continuing metaphor of flowing and
tides, but F, in characteristic Shakespearean manner, is running two different metaphors in parallel (tides and transport by sea). Hanmer's emendation of F's 'lines' ('lunes' = fits of madness)
neatly evokes the moon as mistress of both tides
and lunacy, and has therefore attracted most editors; but it is not really justified. 'Lines' can mean
courses of action (suggested indeed by Q's 'course,

and time') but even more relevantly, *OED* (Line *sb*²
29) cites 'on a line' meaning 'in a rage' (Warwick-
shire dialect) to support its definition of 'lines' as
'caprices or fits of temper' both here and in *Wiv.*
4.2.22 (where modern editors have also frequently
emended to 'lunes').

118 **pettish lines** petulant, ill-humoured fits
(see previous note).

119 **passage . . . action** successful carrying out
of this enterprise (the war); together with 'Rode
on his tide' (120), the image evokes a movement of
ships across the sea.

121 **overhold** overestimate.

122 **engine** machine used for war, such as a large
cannon.

125 **stirring dwarf** a figure of slight significance,
who is nevertheless willing to take action.

125 **allowance** approval.

128 **second voice** a spokesman (someone other
than Achilles).

135 **subscribe** confirm.

AJAX Why should a man be proud? How doth pride grow? – I know
     not what pride is.

AGAMEMNON Your mind is the clearer, Ajax, and your virtues the   140
     fairer. He that is proud eats up himself; pride is his own glass, his
     own trumpet, his own chronicle, and whatever praises itself but in
     the deed devours the deed in the praise.

Enter ULYSSES

AJAX I do hate a proud man as I do hate the engendering of toads.

NESTOR [*Aside*] And yet he loves himself, is't not strange?   145

ULYSSES Achilles will not to the field tomorrow.

AGAMEMNON What's his excuse?

ULYSSES   He doth rely on none,
     But carries on the stream of his dispose
     Without observance or respect of any,
     In will peculiar and in self-admission.   150

AGAMEMNON Why will he not upon our fair request
     Untent his person and share the air with us?

ULYSSES Things small as nothing for request's sake only
     He makes important. Possessed he is with greatness
     And speaks not to himself but with a pride   155
     That quarrels at self-breath; imagined worth
     Holds in his blood such swoll'n and hot discourse
     That 'twixt his mental and his active parts

---

139 pride] Q; it F   140 Ajax] F; *not in* Q   144 as I do] Q; as I F   145 SD] *Capell (subst.); not in* Q, F   145 And yet]
Q; Yet F   152 the air] F; th'ayre Q   156 worth] Q; wroth F

141 eats up himself Another instance of the
motif of self-consumption that runs throughout
the play. As the rest of the speech suggests, the
self-destructiveness of pride is related to the idea
of reflection as Ulysses develops it in his colloquy
with Achilles in 3.3. The application of all this to
Ajax as well as Achilles is evident and is usually
heightened in production, where Ajax's struttings
are often comically absurd.

145 Nestor probably directs this comment to
Diomedes.

148 stream . . . dispose course of his inclinations. The phrase continues the language of 118–
19; the repetition of 'stream' in Q might perhaps
have been one incentive for the revision made to
the earlier passage.

150 Self-willed and relying solely on his own
judgement.

152 Untent his person Emerge from the
tent. Such verbose circumlocution is typical of
Agamemnon and most of the other Greek leaders, and may be one reason why Achilles will have
nothing to do with them. It is a characteristic that
prompts Thersites to satirical invective.

153–4 Things . . . important He regards even
the most trivial request as an insult to his pride.

154 greatness the conviction of his own greatness (which 'possesses' him like an evil spirit).

155–6 And . . . breath Either (1) his haughty
disdain for those who would speak with him extends even to himself when he addresses himself (a
sarcastic hyperbole); or (2) his pride finds even his
own self-praise inadequate.

158–60 That . . . himself Another instance
of self-destructive, self-consuming behaviour; see
1.3.119–24.

Kingdomed Achilles in commotion rages
And batters down himself. What should I say? –   160
He is so plaguy proud that the death-tokens of it
Cry 'No recovery'.
AGAMEMNON   Let Ajax go to him.
Dear lord, go you and greet him in his tent:
'Tis said he holds you well and will be led
At your request a little from himself.   165
ULYSSES O Agamemnon, let it not be so.
We'll consecrate the steps that Ajax makes
When they go from Achilles; shall the proud lord
That bastes his arrogance with his own seam
And never suffers matter of the world   170
Enter his thoughts, save such as doth revolve
And ruminate himself, shall he be worshipped
Of that we hold an idol more than he?
No, this thrice worthy and right valiant lord
Shall not so stale his palm nobly acquired,   175
Nor, by my will, assubjugate his merit,
As amply titled as Achilles' is,
By going to Achilles.
That were to enlard his fat-already pride,
And add more coals to Cancer when he burns   180
With entertaining great Hyperion.
This lord go to him? Jupiter forbid,

---

160 down himself] Q; gainst it selfe F   162 'No recovery'] *Hanmer (subst.)*; no recouerie Q, F *(subst.)*   171 doth] Q;
doe F   175 Shall] Q; Must F   177–8] *Johnson; as one line* Q, F   177 titled] F; liked Q

159 **Kingdomed** The phrase is unusual, but the
idea was a commonplace one – that a person is
structured as a kind of kingdom, with the 'mental' parts (158) ruling like a prince over the body
and the passions ('active parts'). Achilles' passions,
growing out of an inflated sense of his 'imagined
worth' (156), are creating a rebellion in the kingdom of his being.

161–2 **He . . . recovery** His pride is a plague
whose symptoms indicate there is no possibility of
recovery.

162 **Let . . . him** This suggestion and what follows from it are part of a ploy, a trick played on
the obtuse Ajax, whose pride is as extreme as that
of Achilles, and less justified.

169 **seam** fat, grease (Achilles' pride is com-

pared to roast meat basted with its own fat); see
1.3.378 and n.

170–2 **And never . . . himself** He will allow
himself to think about the external world only
when doing so reflects his own greatness. The passage is both verbose and elliptical.

173 **Of that** By him whom (i.e. Ajax).

175 **palm** honour (the palm, like the laurel, was
a sign of military prowess and victory).

176 **assubjugate** subject, debase.

177 Which is as highly reputed as Achilles' is.

179 **enlard** fatten (continuing the image from
earlier in the speech (169 n.)).

180 **Cancer** A sign of the zodiac associated with
hot weather, since the sun ('Hyperion' (181)) enters
Cancer on 21 June.

And say in thunder 'Achilles go to him!'

NESTOR [*Aside to Diomedes*] O this is well – he rubs the vein of him.

DIOMEDES [*Aside to Nestor*] And how his silence drinks up this
    applause!   185

AJAX If I go to him, with my armèd fist
    I'll pash him o'er the face.

AGAMEMNON O no, you shall not go.

AJAX An he be proud with me, I'll feeze his pride.
    Let me go to him.   190

ULYSSES Not for the worth that hangs upon our quarrel.

AJAX A paltry, insolent fellow.

NESTOR [*Aside*] How he describes himself.

AJAX Can he not be sociable?

ULYSSES [*Aside*] The raven chides blackness.   195

AJAX I'll let his humours blood.

AGAMEMNON [*Aside*] He will be the physician that should be the
    patient.

AJAX An all men were o'my mind –

ULYSSES [*Aside*] Wit would be out of fashion.   200

AJAX 'A should not bear it so, 'a should eat swords first; shall pride carry
    it?

NESTOR [*Aside*] An 'twould, you'd carry half.

ULYSSES [*Aside*] 'A would have ten shares.

183] 'Achilles . . . him!'] Hanmer (subst.); Achilles . . . him. Q, F   184, 185 SDS] Johnson (subst.); not in Q, F   185 this] F; his Q   186–7] Rowe²; as prose Q, F   187 pash] F; push Q   189–90] Q; as prose F   193 SD] Capell (subst.); not in Q, F; so too at 195, 197, 200, 203, 204, 206   196 I'll let his humours] F; Ile tell his humorous Q   199 o'my] F; of my Q   204 SH] F; Aiax Q (which assigns 204–5 to Ajax)

184 rubs . . . him plays upon his humour.

187 pash strike, smash.

189 feeze fix (as in the phrase 'I'll fix him'). Compare the quarrelsome opening line of *Shr.*: 'I'll pheeze you, in faith'.

191 our quarrel The war with the Trojans.

193–240 How he . . . Ajax Throughout this sequence the Greek lords mock Ajax behind his back, the various asides being spoken to each other conspiratorially, rather than to the audience. Ajax meanwhile struts about threatening to take Achilles down a peg, when everyone knows that were he to try he would be easily beaten.

196 I'll draw ('let') his blood (and hence purge his pride – as a physician draws blood from a patient in order to reduce the imbalance of bodily 'hu-mours', the fluids which, in proper balance, made for a healthy temperament). Q's 'humorous' is possible, but 'humours' is more likely the object of the verbal phrase 'let blood'.

201–3 carry it . . . carry prevail . . . bear. Nestor's pun implies that Ajax is an ass, an over-proud beast of burden.

204 ten shares the whole burden (of pride). The implication is that ten shares would constitute the whole (Variorum).

204–206 On the speech headings here it seems best to trust F as the text more likely to have theatrical provenance. Hence Ulysses' line at 204 is a response to Nestor's previous aside; meanwhile, Ajax is strutting about, threatening to thrash Achilles who, he says, is not yet thoroughly warmed

AJAX I will knead him, I'll make him supple, he's not yet through warm.   205
NESTOR [*Aside*] Force him with praises, pour in, pour in: his ambition
    is dry.
ULYSSES [*To Agamemnon*] My lord, you feed too much on this dislike.
NESTOR Our noble general, do not do so.
DIOMEDES You must prepare to fight without Achilles.   210
ULYSSES Why, 'tis this naming of him does him harm.
    Here is a man – but 'tis before his face,
    I will be silent.
NESTOR   Wherefore should you so?
    He is not emulous as Achilles is.
ULYSSES Know the whole world he is as valiant –   215
AJAX A whoreson dog that shall palter with us thus. Would he were a
    Trojan.
NESTOR What a vice were it in Ajax now –
ULYSSES If he were proud.
DIOMEDES Or covetous of praise.   220
ULYSSES Ay, or surly borne.
DIOMEDES Or strange or self-affected.
ULYSSES [*To Ajax*] Thank the heavens, lord, thou art of sweet
    composure:
    Praise him that got thee, she that gave thee suck.
    Famed be thy tutor and thy parts of nature   225
    Thrice famed beyond, beyond all erudition.
    But he that disciplined thine arms to fight,

---

205 SH] F; *before 204* Q; *speech continued to Ulysses / Evans*   205 he's not . . . warm] Q, F; *assigned to Nestor as part of ensuing speech / Theobald*   206 praises] F; praiers Q   206 pour in, pour in:] F; poure in, poure, Q   208 SD] *Capell; not in* Q, F   210 You] F; Yon Q   211 does] Q (do's); doth F   212 man –] *Rowe;* man Q; man, F   212–13 Here . . . silent] F; *as one line* Q   215 valiant –] Q; valiant. F   216–17] Q, F; *as verse (thus with us –* / Would*) Pope*   216 with us thus] Q; thus with vs F   222 self-affected] F3; selfe affected Q, F   223 SD] *Oxford; not in* Q, F   225 Famed] Q; Fame F   226 beyond, beyond all] F; beyond all thy Q; beyond all *Steevens*[3]   227 thine] Q; thy F

up (by being 'kneaded') and hence insufficiently flexible. Editorial desire to intervene has been provoked by the appropriateness of Ajax's lines to his own situation, but that has been the joke all along. Nestor's culinary metaphor in 206 develops Ajax's reference to baking, again following the pattern of the lords commenting upon Ajax's language.
206 Force Stuff (cf. French *farcir*).
207 dry barren, sterile (*OED* a 15).
208 Ulysses, in addressing Agamemnon, follows Nestor's suggestion to continue the game.
208 this dislike i.e. Achilles' haughtiness.
212 a man Ajax.

216 palter trifle.
221 surly borne carried himself in a surly manner.
222 self-affected conceited.
223 composure make-up, temperament.
224 got begot.
225 parts of nature natural gifts.
226 beyond, beyond all erudition surpassing what can be accomplished through study and learning – a deliberate and mocking exaggeration, made more pointed by the repetition of 'beyond', which seems to be an F revision. Delius notes that the duplication of 'beyond' also occurs in *Cym.* 3.2.56.

Let Mars divide eternity in twain
And give him half; and for thy vigour
Bull-bearing Milo his addition yield   230
To sinewy Ajax. I will not praise thy wisdom
Which like a bourn, a pale, a shore, confines
Thy spacious and dilated parts. Here's Nestor:
Instructed by the antiquary times
He must, he is, he cannot but be wise;   235
But pardon, father Nestor, were your days
As green as Ajax' and your brain so tempered,
You should not have the eminence of him,
But be as Ajax.
AJAX [*To Nestor*]   Shall I call you father?
NESTOR Ay my good son.
DIOMEDES   Be ruled by him, Lord Ajax.   240
ULYSSES There is no tarrying here: the hart Achilles
Keeps thicket. Please it our great general
To call together all his state of war.
Fresh kings are come to Troy – tomorrow
We must with all our main of power stand fast.   245
And here's a lord, come knights from east to west
And cull their flower, Ajax shall cope the best.
AGAMEMNON Go we to council. Let Achilles sleep:
Light boats sail swift, though greater hulks draw deep.

Exeunt

---

232 bourn] F; boord Q   233 Thy] F; This Q   239 SD] *This edn; not in* Q, F   240 SH NESTOR] Q; *Ulis.* F   242 great]
Q; *not in* F   247 cull] F; call Q   249 sail] Q; may saile F   249 hulks] Q; bulkes F

228 eternity eternal fame.

230 Milo An ancient Greek athlete and weight-
lifter who carried a bull some 40 yards (36.5 me-
tres), killed it with a single blow of his fist, and,
hungry after his exertions, ate it – all in a single day. He is mentioned by Herodotus and Pliny,
among others.

230 addition title (i.e. that of bull-bearer).

232 a bourn, a pale a boundary, a border.
The praise here, as throughout the speech, is slyly
equivocal – his wisdom stretches only so far as his
other 'parts', which is not very far at all.

233 dilated extensive.

234 antiquary ancient.

237 green youthful.

237 so tempered at the same stage of development.

242 Keeps thicket Remains in hiding (a hunting
term).

243 state council.

244 Fresh kings . . . Troy Ready and eager
leaders of reinforcements for the Trojan side.

247 cull their flower choose their very best (the
flower of chivalry).

247 cope match.

249 Despite the deep draw of large ships (like
Achilles), smaller, lighter craft are more valuable
in combat.

[3.1] *Music sounds within.* Enter PANDARUS *and a* SERVANT [*meeting*]

PANDARUS Friend, you, pray you a word – do you not follow the young
    Lord Paris?
SERVANT Ay sir, when he goes before me.
PANDARUS You depend upon him I mean.
SERVANT Sir, I do depend upon the Lord.   5
PANDARUS You depend upon a notable gentleman: I must needs praise
    him.
SERVANT The Lord be praised!
PANDARUS You know me, do you not?
SERVANT Faith sir, superficially.   10
PANDARUS Friend, know me better, I am the Lord Pandarus.
SERVANT I hope I shall know your honour better.
PANDARUS I do desire it.
SERVANT You are in the state of grace.
PANDARUS Grace? Not so, friend, honour and lordship are my titles.   15
    What music is this?
SERVANT I do but partly know sir: it is music in parts.
PANDARUS Know you the musicians?
SERVANT Wholly, sir.
PANDARUS Who play they to?   20
SERVANT To the hearers, sir.
PANDARUS At whose pleasure, friend?
SERVANT At mine sir, and theirs that love music.
PANDARUS Command I mean, friend.
SERVANT Who shall I command, sir?   25
PANDARUS Friend, we understand not one another. I am too courtly
    and thou too cunning. At whose request do these men play?

Act 3, Scene 1   3.1] *Rowe (subst.); not in* Q, F   **0** SD *Music sounds within*] F *(at end of previous scene); not in* Q   **0** SD
Enter . . . SERVANT] F; *Enter Pandarus* Q   **0** SD *meeting*] *This edn; not in* Q, F   **1** do you not] Q; *Doe not you* F
3 SH] F *(subst.); Man* Q *(so throughout scene)*   **6** notable] Q; *noble* F   **15** titles] Q; *title* F   **24** friend] F; *not in* Q
27 thou too] Q; *thou art too* F

Act 3, Scene 1

0 SD Pandarus has come to Paris' dwelling and
accosts the Servant who no doubt emerges from a
different door.

1 follow serve, but the Servant knowingly takes
it in a literal sense.

5 Lord Both 'nobleman' (Paris) and God. As in
his first speech, he uses an evasive pun to confuse
his questioner. He repeats the feeble joke in 8.

12 i.e. I hope I shall see you be a morally better man. Again the Servant twists the sense of
Pandarus' phrase; meanings related to both social
and moral status remain in play through the next
exchange.

14, 15 grace, Grace The state of the soul required for salvation and a ducal title (which Pandarus carefully rules out as inappropriate for him).

17 parts different harmonic lines.

22 pleasure command (as Pandarus explains in
24), but the Servant deliberately misinterprets.

SERVANT That's to't indeed sir. Marry sir, at the request of Paris my
lord, who is there in person, with him the mortal Venus, the heart-
blood of beauty, love's invisible soul.   30

PANDARUS Who, my cousin Cressida?

SERVANT No sir, Helen. Could you not find out that by her attributes?

PANDARUS It should seem, fellow, thou hast not seen the Lady Cressid.
I come to speak with Paris from the Prince Troilus. I will make a
complimental assault upon him, for my business seethes.   35

SERVANT Sodden business? There's a stewed phrase indeed!

Enter PARIS *and* HELEN

PANDARUS Fair be to you, my lord, and to all this fair company, fair
desires in all fair measure fairly guide them – especially to you,
fair queen, fair thoughts be your fair pillow!

HELEN Dear lord, you are full of fair words.   40

PANDARUS You speak your fair pleasure, sweet queen. Fair prince, here
is good broken music.

---

29 who is] Q; who's F   30 invisible] Q, F; visible *Hanmer;* indivisible *Walker*   32 Could you not] F; could not you Q
33 thou] Q; that thou F   33 Cressid] Q; *Cressida* F   36 SD] Q, F *(subst.); Enter . . . Helen attended / Theobald*

30 love's invisible soul The spiritual essence of
love given physical embodiment in Helen. Hanmer
and the many editors who follow him regard 'invisible' as tautological and so emend; but they assume,
first, that the Servant has completed his phrase (in
performance, Pandarus might interrupt him before
he has a chance to finish with a phrase such as
'made visible'); and, second, that he is speaking
with strict logic rather than metaphorical hyperbole.

31 Now it is Pandarus' turn deliberately to mis-
understand the effusive Servant.

35 complimental assault courteous foray.

35 seethes is boiling over. Pandarus means he
is in a rush, but the Servant characteristically misinterprets, pretending in his reply (36) to take the
cooking metaphor literally ('sodden' = overboiled
and hence insipid) and adding a salacious pun to
the mix (stew = brothel).

36 SD Virtually all modern editors bring on attendants with Paris and Helen, presumably because
of 'fair company' (37), though some modern productions (Guthrie, Old Vic 1956; BBC) do without them, while others bring Helen and Paris onto
an already crowded stage. The use of extras as
onlookers can add to the pronounced voyeurism
of the scene. (The Servant, though he has nothing more to say, presumably remains throughout.)
Oxford and Bevington[2] specify that the attendants

are the musicians, who have been playing from the
beginning of the scene. They may enter as strolling
accompanists to the lovers' play (though this would
be awkward if they are a 'broken consort' – an en-
semble with different types of instruments, including viols – as implied by 42); or, more likely, they
could at some point be discovered, playing behind
a curtain. Apparently they have stopped playing by
43, and Pandarus approaches them to borrow an
instrument at 81.

37–9 Here is the first sally in Pandarus' 'complimental assault' (35), pushed almost to the point
of absurdity. This scene with Paris and Helen,
the most famous lovers of the ancient world, is
a favourite of modern producers, who have cap-
tured its brilliant mix of lascivious satire, languid
wit (à la Noel Coward) and poignant melancholy
in a variety of ingenious ways. In 1956 at the Old
Vic (Guthrie), Helen lounged by the piano in a
shocking pink gown, while Paris leaned over it like
a louche Fred Astaire. In 1976 at Stratford, Helen
arrived attached to Paris by a golden chain, and in
1990 at the Swan Theatre, Helen appeared on a litter all wrapped in gold cloth which Paris unwound
by walking around her until she was revealed in
sensuous, scarlet brilliance. See also 91–2 n. and
Introduction, pp. 40–1, 49–50.

42 broken in parts (see 17) and, probably, played
on different kinds of instruments. Shakespeare

PARIS You have broke it, cousin, and by my life you shall make it whole
again – you shall piece it out with a piece of your performance.
Nell, he is full of harmony.   45

PANDARUS Truly lady, no.

HELEN O sir!

PANDARUS Rude in sooth, in good sooth very rude.

PARIS Well said, my lord, well, you say so in fits.

PANDARUS I have business to my lord, dear queen. My lord, will you   50
vouchsafe me a word?

HELEN Nay this shall not hedge us out, we'll hear you sing certainly.

PANDARUS Well, sweet queen, you are pleasant with me. But, marry
thus my lord: my dear lord and most esteemed friend, your brother
Troilus –   55

HELEN My Lord Pandarus, honey-sweet lord –

PANDARUS Go to, sweet queen, go to – commends himself most affectionately to you.

HELEN You shall not bob us out of our melody: if you do, our melancholy upon your head.   60

PANDARUS Sweet queen, sweet queen, that's a sweet queen, i'faith –

HELEN And to make a sweet lady sad is a sour offence.

PANDARUS Nay that shall not serve your turn, that shall it not, in
truth, la! Nay I care not for such words, no, no. And, my lord, he

---

57–8] *Capell; as verse* (go to? / Comends) Q, F *(subst.)*   59–60] *Hanmer; as verse* (melody, / If) Q, F *(subst.)*

apparently enjoyed punning on the different meanings of 'broken,' as, for example, in *H5* 5.2.243–5:
'Come, your answer in broken music; for thy voice
is music and thy English broken', and 'is there any
else longs to see this broken music in his sides?'
AYLI 1.2.141–2.

43 broke interrupted.

44 piece it out put it back together.

45 Nell . . . harmony Some editors, notably
Alexander and Palmer, give this line to Helen,
interpreting Q, F's *Nel* (followed by a period in
Q and a comma in F) as a speech heading. But
the dramatic situation makes excellent sense as
it stands, with Paris both praising and teasing
Pandarus in his comment to his lover, and
Pandarus coyly denying the compliment (the familiar nickname 'Nell,' used again in 119, has a
touch of domestic sweetness but is also ironically
banal for heroes of myth).

47–8 Oxford has Helen tickling Pandarus here,
apparently to explain his repetitiveness in 48 and
Paris' phrase 'in fits' (49). But Pandarus repeats

himself constantly and 'in fits' is a continuation
of the musical allusions (fit = a strain, or part of
a song). Still, tickling would not be out of place –
Helen is generous with her flirtatious touching, and
she has been known to tickle Troilus' chin, as Pandarus tells Cressida in 1.2.119.

48 Rude Rough, unpolished (referring to his
musical skills).

49 fits (1) spasms, (2) parts in music.

50–81 I have business . . . do you spy In this
sequence, Pandarus tries to convey his secret message to Paris, while Helen playfully interrupts, urging him to sing; as a result, most of Pandarus'
speeches are split between his two interlocutors.
It is not certain that Helen overhears his words to
Paris, but there is nothing in the scene to suggest
that she does not. Indeed, it is likely that she knows
what is going on as well as Paris does (see 73 n.).
Hence her repeated interruptions might be acted
as a sort of knowing game.

52 hedge us out put us off, elude us.

59 bob trick, cheat.

desires you that if the King call for him at supper you will make   65
his excuse.

HELEN My Lord Pandarus –

PANDARUS What says my sweet queen, my very, very sweet queen?

PARIS What exploit's in hand? Where sups he tonight?

HELEN Nay but my lord –   70

PANDARUS What says my sweet queen? My cousin will fall out with
you.

HELEN You must not know where he sups.

PARIS I'll lay my life with my disposer Cressida.

PANDARUS No, no, no such matter, you are wide: come, your disposer   75
is sick.

PARIS Well I'll make's excuse.

PANDARUS Ay, good my lord. Why should you say Cressida? – no, your
poor disposer's sick.

PARIS I spy –   80

PANDARUS You spy? What do you spy? [*To a musician*] Come, give me
an instrument: now sweet queen –

73] Q, F; *assigned to Pandarus / Capell*   74 I'll . . . life] Q; *not in* F   77 make's] *Kittredge (conj.   Capell)*; makes Q;
make F   79 poor disposer's] F; disposers Q   81 SD] *Oxford; not in* Q, F

71–2 My cousin . . . you Since Pandarus is trying to keep Cressida's involvement secret, it is
doubtful that 'cousin' here refers to her, though
many editors have read it that way; more likely, he is
suggesting, jokingly, that Paris will become jealous
if Helen continues to flirt with him as she has been
(Tannenbaum, p. 76). Although Paris and Pandarus
are not related, the term 'cousin' was used very
loosely; indeed, Paris refers to Pandarus as 'cousin'
(43).

73 Editors since the eighteenth century have
been divided over the ascription of this line, though
most have followed Capell in giving it to Pandarus.
However, many recent editors have followed Q, F
and given it to Helen (Muir also adds the stage direction, '*to Paris*'). Capell's solution makes logical
sense and continues the pattern of Pandarus trying
to speak to Paris while appeasing Helen (here he
would be answering Paris' question in 69). But Q,
F set up a more intriguing possibility: Helen has
heard Paris' question, noted Pandarus' secrecy, and
now answers for him, in a pointedly mocking way.

74 This line is no doubt addressed, with a glint
of ironic collusion, as much to Helen as to Pandarus
(see 73 n).

74 lay wager.

74, 75, 79 disposer Almost three pages of small
type in Variorum fail to cast much light on this
troublesome word. A similarly long note in *Textual Companion* in favour of Oxford's emendation
to 'dispenser' remains unconvincing. Evans' simple explanation is also the best guess: 'probably a
courtly turn of phrase meaning that he is always at
her disposal or command'.

75 wide off-track, wide of the mark.

77 make's make his. Given that apostrophes
were used very inconsistently in the period (79 provides another example), Capell's suggestion neatly
explains Q's 'makes'.

80 I spy Perhaps, as Steevens[2] suggested, a
reference to the children's game (a version of
hide and seek) though the first citation given in
OED (Hy-spy) is 1777. Clearly, Paris is hinting
that he sees what is going on with Troilus and
Cressida.

81–2 Pandarus finally consents to sing, evidently
to shift the course of the conversation away from
Troilus' tryst with Cressida. He thus borrows an
instrument from one of the musicians who have
been playing. See 36 SD n.

HELEN Why this is kindly done.

PANDARUS My niece is horribly in love with a thing you have, sweet
    queen.   85

HELEN She shall have it my lord, if it be not my Lord Paris.

PANDARUS He? No, she'll none of him: they two are twain.

HELEN Falling in after falling out may make them three.

PANDARUS Come, come, I'll hear no more of this. I'll sing you a song
    now.   90

HELEN Ay, ay, prithee now. By my troth, sweet lord, thou hast a fine
    forehead.

PANDARUS Ay you may, you may –

HELEN Let thy song be love: this love will undo us all, O Cupid,
    Cupid, Cupid –   95

PANDARUS Love, ay, that it shall i'faith.

PARIS Ay good now: [*Sings*] Love, love, nothing but love –

PANDARUS In good troth, it begins so.

    [*Sings*] Love, love, nothing but love, still love, still more!
        For O love's bow   100
        Shoots buck and doe.
        The shaft confounds
        Not that it wounds
        But tickles still the sore.

---

84 horribly] Q; horrible F   91 lord] F; lad Q   97 SD] *This edn; not in Q, F*   98] F *(corr.); as part of Paris' speech* F *(uncorr.); not in* Q   99 SD] *Capell (subst.); not in* Q, F   99 still love] Q; *not in* F   100–1] F; *as one line* Q   102 shaft confounds] F; shafts confound Q   102–3] *Pope; as one line* Q, F

84–5 What the 'thing' is that Cressida would like is unclear – perhaps merely some object, but more likely a princely lover (with a strong sexual suggestion – thing = penis), which gives added point to Helen's reply (86): she does not want to share Paris or his 'thing' with any rivals.

87 twain separate, at odds. This presumed division between Cressida and Paris has fuelled the fires of explanation in regard to 'disposer' (see 74 and n.).

88 Falling in . . . out Tumbling into bed after having an argument ('falling out').

88 make them three produce a child (punning on 'twain' in the previous line).

91–2 On this line in the RSC production in 1990, Sally Dexter as Helen licked Pandarus on the forehead (production photo).

94 this love . . . all Perhaps a phrase from a song. It recurs in Nathan Field's *A Woman is a Weathercock* (Verity, cited in Variorum), but that could be a reminiscence of this passage. The line

has a melancholy air, and lights up a different, much less frivolous side of Helen if spoken seriously, with awareness and depth of feeling, as it was by Sally Dexter in 1990 (RSC); see 37–9 n. and Introduction, p. 41.

97 SD Paris presumably starts the song for Pandarus, though he might simply be indicating which song he wants, or what the musicians are to play.

99–110 The song is quite deliberately naughty; that it turns on a number of sexual puns suits both the voyeurism of Pandarus and the languorous sexuality of Helen. Love and hunting were often linked metaphorically in Renaissance lyrics through images of pursuit and the wounds made by Cupid's arrow. Here, the arrow has obvious phallic implications.

102–104 The arrow of love (the penis) does not damage ('confounds / Not') where it wounds, but continues to tickle the 'sore' (i.e. the 'wound' it either makes or penetrates, with a further pun on 'sore' as a kind of buck or stag).

> These lovers cry, O, O, they die,   105
> Yet that which seems the wound to kill
> Doth turn 'O, O' to 'ha ha he',
> So dying love lives still.
> 'O, O' a while, but 'ha ha ha'
> 'O, O' groans out for 'ha ha ha' – Heigh-ho!   110

HELEN In love, i'faith, to the very tip of the nose.

PARIS He eats nothing but doves, love, and that breeds hot blood, and hot blood begets hot thoughts, and hot thoughts beget hot deeds, and hot deeds is love.

PANDARUS Is this the generation of love: hot blood, hot thoughts,   115
and hot deeds? Why, they are vipers; is love a generation of vipers? Sweet lord, who's afield today?

PARIS Hector, Deiphobus, Helenus, Antenor, and all the gallantry of Troy. I would fain have armed today, but my Nell would not have it so. How chance my brother Troilus went not?   120

HELEN He hangs the lip at something – you know all, Lord Pandarus.

PANDARUS Not I, honey-sweet queen. I long to hear how they sped today. You'll remember your brother's excuse?

PARIS To a hair.

105, 107 O, O] *Pope (subst.)*; oh ho Q, F   109, 110 O, O] *Capell (subst.)*; oh ho Q, F   117 Sweet . . . today?] *Pope; new line* Q, F   120 How . . . not?] *Pope; new line* Q, F   123 You'll . . . excuse?] *Pope; new line* Q, F

105 die come to sexual climax (a ubiquitous Elizabethan pun, repeated in 'dying' (108)).

106 the wound to kill a wound that would kill.

107 turns the seeming pain and groans of 'dying' (108) into sounds of delight.

110 Heigh-ho Possibly a final refrain of the song (as Palmer argues), but more likely a simple exclamation: perhaps a sigh, perhaps even a gesture of self-congratulation.

111 A reference either to Pandarus' nasal singing, or, as Ritson suggests (p. 162), to his concluding interjection, 'Heigh-ho', probably with an additional, salacious suggestion ('nose' = penis), which Paris picks up on in the following speech.

112 doves Associated with Venus, and hence with love, because of their cooing and supposedly amorous behaviour.

115 generation genealogy.

116 a generation of vipers an experience that generates vicious offspring. The phrase appears several times in the gospels, usually in the simple sense of 'evil generations', as in Matthew 3.7, 'O generacions of vipers, who hathe forewarned you to flee from the angre to come?'

117 vipers? Sweet Q, F have a line break before 'Sweet', perhaps to indicate the change of subject. Oxford adds an *Alarum* to motivate the shift. While it may seem odd that there is a battle going on in the midst of what is supposed to be a truce enlivened by Hector's challenge, the inconsistency, of a type common in Shakespeare, underlines the linkage in the play between love and war. Indeed, Hector's chivalric challenge is a salient example of the metaphorical connection. See 1.3.263 n.

118 gallantry gallant warriors.

119–20 I . . . went not Unlike Hector in 5.3, but like Troilus at the outset and like Achilles in 5.1.34 ff., Paris is deflected from battle by his love.

121 hangs the lip looks vexed or sheepish (see *OED* Lip *sb* 2; Hang *v* 4b). Once again Helen and Paris are teasing Pandarus, pressuring him to reveal the secret.

124 To a hair Down to the slightest detail (with a glance at the story, recounted by Pandarus in 1.2.119–43, about Helen's interest in Troilus' chin hair).

PANDARUS Farewell, sweet queen.   125
HELEN Commend me to your niece.
PANDARUS I will, sweet queen.   [*Exit*]
              Sound a retreat
PARIS They're come from field: let us to Priam's hall
              To greet the warriors. Sweet Helen, I must woo you
              To help unarm our Hector: his stubborn buckles,   130
              With these your white enchanting fingers touched,
              Shall more obey than to the edge of steel
              Or force of Greekish sinews; you shall do more
              Than all the island kings t'disarm great Hector.
HELEN 'Twill make us proud to be his servant, Paris;   135
              Yea, what he shall receive of us in duty
              Gives us more palm in beauty than we have,
              Yea, overshines ourself.
PARIS Sweet, above thought I love thee.

                                              Exeunt

[3.2] *Enter* PANDARUS *and Troilus'* MAN [*meeting*]

PANDARUS How now, where's thy master? At my cousin Cressida's?
MAN No sir, he stays for you to conduct him thither.

---

127 SD *Exit*] *Rowe; not in* Q, F   128 field] F; *the field* Q   131 these] F; *this* Q   134 kings t'disarm] *This edn;* Kings, disarme Q, F   139 SH] Q; *not in* F   139 thee.] F; *her?* Q   Act 3, Scene 2   3.2] *Capell (subst.); not in* Q, F   o SD *Enter* . . . MAN] F; *Enter. Pandarus Troylus, man* Q   o SD *meeting*] *Capell; not in* Q, F   2 he stays] F; *stayes* Q

127–39 With Pandarus' exit, the tone, mood, and rhetoric become suddenly lyrical and romantic, adding yet another dimension to this opalescent scene.

134 t'disarm Editors have universally let this line pass without comment or emendation, usually changing the Q, F punctuation from comma to dash or colon before 'disarm'. But nowhere else in the speech does Paris use the imperative, and, much more important, the shift to the imperative obscures both the parallelism with the preceding lines (130–33) and the graceful compliment that Helen will do more than all those Greek warriors to disarm Hector. Since, as I point out in the Textual Analysis (p. 248), this is one of those relatively few parts of the play where F seems to derive directly from Q, emendations can be made with more confidence.

Act 3, Scene 2
    o SD Pandarus and Troilus' manservant no doubt enter from different doors, as specified by Oxford. While this servant may be the Boy who appears at 1.2.231, the texts differentiate between them. It is possible that the actor who played Helen doubled as the Boy in 1.2, and a different actor took this role.

1–2 There is some uncertainty about the location of this scene, since these two lines indicate that the characters are not at or near Cressida's house, whereas subsequent dialogue makes it clear that they are in an orchard (14) or garden adjacent to her dwelling, into which they retire at the end of the scene (Cressida apparently shares the house with Pandarus now that her father, whose house it is (see 4.1.37–8) has gone over to the Greeks). Such flexibility of location was common on Elizabethan stages.

Enter TROILUS

PANDARUS O here he comes: how now, how now!
TROILUS Sirrah, walk off.

[*Exit Man*]

PANDARUS Have you seen my cousin?   5
TROILUS No Pandarus, I stalk about her door
    Like a strange soul upon the Stygian banks
    Staying for waftage. O, be thou my Charon
    And give me swift transportance to those fields
    Where I may wallow in the lily beds   10
    Proposed for the deserver. O gentle Pandar,
    From Cupid's shoulder pluck his painted wings
    And fly with me to Cressid.
PANDARUS Walk here i'th'orchard, I'll bring her straight.   *Exit*
TROILUS I am giddy: expectation whirls me round.   15
    Th'imaginary relish is so sweet
    That it enchants my sense – what will it be
    When that the wat'ry palate tastes indeed

2 SD] F; *not in* Q   4 SD] *Capell (subst.); not in* Q, F   7 Like] F; Like to Q   9 those] F; these Q   11 Pandar] Q; *Pandarus*
F   14 SD] F *(subst.); not in* Q   18 palate tastes] *Hanmer*; pallats taste Q, F

7 **strange** Referring to the feelings of estrangement experienced by the newly arrived soul in
its unfamiliar surroundings. David Thatcher, in
an unpublished paper, suggests that the 'strange
soul' is Ovid's Orpheus, whose 'ghost', in Gold-
ing's translation, 'stalks' the 'fields' of Elysium.
7 **Stygian banks** shores of the river Styx, the
gateway to the classical underworld, overseen by
Charon (8), who ferried souls across the Styx.
8 **staying for waftage** waiting for passage.
9 **transportance** transport (first citation in
OED).
9 **fields** The Elysian fields, the abode of souls in
the classical underworld.
10 **wallow** roll about (*OED v*[1] 3). The word does
not necessarily carry the negative connotations that
it has accrued in modern usage, but there is certainly a hint of sensual self-indulgence.
10 **lily beds** The lilies, while they appear in classical accounts of paradise, derive more from biblical sources, especially the Song of Solomon (6.1),
where they have a distinct sexual ring: 'My welbe-
loued is gone downe into his garden to the beds of
spices, to fede in the gardens, and to gather lilies.'
11 **Proposed** Promised.
12 **painted** variegated, multi-coloured. Cupid,
the diminutive god of love, was traditionally depicted with wings. The bizarre image of the

middle-aged Pandarus donning those wings is an
index of Troilus' feverish state of mind.
14 **orchard** enclosed garden, perhaps, but not
necessarily, with fruit trees.
15 This and several subsequent lines echo and
develop motifs in *MV* 3.2, where Bassanio and Portia express their joys at his success (see Variorum
and Muir). There are, however, important differences between the two scenes. Troilus is caught
up in his fantasies and is giddy with expectation
about sexual delights to come; Bassanio is 'giddy
in spirit' (*MV* 3.2.144) because he has been successful in his quest. Portia is delighted by what
has been achieved, Troilus by his own imagination of what is to come. In general, Troilus'
joys are sensuous, fragile, and elusive, where those
of the lovers in *MV* are more grounded and
mutual.
16 **imaginary relish** imagined pleasure.
17–22 **what will . . . powers** Troilus asks himself what will happen when he moves from imagined to real delights, and answers that they will
prove too exquisite for his 'ruder powers'. The result will be a disintegration of his very personhood.
18 **wat'ry palate** i.e. the mouth watering in
anticipation. Q, F's 'pallats', has been glossed as
'senses', but the singular form works best with
'wat'ry'.

Love's thrice repurèd nectar? Death, I fear me,
Sounding destruction, or some joy too fine,   20
Too subtle-potent, tuned too sharp in sweetness
For the capacity of my ruder powers.
I fear it much and I do fear besides
That I shall lose distinction in my joys,
As doth a battle when they charge on heaps   25
The enemy flying.

      Enter PANDARUS

PANDARUS She's making her ready, she'll come straight; you must be
    witty now. She does so blush and fetches her wind so short as if she
    were frayed with a sprite. I'll fetch her; it is the prettiest villain –
    she fetches her breath as short as a new-ta'en sparrow. *Exit*   30
TROILUS Even such a passion doth embrace my bosom:
    My heart beats thicker than a feverous pulse
    And all my powers do their bestowing lose,
    Like vassalage at unawares encount'ring
    The eye of majesty.   35

---

19 repurèd] Q; reputed F   21 subtle-potent] *Theobald;* subtill, potent Q, F (*subst.*)   21 tuned] Q; and F   24 lose] F3; loose Q, F   26 SD] F; *not in* Q   29 frayed] *Capell* (fray'd); fraid Q, F   30 as short] Q; so short F   30 SD] F (*subst.*); *not in* Q   34 unawares] F; vnwares Q

19 thrice repurèd nectar the elixir of love, refined three times over.

20 Sounding Swooning. In a fully modernised text such as the present one, it might be better to read 'swooning' here (as in Oxford), but other possible connotations of 'sounding' that could be in play (e.g. sounding to battle, sounding the depths) would be lost; I thus retain the Q, F reading.

21 subtle-potent An invented compound, combining the notions of extreme refinement and power; both Q and F treat the two words as separate adjectives (Theobald was the first to hyphenate), so it would be possible for an actor to emphasise the contrast in meaning. Here, as so often, the textual details open up different performance possibilities.

21–2 tuned . . . ruder powers tuned to such a sharp pitch that their sweetness will elude my relatively unrefined capacities. The metaphor shifts deftly from gustatory to musical sensation.

24 distinction in the ability to distinguish between, with a glance at 'distinction' meaning recog-

nition for princely (in this instance sexual) performance. See 1.3.27–30 n.

25 a battle an army. Again, in imagining the delights of love, Troilus' mind turns to thoughts of war, and the joys of wild, bloody pursuit.

25 on heaps helter-skelter.

26 The enemy flying With the enemy in retreat.

28 witty (1) clever, (2) alert (i.e. with your wits about you).

28 fetches . . . short pants, breathes quickly.

29 frayed with frightened by.

29 villain Pandarus uses the word affectionately, the way 'devil' might be used in modern English. 'Villain' referred originally to a rustic or peasant, and only later, through a kind of linguistic snobbery, came to mean evildoer.

32 thicker faster.

33 bestowing ability to function.

34 vassalage vassals, subjects of a lord or king ('majesty', 35). As so often in the play, the abstract terms substitute for the concrete – see Introduction, pp. 22–4.

34 at unawares unexpectedly.

Enter PANDARUS *and* CRESSIDA

PANDARUS Come, come, what need you blush? – shame's a baby. Here
she is now: swear the oaths now to her that you have sworn to me.
[*Cressida draws away*] What are you gone again? – you must be
watched ere you be made tame, must you? Come your ways, come
your ways: an you draw backward, we'll put you i'th'thills. Why do   40
you not speak to her? Come, draw this curtain and let's see your picture [*Removing her veil*]. Alas the day, how loath you are to offend
daylight: an 'twere dark you'd close sooner. So, so, rub on and kiss
the mistress. How now, a kiss in fee-farm! Build there carpenter, the
air is sweet. Nay you shall fight your hearts out ere I part you, the   45
falcon as the tercel, for all the ducks i'th'river. Go to, go to.
TROILUS You have bereft me of all words, lady.
PANDARUS Words pay no debts, give her deeds; but she'll bereave you
o'th'deeds too, if she call your activity in question. What, billing

---

36 blush? – shame's] *Pope (subst.);* blush? / Shames Q, F   38 SD] *White*² *(subst.); not in* Q, F   40 thills] Q *(filles),* F
(fils); files F2, *Rowe*   42 SD] *Bevington*² *(subst., conj. Malone); Snatching her mask / Johnson; not in* Q, F

36–46 Pandarus first speaks to Cressida, then to
Troilus, back to Cressida, then to Troilus and so
on, and, after 43, to both at once.

39 watched . . . tame The reference is to the
training of hawks, which are kept awake ('watched')
in order to be tamed. Shakespeare frequently alludes to such practices, sometimes with a suggestion of overweening male power, as in *Shr.* 4.1.190–
6 and *Oth.* 3.3.261–3.

40 thills shafts of a cart. Q and F give variant
spellings of a dialectal equivalent, modernised as
'fills' in many recent editions. Pandarus speaks to
Cressida as if she were a shy or wayward colt.

41–2 picture i.e. her face. Curtains were often
hung in front of pictures, making the analogy a natural one: compare *TN* 1.5.233: 'we will draw the
curtain [Olivia's veil], and show you the picture'.
The phrasing clearly suggests Cressida is wear-
ing a veil, which Pandarus probably removes here
(though he could do it herself).

43 close (1) come to terms, (2) embrace.

43–44 rub . . . mistress Pandarus speaks to
Troilus, whom he is urging into amorous action.
His witty metaphor derives from the game of
bowls: the small ball at which the players aim is
called the 'mistress', 'rub' describes the curving
movement of the balls, which 'are said to "kiss"
when they touch gently' (Nares, cited in Variorum).

44 kiss in fee-farm prolonged kiss ('fee-
farm' = a grant of land in perpetuity). The lovers
seem to have responded to Pandarus' urging in his

previous lines, and are now kissing, thus prompting
his cheerfully voyeuristic approval.

44–45 Build . . . sweet Building where the air
is sweet is conducive to health and prosperity –
a notion referred to, with dramatic irony, in *Mac.*
1.6.1–10. Here the suggestion is that the sweet air
of the lovers' mingled breaths is an ideal place for
a permanent dwelling.

45 fight . . . out struggle to outdo each other
in love. Some editors and commentators have preferred 'sigh . . .', but Baldwin (Variorum) points
out that the image, as frequently in the play, connects war and love.

46 falcon . . . tercel female ('falcon') as (vigorously as) the male ('tercel').

46 for . . . river The phrasing suggests a bet
(compare 'for all the money in the world'), while
Pandarus' mind no doubt jumps to 'ducks' in association with his reference to falcon and tercel.

47 This line appears almost verbatim in *MV*
3.2.175. See 15 n.

48 deeds With a triple pun: (1) actions, (2) sexual consummation (as in 'doing the deed'), (3) legal
documents (a meaning developed later in the
speech).

48–9 bereave . . . question deprive you of sexual prowess as well, if she puts your virility to
the test ('bereave' follows on Troilus' 'bereft'). The
joke is a sly glance at male sexual exhaustion and
the presumed inexhaustibility of women.

49 billing kissing (as doves and pigeons are said

again? Here's 'In witness whereof the parties interchangeably . . .'   50
Come in, come in, I'll go get a fire.   [*Exit*]

CRESSIDA Will you walk in my lord?

TROILUS O Cressida, how often have I wished me thus!

CRESSIDA Wished my lord? The gods grant – O my lord –

TROILUS What should they grant? What makes this pretty abruption?   55
What too curious dreg espies my sweet lady in the fountain of our
love?

CRESSIDA More dregs than water if my fears have eyes.

TROILUS Fears make devils of cherubims, they never see truly.

CRESSIDA Blind fear that seeing reason leads, finds safer footing than   60
blind reason stumbling without fear: to fear the worst oft cures
the worse.

TROILUS O let my lady apprehend no fear: in all Cupid's pageant there
is presented no monster.

CRESSIDA Nor nothing monstrous neither?   65

TROILUS Nothing but our undertakings, when we vow to weep seas,
live in fire, eat rocks, tame tigers, thinking it harder for our mistress
to devise imposition enough than for us to undergo any difficulty

---

50 'In . . . interchangeably . . .'] *Hanmer (subst.);* in . . . interchangeably. Q, F   51 SD] F2 *(subst.); not in* Q, F
53 Cressida] F; *Cressed* Q   58 fears] *Pope;* teares Q, F   60 safer] Q; safe F   62 worse] Q, F; worst *Hanmer*   63–4] *Pope;
as verse* (feare, / In) Q, F   65 Nor] F; Not Q

to 'bill and coo', hence continuing the many bird
images in this passage).

50 In . . . interchangeably A legal formula
used for contracts signed in duplicate, where each
party delivers his/her signed copy to the other ('interchangeably' = reciprocally). The subtextual legal suggestions in the preceding lines ('debts' and
'deeds') surface in the analogy.

51 fire light, candle; the reference could be to
providing a fire for their bedroom, though judging by what each has said while alone (1.2.242 ff.
and 15–35 of this scene), they seem quite 'warm'
already.

52–84 This passage, neatly framed by Cressida's
repeated invitation to 'walk in', poses a crucial
problem of interpretation for both actor and reader.
Is her 'fear' (58, 60–1) genuine or is she playing
with Troilus, appearing more reluctant than she is
(as suggested by her soliloquy at the end of 1.2)?
See Introduction, pp. 28–31 for a full discussion of
Cressida's hesitations.

55 abruption interruption.

56 too curious over-precise or scrupulous in

inquiry. (Palmer cites *Ham.* 5.1.205–6:"Twere to
consider too curiously, to consider so.') The word
properly describes Cressida's looking into love's
fountain, not the dreg (impurity, sediment) Troilus
imagines she finds there, but this kind of transpo-
sition is common in Shakespeare.

59 One's fears transform angels to devils, they
always mis-perceive; cherubims ('cherubins' is the
usual plural form in early modern English) = one
of the highest orders of angels.

60 seeing reason reason that is able to see.

61–2 to . . . worse Proverbial – see Dent w912.

63–4 Troilus is mistaken, since frequently
Cupid's shows, as in Spenser's *Faerie Queene*, III.12,
do feature monsters such as Fear, Suspicion, and
Cruelty; Troilus clearly has an interest in persuad-
ing Cressida not to be afraid, and he is also prone
to naïveté.

66–9 Nothing . . . imposed Such are the ex-
travagances depicted in conventional Renaissance
love poetry.

68 devise imposition impose difficult
tasks.

imposed. This is the monstrosity in love, lady, that the will is
infinite and the execution confined, that the desire is boundless   70
and the act a slave to limit.

CRESSIDA They say all lovers swear more performance than they are
able, and yet reserve an ability that they never perform, vowing
more than the perfection of ten and discharging less than the tenth
part of one. They that have the voice of lions and the act of hares,   75
are they not monsters?

TROILUS Are there such? Such are not we. Praise us as we are tasted,
allow us as we prove. Our head shall go bare till merit crown it: no
perfection in reversion shall have a praise in present; we will not
name desert before his birth and, being born, his addition shall be   80
humble. Few words to fair faith: Troilus shall be such to Cressid
as what envy can say worst shall be a mock for his truth, and what
truth can speak truest not truer than Troilus.

CRESSIDA Will you walk in my lord?

Enter PANDARUS

PANDARUS What, blushing still? Have you not done talking yet?   85
CRESSIDA Well uncle, what folly I commit I dedicate to you.
PANDARUS I thank you for that: if my lord get a boy of you, you'll give
him me. Be true to my lord; if he flinch chide me for it.

---

69 This is] F; This Q   69 monstrosity] F3; monstruousity Q; monstruositie F   78–9 merit . . . perfection] F; merit
louer part no affection Q   84 SD] F; *not in* Q

69 **monstrosity** The Q, F and F3 readings are
simply variant spellings of what *OED* (Monstru-
osity) recognises as equivalent words, though the
derivation of the latter word comes from Latin
via medieval French, while the more familiar term
comes directly from Latin.

72 **performance** i.e. sexual performance – making wittily explicit what was merely an overtone in
Troilus' rather wistful description of the general
insufficiency of love's 'act' (71) to live up to its
promise.

73 **reserve** keep for future use or enjoyment.
Cressida suggests that lovers make passionate
promises but frequently fail to deliver, not only
from lack of ability, but from a deliberate restraint
or coolness.

74 **discharging** paying, expending. The word
combines economic and explicit sexual/
physiological meanings; cf. Sonnet 129, 1–2
'Th'expense of spirit in a waste of shame / Is
lust in action.'

77–8 **Praise . . . prove** Judge us according to
our results, with, perhaps, an allusion to the biblical adage 'by their frutes ye shal knowe them'
(Matthew 7.20). 'Tasted' is akin to 'tested' in both
sound and meaning.

79 **perfection in reversion** future perfection or
accomplishment; an office was held 'in reversion'
when it was designated to come into a person's possession at some future date (e.g. at the death of the
current holder).

80 **name . . . birth** give a name to our 'desert'
(i.e. what we deserve as faithful lovers) before it is actually born. The analogy is with
a child having to survive birth before being
named.

80 **his addition** its title or name.

82 **what envy . . . truth** the worst that envy can
do will be to mock his constancy.

88 **flinch** fall back through a failure of courage
or endurance (and hence prove untrue), with a sexual innuendo.

TROILUS You know now your hostages: your uncle's word and my firm
    faith.   90

PANDARUS Nay I'll give my word for her too: our kindred, though they
    be long ere they be wooed, they are constant being won; they are
    burrs I can tell you: they'll stick where they are thrown.

CRESSIDA Boldness comes to me now and brings me heart:
    Prince Troilus, I have loved you night and day   95
    For many weary months.

TROILUS Why was my Cressid then so hard to win?

CRESSIDA Hard to seem won, but I was won my lord
    With the first glance that ever – pardon me,
    If I confess much, you will play the tyrant;   100
    I love you now, but till now not so much
    But I might master it – in faith I lie,
    My thoughts were like unbridled children grown
    Too headstrong for their mother – see, we fools!
    Why have I blabbed? Who shall be true to us   105
    When we are so unsecret to ourselves?
    But though I loved you well, I wooed you not,
    And yet, good faith, I wished myself a man
    Or that we women had men's privilege
    Of speaking first. Sweet, bid me hold my tongue,   110
    For in this rapture I shall surely speak
    The thing I shall repent. See, see your silence,
    Coming in dumbness, from my weakness draws

---

92 be wooed] Q; are wooed F   94–6] *Rowe; as prose* Q, F   99 glance . . . me] F2 *(with colon after* ever*)*; glance; that
euer pardon me Q, F   101 till now not] Q; not till now F   103 grown] Q; grow F   113 Coming] Q, F; Cunning *Pope*

98–114 This speech, so full of 'abruption' (55), poses problems of interpretation similar to those mentioned in relation to 52–84 and discussed in the Introduction. The problem for the actor is to determine how tormented she actually is, how flirtatious, how sincere.

106 **unsecret** disloyal in revealing our secret thoughts.

111 **rapture** transport of joy. Bevington[2] notes that this predates *OED*'s earliest citation (1629) of what has become the standard modern meaning and suggests that the older meaning of 'carrying off a woman' may still be in play here.

113 **Coming in dumbness** Virtually all editors since Pope have accepted his deft emendation, 'cunning', though Greg argues cogently for following Q, F (*Principles*, p. 12). 'Coming' can mean 'forward' or 'ready to act,' which fits the context, so that Cressida says that Troilus' silence suits his purposes – his dumbness readily prods her into indiscretion. 'Coming' can even, as Baldwin points out (Variorum), have its usual meaning (Silence is coming dumbly along). Given the relative independence of Q and F discussed in the Textual Analysis, agreement between the two texts needs to be given more weight than it would were F dependent on Q. Nevertheless, 'cunning' gives a sharper sense of paradox, by suggesting that Troilus' silence is a deliberate strategy designed to elicit indiscreet speech, and may be what Shakespeare wrote.

My very soul of counsel. Stop my mouth.

TROILUS And shall, albeit sweet music issues thence.   115

[*Kisses her*]

PANDARUS Pretty i'faith.

CRESSIDA My lord I do beseech you, pardon me –
    'Twas not my purpose thus to beg a kiss;
    I am ashamed – O heavens, what have I done?
    For this time will I take my leave, my lord.   120

TROILUS Your leave, sweet Cressid?

PANDARUS Leave? An you take leave till tomorrow morning –

CRESSIDA Pray you, content you –

TROILUS What offends you lady?

CRESSIDA Sir, mine own company.   125

TROILUS You cannot shun yourself.

CRESSIDA Let me go and try.
    I have a kind of self resides with you,
    But an unkind self that itself will leave
    To be another's fool. I would be gone.   130
    Where is my wit? I know not what I speak.

TROILUS Well know they what they speak that speak so wisely.

CRESSIDA Perchance my lord I show more craft than love
    And fell so roundly to a large confession
    To angle for your thoughts; but you are wise,   135
    Or else you love not – for to be wise and love
    Exceeds man's might; that dwells with gods above.

---

114 My . . . counsel] Q; My soule of counsell from me F   115 SD] *Rowe (subst.); not in* Q, F   130–1 fool . . . speak.] Q; foole. Where is my wit? / I would be gone: I speake I know not what. F   132 speak so] Q; speakes so F

114 very soul of counsel most secret thoughts (i.e. her weakness makes it impossible to keep her own counsel).

119–20 Again, Cressida's sudden decision to leave seems to derive from both anxiety and strategy.

128–30 I have . . . fool One part of me is yours, but that part is unnatural ('unkind') since it has abandoned the other part and become the plaything of another person. The lines succinctly register Cressida's split feelings not only here but throughout much of the play. Similar ideas are woven through the Sonnets; see, for example, Sonnet 133: 'Me from myself thy cruel eye hath taken' (5) and 134: 'And I myself am mortgag'd to thy will, / Myself I'll forfeit . . .' (2–3). Sonnet 88 offers a more positive view of the forfeited self: 'The injuries that to myself I do / Doing thee vantage, double-vantage me' (11–12).

132 Troilus, smitten by Cressida's wit as well as her beauty, nevertheless seems aware of the possible calculation in her words and behaviour.

133–5 Perchance . . . thoughts Cressida cleverly acknowledges the possible 'craft' in her manner, thus disarming suspicion.

134 roundly (1) frankly, (2) glibly.

135 but you are wise i.e. because he has not taken the bait she has used to 'angle' (fish) for his thoughts.

136 else in other words (?). As Evans notes, following Malone, the confusion, created by the word 'not' later in the line, may be Shakespeare's ('Our author,' says Malone, 'sometimes entangles himself in inextricable difficulties of this kind' (quoted in Variorum)). Cressida's meaning is nevertheless fairly clear: Troilus, in refusing her bait, has shown wisdom, which is incompatible with his being in love.

TROILUS O that I thought it could be in a woman –
As, if it can, I will presume in you –
To feed for aye her lamp and flames of love,   140
To keep her constancy in plight and youth,
Outliving beauty's outward with a mind
That doth renew swifter than blood decays,
Or that persuasion could but thus convince me
That my integrity and truth to you   145
Might be affronted with the match and weight
Of such a winnowed purity in love –
How were I then uplifted! But, alas,
I am as true as truth's simplicity
And simpler than the infancy of truth.   150
CRESSIDA In that I'll war with you.
TROILUS   O virtuous fight,
When right with right wars who shall be most right!
True swains in love shall in the world to come
Approve their truth by Troilus: when their rhymes,
Full of protest, of oath and big compare,   155
Want similes, truth tired with iteration –
As true as steel, as plantage to the moon,

140 aye] F; age Q   142 beauty's] Capell; beauties Q, F   154 truth] Q; truths F   156 Want] F2; Wants Q, F

138–50 Troilus constructs his own simplicity and truth in contrast to the presumed incapacity of women to remain faithful, which was the legacy of anti-feminist tradition (and part of the legend of Cressida as it developed after Chaucer). See Introduction, pp. 27, 33–4, and Sources of the play, pp. 255–6.
140 for aye forever.
141 in . . . youth as fresh as when it was pledged.
142 beauty's outward the (mere) externals of beauty (the contrast is with the 'mind' that 're-news' as beauty and passion wane). I take Q, F's 'beauties' to be a possessive, on the analogy of such usages as 'Enemies waight' (1.3.204, TLN 663), so that 'beauty's' is merely a modernisation; but it is possible that 'beauties' should be read as a plural noun, and 'outward' as an adjective.
143 renew . . . decays revivify itself more quickly than youthful vigour, beauty, and passion fade.
144 Or if I could be persuaded.
146–7 affronted . . . love balanced by the matching weight of a pure, unmixed love such as mine ('winnowed' = refined, like grain after it is separated from the chaff).

148–50 But, alas . . . truth Troilus' logic breaks down here – to follow through on his think-ing, he would have to accuse Cressida directly of future falsehood. Instead he falls back on a charac-teristic declaration of his own truth.
153–85 This highly contrived, almost operatic passage sets up each of the three characters in the roles that by Shakespeare's time they had come to play in the popular imagination, though only 'pander' (181, 182) had actually become a common part of the language. See Bowen, Charnes, Gaudet 'Troilus', James, and Introduction, pp. 32–5.
153 swains lovers (originally shepherds).
154 Approve Attest authoritatively to (OED v[1] 2).
155 protest protestations.
155 big compare extravagant comparisons.
156 truth . . . iteration truth having been worn out by too much repetition (of clichéd similes).
157 plantage vegetation. The word and the idea have caused difficulty for commentators; even if we are aware of the apparent belief among Elizabethan farmers that 'the increase of the moone maketh plants . . . frutefull' (Reginald Scot, cited in Var-iorum), the image seems ill-suited to the idea of constancy.

As sun to day, as turtle to her mate,
As iron to adamant, as earth to th'centre –
Yet after all comparisons of truth,   160
As truth's authentic author to be cited,
'As true as Troilus' shall crown up the verse
And sanctify the numbers.

CRESSIDA   Prophet may you be!
If I be false or swerve a hair from truth,
When time is old and hath forgot itself,   165
When waterdrops have worn the stones of Troy
And blind oblivion swallowed cities up
And mighty states characterless are grated
To dusty nothing, yet let memory
From false to false among false maids in love   170
Upbraid my falsehood: when they've said 'as false
As air, as water, wind or sandy earth,
As fox to lamb, or wolf to heifer's calf,
Pard to the hind or stepdame to her son',
Yea, let them say to stick the heart of falsehood,   175
'As false as Cressid'.

PANDARUS Go to, a bargain made: seal it, seal it, I'll be the witness.
Here I hold your hand, here my cousin's. If ever you prove false
one to another, since I have taken such pains to bring you together,
let all pitiful goers-between be called to the world's end after my 180
name: call them all panders; let all constant men be Troiluses, all
false women Cressids, and all brokers-between panders. Say Amen.

---

160 Yet] F; *not in* Q   162 'As . . . Troilus'] *Johnson (subst.)*; As . . . *Troylus* Q, F   165 and] F; or Q   171–4 'as . . .
son'] *Capell*; as . . . Sonne Q, F   172 wind or sandy] Q; as Winde, as sandie F   173 or] Q; as F   176 'As . . . Cressid']
Staunton (subst.); As . . . *Cressid* Q, F   177–8 witness. Here] *Rowe*; witnes here Q, F *(subst.)*   179 pains] F; paine Q
181 panders] Q, F *(subst.)*; Pandars *Pope (so too at 182)*

158 **turtle** dove.
159 **adamant** magnet.
159 **earth . . . centre** as objects at the surface of
the earth are to the force at the centre. Elizabethans
understood gravity as a kind of magnet-
ism.
161 As the most authoritative text that can be
cited.
163 **sanctify the numbers** give a kind of im-
primatur to the verses.
168 **characterless** all their written records expunged (the accent is on the second syllable).
169–71 **let memory . . . falsehood** let history,

as it records one instance of feminine falsehood
after another, condemn my infidelity.
174 **Pard . . . hind** Leopard . . . doe.
175 **stick** pierce to.
181 **constant** Why Pandarus, after saying 'if
ever you prove false to one another' should now
speak of Troilus as an image of constancy has puzzled many readers. While the main point of the
speech is to provide a symbolic declaration that already knows, as it were, the future of these mythol-
ogised figures, nevertheless the odd linkage of falseness and truth can suggest that Troilus is in some
sense unfaithful.

TROILUS Amen.

CRESSIDA Amen.

PANDARUS Amen. Whereupon I will show you a chamber with a bed,   185
    which bed, because it shall not speak of your pretty encounters,
    press it to death, away!

Exeunt [*Troilus and Cressida*]

        And Cupid grant all tongue-tied maidens here
        Bed, chamber, pander, to provide this gear.   *Exit*

[3.3] *Flourish. Enter* AGAMEMNON, ULYSSES, DIOMEDES, NESTOR,
[AJAX,] MENELAUS, and CALCHAS

CALCHAS Now, princes, for the service I have done,
        Th'advantage of the time prompts me aloud
        To call for recompense. Appear it to your mind
        That through the sight I bear in things to come
        I have abandoned Troy, left my possession,   5
        Incurred a traitor's name, exposed myself
        From certain and possessed conveniences
        To doubtful fortunes, sequest'ring from me all
        That time, acquaintance, custom, and condition
        Made tame and most familiar to my nature,   10
        And here to do you service am become
        As new into the world – strange, unacquainted.

---

185 chamber with a bed] *Hanmer;* Chamber Q, F   187 SD] *Capell; Exeunt* Q; *not in* F   189 pander] Q *(Pander);* and Pander F   189 SD] Q; *Exeunt* F   **Act 3, Scene 3**   3.3] *Capell (subst.); not in* Q, F   0 SD.1 *Flourish*] F *(after / Chalcas); not in* Q   0 SD.2 AJAX] *Theobald; not in* Q, F   0 SD.2 MENELAUS] F; *not in* Q   0 SD.2 CALCHAS] Q, F *(Chalcas)*   1 done] Q; done you F   3 your mind] F; mind Q   4 come] F4; loue Q, F; *Jove / Johnson*

185 **with a bed** Hanmer's addition is logical, and
has been adopted by most editors; but Pandarus
is not always logical, and often speaks in elliptical
phrases.

187 **press it to death** The phrase ominously recalls the punishment of criminals sentenced to tor-
ture by pressing, a procedure that sometimes led to
death, though Pandarus is alluding to the common
metaphor for sexual consummation (as in French
le petit mort); see Achilles' 'pressed bed' (1.3.163
and n.).

188–9 Pandarus again addresses the audience directly in his epilogue (see 5.11.44 ff.), but for the
actor to step outside the character in the middle of
the play and speak to specific members of the audience is unusual in Shakespeare; cf. *Shr.* 4.1.210–
11.

189 **gear** stuff, material (such as bed and chamber).

Act 3, Scene 3

0 SD With ominous dramatic irony, Calchas appears to request the exchange immediately after the
love scene between his daughter and Troilus.

2 **advantage** suitability.

3 **Appear it** Let it appear.

4 **sight . . . come** my visionary knowledge of
the future.

7 **From** By turning from.

8 **sequest'ring** separating.

12 **As** As though.

12 **strange, unacquainted** i.e. as a stranger, unknown and without acquaintances.

I do beseech you, as in way of taste,
To give me now a little benefit
Out of those many registered in promise   15
Which you say live to come in my behalf.
AGAMEMNON What wouldst thou of us, Trojan? Make demand.
CALCHAS You have a Trojan prisoner called Antenor
Yesterday took: Troy holds him very dear.
Oft have you (often have you thanks therefor)   20
Desired my Cressid in right great exchange
Whom Troy hath still denied; but this Antenor
I know is such a wrest in their affairs
That their negotiations all must slack
Wanting his manage, and they will almost   25
Give us a prince of blood, a son of Priam,
In change of him. Let him be sent, great princes,
And he shall buy my daughter, and her presence
Shall quite strike off all service I have done
In most accepted pain.
AGAMEMNON   Let Diomedes bear him   30
And bring us Cressid hither; Calchas shall have
What he requests of us. Good Diomed,
Furnish you fairly for this interchange;
Withal bring word if Hector will tomorrow
Be answered in his challenge: Ajax is ready.   35
DIOMEDES This shall I undertake and 'tis a burden
Which I am proud to bear.

[Exeunt Diomedes and Calchas]

---

37 SD.1] *Capell; Exit* Q, F

13 **taste** foretaste, advance payment.
15 **registered in promise** recorded as promises, pledged.
20 **often ... therefor** you have often been thanked for it.
21 **in ... exchange** in exchange for a Trojan of high rank.
23 **wrest** device for tuning a stringed instrument (the implication being that Antenor is crucial for maintaining the harmony of Trojan deliberations).
25 **Wanting his manage** Lacking his guiding hand.

29 **strike off** recompense.
30 **accepted pain** i.e. the pains I have willingly taken (though Calchas could be referring, with a touch of sarcasm, to the ease with which the Greeks have accepted his treasonous labours).
30–1 **Let ... hither** The decision on which the main plot of the play hinges is quickly and easily taken, without the tortuous discussion typically devoted to other matters.
33 **Furnish you fairly** Prepare yourself fully (with everything you need).

ACHILLES *and* PATROCLUS [*appear in the doorway of*] *their tent*

ULYSSES Achilles stands i'th'entrance of his tent:
    Please it our general pass strangely by him
    As if he were forgot, and, princes all,   40
    Lay negligent and loose regard upon him;
    I will come last. 'Tis like he'll question me
    Why such unplausive eyes are bent, why turned, on him;
    If so, I have derision medicinable
    To use between your strangeness and his pride,   45
    Which his own will shall have desire to drink.
    It may do good: pride hath no other glass
    To show itself but pride, for supple knees
    Feed arrogance and are the proud man's fees.
AGAMEMNON We'll execute your purpose and put on   50
    A form of strangeness as we pass along;
    So do each lord and either greet him not
    Or else disdainfully, which shall shake him more
    Than if not looked on – I will lead the way.
                    [*They file past Achilles' tent*]
ACHILLES What, comes the general to speak with me?   55
    You know my mind, I'll fight no more 'gainst Troy.
AGAMEMNON What says Achilles? Would he aught with us?
NESTOR Would you, my lord, aught with the general?
ACHILLES No.
NESTOR Nothing, my lord.   60

37 SD.2] *Hanmer* (*subst.*); Achilles *and* Patro *stand in their tent* Q; *Enter* Achilles *and* Patroclus *in their tent* F   39 pass] Q; to pass F   43 are bent, why turned] Q, F (*subst.*); are bent *Pope*   54 SD] *This edn; they pass forward. / Capell; not in* Q, F

37 SD.2 The ensuing stage action demands that Achilles and Patroclus be visible from this point, presumably just at the entrance to their tent, which also formed the backdrop to 2.3 (see 2.3.18 and 19 SDs and n.). On Shakespeare's stage, the tent might have been a separate structure placed before an entry door at the rear of the stage, or it might simply, and effectively, have been a curtained recess, the very one that Cressida and Troilus had retired into just moments before. Both the Q and F directions imply that Achilles and Patroclus stand just in front of their tent, perhaps staring at the generals, challenging them once again to come begging.

39 **strangely** distantly, as a stranger.

41 Observe him with a deliberately casual and detached air.

43 **unplausive** disdainful (only citation in *OED*).

44 **derision medicinable** i.e. a way of making

your disdain ('derision') healthful to Achilles (by using it as a cure for his 'pride' (45)).

46 Which (medicine) he will be eager to swallow (because he will notice their scorn and ask Ulysses about it).

47–8 **pride . . . pride** only pride can be a mirror to pride. Hence, the proud behaviour that Ulysses is urging on Agamemnon and the rest will serve as a mirror to Achilles.

48–9 **supple . . . fees** kneeling to the proud man (and thus paying the 'fees' he expects) only feeds his arrogance the more.

55–69 During this sequence, the Greek leaders follow Ulysses' advice, by walking past Achilles with only the slightest acknowledgement; talking among themselves, they offer none of the adulation that Achilles is used to. For their departure, I have rejected Capell's revisions accepted by almost all subsequent editors (see collation 61, 63,

AGAMEMNON The better.

ACHILLES Good day, good day.

MENELAUS How do you, how do you?

ACHILLES What, does the cuckold scorn me?

AJAX How now, Patroclus?   65

ACHILLES Good morrow, Ajax.

AJAX Ha!

ACHILLES Good morrow.

AJAX Ay, and good next day too.

          Exeunt [Agamemnon, Nestor, Menelaus, and Ajax]

ACHILLES What mean these fellows? Know they not Achilles?   70

PATROCLUS They pass by strangely: they were used to bend,

    To send their smiles before them to Achilles,

    To come as humbly as they use to creep

    To holy altars.

ACHILLES   What, am I poor of late?

    'Tis certain greatness, once fall'n out with fortune,   75

    Must fall out with men too. What the declined is,

    He shall as soon read in the eyes of others

    As feel in his own fall; for men, like butterflies,

    Show not their mealy wings but to the summer,

    And not a man for being simply man   80

    Hath any honour, but honour for those honours

    That are without him, as place, riches, and favour –

    Prizes of accident as oft as merit,

    Which, when they fall, as being slippery standers,

    The love that leaned on them, as slippery too,   85

61 The better.] Q, F; The better. *Exeunt* Agamemnon *and* Nestor / *Capell (subst.)*   **63 how do you?**] Q, F; how do you? *Exit / Capell*   **66** Ajax.] F4; *Aiax?* Q, F   **69 SD**] *This edn; Exeunt* Q, F; *Exit* Ajax *Capell*   **73–4 To . . . altars**] *Rowe²; as one line* Q, F   **73** use] *Dyce² (conj. W. S. Walker)*; vs'd Q, F   **81 honour for**] Q; honour'd for F

69), because, while possible, they seem too rigid. I instead follow the direction of Q and F, which both indicate a collective exit (69 SD). Of course, a theatre company, then as now, would sort out the exit in a convenient way, not necessarily keeping Agamemnon and Nestor onstage until the very end of the exchange between Ajax and Achilles. While the others are leaving, Ulysses takes out a book and begins to read.

71 used accustomed.

73 use are accustomed. Dyce's emendation is appropriate since presumably the Greeks have not stopped revering the gods.

74 poor devalued, unpopular.

76 declined person whose fortune has declined.

79 mealy powdery.

80–3 No man is esteemed for his intrinsic merits, but only for external 'honours' such as status, wealth, and popularity, which are rewards that are the product of chance ('accident') as often as 'merit'. Shakespeare may have adopted this familiar idea from Montaigne ('A man should be judged by himselfe, and not by his complements'), who himself was following Seneca (Variorum).

84 slippery standers unstable props (for the love they are meant to support, as the next line makes clear).

    Doth one pluck down another and together
    Die in the fall. But 'tis not so with me;
    Fortune and I are friends: I do enjoy
    At ample point all that I did possess,
    Save these men's looks, who do methinks find out   90
    Something not worth in me such rich beholding
    As they have often given. Here is Ulysses,
    I'll interrupt his reading. How now, Ulysses!
ULYSSES Now, great Thetis' son!
ACHILLES What are you reading?
ULYSSES   A strange fellow here   95
    Writes me that man, how dearly ever parted,
    How much in having, or without or in,
    Cannot make boast to have that which he hath,
    Nor feels not what he owes, but by reflection –
    As when his virtues shining upon others   100
    Heat them, and they retort that heat again
    To the first givers.
ACHILLES   This is not strange, Ulysses:
    The beauty that is borne here in the face
    The bearer knows not, but commends itself
    To others' eyes; nor doth the eye itself,   105
    That most pure spirit of sense, behold itself,
    Not going from itself, but eye to eye opposed,
    Salutes each other with each other's form,
    For speculation turns not to itself

86–7] F; Doth . . . fall, / But . . . mee, Q   100 shining] F; ayming Q   102 givers] Q; giuer F   105–6] Q; *not in* F

89 At ample point To the fullest.
91 rich beholding high regard.
95 A strange . . . here Who the 'strange fellow' might be has been the subject of much speculation: Plato, Seneca, and Montaigne have all been named, though the parallels are more with Achilles' reply than with Ulysses' analysis of 'reflection'. It is likely that Shakespeare had no one author in mind, but invented him for dramatic and thematic purposes, as he apparently did the 'satirical rogue' whom Hamlet invokes against Polonius' snooping (2.2.196). See Introduction, pp. 35–8, for a discussion of this whole passage.
96 how dearly ever parted no matter how richly endowed, with an added suggestion of 'divided'.
97 or . . . in either externally or internally.
99 owes owns, possesses.

99 reflection The metaphor derives from reflected heat and light, more than from mirroring, though both senses are relevant.
100 others other people.
101 retort reflect (as objects reflect the heat of the sun).
106 most . . . sense most refined of the senses (each of which was thought to have its own vaporous spirit – see 1.1.54 n.).
107 Not . . . itself Since it cannot go out from itself.
107–11 but eye . . . itself Achilles makes the relatively simple point that the eye, being fixed, can only see itself when it is set opposite to another person's eye and is 'mirrored there'. See Variorum, pp. 411–15, and Bowen, pp. 98 ff., for extended discussions of the background to this passage.
109 speculation sight.

Till it hath travelled and is mirrored there   110
Where it may see itself. This is not strange at all.
ULYSSES I do not strain at the position –
It is familiar – but at the author's drift,
Who in his circumstance expressly proves
That no man is the lord of anything,   115
Though in and of him there be much consisting,
Till he communicate his parts to others;
Nor doth he of himself know them for aught
Till he behold them formed in the applause
Where they're extended, who like an arch reverb'rate   120
The voice again, or like a gate of steel
Fronting the sun, receives and renders back
His figure and his heat. I was much rapt in this,
And apprehended here immediately
The unknown Ajax.   125
Heavens what a man is there! – a very horse
That has he knows not what. Nature, what things there are
Most abject in regard and dear in use!
What things again most dear in the esteem
And poor in worth! Now shall we see tomorrow –   130
An act that very chance doth throw upon him –
Ajax renowned. O heavens, what some men do

110 mirrored] *Hudson (Singer MS.);* married Q, F   112 strain at] Q; straine it at F   115 man] Q; may F   116 be] Q; is F   119 the applause] Q; th'applause F   120 they're] Q (th'are); they are F   120 reverb'rate] Q, F; reverb'rates F2, *Rowe*   125–7] F; Th'vnknowne . . . there? / A . . . what / Nature . . . are. Q   128 abject] F; obiect Q

110 **travelled** Q's reading ('trauel'd') suggests motion, but F's 'trauail'd', an alternate spelling of 'travelled', points also to the further meaning 'worked' or 'laboured'.

112 **strain at** find difficulty in (cf. 1.3.328 where 'strain' in a similar sense is used as a noun).

114 **his circumstance** the details of his argument.

118–20 **Nor doth . . . extended** He is incapable of assessing his own virtues ('parts', 117) until those to whom he extends himself recognise (and thereby 'form') those virtues. The idea links to the recurrent questioning of value in the play, as, for example, in the Trojan council scene (2.2) – see Introduction, pp. 38–41. For a similar interrogation of value, see *Cor.* 4.7.49–50 ff.: 'So our virtues / Lie in th' interpretation of the time . . .'

120 **who** Referring to those who applaud the

man's virtues (although the shift to singular verb forms in 122 betrays the grammatical uncertainty, since 'who' (= which) could also refer to the 'applause' itself).

123 **His** Its (the sun's).

123 **rapt in** struck by.

125 **unknown** unacknowledged, not yet the subject of others' 'reflection'.

126–7 **Heavens . . . not what** The seeming compliment in these lines cuts two ways, especially if we compare Thersites' remark later in the scene that Ajax's horse is 'more capable' than he is (296–7).

128 **abject . . . use** low in esteem but valuable when put to use.

131 **chance** Chance, of course, had nothing to do with it, but Ulysses' irony reminds us that this seemingly abstract discussion is actually part of a manipulative strategy.

While some men leave to do;
How some men creep in skittish Fortune's hall,
Whiles others play the idiots in her eyes;   135
How one man eats into another's pride,
While pride is fasting in his wantonness!
To see these Grecian lords – why even already
They clap the lubber Ajax on the shoulder
As if his foot were on brave Hector's breast   140
And great Troy shrieking.
ACHILLES I do believe it, for they passed by me
As misers do by beggars: neither gave to me
Good word nor look. What, are my deeds forgot?
ULYSSES Time hath, my lord, a wallet at his back   145
Wherein he puts alms for oblivion,
A great-sized monster of ingratitudes;
Those scraps are good deeds past, which are devoured
As fast as they are made, forgot as soon
As done. Perseverance, dear my lord,   150
Keeps honour bright: to have done is to hang
Quite out of fashion like a rusty mail
In monumental mock'ry. Take the instant way,
For honour travels in a strait so narrow
Where one but goes abreast; keep then the path,   155

---

137 fasting] Q; feasting F   140 on] Q *(one),* F   141 shrieking] Q *(shriking);* shrinking F   148–50] *Steevens;*
Those . . . past, / Which . . . made, / Forgot . . . Lord Q, F; Those . . . are / Devoured . . . forgot / As . . . lord
Bevington²   155 one] F; on Q

133 **leave** neglect.

134–5 Ajax's creeping (as opposed to the potentially bold steps of Achilles) has gained him Fortune's favour, while Achilles plays the fool and thus
misses his chance. The first of these lines thus
probably applies to Ajax, the second to Achilles,
as is the case with the pairs of lines that immediately precede and follow these. However, as Malone and many modern commentators have argued,
Ulysses could be saying: 'While some [i.e. Achilles]
remain tamely inactive ("creep") in fickle Fortune's
hall, others gain her attention, even by playing the
fool.'

136–7 How Ajax feeds himself with his rival's
glory ('pride', 136) while Achilles foolishly fasts
because of his own egotism ('pride', 137).

139 **lubber** oaf or oafish (it could be either noun
or adjective).

145 **wallet** sack. The image of Time with such
a sack full of good deeds is original to Shakespeare,

although the emblem of a backpack laden with
faults that one cannot see and can hence forget
about was traditional. It occurs in many ancient
writers and in Erasmus' *Adages,* 1.vi.90. See Variorum.

147 **monster** Properly refers to 'oblivion', i.e.
forgetfulness, the source of the ingratitudes, though
of course Time, as the source of oblivion, is also
implicated. The grammatical uncertainty is part of
the point: time and oblivion are inextricably linked.
Palmer notes a parallel in *MM* 5.1.12–13, where the
Duke speaks of constructing 'A forted residence
'gainst the tooth of time / And razure of oblivion'.

152 **mail** suit of armour.

153 **In monumental mock'ry** Standing as a
mocking tribute, or monument, to forgotten glory.

153 **instant** most direct.

154 **strait** course, passageway.

155 **one . . . abreast** only one person at a time
can travel (in pursuit of honour).

For emulation hath a thousand sons
That one by one pursue. If you give way
Or hedge aside from the direct forthright,
Like to an entered tide they all rush by
And leave you hindmost;   160
Or like a gallant horse fall'n in first rank,
Lie there for pavement to the abject rear,
O'er-run and trampled on: then what they do in present,
Though less than yours in past, must o'er-top yours;
For Time is like a fashionable host   165
That slightly shakes his parting guest by th'hand,
And with his arms outstretched as he would fly
Grasps in the comer; Welcome ever smiles
And Farewell goes out sighing. O let not virtue seek
Remuneration for the thing it was,   170
For beauty, wit,
High birth, vigour of bone, desert in service,
Love, friendship, charity, are subjects all
To envious and calumniating Time.
One touch of nature makes the whole world kin: 175
That all with one consent praise new-born gauds,
Though they are made and moulded of things past,
And give to dust that is a little gilt
More laud than gilt o'er-dusted.

---

158 hedge] F; turne Q   160 hindmost] F; him, most Q   161–3 Or . . . trampled on] F; *not in* Q   162 abject rear]
Hanmer; abiect, neere F   164 past] F; passe Q   168 Welcome] *Pope;* the welcome Q, F   169 Farewell] Q *(subst.);*
farewels F   169 O let] F; Let Q   170–1] *Steevens³; as one line* Q, F   178 give] *Theobald (conj. Thirlby);* goe Q, F

158 hedge dodge, shift; leave open a way of retreat or escape (*OED v* 9).

158 forthright straight and narrow path (usually an adverb or adjective, the word is used here as a noun for the first time – *OED sb*).

159 entered tide The image suggests the force of the tide as it enters a small bay through a narrow passage.

161–3 Or . . . on These F-only lines probably represent a first shot, later cancelled and hence absent from Q, though they could have been accidentally omitted. The lines create confusion about the implied subject of 'Lie', since the simile of the fallen horse shifts the referent from that of the previous simile (from those who rush by to the person who is ignored). See Textual Analysis, p. 239.

162 pavement . . . rear i.e. the noble horse and horseman become the roadway for the less worthy

soldiers in the 'rear' (Hanmer's emendation being generally accepted).

164 o'er-top surpass.

166 slightly indifferently, with a suggestion of insult or 'slight'.

174 calumniating slanderous (spreading calumny).

175 One natural trait creates a common bond among all people. The implication, spelled out in what follows, is that the 'touch' is a failing or weakness.

176 with one consent in mutual agreement.

176 gauds trifles, mere toys.

177 Even though they may simply be old things made to look new.

178, 179 gilt The contrast is between that which is merely gilded (178) and that which is true gold (179).

179 laud praise.

The present eye praises the present object;   180
Then marvel not, thou great and complete man,
That all the Greeks begin to worship Ajax,
Since things in motion sooner catch the eye
Than what stirs not. The cry went once on thee,
And still it might, and yet it may again,   185
If thou wouldst not entomb thyself alive
And case thy reputation in thy tent,
Whose glorious deeds but in these fields of late
Made emulous missions 'mongst the gods themselves
And drove great Mars to faction.

ACHILLES   Of this my privacy   190
I have strong reasons.

ULYSSES   But 'gainst your privacy
The reasons are more potent and heroical.
'Tis known, Achilles, that you are in love
With one of Priam's daughters.

ACHILLES Ha, known?   195

ULYSSES Is that a wonder?
The providence that's in a watchful state
Knows almost every grain of Pluto's gold,
Finds bottom in th'uncomprehensive deeps,
Keeps place with thought and, almost like the gods,   200

---

183 sooner] Q; begin to F   184 stirs not] Q; not stirs F   184 once] Q; out F   198 grain . . . gold] F; thing Q
199 deeps] F; depth Q; deep *Rowe*   200 place] Q, F; pace *Hanmer*

180 i.e. the eye, functioning strictly in the present, can only see (and hence praise) what is before it. Ulysses summarises what he has been saying in the previous five lines.

184 cry acclaim.

185 Ulysses would seem again to be repeating himself since the two halves of the line are almost identical in meaning, but 'still' can mean 'always' as well as 'even now'.

187 case imprison, shut in.

189 emulous missions forays motivated by envy.

190 faction taking sides (Mars takes the Trojan side in Book v of *The Iliad*).

193–4 This is the first mention of Achilles' clandestine affair with Polyxena, the daughter of Priam and Hecuba (see 209 ff. and 5.1.34–9), a feature of the story that plays a more important role in Homer and many subsequent versions.

197 The spying practised by the state is compared, with ironic overtones, to the watchful 'providence' of God. In one recent production (RSC 1998), Ulysses showed secret photos to Achilles as proof of the effectiveness of his spy network.

198 Pluto's gold Shakespeare, like many before him, might have mistakenly conflated Pluto, the god of the underworld, and Plutus, god of riches. The two figures were in fact closely connected, both names ultimately deriving from a Greek root associated with 'earth', so it is not surprising that Pluto as well as Plutus came to be associated with mines and gold. The Latin name for Pluto, Dis, is a contraction of Latin *dives* (= wealth), suggesting an ancient link between the two Greek figures.

199 uncomprehensive unfathomable.

200 Keeps place Stays abreast.

Does thoughts unveil in their dumb cradles.
There is a mystery, with whom relation
Durst never meddle, in the soul of state,
Which hath an operation more divine
Than breath or pen can give expressure to.   205
All the commerce that you have had with Troy
As perfectly is ours as yours, my lord,
And better would it fit Achilles much
To throw down Hector than Polyxena.
But it must grieve young Pyrrhus now at home,   210
When fame shall in our islands sound her trump,
And all the Greekish girls shall tripping sing:
'Great Hector's sister did Achilles win
But our great Ajax bravely beat down him.'
Farewell my lord; I as your lover speak –   215
The fool slides o'er the ice that you should break.   [*Exit*]

PATROCLUS To this effect, Achilles, have I moved you.
A woman impudent and mannish grown
Is not more loathed than an effeminate man

---

201 Does] F2; Do Q, F *(subst.)*   201 thoughts unveil] Q, F; infant thoughts unveil *Oxford (conj. Malone)*; hidden
thoughts unveil *(conj. Kinnear)*   211 our islands] Q; her Iland F   213–14 'Great . . . him.'] *Hanmer*; Great . . . him:
Q, F *(subst.)*   216 SD] *Pope; not in* Q, F

---

201 i.e. Discovers thoughts as soon as they are
conceived and before they are spoken – a slightly
paranoid, but not entirely unjustified, tribute to
Elizabethan spy networks. Though Isabella in *MM*.
5.1.453 declares that 'thoughts are no subjects',
there were instances, such as treason, where what a
person thought could become legally actionable –
see Maus.
   202 mystery Like 'providence' (197) and 'divine' (204), the word gives a deceptive theological
colouration to what is actually an account of political surveillance.
   202–3 with . . . meddle which one dare not discuss; 'relation' = account, report.
   205 expressure expression. Shakespeare seems
to have invented the word – at least the first
three citations in *OED* are all his (*Wiv* 5.5.67, *TN*
2.3.157, and this one).
   206 commerce dealings.
   207 perfectly . . . yours is known as well to us
as to you.
   209 throw down A deft example of *zeugma*,
where a single verb with two different meanings
takes two differently appropriate objects. In the
present instance, throwing down Hector in battle
is contrasted with throwing down his sister on a

bed, thus wittily joining the play's twin themes of
war and love.
   210 Pyrrhus Achilles' son.
   211 trump trumpet.
   212 tripping lightly, 'trippingly' (as in Hamlet's
'Speak the speech, I pray you . . . trippingly on the
tongue' (3.2.1–2)). There may also be a suggestion of
dancing (as in the phrase, 'trip the light fantastic').
   214 him Hector.
   215 lover dear friend (without any implication
of a sexual relationship); frequently used in Shakespeare.
   216 This curious and difficult line seems to contain a pointless allusion to an incident in Robert
Armin's *Nest of Ninnies*, which describes a fool
crossing thin ice in order to join a troupe of travel-
ling players. Ulysses apparently means that Ajax
is getting away with mere foolish sliding, when
Achilles should be out there breaking the ice, i.e.
making something serious happen. But the contrary implications of the line (sliding over thin
ice seems preferable to breaking through it, which
would land Achilles in cold water) undercut the
main point.
   218–20 A woman . . . action In most modern
productions, Achilles and Patroclus share a clear

In time of action. I stand condemned for this: 220
They think my little stomach to the war,
And your great love to me, restrains you thus.
Sweet, rouse yourself, and the weak, wanton Cupid
Shall from your neck unloose his amorous fold
And, like a dew-drop from the lion's mane,   225
Be shook to air.
ACHILLES   Shall Ajax fight with Hector?
PATROCLUS Ay, and perhaps receive much honour by him.
ACHILLES I see my reputation is at stake,
    My fame is shrewdly gored.
PATROCLUS   O then beware!
Those wounds heal ill that men do give themselves;   230
Omission to do what is necessary
Seals a commission to a blank of danger,
And danger like an ague subtly taints
Even then when we sit idly in the sun.
ACHILLES Go call Thersites hither, sweet Patroclus,   235
    I'll send the fool to Ajax and desire him
    T'invite the Trojan lords after the combat
    To see us here unarmed. I have a woman's longing,

225 like a] F; like Q   226 air] Q; ayrie ayre F   234 we] F; they Q

and obvious homosexual relationship, an interpretation that various aspects of the play support. But
in Elizabethan England, homosexual involvement
did not imply effeminacy. Quite the contrary, paying too much attention to *women* made men effeminate, as Patroclus clearly hints, since he is presumably referring to Polyxena and what Ulysses
has said about her. As for the 'mannish' woman,
this was a contested issue in Shakespeare's culture,
erupting full force about a decade after this play
was written, when it became fashionable among
certain women to dress in men's clothing. For discussion of such issues, see, among many others,
Orgel and Woodbridge.

221 stomach to appetite for.

223–4 Cupid's power is typically invoked in relation to heterosexual desire only, but there is a telling slide from Patroclus' mention of Achilles love
for *him* to his talk of throwing off Cupid's hold.

226 air F's 'ayrie ayre' may be right, though it
seems likely that the MS. contained both words,
either because of mistaken repetition by a copyist
which was then 'sophisticated into sense' (*Textual
Companion*) or because the first was meant to be
deleted. As with many textual details, this one casts

doubt on the prevailing view that F was printed
from a revised copy of Q – see Textual Analysis,
pp. 245–50.

226 Shall . . . Hector It may seem surprising
that Achilles only now figures out that Ajax has
been chosen to combat Hector, but no one has told
him, and even Ulysses' previous speech only hinted
at it.

229 shrewdly gored deeply wounded.

232 i.e. gives a free hand to whatever might
threaten one's well-being. The reference is to the
practice of giving government officials a 'blank'
warrant, or 'commission', to be filled in as they
desired (cf. 'blank cheque'). Patroclus plays on
'Omission' (231) and 'commission.'

233 ague fever – supposedly worsened by sit-
ting in the sun (compare Hotspur's reaction to the
heroic description of Prince Hal: 'worse than the
sun in March, / This praise doth nourish agues'
[*1H4* 4.1.110–11]).

233 taints infects.

238 woman's longing Perhaps referring to the
supposedly irrational cravings of pregnant women,
or perhaps simply an instance of casual stereo-
typing.

An appetite that I am sick withal,
To see great Hector in his weeds of peace,   240
Enter THERSITES
To talk with him and to behold his visage
Even to my full of view. A labour saved!

THERSITES A wonder!

ACHILLES What?

THERSITES Ajax goes up and down the field asking for himself.   245

ACHILLES How so?

THERSITES He must fight singly tomorrow with Hector and is so
   prophetically proud of an heroical cudgelling that he raves in saying nothing.

ACHILLES How can that be?   250

THERSITES Why 'a stalks up and down like a peacock – a stride and
   a stand; ruminates like an hostess that hath no arithmetic but her
   brain to set down her reckoning; bites his lip with a politic regard
   as who should say 'There were wit in this head an 'twould out';
   and so there is, but it lies as coldly in him as fire in a flint, which   255
   will not show without knocking. The man's undone for ever: for
   if Hector break not his neck i'th'combat, he'll break't himself in
   vainglory. He knows not me – I said 'Good morrow, Ajax' and he
   replies 'Thanks, Agamemnon.' What think you of this man that
   takes me for the general? He's grown a very land-fish, language-   260
   less, a monster. A plague of opinion! – A man may wear it on both
   sides like a leather jerkin.

ACHILLES Thou must be my ambassador to him, Thersites.

---

240 SD] F; *after 242* Q   254 'There . . . out'] *Dyce²;* there . . . out Q, F   254 this] Q; his F   263 to him] F; *not in* Q

240 weeds garments.

240 SD I follow F's placement of Thersites' entrance, thus giving him time to move downstage
before Achilles exclaims 'A labour saved!' (242),
which marks the moment when he actually sees
Thersites. The latter has been absent since 2.3.

251–2 a stride and a stand stopping and starting. Throughout this speech, Thersites no doubt
mimics some of Ajax's absurd behaviour.

252–3 hostess . . . reckoning barmaid or
tavern-keeper who must rely on her weak brain
to sum up the bill.

253 politic regard attempt to look shrewd
(like Malvolio in *TN* or Ben Jonson's Sir Politic
Wouldbe in *Volpone*).

254 an 'twould out if it would only come
forth.

260 land-fish monstrosity (neither fish nor
fowl). Shakespeare later created a memorable character out of just such a 'monster' – Caliban in
Temp., who is described as a 'strange fish' with
'fins like arms' (2.2.27–34) but who turns out to be
far from 'languageless'.

261 opinion reputation.

261–2 A man . . . jerkin The idea is an ironic
version of that propounded earlier by Ulysses (95–
102): Ajax's 'parts' have been 'reflected' by the
'opinion' of others, and he can now claim to possess
them.

262 jerkin jacket (here, one that is reversible).

THERSITES Who, I? Why, he'll answer nobody, he professes not answering – speaking is for beggars; he wears his tongue in's arms.   265
I will put on his presence: let Patroclus make demands to me, you
shall see the pageant of Ajax.

ACHILLES To him Patroclus. Tell him I humbly desire the valiant Ajax
to invite the most valorous Hector to come unarmed to my tent,
and to procure safe-conduct for his person of the magnanimous   270
and most illustrious six-or-seven-times-honoured captain-general
of the Grecian army, Agamemnon, *et cetera*. Do this.

PATROCLUS Jove bless great Ajax!

THERSITES H'm –

PATROCLUS I come from the worthy Achilles –   275

THERSITES Ha?

PATROCLUS Who most humbly desires you to invite Hector to his
tent –

THERSITES H'm –

PATROCLUS And to procure safe-conduct from Agamemnon –   280

THERSITES Agamemnon?

PATROCLUS Ay, my lord.

THERSITES Ha!

PATROCLUS What say you to't?

THERSITES God be wi'you, with all my heart.   285

PATROCLUS Your answer, sir?

THERSITES If tomorrow be a fair day, by eleven o'clock it will go one
way or other; howsoever, he shall pay for me ere he has me.

PATROCLUS Your answer, sir?

THERSITES Fare ye well, with all my heart.   290

ACHILLES Why, but he is not in this tune is he?

THERSITES No, but he's out o'tune thus. What music will be in him
when Hector has knocked out his brains I know not, but I am sure
none, unless the fiddler Apollo get his sinews to make catlings on.

---

266 demands] Q; his demands F   269 most valorous] F; valorous Q   272 the Grecian army, Agamemnon, *et cetera*] F;
the armie, Agamemnon Q   274, 279 H'm] Q, F *(Hum)*   285 be wi'you] *Rowe;* buy you Q, F; b'you F4   290 ye] Q;
you F   292 he's] F; *not in* Q   292 o'tune] F *(a tune);* of tune Q

265 he . . . arms he will only speak with his
weapons or his brawn, with perhaps a further
grotesque pun on 'coat of arms'.
266 put . . . presence assume his manner.
Thersites here clearly adopts his persona as a court
'fool' (236) to present his satirical 'pageant' (267).
268–72 Achilles eagerly takes up the mock-
heroic style.

288 pay . . . has me pay a price (of blows) before he defeats me.
291 in this tune acting in this way. Achilles'
question effectively breaks off the 'pageant' (267).
294 fiddler Apollo As the god of music and poetry, Apollo was often pictured with a lyre or lute.
Thersites uses suitably burlesque language.
294 catlings lute or viol strings (typically

ACHILLES Come, thou shalt bear a letter to him straight.   295
THERSITES Let me bear another to his horse, for that's the more capable
    creature.
ACHILLES My mind is troubled like a fountain stirred,
    And I myself see not the bottom of it.
                                    [*Exeunt Achilles and Patroclus*]
THERSITES Would the fountain of your mind were clear again, that I   300
    might water an ass at it. I had rather be a tick in a sheep than
    such a valiant ignorance.   [*Exit*]

[**4.1**]   *Enter at one door* AENEAS *with a torch, at another* PARIS,
DEIPHOBUS, ANTENOR, DIOMEDES *the Grecian, with torches*

PARIS See ho, who is that there?
DEIPHOBUS It is the Lord Aeneas.
AENEAS Is the prince there in person?
    Had I so good occasion to lie long
    As you, Prince Paris, nothing but heavenly business   5
    Should rob my bed-mate of my company.
DIOMEDES That's my mind too. Good morrow, Lord Aeneas.
PARIS A valiant Greek, Aeneas, take his hand,
    Witness the process of your speech, wherein
    You told how Diomed a whole week by days   10
    Did haunt you in the field.

295 bear] Q; carry F   **299** SD] Capell (subst.); Exit / Rowe; not in Q, F   **302** SD] Capell; Exeunt / Rowe; not in Q, F
Act 4, Scene 1   **4.1**] Rowe (subst.); not in Q, F   **0** SD.1 AENEAS with a torch] F; Æneas Q; Æneas; Servant, with a torch,
preceding / Capell   **0** SD.2 DIOMEDES the Grecian] Q, F (subst.); and Diomede Rowe; Diomedes and Others / Malone
5 you] F; your Q   **9** wherein] Q; within F   **10** a] Q; in a F

made of catgut). Shakespeare seems to have invented the word in this sense; one of the comically named musicians in *Rom.* 4.5 is Simon
Catling.
    298–9 Another example of Shakespeare's re-
markable capacity to shift the tone: from burlesque
satire, we move abruptly to poetic self-scrutiny, and
then, in Thersites' final comments, to bitter mockery.
    302 ignorance fool.

Act 4, Scene 1
    0 SD Before dawn (hence the need for torches),
the Trojan lords go with Diomedes to complete the

exchange of Cressida for Antenor. Though Antenor
says not one word in the play, his silent presence
can have a powerful theatrical effect, since he embodies the forces that separate Troilus and Cressida.
    3 prince Paris.
    4–6 The banter here ironically foreshadows the
impending departure of Troilus from Cressida's
bed (4.2).
    4 occasion reason (*OED sb*[1] 2).
    9 Witness Attest to.
    9 process drift, tenor. Aeneas has presumably
praised Diomedes on some previous occasion.
    10 by days daily.

AENEAS   Health to you, valiant sir,
    During all question of the gentle truce;
    But when I meet you armed, as black defiance
    As heart can think or courage execute.

DIOMEDES The one and other Diomed embraces.   15
    Our bloods are now in calm and, so long, health!
    But when contention and occasion meet,
    By Jove I'll play the hunter for thy life
    With all my force, pursuit, and policy.

AENEAS And thou shalt hunt a lion that will fly   20
    With his face backward. In humane gentleness,
    Welcome to Troy; now, by Anchises' life,
    Welcome indeed! By Venus' hand I swear
    No man alive can love in such a sort
    The thing he means to kill more excellently.   25

DIOMEDES We sympathise. Jove, let Aeneas live,
    If to my sword his fate be not the glory,
    A thousand complete courses of the sun;
    But in mine emulous honour let him die
    With every joint a wound, and that tomorrow.   30

AENEAS We know each other well.

DIOMEDES We do and long to know each other worse.

PARIS This is the most despiteful gentle greeting,
    The noblest hateful love, that e'er I heard of.
    What business, lord, so early?   35

---

17 But] F; Lul'd Q   17 meet] Q; meetes F   33 despiteful] Q; despightful'st F   34–5] F; *as prose* Q

12–14 Throughout any peaceful interchanges occasioned by the truce; but when I meet you on the battlefield (I will salute you) with as grim defiance as my heart can muster and my daring put into effect.

16 As long as 'our bloods' remain 'calm', I wish you health.

17 contention . . . meet opportunity to fight arises.

19 policy strategy, cunning.

21 backward turned towards his pursuer.

22, 23 Anchises, Venus Aeneas' mortal father and immortal mother.

24 sort manner.

25 more excellently The phrase can refer to Aeneas' 'excellent' love for Diomedes or the manner in which he will kill him; given the circumstances, the two possibilities are closely related.

26 sympathise agree, feel the same way.

26–8 let . . . sun let Aeneas live a thousand years if my sword does not gloriously determine his fate.

29 in . . . honour for the sake of the glory that I am jealous to preserve and augment.

33 despiteful gentle contemptuous (and) courteous; that Shakespeare thought of the two words as opposites is clear from Rosalind's remark in *AYLI*: 'It is my study / To seem despiteful and ungentle to you' (5.2.79–80). Paris' oxymoron, like his 'noblest hateful' (34), catches the ambivalence of the previous exchange, which is marked by a mix of elaborate courtesy and vengeful hostility. The hostility derives from Shakespeare's sources, the extravagantly chivalrous tone is his own addition.

AENEAS I was sent for to the king, but why I know not.
PARIS His purpose meets you: 'twas to bring this Greek
          To Calchas' house and there to render him
          For the enfreed Antenor the fair Cressid.
          Let's have your company or, if you please,   40
          Haste there before us. [*Aside to Aeneas*] I constantly believe –
          Or rather call my thought a certain knowledge –
          My brother Troilus lodges there tonight.
          Rouse him and give him note of our approach,
          With the whole quality wherefore; I fear   45
          We shall be much unwelcome.
AENEAS [*To Paris*]   That I assure you.
          Troilus had rather Troy were borne to Greece
          Than Cressid borne from Troy.
PARIS [*To Aeneas*]   There is no help:
          The bitter disposition of the time
          Will have it so. – On, lord, we'll follow you.   50
AENEAS Good morrow all.   *Exit*
PARIS And tell me, noble Diomed, faith, tell me true,
          Even in the soul of sound good fellowship,
          Who in your thoughts deserves fair Helen best,
          Myself or Menelaus?
DIOMEDES   Both alike: 55
          He merits well to have her that doth seek her,
          Not making any scruple of her soil,
          With such a hell of pain and world of charge;
          And you as well to keep her that defend her,

37 'twas] Q; it was F   41 SD] *Walker (subst.); not in* Q, F; *so too at 46 and 48*   41 believe] Q; doe thinke F   45–6] F; With
. . . wherefore: / I . . . vnwelcome. Q   45 wherefore] Q; whereof F   46–8 That . . . Troy] F; *as prose* Q   51 SD] F
(*Exit Æneas*); *not in* Q   53 the] F; *not in* Q   54 deserves . . . best] Q; merits faire *Helen* most F   57 soil] Q; soylure F

37 **meets** Both literal and figurative: Priam's
'purpose' (the exchange) is personified in Antenor
and Diomedes.
    41–50 **I constantly believe . . . follow you**
Paris, sensitive to the feelings of Troilus, sends Aeneas ahead to warn him. The little colloquy with
Aeneas takes place as the latter prepares to exit,
while the Trojan warriors entertain Diomedes on
another part of the stage.
    41 **constantly** firmly.
    42 **call my thought** let my belief be called.
    44 **give him note** tell him.
    45 **quality wherefore** reason or cause for it (i.e.

for 'our approach').
    49 **disposition** circumstances.
    56 **He** Menelaus.
    57–8 In that he remains untroubled by the taint
of her infidelity ('soil') and the painful war that followed upon it. F's 'soylure' is cited by *OED* as the
first figurative use, though the word in the literal
sense had appeared once before in 1297.
    57 **scruple** (1) moral qualm, (2) tiny unit of
weight (a meaning which only comes into play later
in the speech – see 66–7 and 71–2).
    58 **world of charge** huge cost (both financial
and human).

Not palating the taste of her dishonour,   60
With such a costly loss of wealth and friends.
He like a puling cuckold would drink up
The lees and dregs of a flat tamèd piece;
You like a lecher out of whorish loins
Are pleased to breed out your inheritors.   65
Both merits poised, each weighs nor less nor more,
But he as he, the heavier for a whore.

PARIS You are too bitter to your countrywoman.

DIOMEDES She's bitter to her country. Hear me Paris,
For every false drop in her bawdy veins,   70
A Grecian's life hath sunk; for every scruple
Of her contaminated carrion weight,
A Trojan hath been slain; since she could speak
She hath not given so many good words breath
As for her Greeks and Trojans suffered death.   75

PARIS Fair Diomed, you do as chapmen do,
Dispraise the thing that you desire to buy;
But we in silence hold this virtue well:
We'll not commend what we intend to sell.
Here lies our way.   80

Exeunt

---

66 nor less] Q; no lesse F   67 the] Q; which F; each *Dyce (conj. Johnson)*   77 you] F; they Q   79] Q, F; We'll . . . intend not sell *Warburton*; We'll but commend . . . sell *Collier² (conj. Z. Jackson)*; We'll not commend that not intend to sell *Palmer (conj. Lettsom)*

60 palating the taste sensing the (bitter) taste. This is the first instance of 'palate' being used as a verb; see also *Ant.* 5.2.7 and *Cor.* 3.1.104.

62 puling feebly querulous.

63 lees sediment (at the bottom of a container of wine).

63 piece (1) cask of wine, (2) a woman (usually derogatory). 'Flat' and 'tamèd' refer to (1) a cask that has been opened or pierced (*OED* Tame *v²* 1b), so that the wine, in being exposed to the air, has spoiled; and (2) a woman that has been similarly penetrated and used up. Diomedes' metaphor is characteristically savage and precise.

64 loins genitals; in particular, those of Helen.

66 poised set in the balance.

67 But each like the other, (is) burdened by the heaviness (sadness) of loving a whore. As Baldwin suggests, referring to the original question posed by Paris (54–5), 'neither's weight of merit would be increased' by a traditionally 'light' whore (Variorum). Once again, Diomedes' thinking is as pre-cise as it is brutal – the whole speech is sharply symmetrical.

71 scruple tiny fraction. Diomedes continues his earlier metaphor of weighing. See 57 n.

72 carrion putrefied (like a rotting carcass).

76 chapmen traders.

79 This line has generated editorial frustration, emendation, and commentary. Paris seems to imply that he intends to sell Helen, which is clearly not the case. Hence editors have emended 'not' to 'but', or 'what we' to 'that not', both of which imply that Helen is not for sale. The main point is that Paris wants to avoid a contest with Diomedes – not only because he refuses to practise the seller's art by praising Helen (as Johnson suggests – i.e. he won't play the marketing game since Helen is not for sale), but also because he has been put on the defensive by Diomedes' harsh and aggressive response to his courtly inquiry about deserving Helen. He is looking, not too successfully, for a graceful way out of an awkward situation.

[4.2] *Enter* TROILUS *and* CRESSIDA

TROILUS Dear, trouble not yourself, the morn is cold.

CRESSIDA Then, sweet my lord, I'll call mine uncle down,
                He shall unbolt the gates.

TROILUS   Trouble him not.
                To bed, to bed; sleep kill those pretty eyes,
                And give as soft attachment to thy senses   5
                As infants empty of all thought.

CRESSIDA Good morrow then.

TROILUS   I prithee now to bed.

CRESSIDA Are you a-weary of me?

TROILUS O Cressida, but that the busy day,
                Waked by the lark, hath roused the ribald crows   10
                And dreaming night will hide our joys no longer,
                I would not from thee.

CRESSIDA   .   Night hath been too brief.

TROILUS Beshrew the witch! With venomous wights she stays
                As tediously as hell, but flies the grasps of love
                With wings more momentary-swift than thought.   15
                You will catch cold and curse me.

CRESSIDA   Prithee tarry;
                You men will never tarry.
                O foolish Cressid, I might have still held off
                And then you would have tarried. Hark, there's one up.

Act 4, Scene 2   4.2] *Pope (subst.); not in* Q, F   4 kill] Q, F; seal *Rowe²;* lull *Hudson² (conj. Lettsom)*   11 joys] Q;
eyes F   14 tediously] Q; hidiously F   15 momentary-swift] *Pope;* momentary swift Q; momentary, swift F

Act 4, Scene 2
1 The line places the scene outdoors; subsequent
dialogue makes it clear that the setting is a courtyard within the gates of Calchas and Cressida's
house.
4 **kill** close, overpower. While Troilus clearly has
a gentle meaning in mind, the unconscious violence
of the phrase connects this moment of 'sweet sorrow' (*Rom.* 2.2.184) to the harsher realities of war.
5 **attachment** imprisonment.
6 **As** As do.
10 **ribald** raucously abusive. The implication is
that the crows, having drowned out the sweet sound
of the lark, the traditional bird of dawn that separates young couples (cf. *Rom.* 3.5.1–7), are irrev-
erently mocking the lovers. The crows may also be
associated with carrion on the battlefield and hence
serve as a reminder of war in the midst of love.

13 **Beshrew** Curse.
13 **witch** night (personified).
13–15 **With venomous ... thought** Night
drags by ('stays') tediously for people ('wights')
burdened by hateful ('venomous') feelings, but flies
rapidly away from the 'grasps' of lovers who would
like to slow her passage.
17–19 These lines reveal much about Cressida's
sense of vulnerability; she is painfully aware that
she has thrown away the protective cover she had
consciously created for herself while still 'holding
off' (see 1.2.242–55). The phrasing may also suggest previous experience of men not 'tarrying' (running off after getting their sexual pleasure? Having
insufficient staying power?), though such a possi-
blility remains ambiguous. Troilus' unwillingness
to 'tarry' is strongly emphasised in his first appearance (1.1.14–24).

PANDARUS (*Within*) What's all the doors open here? 20
TROILUS It is your uncle.
CRESSIDA A pestilence on him! Now will he be mocking – I shall have
such a life.

Enter PANDARUS

PANDARUS How now, how now, how go maidenheads? Hear you, maid,
where's my cousin Cressid? 25
CRESSIDA Go hang yourself, you naughty mocking uncle!
You bring me to do, and then you flout me too.
PANDARUS To do what? To do what? Let her say what. What have I
brought you to do?
CRESSIDA Come, come, beshrew your heart! You'll ne'er be good nor 30
suffer others –
PANDARUS Ha, ha! Alas, poor wretch, ah, poor *chipochia*! Has't not slept
tonight? Would he not, a naughty man, let it sleep? A bugbear take
him!

---

20 SD] F; *not in* Q   23 SD] F (*after 21*); *placed here* / Capell; *not in* Q   24 Hear you] F; Heere you Q; Here, you Capell
24–5] Pope; *as verse* (maiden-heads, / Heere) Q, F (*subst.*)   28–9] Pope; *as verse* (what, / What) Q, F (*subst.*)   32 ah]
Dyce; a Q, F   32 chipochia] Q, F (*subst.*); capocchia / Theobald   32 Has't] Walker (*conj. Tannenbaum*); hast Q, F

24 maid virgin. Pandarus pretends not to recognise Cressida, presumably because the girl in front of him looks like a 'maid' and therefore could not be Cressida.
26 naughty wicked (used playfully but with an edge of bitterness); see 38n.
27 do have sex (though Pandarus, in his reply, mockingly interprets the word in its ordinary sense). See also 50, 54.
31 suffer allow.
32 chipochia vagina or clitoris (and, by extension, woman or girl). Theobald (1733) thought that Q, F's '*chipochia*' was 'a Word in no living Language that I can find', and so he substituted *cappochia*, which he derived from '*capocchio*' an Italian word for blockhead or simpleton. Malone, looking up *capocchia* in John Florio's Italian–English dictionary of 1598, *A World of Words*, found that it meant 'foreskin of a man's priuie member' (Florio distinguishes *capocchio* = 'doult' or 'noddie' from '*capocchia*' though Theobald did not). Theobald's emendation has been accepted by every editor since, but no one has explained why Pandarus, who is clearly speaking to Cressida, should associate her with a man's 'priuie member'. '*Chipochia*' does not appear in Florio (though he does include '*poccia*' =

teat or nipple), but the word (as Paul Harvey has told me) seems to derive from a combination of '*che*' (= what, in the sense of 'what a – !') and '*poccia*' in a general sense of sexual parts. Though Florio doesn't say so, *poccia* was in vernacular use in a specifically genital sense: see Valter Buggione & Giovanni Casalegno, *Dizionario storico del lessico erotico italiano* (1996), p. 474, and Giacomo Devoto and Gian Carlo Oli, *Il dizionario della lingua italiana* (1990), p. 1428, who both explain '*poccia dell'amore*' as a woman's vulva. *Chipochia* thus probably derives from the simple phrase *che poccia*, which Shakespeare, having heard, understood not as an exclamatory synecdoche (a part for the whole) for a desirable woman, but as a single word connoting the most desirable sexual part. He therefore made it part of Pandarus' mock sympathy (while spelling it in his characteristically casual way).
32 Has't The use of the neuter pronoun to refer to Cressida both here and in the next line signals a kind of baby-talk still in use today. But 'it' also refers suggestively to Cressida's *chipochia* (see previous note), so that, in teasing Cressida, Pandarus keeps up the anatomical byplay.
33 bugbear goblin supposed to devour naughty children, and hence an imaginary creature typically

CRESSIDA Did not I tell you? Would he were knocked i'th'head.   35
                    One knocks
Who's that at door? Good uncle, go and see.
My lord, come you again into my chamber.
You smile and mock me as if I meant naughtily.
TROILUS Ha, ha!
CRESSIDA Come, you are deceived: I think of no such thing.   40
                    Knock
How earnestly they knock. Pray you, come in –
I would not for half Troy have you seen here.
                    Exeunt [Troilus and Cressida]
PANDARUS Who's there? What's the matter, will you beat down the
    door? [*He opens the door*]

                [*Enter* AENEAS]

How now, what's the matter?   45
AENEAS Good morrow, lord, good morrow.
PANDARUS Who's there? My Lord Aeneas! By my troth, I knew you
    not; what news with you so early?
AENEAS Is not Prince Troilus here?
PANDARUS Here? What should he do here?   50
AENEAS Come, he is here, my lord, do not deny him.
    It doth import him much to speak with me.
PANDARUS Is he here say you? It's more than I know, I'll be sworn –
    for my own part, I came in late. What should he do here?
AENEAS Whoa – nay then! Come, come, you'll do him wrong ere   55

---

35 SD] *placed as in Capell; after 36* Q; *after 34* F   40 SD] *Capell; after 41* Q, F   42 SD *Troilus and Cressida*] *Capell; not in* Q, F   44 SD.1 *He . . . door*] *Capell (subst.); not in* Q, F   44 SD.2 *Enter* AENEAS] *Rowe (after 45); not in* Q, F   53 It's] Q *(its);* 'tis F   55 Whoa] Q, F *(Who); Pho Theobald; Whoo Johnson; Ho Walker (conj. Tannenbaum)*

invoked by nurses to frighten children into obedience (*OED*). The term continues the baby-talk motif (see previous note).

38 meant naughtily had wicked intentions. The word 'naughty' echoes through this sequence, usually with sexual overtones; it could carry a much stronger meaning in Elizabethan English than it typically does now, but Cressida's use of it here is both playful and defensive. She insists, no doubt sincerely, that her suggestion that Troilus return to her chamber (37) arose not from seductiveness but from a sensible caution that he avoid discovery.

43–7 The stage action here is a little difficult to reconstruct. Q, F give no directions at all. Presumably, Pandarus goes to a door at the rear of the stage, on the other side from that through which the lovers are leaving; when he opens it, Aeneas either bursts quickly into the 'courtyard', past Pandarus, looking around for Troilus, or he remains hidden in the recesses of the opening. Some such action seems required by the fact that Pandarus does not at first recognise Aeneas ('Who's there? My Lord Aeneas!', 47), even though the dawn is well advanced.

52 doth . . . much is very important for him.

55 Whoa Baldwin (Variorum) points out that *OED* gives 'Who' (as in Q, F) as a possible spelling for 'Whoa,' the common 'stop' command used with horses (*OED* Who *int*).

55–6 do him . . . ware you will unintentionally do him harm (in feigning ignorance of his whereabouts).

you are ware; you'll be so true to him to be false to him. Do not
you know of him, but yet go fetch him hither, go.

Enter TROILUS

TROILUS How now, what's the matter?
AENEAS My lord, I scarce have leisure to salute you,
    My matter is so rash: there is at hand   60
    Paris your brother, and Deiphobus,
    The Grecian Diomed, and our Antenor
    Delivered to us, and for him forthwith,
    Ere the first sacrifice, within this hour,
    We must give up to Diomedes' hand   65
    The Lady Cressida.
TROILUS   Is it so concluded?
AENEAS By Priam and the general state of Troy;
    They are at hand and ready to effect it.
TROILUS How my achievements mock me!
    I will go meet them, and, my Lord Aeneas,   70
    We met by chance – you did not find me here.
AENEAS Good, good, my lord, the secrets of nature
    Have not more gift in taciturnity.

Exeunt [Troilus and Aeneas]

56 you are] Q; y'are F   57 SD] F; *not in* Q   63 to us, and for him] F; to him, and Q   66 so concluded] Q; concluded
so F   72 nature] F; neighbour *Pandar* Q   73 SD] *Capell; Exeunt* Q; *Exennt. / Enter Pandarus and Cressid* F

56–7 Do not . . . of him Keep pretending that
you know nothing of him.
  57 SD Troilus enters before Pandarus has time
to follow Aeneas' demand to 'fetch' him. Pandarus
remains onstage eavesdropping on the subsequent
dialogue between Aeneas and Troilus, and is thus
in a position to tell Cressida the news when she
comes in. See 73 SD n. and Textual Analysis, pp.
243–4.
  60 rash urgent.
  64 sacrifice religious observance. The reference
seems to be to pagan ceremonies performed at regular intervals during the day, and is in keeping with
many details in the play that highlight the foreign,
pre-Christian culture of the play's milieu.
  66 Is . . . concluded? However regretful he may
be, Troilus seems to accept the new situation immediately, giving up without a fight. His response
contrasts sharply with Cressida's 'I will not go from
Troy' (106), the final words of the scene.
  67 state council.
  69 Troilus thinks only of the dark irony of his
own situation – he has no sooner achieved his goal
than he is mocked by his very success. He says
nothing about Cressida or her feelings.

  71 We . . . chance Tell the others that we met
by chance. Now that the prospect of losing Cressida is imminent, Troilus has even stronger reasons
for wanting to keep the affair secret.
  72 secrets of nature Before the advent of modern science, nature was traditionally viewed as unwilling to part with her secrets. Nevertheless the
text here is problematic; commentators have noted
the metrical irregularity and either argued that 'secrets' is trisyllabic ('sec-er-ets') or suggested alternatives (such as 'secrecies'). More puzzling is
the Q reading, 'secrets of neighbour *Pandar*.' For
one thing, Pandarus is anything but close-lipped;
moreover, as Palmer points out, in Shakespeare
the word 'neighbour' is used exclusively by and
about those of middle or lower status. Perhaps
Shakespeare originally thought to draw ironic attention to Pandarus' onstage eavesdropping (he is
no doubt straining to hear what Troilus and Aeneas are saying), but then changed his mind and
selected the more appropriate and conventional
phrase.
  73 taciturnity keeping silent.
  73 SD Since Pandarus has been onstage for some
time, though he has been silent for the previous

PANDARUS Is't possible? No sooner got but lost? The devil take Antenor! The young prince will go mad – a plague upon Antenor! I   75
would they had broke 's neck.

Enter CRESSIDA

CRESSIDA How now, what's the matter? Who was here?

PANDARUS Ah, ah!

CRESSIDA Why sigh you so profoundly? Where's my lord?
        Gone? Tell me, sweet uncle, what's the matter?   80

PANDARUS Would I were as deep under the earth as I am above.

CRESSIDA O the gods! what's the matter?

PANDARUS Pray thee, get thee in; would thou hadst ne'er been born!
I knew thou wouldst be his death. O poor gentleman! A plague
upon Antenor!   85

CRESSIDA Good uncle I beseech you, on my knees I beseech you, what's
the matter?

PANDARUS Thou must be gone, wench, thou must be gone: thou art
changed for Antenor. Thou must to thy father and be gone from
Troilus; 'twill be his death, 'twill be his bane, he cannot bear it.   90

CRESSIDA O you immortal gods, I will not go.

PANDARUS Thou must.

CRESSIDA I will not uncle: I have forgot my father,
    I know no touch of consanguinity,
    No kin, no love, no blood, no soul so near me   95
    As the sweet Troilus. O you gods divine,
    Make Cressid's name the very crown of falsehood
    If ever she leave Troilus. Time, force, and death

---

74 lost?] *Hanmer;* lost, Q; lost: F   76 SD] *Theobald (Enter* Cressida *to* Pandarus*); Enter Cress.* Q *(as speech head-ing before 77); Enter Pandarus and Cressid* F *(after 73)*   78 Ah, ah] Q; Ah, ha F   79–80] *Malone; as prose* Q, F   83 Pray thee] Q; Prythee F   86 I beseech you, what's] F; whats Q

twenty lines, the *Exeunt* in both texts must refer to Troilus and Aeneas. F's direction, *Enter Pandarus and Cressid*, is probably the result of a book-keeper who, noting that the next lines after *Exeunt* in the MS. belong to Pandarus and Cressida, wrote in Pandarus' unnecessary entry. Almost all editors, with the exception of Oxford, therefore follow Q, adjusting the speech heading (77) into an entry for Cressida alone. Cressida enters to Pandarus, who is momentarily alone onstage, wringing his hands; indeed, her line makes sense only in that context. See Textual Analysis, pp. 243–4.

75 The young . . . mad Like Troilus, Pandarus seems unconcerned with Cressida's reaction to the news.

86 The repetition of 'I beseech you' in F may be a theatrical interpolation, but it nicely expresses Cressida's sense of urgency.

90 bane ruin (literally, poison).

94–6 I know . . . Troilus Noble cites Matthew 19.5: 'For this cause, shal a man leaue father and mother, and cleaue vnto his wife, and they twaine shalbe one flesh', but the allusion, if it is one, is tinged with irony.

94 touch feeling (*OED* Touch *sb* 13b; see *TGV* 2.7.18: 'Didst thou but know the inly touch of love . . .').

94 consanguinity blood relationship.

97 crown utmost top, consummation.

98 force violence.

    Do to this body what extremes you can,
    But the strong base and building of my love   100
    Is as the very centre of the earth
    Drawing all things to it. I'll go in and weep –
PANDARUS Do, do.
CRESSIDA Tear my bright hair and scratch my praisèd cheeks,
    Crack my clear voice with sobs and break my heart   105
    With sounding Troilus. I will not go from Troy.

                                     Exeunt

[4.3] *Enter* PARIS, TROILUS, AENEAS, DEIPHOBUS, ANTENOR, *and*
DIOMEDES

PARIS It is great morning, and the hour prefixed
    For her delivery to this valiant Greek
    Comes fast upon. Good my brother Troilus,
    Tell you the lady what she is to do,
    And haste her to the purpose.
TROILUS   Walk into her house;   5
    I'll bring her to the Grecian presently,
    And to his hand, when I deliver her,
    Think it an altar and thy brother Troilus
    A priest there off'ring to it his own heart.   *[Exit]*
PARIS *[Aside]* I know what 'tis to love   10
    And would, as I shall pity, I could help! –
    Please you walk in, my lords.

                                     Exeunt

99 extremes] Q; extremitie F   **102** I'll] Q; I will F   **102** weep –] *Theobald;* weepe. Q, F   **106** SD] F; *not in* Q   Act 4, Scene 3   **4.3**] *Capell (subst.); not in* Q, F   **0** SD.1 *and*] F; *not in* Q   **2** For] Q; Of F   **9** his own] Q; his F   **9** SD] *Capell (subst.); not in* Q, F   **10** SD] *This edn; not in* Q, F

100–2 Cressida compares her love to the magnetic force (gravity) that was thought to reside at the earth's core. See 3.2.159, where Troilus expresses his faithfulness in the same terms.

106 sounding echoing. The word carries other meanings: (1) 'swooning' or fainting, and (2) 'measuring the depths of', both of which may be in play, at least by association.

Act 4, Scene 3

0 SD.1 Troilus has come out of Calchas' house to meet the others involved in the exchange.

1 great morning broad daylight.

3–5 Good my brother … purpose Paris,

aware of Troilus' grief and his need to be alone with Cressida, sends him in ahead of the others.

7–9 Probably spoken *sotto voce* to Paris, since Troilus presumably does not want to broadcast his feelings.

9 SD Capell's direction makes sense, since clearly Troilus goes in ahead of the others. He could, however, exit after 11; if so, Paris' next two lines (10–11) would be addressed quietly to Troilus, in sympathetic response to the latter's anguish.

10 SD See 9 SD n. Assuming Troilus exits after 9, then 10–11 are a meditative aside; they certainly are not addressed to the rest of the group.

[4.4] *Enter* PANDARUS *and* CRESSIDA

PANDARUS Be moderate, be moderate.
CRESSIDA Why tell you me of moderation?
     The grief is fine, full, perfect that I taste
     And violenteth in a sense as strong
     As that which causeth it. How can I moderate it?   5
     If I could temporise with my affection,
     Or brew it to a weak and colder palate,
     The like allayment could I give my grief.
     My love admits no qualifying dross,
     No more my grief in such a precious loss.   10

Enter TROILUS

PANDARUS Here, here, here he comes! Ah, sweet ducks!
CRESSIDA [*Embracing him*] O Troilus, Troilus!
PANDARUS What a pair of spectacles is here – let me embrace too! 'O
  heart', as the goodly saying is,
     O heart, heavy heart!   15
     Why sigh'st thou without breaking?
  where he answers again:
     Because thou canst not ease thy smart
     By friendship nor by speaking.
  There was never a truer rhyme. Let us cast away nothing, for we   20
  may live to have need of such a verse – we see it, we see it. How
  now, lambs!

Act 4, Scene 4   4.4] *Capell (subst.); not in* Q, F   **4** violenteth] Q; *no lesse* F   **6** affection] F; affections Q   **9** dross] Q; *crosse* F   **10** SD] Q; *after 9* F   **11** Ah] *Johnson (subst.);* a Q, F   **11** ducks] Q; *ducke* F   **12** SD] *Malone, after Capell (throwing herself upon him); not in* Q, F   **13–14** 'O heart'] *Theobald (subst.);* Oh heart Q, F *(subst.)*   **15–16, 18–19]** *Pope; as prose* Q, F   **16** sigh'st] Q *(subst.);* sighest F

Act 4, Scene 4
4 violenteth rages, disturbs. Shakespeare frequently turns adjectives and nouns into verbs. While 'violent' was occasionally used as a transitive verb before Shakespeare, this is the only instance cited in *OED* of the word being used intransitively.
6 temporise with moderate.
7 brew . . . palate water down (my affection) to make it less passionate.
8 allayment tempering, dilution.
9–10 My love . . . grief Since my love contains no diluting impurity ('qualifying dross'), my grief too must be undiluted (for qualify = dilute, see

Oth. 2.3.39–40 'one cup . . . and that was craftily qualified').
13 pair of spectacles sight, with a gratuitous pun on eye-glasses.
14 goodly saying Pandarus' 'rhyme' (20), may be a traditional ballad, but is more likely an invention illustrating his sententiousness. It has not been identified, but Bevington[2] links it to the proverb, 'Grief pent up will break the heart' (Dent G449).
17–19 The heart ('he') responds to the lover ('thou'), who has no way except sighing to assuage his grief.

TROILUS Cressid, I love thee in so strained a purity
              That the blest gods, as angry with my fancy,
              More bright in zeal than the devotion which   25
              Cold lips blow to their deities, take thee from me.
CRESSIDA Have the gods envy?
PANDARUS Ay, ay, ay, ay, 'tis too plain a case.
CRESSIDA And is it true that I must go from Troy?
TROILUS A hateful truth.
CRESSIDA   What, and from Troilus too?   30
TROILUS From Troy and Troilus.
CRESSIDA   Is't possible?
TROILUS And suddenly – where injury of chance
              Puts back leave-taking, jostles roughly by
              All time of pause, rudely beguiles our lips
              Of all rejoindure, forcibly prevents   35
              Our locked embrasures, strangles our dear vows
              Even in the birth of our own labouring breath.
              We two that with so many thousand sighs
              Did buy each other must poorly sell ourselves
              With the rude brevity and discharge of one.   40
              Injurious time now with a robber's haste
              Crams his rich thiev'ry up he knows not how:
              As many farewells as be stars in heaven,

---

23 strained] Q; strange F   40 one] Q; our F   42 thiev'ry] Q *(theeu'ry)*; theeuerie F

23 so strained a purity such a pure, unqualified way. Troilus adopts the language of purity and dilution that Cressida introduced before his entrance (7–10).
24 fancy love.
25 More . . . zeal (Which is) more passionate and devoted.
26 Cold lips i.e. the lips of those whose religious devotion is so much less 'bright in zeal' (25) than Troilus' love.
32–47 Troilus seems more concerned with rhetoric than Cressida in this speech; he is suffering, not strictly because of the impending separation, but because chance and time are robbing the lovers of an opportunity for a proper good-bye. His attitude has contributed, in several recent productions, to Cressida's dawning awareness that he may not measure up to her expectations.
32 injury of chance the cruelty of fortune
33 Puts back Thwarts.
33 jostles . . . by shunts . . . aside.

34 beguiles cheats.
35 rejoindure response (in this case, kisses). As with 'embrasures' in the next line, this is the sole citation for this word in this sense in *OED*. Shakespeare seems to have been particularly inventive with '–ure' words in composing this play. See Introduction, p. 23, and 1.3.87 n.
36 embrasures embraces.
37 Even as we labour to give them ('our dear vows' (36)) voice.
40 one one sigh. The metaphor is a commercial one: the lovers bought high and are forced to sell low. F's 'our' is an instance of misreading of MS., inexplicable if, as recent editors have assumed, F were printed from a copy of Q; see Textual Analysis, pp. 247–8.
41–2 The image of Time as a thief with a sack into which he 'Crams' his loot recalls Ulysses' metaphor of Time's wallet and its 'alms for oblivion' in 3.3.145–6.
42 Stuffs away his valuable stolen goods all in a jumble.

With distinct breath and consigned kisses to them,
He fumbles up into a loose adieu,   45
And scants us with a single famished kiss
Distasted with the salt of broken tears.
AENEAS (*Within*) My lord, is the lady ready?
TROILUS Hark, you are called. Some say the Genius so
Cries 'come' to him that instantly must die.   50
[*To Pandarus*] Bid them have patience, she shall come anon.
PANDARUS Where are my tears, rain to lay this wind, or my heart will
be blown up by the root!   [*Exit*]
CRESSIDA I must then to the Grecians?
TROILUS   No remedy.
CRESSIDA A woeful Cressid 'mongst the merry Greeks.   55
When shall we see again?
TROILUS Hear me my love, be thou but true of heart –
CRESSIDA I true? How now, what wicked deem is this?
TROILUS Nay, we must use expostulation kindly,
For it is parting from us.   60
I speak not 'be thou true' as fearing thee,

47 Distasted] Q; Distasting F   47 tears.] Q; teares. Enter Æneus F   49–50 Genius so / Cries 'come'] F (*subst.*); Genius / Cries so Q   50 'come'] Hanmer (*subst.*); come F   51 SD] Oxford; not in Q, F; To Aeneas / Muir   52 tears, rain] *This edn*; teares rain Q; teares? rain, F; tears? Rain, Rowe   53 by the root] F; by my throate Q   53 SD] Theobald (*subst.*); not in Q, F   56] Q; assigned to Troilus F   57 my love] F; loue Q   61 'be thou true'] Hanmer (*subst.*); be thou true Q, F; also quotation marks in 64, 73

44 distinct . . . consigned specifically marked . . . reserved. Each farewell, that is, has its own distinctive sigh and kiss.
45 fumbles up throws together.
45 loose (1) heedless, (2) jumbled.
46 scants starves. The word brings in the recurrent language of eating and tasting, continued in 'famished' (46), 'distasted', and 'salt' (47).
47 broken tears A typical Shakespearean synecdoche: it is not of course the tears, but the lovers themselves, that are broken.
47–8 Despite F's Enter Æneus after 47, the SD *within* in both texts in 48 has led most recent editors to follow Q, though Oxford has Aeneas enter and omits 'within'. (See Textual Analysis, p. 243, for a full discussion.) The scene itself is simple but telling: we hear Aeneas call, Troilus sends Pandarus to stall the visitors so he and Cressida can share a brief farewell, Aeneas (this time with Paris) interrupts again at 97, and finally the intruders enter at 107. For any of them actually to appear before this would render their eventual entrance anti-climactic.

49 Genius Guardian spirit assigned to attend on an individual during life and usher him into the underworld after death.
52–3 tears . . . root Refers to the ancient belief that rain reduces the wind (Dent R16). Pandarus wants his tears to allay ('lay') the hurricane of his feelings, or else his heart, like a great tree, will be uprooted. Q's 'by my throate' makes a kind of grotesque sense (his heart will be broken or forced up his throat), but is probably a misreading of MS.
55 merry Greeks A slang term for scurrilous or wanton rogues. Cressida puns on the literal and proverbial meanings. Compare 1.2.95.
56 see i.e. see each other.
58 deem suspicion, surmise. Cressida's anger at her lover's apparent lack of faith in her has, in several recent performances, been accompanied by a sudden awareness that Troilus may be less than she had thought. See Introduction, pp. 30–1, 63.
59–60 We must not converse roughly with each other, since the opportunity for talk between us is being cut short.
61 as fearing thee because I doubt your fidelity.

For I will throw my glove to Death himself
That there's no maculation in thy heart,
But 'be thou true' say I to fashion in
My sequent protestation: be thou true   65
And I will see thee.

CRESSIDA O you shall be exposed, my lord, to dangers
As infinite as imminent – but I'll be true.

TROILUS And I'll grow friend with danger. Wear this sleeve.

CRESSIDA And you this glove. When shall I see you?   70

TROILUS I will corrupt the Grecian sentinels
To give thee nightly visitation.
But yet be true!

CRESSIDA   O heavens, 'be true' again?

TROILUS Hear why I speak it, love:
The Grecian youths are full of quality,   75
Their loving well composed, with gifts of nature flowing,
And swelling o'er with arts and exercise;
How novelty may move, and parts with person –
Alas a kind of godly jealousy,
Which I beseech you call a virtuous sin,   80
Makes me afeard.

CRESSIDA   O heavens, you love me not!

TROILUS Die I a villain then!
In this I do not call your faith in question
So mainly as my merit: I cannot sing,
Nor heel the high lavolt, nor sweeten talk,   85

---

63 there's] F; there is Q   65–6] F; *as one line* Q   69–70] Q; And . . . danger; / Weare . . . Sleeue. / And . . .
Gloue. / When . . . you? F   72–3 To . . . true!] F; *as one line* Q   76] F (Their . . . guift of nature, / Flawing); *not in* Q
76 gifts] *Theobald²*; guift F   76 flowing] F2; Flawing F   76–7 nature flowing, / And] *Hanmer*; nature, / Flawing and
F; And Q   78 novelty] Q; nouelties F   78 person] F; portion Q   81 afeard] Q (*subst.*); affraid F

62 throw my glove extend a challenge.

63 maculation stain, imperfection.

64–5 fashion . . . protestation introduce the
following ('sequent') declaration.

69 sleeve detachable garment covering the arm,
given as a favour or token. Shakespeare probably
took the idea from Chaucer, whose Criseyde gives
Diomede a sleeve (v.1043).

71 corrupt bribe.

75–87 Troilus' depiction of the Greeks hardly
seems to match what we have seen of their behaviour.

76–7 with . . . exercise The Greek youths' skill
in loving overflows with both natural gifts and

practised art. I adopt Hanmer's lineation, which is
based on the likelihood that the Q compositor left
out one whole line, and also makes the rhetorical
parallel clear.

78 move incite to love.

78 parts with person natural gifts ('parts') together with good looks.

79 jealousy suspicion.

81 O . . . not This can be, as it was for Sophie
Okonedo's Cressida at London's National Theatre
in 1999, a terrible realisation.

84 mainly much.

85 heel the high lavolt kick up my heels in a
lively dance.

> Nor play at subtle games – fair virtues all
> To which the Grecians are most prompt and pregnant.
> But I can tell that in each grace of these
> There lurks a still and dumb-discoursive devil
> That tempts most cunningly. But be not tempted.   90

CRESSIDA Do you think I will?

TROILUS No,
> But something may be done that we will not,
> And sometimes we are devils to ourselves
> When we will tempt the frailty of our powers,   95
> Presuming on their changeful potency.

AENEAS (*Within*) Nay, good my lord –

TROILUS   Come, kiss and let us part.

PARIS (*Within*) Brother Troilus!

TROILUS   Good brother, come you hither,
> And bring Aeneas and the Grecian with you.

CRESSIDA My lord, will you be true?   100

TROILUS Who I? Alas it is my vice, my fault:
> Whiles others fish with craft for great opinion,
> I with great truth catch mere simplicity;
> Whilst some with cunning gild their copper crowns,
> With truth and plainness I do wear mine bare;   105
> Fear not my truth. The moral of my wit
> Is 'plain and true': there's all the reach of it.

92–3 No, / But] *Pope; No, but* Q, F   100 true?] Q; *true? Exit.* F   107 'plain . . . true'] *Johnson (subst.); plaine . . . true* Q, F

87 **pregnant** ready.
89 **dumb-discoursive** discoursing eloquently, though silently.
93 **will not** do not wish.
95–6 When we persist in tempting our weak powers, taking for granted our ability ('potency') to resist temptation even though it is in fact quite unstable ('changeful').
97–9 Once again voices from behind the stage wall impinge on the lovers, and again Troilus calls out an answer (see 47–8 n.). F's *Exit* after Cressida's next line (100) may suggest, as Gary Taylor argues in the *Textual Companion*, that Paris appears briefly at the door; but more likely the *Exit* was necessitated by Aeneas' presumed entrance at 47 (see 47–8 n.) and seeming re-entrance at 107.

100 From this moment till the end of the scene, Cressida remains silent.
103 **simplicity** (1) sincerity, (2) naïveté. Troilus invokes both meanings, putting his simplicity above the high reputation ('opinion', 102) that others achieve through duplicity.
104 **gild . . . crowns** counterfeit by adding a thin layer of gilt to copper coins, making them seem like gold ('crown' = a kind of coin). The image continues the contrast between craft and truth from the two previous lines and might also suggest the donning of a false or illegitimate crown.
105 **mine** i.e. his head; Troilus has cleverly shifted to yet another meaning of 'crown' (see previous note) in order to make his point about his plainness and lack of craft.

Enter [AENEAS, PARIS, ANTENOR, DEIPHOBUS, *and* DIOMEDES]

Welcome Sir Diomed! Here is the lady
Which for Antenor we deliver you;
At the port, lord, I'll give her to thy hand   110
And by the way possess thee what she is.
Entreat her fair and by my soul, fair Greek,
If e'er thou stand at mercy of my sword,
Name Cressid and thy life shall be as safe
As Priam is in Ilium.

DIOMEDES   Fair Lady Cressid,   115
So please you save the thanks this prince expects:
The lustre in your eye, heaven in your cheek,
Pleads your fair usage, and to Diomed
You shall be mistress and command him wholly.

TROILUS Grecian, thou dost not use me courteously   120
To shame the seal of my petition to thee
In praising her. I tell thee, lord of Greece,
She is as far high-soaring o'er thy praises
As thou unworthy to be called her servant.
I charge thee use her well, even for my charge,   125
For by the dreadful Pluto, if thou dost not,
Though the great bulk Achilles be thy guard,
I'll cut thy throat.

DIOMEDES   O be not moved, Prince Troilus.
Let me be privileged by my place and message

---

107 SD] *Malone; Enter the Greekes* F (*after 105*); *not in* Q   118 usage] Q; *visage* F   121 seal] Q, F; *zeal Theobald*
121 to thee] Q; *towards* F   122 In] Q; *I* F

107 SD F's direction (*Enter the Greekes*) again looks like the work of a book-keeper, since the author, we can assume, knew that only one of the newcomers is actually a Greek.
110 **port** gate.
111 **possess** tell.
116 **save the thanks** do not bother thanking Troilus for his chivalry. Diomedes insultingly ignores Troilus, turning his seductive 'arts and exercise' (77) on Cressida, thus mirroring Troilus' anxious description of Greek wiles in 75 ff.
118 **Pleads . . . usage** Assures your proper treatment.
119 **mistress** object of his courtly love – without the connotation of a sexual relationship that

the word later acquired. However, the courtly language here, as so often in the play, is a mask for predatory behaviour.
121 **seal** Editors follow Theobald almost universally in preferring 'zeal'; while 'zeal' works better with 'shame', 'seal' fits the legal metaphor ('petition') better. In any event, both meanings are clearly in play, and their sound was almost indistinguishable in some forms of Elizabethan (as modern) speech.
124 **servant** suitor or would-be courtly lover; Troilus is reacting to Diomedes' desire that Cressida become his 'mistress' (119).
125 **for my charge** because I insist on it.
126 **Pluto** The god of the underworld.

To be a speaker free; when I am hence   130
I'll answer to my lust. And know you, lord,
I'll nothing do on charge: to her own worth
She shall be prized, but that you say be't so,
I speak it in my spirit and honour, no.
TROILUS Come, to the port. I tell thee Diomed,   135
This brave shall oft make thee to hide thy head.
Lady, give me your hand and as we walk
To our own selves bend we our needful talk.
                    [*Exeunt Troilus, Cressida, and Diomedes*]
                            Sound trumpet
PARIS Hark, Hector's trumpet!
AENEAS How have we spent this morning!   140
The prince must think me tardy and remiss
That swore to ride before him to the field.
PARIS 'Tis Troilus' fault. Come, come to field with him.
DEIPHOBUS Let us make ready straight.
AENEAS Yea, with a bridegroom's fresh alacrity   145
Let us address to tend on Hector's heels:
The glory of our Troy doth this day lie
On his fair worth and single chivalry.

                                            Exeunt

131 you] Q; my F   135 I] Q; Ile F   138 SD.1] *Rann (conj. Ritson); not in* Q, F   138 SD.2] F; *not in* Q   142 to the] Q; in the F   143 him.] *Rowe;* him. Exeunt Q (subst.), F   144–8] F; *not in* Q   144 SH] *Malone (conj. Ritson); Dio.* F   148 SD] *Rowe; after 143* Q, F

131 answer . . . lust Either (1) do what I please, or (2) respond (to you) according to my desires, or perhaps both. Diomedes uses 'lust' in the general sense of 'desire', but there is deliberate provocation in his choice of a word with obvious sexual implications.
132 charge command.
136 brave boast.
138 SD.1 Neither Q nor F has an exit for the lovers and Diomedes, though Troilus' last lines seem to require one; moreover, it would be inappropriate for Paris to speak as he does (143) if his brother were still present.
143 him Hector.
144–8 These lines may have been cut in the MS. behind Q while remaining in that behind F,

though it is equally possible that they were added in the theatre to give Diomedes and Cressida a little more time to prepare for their re-entry near the beginning of the next scene. Either way, it is difficult to account for F's erroneous placement of *Exeunt* after 143 instead of at the end of the scene.
145 The irony of the bridegroom simile glances retrospectively at Troilus' 'alacrity' in 3.2.15–35, and the contrasting reluctance of the parting lovers earlier in this scene.
146 address prepare ourselves (*OED v* 3b).
148 single chivalry unique personal valour. The phrase points forward to Hector's one-on-one combat with Ajax, which follows almost immediately.

[4.5] *Enter* AJAX, *armed*, ACHILLES, PATROCLUS, AGAMEMNON,
MENELAUS, ULYSSES, NESTOR [*and others, with a trumpeter*]

AGAMEMNON Here art thou in appointment fresh and fair,
    Anticipating time with starting courage.
    Give with thy trumpet a loud note to Troy,
    Thou dreadful Ajax, that the appallèd air
    May pierce the head of the great combatant   5
    And hale him hither.
AJAX   Thou, trumpet, there's my purse:
    Now crack thy lungs and split thy brazen pipe,
    Blow, villain, till thy spherèd bias cheek
    Outswell the colic of puffed Aquilon;
    Come stretch thy chest and let thy eyes spout blood,   10
    Thou blowest for Hector.
                   [*Trumpet sounds*]
ULYSSES No trumpet answers.
ACHILLES   'Tis but early days.

Act 4, Scene 5   4.5] *Capell (subst.); not in* Q, F   0 SD.2 NESTOR] *Theobald; / Nester, Calcas. &c.* Q, F   0 SD.2 *and others*] *Capell; &c.* Q, F   0 SD.2 *with a trumpeter*] *Oxford (subst.); not in* Q, F   2 time . . . courage.] *Theobald;* time. With . . . courage, Q, F   5–6 May . . . hither] F; *as one line* Q   11 SD] *Hanmer; not in* Q, F

Act 4, Scene 5

0 SD.2 Both Q and F give an entry for Calchas here. Perhaps Shakespeare originally intended to include Calchas in the scene, but then changed his mind without deleting his name from the initial direction. That he did change his mind is reasonably clear from Diomedes' 'Lady, a word. I'll bring you to your father' (53) and Agamemnon's later greeting 'Here is Sir Diomed' which seems to indicate a re-entry. Still, as Gaudet has suggested ('Father'), the possibility of Calchas being onstage until line 63 when he presumably would exit with Cressida (and perhaps Diomedes) offers interesting choices for production (e.g. that Cressida, when she enters at 13, sees her father but wants nothing to do with him, angry as she is at the exchange that he has initiated). See Williams, 'Calchas'.

1 **appointment** looks and apparel (Ajax is well 'appointed', handsomely armed).

2 Arriving early and so displaying an eager and lively courage.

4 **appallèd** frightened.

6 **hale** draw, pull. The figure imagines the trumpet driving the frightened air into the very skull of Hector and drawing him to the combat with Ajax. See 1.3.66–8.

6 **trumpet** trumpeter.

7 **brazen pipe** While this could refer to the brass trumpet itself, more likely it means the trumpeter's wind-pipe, 'brazen' not only in association with the instrument he plays, but also in the insolent way he should affront Hector.

8 **villain** Like 'sirrah', the term denotes simply a social inferior, with no connotation of malice.

8 **spherèd bias** puffed up and rounded like a ball used in the game of bowls ('bias' = a weight or protruberance in the ball causing it to run on an oblique line).

9 The reference is to the north wind (Aquilon), frequently pictured with distended cheeks. Ajax, in an image that becomes more and more absurd as it develops, suggests that Aquilon suffers from colic, an excess of pent-up wind.

10 **spout blood** i.e. from blowing so hard.

AGAMEMNON Is not yond Diomed with Calchas' daughter?

[*Enter* DIOMEDES *and* CRESSIDA]

ULYSSES 'Tis he – I ken the manner of his gait:
He rises on the toe; that spirit of his,   15
In aspiration lifts him from the earth.
AGAMEMNON Is this the Lady Cressid?
DIOMEDES   Even she.
AGAMEMNON Most dearly welcome to the Greeks, sweet lady.
[*Kisses her*]
NESTOR Our general doth salute you with a kiss.
ULYSSES Yet is the kindness but particular –   20
'Twere better she were kissed in general.
NESTOR And very courtly counsel. I'll begin.
[*Kisses her*]
So much for Nestor.
ACHILLES I'll take that winter from your lips, fair lady.
Achilles bids you welcome.   25
[*Kisses her*]
MENELAUS I had good argument for kissing once.
PATROCLUS But that's no argument for kissing now,
For thus popped Paris in his hardiment,
And parted thus you and your argument.
[*Kisses her*]

---

13 yond] Q; yong F   13 SD] F2 *(after 12); not in* Q, F   15 toe] F; too Q   18 SD] *Collier² (subst.); not in* Q, F; *so too at*
22, 25, 29, 32   20–3] *Pope; as prose* Q, F   29 Q; *not in* F

13 SD Just when characters and audience are expecting Hector, a different visitor from Troy arrives, suggesting a structural and thematic parallel. The 'kissing' sequence that follows has become in recent productions one of the keynotes; since 1985 when Juliet Stevenson was manhandled while she stood vulnerable and shocked in her nightgown (barely covered by Troilus's greatcoat), productions have tended to emphasise Cressida's victimisation and the consequent importance of Diomedes in 'rescuing' her from male aggression. A few have sought to balance this with a sense of Cressida's growing awareness of her own power. See Introduction, pp. 56–7, 61–3.
14 ken recognise.
20 particular individual, belonging to only one person.
21 in general by all of us (not only by the 'general', Agamemnon), with the added sugges-

tion that it should be general practice to treat her so.
24 winter The supposed coldness attendant upon Nestor's advanced age.
26 argument theme, reason. Menelaus is thinking of when he had Helen with him; in response, Patroclus mocks him by using the word in its usual modern sense (27).
28 hardiment (1) boldness, (2) erect penis; the joke turns on the word 'in': *in* his boldness, Paris thrust ('popped') his penis *in*. Shakespeare may have taken the pun from Chaucer: 'Artow in Troie, and hast non hardyment / To take a womman which that loveth the' (IV. 533–4).
29 parted separated, but with the added suggestion of Paris' sexual endowment, and even perhaps a graphic image of his 'parting' Helen's labia as he 'popped in'.

ULYSSES O deadly gall and theme of all our scorns   30
       For which we lose our heads to gild his horns.
PATROCLUS The first was Menelaus' kiss, this mine:
             [*Kisses her again*]
       Patroclus kisses you.
MENELAUS   O this is trim.
PATROCLUS Paris and I kiss evermore for him.
MENELAUS I'll have my kiss, sir. Lady, by your leave –   35
CRESSIDA In kissing do you render or receive?
MENELAUS Both take and give.
CRESSIDA   I'll make my match to live,
       The kiss you take is better than you give.
       Therefore, no kiss.
MENELAUS I'll give you boot: I'll give you three for one.   40
CRESSIDA You're an odd man: give even or give none.
MENELAUS An odd man, lady? Every man is odd.
CRESSIDA No, Paris is not, for you know 'tis true
       That you are odd and he is even with you.
MENELAUS You fillip me o'th'head.
CRESSIDA   No, I'll be sworn.   45
ULYSSES It were no match, your nail against his horn.
       May I, sweet lady, beg a kiss of you?

---

37 SH MENELAUS] *White (conj. Tyrwhitt); Patr.* Q, F   38–9] *Pope; as prose* Q, F   41 You're] *Capell; You are* Q, F
43 not] F; *nor* Q

30 gall bitterness.
30 theme . . . scorns (1) reason why we are held in contempt, (2) cause of our scorn (for Menelaus and Helen).
31 lose our heads (1) put our lives in danger, (2) lose our judgement.
31 gild his horns add a false lustre to Menelaus' disgrace (horns being the sign of the cuckold).
33 trim great (spoken sarcastically).
34 Both Paris and I repeatedly 'pop in' (28) ahead of Menelaus to steal a kiss, thus preventing him from ever having the chance.
36 Cressida has been silent up to this point, a fact that many recent performances and feminist critics have stressed in order to underline her vulnerability and her need to find ways to protect herself.
36 render give.
37 I'll . . . live I'll stake my life, I'll bet.
38–9 Cressida keeps up the mockery of Menelaus, declaring that, since his kisses are less

valuable than hers, she will not make the exchange.
40 boot odds (continuing the betting metaphor).
41 odd singular (both 'strange' and 'single' – i.e. without a mate). Cressida moves wittily from one meaning to another: from betting odds, to singularity, to odd as the opposite of even.
42–4 Menelaus, struggling to keep up, retorts that every man is a unique individual; but Cressida, showing her ability to juggle a number of meanings, refutes this, saying that Paris cannot be 'odd' since he is 'even' with Menelaus, i.e. he has both settled accounts and is part of a couple, while Menelaus is still odd man out, and no doubt still at odds with Paris.
45 fillip flick your finger (implying that her wit is getting close to the bone).
46 Her fingernail can do no harm against his cuckold's horn (both are made of the same material). Ulysses hence expresses agreement with Cressida's denial in the previous line.

CRESSIDA You may.

ULYSSES   I do desire it.

CRESSIDA   Why, beg then.

ULYSSES Why then, for Venus' sake, give me a kiss

When Helen is a maid again and his.   50

CRESSIDA I am your debtor: claim it when 'tis due.

ULYSSES Never's my day, and then a kiss of you.

DIOMEDES Lady, a word. I'll bring you to your father.

[Diomedes and Cressida talk aside]

NESTOR A woman of quick sense.

ULYSSES   Fie, fie upon her!

There's language in her eye, her cheek, her lip,   55

Nay her foot speaks, her wanton spirits look out

At every joint and motive of her body.

O these encounterers, so glib of tongue,

That give a coasting welcome ere it comes,

48 then] Q, F; two *conj. Johnson;* too *conj. Ritson*   50 his.] *Capell;* his – Q, F   53 SD] *Oxford (subst.); not in* Q, F
55 language] Q; a language F   59 a coasting] Q, F; accosting *Hudson (conj. Theobald)*

48 then Most recent editors have emended 'then' to 'too' (or, following Johnson, 'two') in order to maintain the pattern of rhymed couplets running through this section of witty repartee. However, the pattern is broken at 32, 39, and 42, and disturbed at 37; so making an emendation that strains the sense instead of improving it seems unjustified. (While Ritson first suggested 'too', he did so in the context of refuting Johnson, and indicated that it did unnecessary 'violence' to the text.)

50 his i.e. Menelaus'.

51 when 'tis due i.e. never, since Helen will never be a maid again, nor will she belong to Menelaus.

53 SD Most editors have Diomedes and Cressida exit here, which is certainly possible; it seems clear that they must go off before the arrival of Troilus at 64. Oxford, followed by Bevington[2], takes F's *Exeunt* at 63 to refer to Diomedes and Cressida only, since it can hardly mean a full clearing of the stage. It makes for effective theatre if Cressida remains onstage while she is vilified by Ulysses (54ff.), especially if her behaviour contrasts with, instead of confirms, what he has to say. Perhaps the most appropriate stage action would be to have the two speak briefly apart and then begin to move offstage, so that the lines of Ulysses' speech that refer directly to Cressida (54–7) are spoken with her in full view, while the more general lines (58–63) could cover her exit with Diomedes and offer a moment of sexist solidarity

among the Greeks before the arrival of the Trojan warriors.

54 sense Either (1) wit, or (2) sensuality, or perhaps both; Nestor's comment is not necessarily negative.

55–6 There's language ... speaks Palmer notes a parallel with Proverbs 6.12–3: 'The wicked man ... maketh a signe with his eyes: he signifieth with his fete: he instructeth with his fingers.'

57 motive moving limb, movement. This meaning seems to be strictly Shakespearean (*OED sb* 6).

58 encounterers coquettes.

59 a coasting a sidelong or oblique approach. *Textual Companion* regards the popular emendation to 'accosting' as merely a modernisation, yielding the sense that she welcomes any advance (accosting = an amorous advance, as suggested by *TN* 1.3.56–7: '"Accost" is front her, board her, woo her'). But the sense here is a little different, since the point is that she welcomes what is only an oblique hint (implied by 'ere it comes'), not a frontal attack. While 'coasting' seems initially to have derived from nautical usage, it could be, as here, used metaphorically. Compare William Scott, *An Essay of Drapery* ((1635), ed. S. Thrupp, 1953), p. 35: 'he [the thrifty merchant] must never turne his back to honesty; yet sometimes goe about and coast it, using an extraordinary skil, which may be better practis'd than exprest'. A similar meaning is suggested by *H8* 3.2.38–9: 'The King in this perceives him, how he coasts / And hedges his own way.'

And wide unclasp the tables of their thoughts   60
To every ticklish reader. Set them down
For sluttish spoils of opportunity
And daughters of the game.

Exeunt [*Diomedes and Cressida*]
Flourish

ALL The Trojans' trumpet!
AGAMEMNON   Yonder comes the troop.

Enter all of Troy: HECTOR [*armed*], PARIS, AENEAS,
[TROILUS], HELENUS, *and Attendants*

AENEAS Hail all the state of Greece! What shall be done   65
To him that victory commands, or do you purpose
A victor shall be known? Will you the knights
Shall to the edge of all extremity
Pursue each other, or shall they be divided
By any voice or order of the field?   70
Hector bade ask.

---

61 ticklish] Q; tickling F   63 SD.1 *Exeunt*] F; *not in* Q   63 SD.1 *Diomedes and Cressida*] *Pope²* (subst., after 53); not in Q,
F; placed here Oxford   63 SD.2] Evans; part of following SD Q, F   64 Trojans'] Theobald; Troyans Q, F (subst.); Trojan's
Palmer   64 SD] Evans (subst.); Flowrish enter all of Troy. Q (after 63); Exennt. Enter all of Troy, Hector, Paris, Æneas,
Helenus and Attendants. Florish. F (after 63)   64 SD.1 armed] Capell; not in Q, F   64 SD.2 TROILUS] Rowe; not in Q, F
65 the] Q; you F   69 shall they] Q; shall F   70–1 By . . . ask] Rowe²; as one line Q, F

60 tables writing-tablet (often hinged). The image misogynistically links opened thoughts to an open body.

61 ticklish lecherous, easily aroused.

61 Set them down Record them (continuing the image of writing).

62 sluttish . . . opportunity 'corrupt wenches, of whose chastity every opportunity may make prey' (Johnson). Johnson's gloss almost inadvertently catches the doubleness of this condemnation, in which the so-called slut is both instigator and 'prey' of the debasement that Ulysses decries. The role of the men who despoil, while submerged, is present throughout the whole speech – and indeed has been enacted in the kissing game which immediately precedes it.

63 game i.e. the sexual game, prostitution.

63 SD See 53 SD n. Diomedes and Cressida have probably left before Ulysses finishes speaking. Productions which keep Cressida onstage after 53 have differed as to whether she should overhear Ulysses. In the 1985 RSC production at Stratford, it was unclear whether a crudely manhandled Juliet Stevenson did so, but in 1998, in Michael Boyd's production, also for the RSC, Victoria Hamilton clearly did, and it crushed her.

64 Trojans' trumpet Since Rossiter (p. 133) first proposed it, many commentators have taken up the idea that this shout puns on 'Trojan strumpet'. This seems doubtful to me, though in the theatre one might hear the sound that way – and it has been made explicit in some performances (Boyd's, for example, where it was the final blow – see 63 SD n).

67 Will you Do you wish that.

68 edge . . . extremity death.

69–70 be divided . . . field be separated according to the rules of chivalric combat. The match between Hector and Ajax is represented as a medieval tournament, which can be terminated by order of the marshals.

AGAMEMNON   Which way would Hector have it?

AENEAS He cares not, he'll obey conditions.

AGAMEMNON 'Tis done like Hector.

ACHILLES   But securely done:
A little proudly and great deal misprizing
The knight opposed.

AENEAS   If not Achilles, sir,   75
What is your name?

ACHILLES   If not Achilles, nothing.

AENEAS Therefore Achilles. But, whate'er, know this:
In the extremity of great and little,
Valour and pride excel themselves in Hector,
The one almost as infinite as all,   80
The other blank as nothing. Weigh him well,
And that which looks like pride is courtesy:
This Ajax is half made of Hector's blood,
In love whereof half Hector stays at home,
Half heart, half hand, half Hector comes to seek   85
This blended knight, half Trojan and half Greek.

ACHILLES A maiden battle, then. O, I perceive you.

[*Enter* DIOMEDES]

AGAMEMNON Here is Sir Diomed. Go, gentle knight,
Stand by our Ajax; as you and Lord Aeneas
Consent upon the order of their fight,
So be it, either to the uttermost   90
Or else a breath. The combatants being kin
Half stints their strife before their strokes begin.

---

73 SH ACHILLES] *Walker; speech continued to Agamemnon* Q, F; *whole speech, 73–5 ('*Tis . . . opposed), assigned to Achilles, Theobald*   74 misprizing] Q; *disprising* F   75–6 If . . . name] *Pope²; as one line* Q, F   77 whate'er] Q, F *(what ere)*   87 SD] *Theobald (subst.); not in* Q, F   92 breath] Q; *breach* F

73 securely over-confidently.

74 misprizing undervaluing, disdaining.

78–81 In . . . nothing On scales of valour and pride, Hector (as compared to other men) is at the extreme end in both: his valour infinite and his pride non-existent.

81 Weigh Judge.

83 Ajax is Hector's cousin (his mother being Priam's sister – see 120–1) so that half his blood derives from the same source as Hector's.

84–6 These images stressing the close relations between Ajax and Hector, suggest, by implication, the basic similarity between Greeks and Trojans

and the arbitrariness of their differences.

87 maiden bloodless, without issue (though the tone is contemptuous, implying weakness or effeminacy).

87 SD Diomedes returns after delivering Cressida to her father. If however, Calchas were onstage at the beginning of the scene, Diomedes' exit and reentry would be unnecessary. See 0 SD.2 n. and 53 SD n.

91 to the uttermost to the death.

92 breath a friendly fight, done for exercise (wherein each combatant can take a 'breather').

93 stints checks.

[Ajax and Hector enter the lists]

ULYSSES They are opposed already.

AGAMEMNON What Trojan is that same that looks so heavy?   95

ULYSSES The youngest son of Priam, a true knight,
        Not yet mature, yet matchless firm of word,
        Speaking in deeds and deedless in his tongue,
        Not soon provoked nor, being provoked, soon calmed;
        His heart and hand both open and both free,   100
        For what he has he gives, what thinks he shows,
        Yet gives he not till judgement guide his bounty
        Nor dignifies an impare thought with breath;
        Manly as Hector, but more dangerous:
        For Hector in his blaze of wrath subscribes   105
        To tender objects, but he in heat of action
        Is more vindicative than jealous love.
        They call him Troilus and on him erect
        A second hope as fairly built as Hector.
        Thus says Aeneas, one that knows the youth   110
        Even to his inches and with private soul

93 SD] *Capell; not in* Q, F   **94**] F; *not in* Q   **95** SH] F; *Vlisses: / (as part of Agamemnon's speech)* Q   **96**] Q; *The . . . Priam; / A true Knight; they call him Troylus;* F   **98** in deeds] F; deeds Q   **103** impare] Q, F; impure *Hudson (conj. Johnson)*

93 SD **lists** a space set apart for the tournament (probably downstage). Ajax and Hector fight in full view of the audience (always an exciting spectacle), while the onstage spectators shout encouragement from behind, and Diomedes and Aeneas act as umpires. Oxford arranges the fight differently, beginning it offstage, with the combatants exiting here, and all the spectators going off at 117; a new scene then presents Ajax and Hector fighting. Oxford's interpretation is based on the F SD at 158, which gives an entrance to Agamemnon and the other spectators (see *Textual Companion*, pp. 435–6). Most editors since Rowe, however, have interpreted F's *Enter* at 158 as 'Come forward', yielding a much simpler and more effective arrangement, the one followed here. When Aeneas says, 'There is expectance *here* from both the sides / What further you will do' (146–7), he seems to indicate that representatives of both Greeks and Trojans are on-stage at that point, though it is true that Hector's lines at 154–6 could suggest otherwise.

94 opposed face to face (the length of the following dialogue, however, seems to indicate that some preparation is necessary before the fight can actually begin).

95 heavy sad.

96–109 Ulysses' chivalric description of Troilus is structurally parallel to his misogynistic description of Cressida (55–63).

96 F's doubling of 'They call him Troilus' has been much discussed in attempts to establish the provenance of Q and F – see Textual Analysis, pp. 240–2.

98 deedless . . . tongue modest, not boasting of his achievements.

100 free generous.

103 impare unconsidered (?), unworthy (?). Shakespeare seems to have invented the word in this sense (*OED* gives 'unequal' (from Latin *impar*) as the usual meaning). Deighton notes that as 102 qualifies the first half of 101 ('what he has he gives'), so this line qualifies the second half ('what thinks he shows'), i.e. he does not express any 'uneven' thoughts he may have.

105–6 subscribes . . . objects shows mercy to those who excite pity or 'tender' feelings. Later Troilus accuses Hector of having a 'vice of mercy' (5.3.37).

107 vindicative vindictive.

111 Even . . . inches In every detail, from top to toe (Deighton). As Bevington[2] notes, there is an 'oddly amorous' (and homoerotic) tinge to some of the language here – 'inches', 'jealous love' (107), 'erect' (108) – a feature that connects to the erotics of combat that characterise the scene as a whole. See Introduction, pp. 19–21.

111 with private soul confidentially, privately.

Did in great Ilium thus translate him to me.
                    Alarum [*Hector and Ajax fight*]
AGAMEMNON They are in action.
NESTOR Now, Ajax, hold thine own!
TROILUS Hector thou sleep'st; awake thee!   115
AGAMEMNON His blows are well disposed; there, Ajax!
DIOMEDES You must no more.
                              Trumpets cease
AENEAS   Princes, enough, so please you.
AJAX I am not warm yet: let us fight again.
DIOMEDES As Hector pleases.
HECTOR   Why then will I no more.
Thou art, great lord, my father's sister's son,   120
A cousin-german to great Priam's seed.
The obligation of our blood forbids
A gory emulation 'twixt us twain.
Were thy commixtion Greek and Trojan so
That thou couldst say 'This hand is Grecian all,   125
And this is Trojan, the sinews of this leg
All Greek and this all Troy, my mother's blood
Runs on the dexter cheek and this sinister
Bounds in my father's', by Jove multipotent,
Thou shouldst not bear from me a Greekish member   130
Wherein my sword had not impressure made
Of our rank feud. But the just gods gainsay
That any drop thou borrow'dst from thy mother,
My sacred aunt, should by my mortal sword
Be drained. Let me embrace thee, Ajax;   135

---

112 SD *Hector . . . fight*] *Rowe; not in* Q, F   117 SD] *This edn; after 116* Q, F   125–9 'This . . . father's'] *Capell (subst.);*
this . . . fathers Q, F   132 Of . . . feud] F; *not in* Q   133 drop] F; day Q

112 **translate** describe.
112 SD The sounding of trumpets (*Alarum*) announced here lasts throughout the combat, as indicated by the 117 SD *Trumpets cease* (placed beside 116–17 in Q, F). During the combat, the men on each side cheer for their champion.
116 **disposed** placed.
117 Diomedes and then Aeneas intervene to stop the fight, which has, perhaps, become dangerously heated.
121 **cousin-german** close relative, here specifi-

cally first cousin.
122 **obligation . . . blood** duties and responsibilities of our kinship.
124 Were your Greek and Trojan parts combined in such a way.
128 **dexter . . . sinister** right . . . left.
129 **multipotent** all-powerful (first *OED* citation).
130 **member** limb, body part.
131 **impressure** mark, impression.
132 **rank** impetuous, headlong.
132 **gainsay** forbid.

By him that thunders, thou hast lusty arms!
Hector would have them fall upon him thus.
Cousin, all honour to thee.

AJAX   I thank thee, Hector,
Thou art too gentle and too free a man.
I came to kill thee, cousin, and bear hence   140
A great addition earnèd in thy death.

HECTOR Not Neoptolemus so mirable,
On whose bright crest Fame with her loud'st Oyez
Cries 'This is he', could promise to himself
A thought of added honour torn from Hector.   145

AENEAS There is expectance here from both the sides
What further you will do.

HECTOR   We'll answer it:
The issue is embracement. Ajax, farewell.

AJAX If I might in entreaties find success,
As seld I have the chance, I would desire   150
My famous cousin to our Grecian tents.

DIOMEDES 'Tis Agamemnon's wish, and great Achilles
Doth long to see unarmed the valiant Hector.

HECTOR Aeneas, call my brother Troilus to me,
And signify this loving interview   155

---

143 Oyez] *Dyce (subst.);* (O yes) Q, F   144 'This . . . he'] *Hanmer (subst.);* this . . . he Q, F *(subst.)*   144 could] Q; could'st F

---

136 **him that thunders** Zeus (Jupiter).

136 **lusty** powerful, muscular (with, no doubt, a homoerotic edge – the passion of combat sliding easily into sexualised passion, as in *Cor.* 4.5.105 ff.).

137 **thus** i.e. with an embrace, clearly called for by the language.

139 **free** generous, magnanimous.

141 **addition** honorific title and thus, by extension, an augmented reputation.

142–5 **Not even** the marvellous ('mirable') Achilles, whom Fame proclaims the greatest of men, could expect to claim additional honour by tearing it from Hector.

142 **Neoptolemus** Refers to Achilles himself, though the name actually belongs to his son Pyrrhus, as Johnson was the first to point out. See Variorum.

143 **crest** Either (1) a helmet (*OED sb* 4), or possibly (2) a heraldic device placed on a coat of arms (*OED sb* 3). The figure here asks us to imagine Fame writing 'This is he, the great man' on the crest and at the same time proclaiming it like a town-crier or court official, whose defining cry was 'Oyez, oyez' – hear ye, hear ye.

146 **expectance . . . sides** i.e. both sides are waiting to hear. The line, as noted above (93 SD n.), implies that the spectators are onstage.

148 **issue is embracement** outcome is an embrace.

150 **seld** seldom.

150 **chance** i.e. to invite Hector to dinner.

153 Achilles' desire to see Hector unarmed is fulfilled not only now but later, on the field of battle, in a darker and more ironic way (5.9.5–10).

154–6 These lines indicate that the Greek and Trojan spectators are still a distance away from the 'lists', though probably still onstage (see 93 SD n.).

To the expecters of our Trojan part;
Desire them home. [*To Ajax*] Give me thy hand, my cousin,
I will go eat with thee and see your knights.

Agamemnon and the rest [come forward]

AJAX Great Agamemnon comes to meet us here.

HECTOR The worthiest of them tell me name by name –   160
But for Achilles my own searching eyes
Shall find him by his large and portly size.

AGAMEMNON Worthy all arms! As welcome as to one
That would be rid of such an enemy –
But that's no welcome; understand more clear,   165
What's past and what's to come is strewed with husks
And formless ruin of oblivion.
But in this extant moment, faith and truth,
Strained purely from all hollow bias-drawing,
Bids thee with most divine integrity,   170
From heart of very heart, great Hector, welcome!

HECTOR I thank thee, most imperious Agamemnon.

AGAMEMNON [*To Troilus*] My well-famed lord of Troy, no less to you.

MENELAUS Let me confirm my princely brother's greeting:
You brace of warlike brothers, welcome hither!   175

---

157 SD] *Bevington²; not in* Q, F   158 SD] *Rowe (subst.); Enter Agamemnon and the rest* F; *not in* Q   161 my] Q; *mine* F
163 all] Q; *of* F   165–70] F; *not in* Q   173 SD] *Rowe; not in* Q, F

156 expecters those waiting to discover the outcome of the combat.

157 Desire them home Send them back to Troy. Hector, in calling Troilus to him (154), seems to exempt his brother from the general command to the others. Perhaps he knows that Troilus intends to see Cressida, or perhaps he simply wishes to honour Troy's 'second hope' (109) by inviting him along.

158 SD See 93 SD n.; most likely the Trojans and Greeks have been on opposite sides towards the back. As Hector and Ajax clasp hands, the spectators realise that the combat is not just suspended but over, and they move forward.

162 portly imposing.

163 Worthy all arms Altogether worthy as a knight. F's 'of arms' is a much weaker phrase.

163–4 As . . . enemy You are as welcome as you can be to someone, such as myself, who would like to kill you. The hostile edge in this remark, which Agamemnon moves to withdraw in his next line, is characteristic of this part of the scene, especially the exchanges between Achilles and Hector. It

recalls, too, the verbal sparring between Aeneas and Diomedes in 4.1.11–32.

165–70 These lines, not in Q, might indicate a revision designed to soften the harshness of Agamemnon's 'welcome', or to ease the awkward movement from 164 to 171.

166–7 The destructiveness of time and the insistence on the value of the present moment are recurring motifs in the play. See especially 3.3.145–90 and 4.4.41–2. While, unlike the past, the future cannot strictly be said to be strewn with the 'husks . . . of oblivion' ('empty shells . . . of things forgotten'), Agamemnon perhaps means that the future is as much a blank as the forgotten past, or he may be saying that, once it is behind us, the future will be as irrevocably lost as the past.

169 Purified and free from any insincere deviation ('bias-drawing' refers to the curving motion of a weighted bowls ball – see 8 n.).

170 divine integrity godlike wholeness and sincerity.

171 heart . . . heart the bottom of my heart.

172 imperious imperial.

175 brace pair.

HECTOR Who must we answer?

AENEAS   The noble Menelaus.

HECTOR O you, my lord, by Mars his gauntlet thanks!
    Mock not that I affect th'untraded oath:
    Your quondam wife swears still by Venus' glove.
    She's well, but bade me not commend her to you.   180

MENELAUS Name her not now, sir, she's a deadly theme.

HECTOR O pardon, I offend.

NESTOR I have, thou gallant Trojan, seen thee oft,
    Labouring for destiny, make cruel way
    Through ranks of Greekish youth; and I have seen thee   185
    As hot as Perseus spur thy Phrygian steed,
    Despising many forfeits and subduements,
    When thou hast hung thy advancèd sword i'th'air
    Not letting it decline on the declined,
    That I have said to some my standers-by   190
    'Lo, Jupiter is yonder dealing life';
    And I have seen thee pause and take thy breath
    When that a ring of Greeks have hemmed thee in,
    Like an Olympian wrestling. This have I seen
    But this thy countenance, still locked in steel,   195
    I never saw till now. I knew thy grandsire
    And once fought with him; he was a soldier good,
    But by great Mars, the captain of us all,

---

178 that I affect th'untraded oath] F; thy affect, the vntraded earth Q   179 glove.] *Pope;* gloue, Q; Gloue F; glove; F3
187 Despising many] Q; And seene thee scorning F   188 thy] F; th' Q   190 to some] Q; vnto F   191 'Lo . . . life']
Hanmer (subst.); Loe . . . life Q, F   193 hemmed] F; shrupd Q; shrap'd *Sisson*

178 **untraded** unfamiliar, not often used. Hector
pretends to apologise for his affectation in swearing
by Mars' gauntlet, but his oath sets up the parallel with Venus' glove in the next line, and thus
allows him to mock Menelaus by reminding everyone that someone else now plays Mars to Helen's
Venus.

179 **quondam** former.

181 **deadly theme** subject for a mortal quarrel.

184 **Labouring for destiny** Doing the work of
fate (by cutting off the youth of Greece).

186 Nestor compares Hector's Trojan (Phrygian) steed to Pegasus, the winged horse that
Bellerophon, not Perseus, typically rode – see
1.3.42 and n.

187 Disdaining the opportunity to kill men already dying or subdued.

188 **hung . . . air** suspended the swing of

your raised sword. Cf. *Ham* 2.2.477–9: 'for lo
his sword, / Which was declining on the milky
head / Of reverent Priam, seem'd i' th' air to stick'.

189 **declined** those already fallen.

191 Jupiter dealing life is in direct contrast with
Fate dealing death in 184–5. Nestor's speech highlights three sides of Hector: the implacable warrior
(184–5), the merciful knight (186–91 – and see also
105–6 above), and the courageous, cool-headed soldier (192–4).

193 **hemmed** Q's 'shrupd' seems an error of
some kind. 'Shut' and 'shraped' (from 'shrape'
meaning a snare) have been suggested as corrections. F's 'hem'd' may well be a deliberate revision
(author's or actor's) or perhaps a guess by a scribe
or compositor.

195 **still . . . steel** always covered by your helmet.

Never like thee. O, let an old man embrace thee,
And, worthy warrior, welcome to our tents!   200

AENEAS 'Tis the old Nestor.

HECTOR Let me embrace thee, good old chronicle,
That hast so long walked hand in hand with time;
Most reverend Nestor, I am glad to clasp thee.

NESTOR I would my arms could match thee in contention   205
As they contend with thee in courtesy.

HECTOR I would they could.

NESTOR Ha!
By this white beard, I'd fight with thee tomorrow.
Well, welcome, welcome – I have seen the time.   210

ULYSSES I wonder now how yonder city stands,
When we have here her base and pillar by us.

HECTOR I know your favour, Lord Ulysses, well.
Ah sir, there's many a Greek and Trojan dead
Since first I saw yourself and Diomed   215
In Ilium on your Greekish embassy.

ULYSSES Sir, I foretold you then what would ensue;
My prophecy is but half his journey yet.
For yonder walls that pertly front your town,
Yon towers whose wanton tops do buss the clouds,   220
Must kiss their own feet.

HECTOR   I must not believe you.
There they stand yet, and modestly I think
The fall of every Phrygian stone will cost
A drop of Grecian blood; the end crowns all,

---

199 O, let] Q; Let F   206] F; *not in* Q   208–9] *Capell; as one line* Q, F   209–10] Q; *as prose* F

202 chronicle storehouse of memories. Hector's warmth seems genuine, though 'chronicle' suggests an awareness of Nestor's penchant for lengthy narrative.
205 arms With a pun on weapons.
205 contention battle.
210 I . . . time I remember those days (when I could have fought with the likes of Hector).
212 base and pillar i.e. Hector, the very foundation of Troy.
213 favour looks, countenance.
216 embassy This, like Ulysses' comment in 112 about meeting Aeneas in Ilium, refers to an unsuccessful meeting held in Troy early in the war, described in Caxton III.8. At that time, Ulysses,

demanding reparation for the loss of Helen, had threatened that Priam would 'die an euill death, and all thy men, and this noble and famous citie shall be destroyed'.
218 What I then prophesied is but half fulfilled.
219 pertly front stand cockily in front of.
220 wanton (1) sportive (by association with 'pertly', 219), (2) amorous (by association with 'buss').
220 buss kiss.
222 modestly at a modest estimate.
224 the end . . . all the eventual outcome is what matters (a version of the Latin proverb, *finis coronat opus* and more or less equivalent to the modern proverb, 'Time will tell'; Dent E116).

And that old common arbitrator Time   225
Will one day end it.
ULYSSES   So to him we leave it.
Most gentle and most valiant Hector, welcome!
After the general I beseech you next
To feast with me and see me at my tent.
ACHILLES I shall forestall thee, Lord Ulysses, thou!   230
Now Hector I have fed mine eyes on thee,
I have with exact view perused thee, Hector,
And quoted joint by joint.
HECTOR   Is this Achilles?
ACHILLES I am Achilles.
HECTOR Stand fair, I pray thee, let me look on thee.   235
ACHILLES Behold thy fill.
HECTOR   Nay I have done already.
ACHILLES Thou art too brief. I will the second time,
As I would buy thee, view thee limb by limb.
HECTOR O, like a book of sport thou'lt read me o'er,
But there's more in me than thou understand'st.   240
Why dost thou so oppress me with thine eye?
ACHILLES Tell me, you heavens, in which part of his body
Shall I destroy him – whether there or there or there? –
That I may give the local wound a name,
And make distinct the very breach whereout   245

225–6 And . . . end it] F; *as one line* Q   230 Ulysses, thou] Q *(subst.)*, F; Ulysses. [*To Hector*] Thou! *Oxford*
232–3 I . . . joint.] F; *as one line* Q   235 pray thee] Q; prytheeF

225–6 arbitrator . . . it Time, like an umpire,
will eventually bring the contest, and everything
else, to an end.
226 him Time.
230 thou Whether Achilles addresses this word
to Ulysses or, as in Oxford, to Hector, is uncertain, though it is probably a concluding sneer at
Ulysses before Achilles turns to his mortal enemy.
In either case, the use of the second person singular has a deliberately insulting edge – not just
here but throughout the exchange between Achilles
and Hector that follows. This dimension is lost to
speakers of modern English, though it exists in
many other languages.
233 quoted scrutinised.
233 joint limb. Palmer notes an allusion to
butchering, consistent with Achilles' subsequent
interest in hacking Hector to pieces.

233 Is this Achilles? The deliberate naïveté of
the question marks Hector's scorn. His disdain for
his opponent's pride and self-regard is reiterated
at 236, when he quickly turns away from 'quoting' Achilles. The whole exchange (233–60) is tense
with barely suppressed homoerotic violence. See
Introduction, p. 19.
239 book of sport handbook for hunters. Hector
turns the metaphor from buying livestock or human slaves to pursuing game, but he rightly finds
both comparisons insulting.
242–6 Achilles' reply continues the image
of war as a hunt, with Hector as prey. His
concentrated scrutiny of Hector's body registers an intense intimacy between hunter and
hunted.
245 And precisely identify the actual wound
from which.

Hector's great spirit flew. Answer me, heavens.

HECTOR It would discredit the blest gods, proud man,
        To answer such a question. Stand again!
        Think'st thou to catch my life so pleasantly
        As to prenominate in nice conjecture   250
        Where thou wilt hit me dead?

ACHILLES   I tell thee yea.

HECTOR Wert thou an oracle to tell me so
        I'd not believe thee. Henceforth guard thee well,
        For I'll not kill thee there, nor there, nor there,
        But, by the forge that stithied Mars his helm,   255
        I'll kill thee everywhere, yea o'er and o'er.
        You wisest Grecians, pardon me this brag:
        His insolence draws folly from my lips,
        But I'll endeavour deeds to match these words
        Or may I never –

AJAX   Do not chafe thee, cousin.   260
        And you, Achilles, let these threats alone
        Till accident or purpose bring you to't.
        You may have every day enough of Hector
        If you have stomach; the general state, I fear,
        Can scarce entreat you to be odd with him.   265

HECTOR I pray you, let us see you in the field.
        We have had pelting wars since you refused
        The Grecians' cause.

ACHILLES   Dost thou entreat me Hector?
        Tomorrow do I meet thee fell as death,

---

252 an] Q; the F   263 may have] Q; may F   267–8 We . . . cause] F; *as one line* Q   269–70 Tomorrow . . . friends] F;
as one line Q

246 **flew** Achilles' use of the past tense makes
his boast a foregone conclusion.

248 **Stand again** Perhaps Achilles has knelt during his speech to the gods, though more likely Hector simply means 'Stand forward so I can confront
you directly.'

249 **pleasantly** (1) easily, (2) mockingly.

250 **prenominate** specify in advance (continuing the language and writing metaphors
in 'quoted' (233), 'book' (239), and 'name'
(244)).

250 **in nice** with precise.

255 **stithied . . . helm** forged Mars' helmet
('stithy' being a blacksmith's anvil and, by extension, his forge).

258 **folly** foolish words.

260 **chafe thee** let yourself become angry.
Palmer notes that Ajax addresses his cousin famil-
iarly as 'thee' and Achilles formally as 'you' (261).
In contrast to his earlier absurdities, Ajax appears
here as a peacemaker.

262 Until either chance or deliberate choice
bring you to fight (which, of course, Achilles has
been avoiding up to now).

264 **stomach** (1) inclination, (2) courage.

264 **general state** whole Greek leadership.

265 **odd** at odds, willing to fight.

266–8 **I pray you . . . cause** Hector, now somewhat mollified, reverts to the more polite and formal 'you'.

267 **pelting** paltry.

269 **fell** fierce, savage.

Tonight all friends.

HECTOR   Thy hand upon that match.   270

AGAMEMNON First, all you peers of Greece, go to my tent;
There in the full convive we. Afterwards,
As Hector's leisure and your bounties shall
Concur together, severally entreat him.
Beat loud the tabourins, let the trumpets blow,   275
That this great soldier may his welcome know.
                    [*Trumpets and drums*]
                            Exeunt [*all but Troilus and Ulysses*]

TROILUS My Lord Ulysses, tell me I beseech you
In what place of the field doth Calchas keep?

ULYSSES At Menelaus' tent, most princely Troilus.
There Diomed doth feast with him tonight,   280
Who neither looks on heaven nor on earth
But gives all gaze and bent of amorous view
On the fair Cressid.

TROILUS Shall I, sweet lord, be bound to you so much
After we part from Agamemnon's tent   285
To bring me thither?

ULYSSES   You shall command me, sir.
But gentle tell me, of what honour was
This Cressida in Troy? Had she no lover there
That wails her absence?

TROILUS O sir, to such as boasting show their scars   290
A mock is due. Will you walk on, my lord?

---

272 we] Q; you F   274–5 him. / Beat . . . tabourins] F; him / To taste your bounties Q   276 SD.1 *Trumpets and drums*]
This edn (after Capell and Palmer); not in Q, F   276 SD.2 *all . . . Ulysses*] *Malone (after Rowe); not in* Q, F   281 on . . .
earth] F; vpon the heauen nor earth Q   284 you] Q; thee F   287 But] Q; As F

270 match agreement, compact (*OED sb*[1] 11),
punning as well on 'match' = contest.
272 in . . . we let us feast together in the most
convivial way possible (only *OED* citation for
'convive' as a verb).
273 bounties generosity.
274 severally entreat individually invite him
(to feast further).
275 tabourins small drums.
279 Menelaus' tent As Bevington[2] notes, this
is an ironically apt setting for the display of Cressida's infidelity.
281–3 While Ulysses has no realistic way
of knowing about Troilus' interest in Cressida
nor about the persistence of Diomedes' amorous
glances, Shakespeare indulges in a bit of theatrical

sleight of hand in order both to advance the plot
by setting up the betrayal scene (5.2) and to initiate
the discomforting of Troilus.
282 bent inclination.
284–6 Shall . . . thither Troilus seems hardly
to have noticed Ulysses' remarks on Diomedes' infatuation; or it may be that his host's description
confirms his own anxieties.
287 gentle courteously.
288–9 Had . . . absence Again, Ulysses, for all
his courtly rhetoric, seems to be rubbing salt in
Troilus' wound.
290–1 to . . . due Troilus answers Ulysses' question indirectly, by saying that to boast about
the wounds of love is to subject oneself to
mockery.

> She was belov'd, she loved, she is and doth,
> But still sweet love is food for Fortune's tooth.

Exeunt

[**5.1**] *Enter* ACHILLES *and* PATROCLUS

ACHILLES I'll heat his blood with Greekish wine tonight,
    Which with my scimitar I'll cool tomorrow.
    Patroclus, let us feast him to the height.
PATROCLUS Here comes Thersites.

Enter THERSITES

ACHILLES How now, thou cur of envy,   5
    Thou crusty botch of nature, what's the news?
THERSITES Why thou picture of what thou seem'st, and idol of idiot
    worshippers, here's a letter for thee.
ACHILLES From whence, fragment?

---

292 she loved] F; my Lord' Q   Act 5, Scene 1   5.1] *Rowe (subst.); not in* Q, F   5 cur] Q; core F   6 botch] *Theobald;* batch Q, F   7–8] F; *as verse (*Idoll, / Of*)* Q   7 seem'st] F; seemest Q

293 Fortune has the proverbial 'sweet tooth' (Dent T420) and will readily devour the confections of love. Troilus' phrasing, like his insistent repetition of 'Be true' in the departure scene (4.4.57–96), suggests that he expects to be betrayed.

Act 5, Scene 1
1 **heat his blood** warm Hector's blood both literally (wine being thought to have a caloric effect) and metaphorically (i.e. stir his passions). This contrasts with the two senses of 'cool' in the next line – cool his blood by shedding it (literal) and freeze him in fear (metaphorical).
2 **scimitar** a curved Turkish or Persian sword that Shakespeare elsewhere associates with exotic figures (Aaron in *Tit.* (4.2.91) and the Prince of Morocco in *MV* (2.1.24)).
3 **height** utmost.
5 **cur of envy** envious dog. This, along with 'batch'/'botch' in the next line, is a difficult but richly revealing crux. Thersites is often called a dog or cur (see 27, and 2.1.6, 44, 46). The F reading, 'core' of envy, where core = (1) centre, and (2) a hard mass of tissue at the centre of a boil, is more difficult but nevertheless works well with surrounding images and may be a revision (or Q's 'Curre' may be a misreading). See following note and 5.9.1 n.

6 **crusty botch** ill-tempered, scabby mistake (nature, in making you, has 'botched' her work). Q, F's 'batch' has been accepted by some recent editors (Evans, Bevington[2]), on the basis of a submerged baking metaphor (linking to 'crusty'). But associating Thersites with a fresh batch of bread hardly seems insulting; 'botch' (Theobald's emendation) has the added meaning of tumour, boil, or ulcer (*OED sb*[1]) which is clearly relevant as well and connects with F's 'core' in the previous line (Thersites himself uses the phrase 'botchy core' (2.1.5), meaning rotten or ulcerous centre). Taken together, the two insults in lines 5–6 illustrate the textual difficulties of the play: both 'core of envy' and 'cur of envy' make sense, both are relevant to Thersites, and both are consistent with the play's language. 'Core' links nicely with 'botch' = ulcer and with 'crusty' = scabby, while 'cur' links to 'botch' in the sense of nature's mistake (Shakespeare did not much care for dogs) as well as to 'crusty' = harsh, bad-tempered; there could even be a further association with 'bitch'. And 'batch', while it may simply be a peculiar Shakespearean spelling, connects with 'crusty' (bread).
7 **picture . . . seem'st** i.e. your outward appearance matches what you are (an idiot).
9 **fragment** leftover bit, scrap.

THERSITES Why thou full dish of fool, from Troy. 10
    [*Achilles takes letter and reads apart*]
PATROCLUS Who keeps the tent now?
THERSITES The surgeon's box or the patient's wound.
PATROCLUS Well said, adversity, and what need these tricks?
THERSITES Prithee be silent, boy, I profit not by thy talk. Thou art
    said to be Achilles' male varlet. 15
PATROCLUS Male varlet, you rogue, what's that?
THERSITES Why, his masculine whore. Now the rotten diseases of the
    south, the guts-griping, ruptures, catarrhs, loads o'gravel in the
    back, lethargies, cold palsies, raw eyes, dirt-rotten livers, wheezing
    lungs, bladders full of imposthume, sciaticas, lime-kilns i'th'palm, 20
    incurable bone-ache, and the rivelled fee-simple of the tetter, take
    and take again such preposterous discoveries.
PATROCLUS Why thou damnable box of envy, thou, what mean'st thou
    to curse thus?
THERSITES Do I curse thee? 25

---

10 SD] *Capell (subst.); not in* Q, F **13** need these] F*; needs this* Q **14–15**] F*; as verse (*talke, / Thou*)* Q **14** boy] F*;*
box Q **15** said] Q*;* thought F **18** the guts-griping] Q *(hyphen omitted);* guts-griping F **18** catarrhs] F*; not in* Q
18 in the] Q*;* i'th' F **19–21** raw . . . tetter] Q*; and the like* F **20** lime-kilns] Q *(*lime-kills*)* **23** mean'st] F*;* means Q

10 full dish of complete (playing on 'frag-ment' from the previous line and perhaps hinting at 'fool' = a dessert made with cream and fruit).

11 keeps stays in. Patroclus is indicating with his rhetorical question what Achilles has already told us in 1–2, that he will no longer keep to his tent but prepare to fight Hector.

12 Thersites puns on 'tent' (11) meaning a sur-geon's probe or piece of gauze used for cleaning a wound.

13 adversity i.e. a person who goes against the grain, referring to Thersites' enjoyment of perverse word-play.

13 what . . . tricks why keep playing these (verbal) games.

15 male varlet homosexual lover. 'Varlet' means simply 'servant', but the sense in which Thersites uses it here clearly suggests a sexual relationship, and, given 'masculine whore' (17), an unequal one (the word chimes with 'harlot'). Classical writers frequently mention an erotic bond between Achilles and Patroclus (see Variorum), though usually without Thersites' characteristically cyni-cal, even debased, attitude towards it. Productions since the 1960s have typically exploited this as-pect, sometimes ludicrously, sometimes with great sensitivity – as in Nunn's 1999 production, in which theirs seemed the play's most deeply felt relationship.

17–22 Now . . . discoveries Thersites' imagina-tive list of diseases catalogues the unfortunate re-sults of 'preposterous' (22) sexual activity.

17–18 diseases of the south venereal dis-eases, supposed to come from 'warmer' climes. See 'Neapolitan bone-ache' (2.3.15).

18 guts-griping colic.

18 catarrhs profusion of mucus.

18–19 gravel in the back kidney stones.

19 palsies paralysis.

20 imposthume abscess.

20 sciaticas back-aches.

20 lime-kilns extreme heat (from psoriasis).

21 rivelled . . . tetter permanent ('fee-simple' = absolute possession of land) shrivelling eruptions of the skin ('tetter' = impetigo, ring-worm, and other such skin diseases).

21 take strike.

22 preposterous discoveries perverse mani-festations. Literally, preposterous means backside foremost (cf. modern slang 'ass-backwards'), with obvious sodomitical overtones (see Parker, pp. 20–55, for a full discussion). Some early editors re-garded 'discoveries' as the direct object of 'take' and emended to 'discoverers'; however, what Ther-sites seems to be saying is 'May these diseases strike you and, by doing so, make manifest your perversity.'

23 box of envy container stuffed with envy.

PATROCLUS Why no, you ruinous butt, you whoreson indistinguishable
   cur, no.
THERSITES No? Why art thou then exasperate, thou idle immaterial
   skein of sleave-silk, thou green sarcenet flap for a sore eye, thou
   tassel of a prodigal's purse thou? Ah, how the poor world is   30
   pestered with such waterflies, diminutives of nature!
PATROCLUS Out, gall!
THERSITES Finch egg!
ACHILLES My sweet Patroclus, I am thwarted quite
   From my great purpose in tomorrow's battle: 35
   Here is a letter from Queen Hecuba,
   A token from her daughter, my fair love,
   Both taxing me and gaging me to keep
   An oath that I have sworn. I will not break it.
   Fall Greeks, fail fame, honour or go or stay,   40
   My major vow lies here: this I'll obey.
   Come, come Thersites, help to trim my tent,
   This night in banqueting must all be spent.
   Away, Patroclus.

                              [*Exeunt Achilles and Patroclus*]

---

27 cur, no.] Q; Curre. F   29 sleave] Q *(sleiue)*; Sleyd F   43–4] F; *as one line* Q   44 SD] Hanmer; *Exit.* F; *not in* Q

26–7 Patroclus' denial is in one sense sarcastic,
since it is obvious that Thersites *has* been cursing
him, but it would also seem to indicate a refusal to
be branded as a sodomite.
26 ruinous butt broken-down cask.
26 indistinguishable (1) without shape, deformed (2) without distinction, socially inferior.
28 exasperate aggravated.
28–9 idle . . . silk worthless bundle of silk
strands. Johnson comments that Thersites' insults
in this passage are all 'expressive of flexibility, com-
pliance, and mean officiousness' (Variorum), and
Palmer adds effeminacy and dependency; a further
similarity is that all of them emphasise the 'diminutive' (31).
29 sarcenet silk taffeta (coloured green presumably because of Patroclus' raw youth and inexperi-
ence).
30 tassel dangling ornament. With 'purse' (=
scrotum), the word also carries a genital suggestion, Patroclus as a 'prodigal' (spent) penis.
31 waterflies affected courtiers – such as Osric,
who prompts Hamlet to mockery ('Dost know this
waterfly?' *Ham.* 5.2.83–4).
31 diminutives of nature tiny insignificant
creatures.

32 gall lump of bitterness.
33 Finch egg Continuing the idea of natural
'diminutives' (31) – both bird and egg are tiny and
inconsequential.
34 Achilles, having read his letter, breaks into
the snarling row between Patroclus and Thersites just when it is threatening to become
tedious.
37 my fair love Polyxena, mentioned derisively
by Ulysses (3.3.209).
38 taxing chiding (because he had threatened to
break his oath to her).
38 gaging binding, engaging.
39 oath Upon seeing Polyxena and falling in love
with her, Achilles swore to Hecuba that he would
stop fighting and try to prevail upon the Greeks
to give up the siege if only she would grant him
Polyxena as his lover. In Caxton, all this happens
after the death of Hector; Shakespeare adapts the
story to serve his own purposes. Note that Achilles'
love for the Trojan princess is compatible with his
erotic relation with Patroclus.
40 Regardless of whether the Greeks lose, or my
reputation ('fame') suffers, whether my honour disappears or remains.
42 trim spruce up, tidy.

THERSITES With too much blood and too little brain, these two may   45
run mad; but if with too much brain and too little blood they do,
I'll be a curer of madmen. Here's Agamemnon, an honest fellow
enough and one that loves quails, but he has not so much brain as
earwax, and the goodly transformation of Jupiter there, his brother
the bull, the primitive statue and oblique memorial of cuckolds, a   50
thrifty shoeing-horn in a chain hanging at his brother's leg – to
what form but that he is should wit larded with malice and malice
farced with wit turn him to? To an ass were nothing, he is both
ass and ox; to an ox were nothing, he is both ox and ass. To be a
dog, a mule, a cat, a fitchew, a toad, a lizard, an owl, a puttock,   55
or a herring without a roe, I would not care, but to be Menelaus
I would conspire against destiny. Ask me not what I would be if
I were not Thersites, for I care not to be the louse of a lazar, so I
were not Menelaus. Hey-day, sprites and fires!

---

49 brother] F; be Q   51 hanging at his brother's] F; at his bare Q   53 farced] F (forced); faced Q   54 he is] F; her's
Q   55 dog] F; day Q   55 mule] Q (Moyle), F   57 not what] F; what Q   59 Hey-day, sprites] Q (subst.); Hoy-day,
spirits F

45 blood both (1) sexual desire, and more generally (2) passion and irrationality.

46–7 but . . . madmen but if they were to run mad from having more brain than 'blood' (clearly an impossibility in that they have so little brain and so much irrational desire), I'll profess myself a doctor who can cure madness (another highly unlikely eventuality).

48 quails prostitutes. 'The bird . . . was from ancient times associated with lustful aggressiveness' (Williams, *Glossary*).

50 bull Menelaus, with reference to his cuckold's horns, and by extension, an ironic version of Jupiter who transformed himself into a bull in pursuit of Europa.

50 primitive . . . memorial original and (paradoxically) indirect or inexact image. 'Primitive statue' refers to Menelaus as the archetypal cuckold, but the second half of the epithet seems to have slipped over to refer more generally to the bull whose horns make him only an oblique rather than a direct image ('memorial') of cuckoldry. Thersites' mind sometimes runs ahead of his expression.

51 thrifty . . . leg handy instrument ready at any time to be used by Agamemnon. The cuckold's 'horn' suggests another kind of horn to Thersites, who remarks on Menelaus' dependent position as well as his usefulness to his brother as a 'pretext for invading Troy' (Nares, quoted in Variorum).

Thersites' extravagant flights should not be taken realistically – Elizabethan gentlemen did not normally walk around with shoe-horns dangling from their legs.

51–3 to what . . . him to? i.e. what more appropriate shape, different from what he is already, could a malicious wit (such as mine) invent for him? Implicit throughout this speech are references to Ovid's *Metamorphoses*, a text whose stories of transformation fascinated Shakespeare throughout his career.

52, 53 larded, farced stuffed (the terms are both from cookery and mean almost the same thing). See 2.3.206 n.

53–4 To an . . . and ass To transform him to either ass or ox would be redundant since he is already both (i.e. a fool and a cuckold).

55 fitchew polecat (a kind of weasel).

55 puttock kite or buzzard.

57 conspire against destiny fight against my fate (of being transformed into Menelaus).

58 I care . . . lazar I would not mind being a louse on a leper (i.e. vermin on the most feared and despised category of person).

59 Hey-day An exclamation denoting wonder or surprise.

59 sprites and fires Thersites pretends to take the approaching torches as supernatural flames, or 'will o' the wisps'.

Enter HECTOR, [TROILUS,] AJAX, AGAMEMNON, ULYSSES,
NESTOR, [MENELAUS,] *and* DIOMEDES, *with lights*

AGAMEMNON We go wrong, we go wrong.
AJAX   No, yonder 'tis,   60
   There, where we see the lights.
HECTOR   I trouble you.
AJAX No, not a whit.

Enter ACHILLES

ULYSSES   Here comes himself to guide you.
ACHILLES Welcome brave Hector, welcome princes all!
AGAMEMNON So now, fair prince of Troy, I bid good night.
   Ajax commands the guard to tend on you.   65
HECTOR Thanks and good night to the Greeks' general.
MENELAUS Good night, my lord.
HECTOR Good night, sweet lord Menelaus.
THERSITES Sweet draught! 'Sweet' quoth'a, sweet sink, sweet sewer.
ACHILLES Good night and welcome, both at once to those   70
   That go or tarry.
AGAMEMNON Good night.
                          Exeunt Agamemnon [and] Menelaus
ACHILLES Old Nestor tarries, and you too, Diomed,
   Keep Hector company an hour or two.
DIOMEDES I cannot, lord, I have important business,   75
   The tide whereof is now. Good night, great Hector.
HECTOR Give me your hand.
ULYSSES [*Aside to Troilus*] Follow his torch, he goes to Calchas' tent;
   I'll keep you company.
TROILUS   Sweet sir, you honour me.
HECTOR And so good night.
                  [*Exit Diomedes, Ulysses and Troilus following*]

59 SD.1 HECTOR . . . AJAX] *Theobald; Hector, Aiax* F; *not in* Q   59 SD.2 MENELAUS] *Capell; not in* Q, F   59 SD.2 *and*]
Q; *not in* F   60–1 No . . . lights] *Capell; as one line* Q, F   61 lights] Q; *light* F   62 SD] F; *not in* Q   64 good night] Q
(God night), F   69 'Sweet'] *Staunton (subst.)*; sweet Q, F   69 sewer] Q, F *(sure)*   70–1] *Theobald; as prose* Q, F   70
both at once] F; *both* Q   72 SD] Q *(subst.)*; *not in* F   72 SD *and*] *Capell; not in* Q   78 SD *Capell (subst.); not in* Q, F
78–9 Follow . . . company] F; *as prose* Q   80 SD.1 *Exit . . . following*] *Capell (subst.); not in* Q, F

60–2 The Greek heroes, having no doubt eaten   69 **draught** cesspool, privy (so also 'sink').
and drunk too copiously, have lost their way in their   Thersites comments sarcastically on Hector's ad-
own camp.   dressing Menelaus as 'sweet'.
65 **to tend on you** that have been assigned to   76 **tide whereof** time for which.
escort you back to Troy.

ACHILLES   Come, come, enter my tent.   80
                    Exeunt [Achilles, Hector, Ajax, and Nestor]
THERSITES That same Diomed's a false-hearted rogue, a most unjust
    knave. I will no more trust him when he leers than I will a serpent
    when he hisses; he will spend his mouth and promise like Brabbler
    the hound, but when he performs, astronomers foretell it, it is
    prodigious: there will come some change; the sun borrows of the   85
    moon when Diomed keeps his word. I will rather leave to see
    Hector than not to dog him. They say he keeps a Trojan drab and
    uses the traitor Calchas' tent. I'll after. Nothing but lechery – all
    incontinent varlets!   *[Exit]*

[5.2] *Enter* DIOMEDES

DIOMEDES What, are you up here, ho? Speak.
CALCHAS *[Within]* Who calls?
DIOMEDES Diomed. Calchas, I think. Where's your daughter?
CALCHAS *[Within]* She comes to you.

Enter TROILUS *and* ULYSSES *[at a distance; after them* THERSITES]

ULYSSES Stand where the torch may not discover us.   5

80 SD.2 *Achilles . . . Nestor*] *Capell; not in* Q, F   84 it, it] Q; it, that it F   88 Calchas'] Q *(Calcas); Chalcas his* F
89 SD] *Hanmer; Exeunt* F; *not in* Q   Act 5, Scene 2   5.2] *Rowe (subst.); not in* Q, F   2, 4 SDS *Within*] *Hanmer; not in*
Q, F   3 your] Q; you F   4 SD.2] *Capell (subst.), after Rowe; Enter Troylus and Vlisses* F; *not in* Q

82 leers casts a seductive glance. Like the ser-
pent's hiss, Diomedes' leer is a prelude to a nasty
strike.
83–4 spend . . . hound like the misleading bay-
ing of a hound who is off the scent (called a
'babbler' or 'brabbler'), Diomedes' words promise
much. Since Diomedes typically does exactly
what he says he will do, Thersites' criticism,
that he doesn't act on his 'word' (86), seems
more like generalised invective than an accurate
portrayal.
85 prodigious momentous (like a heavenly
portent).
85–6 there . . . moon some great change, such
as the sun taking its light from the moon, will come
upon us (continuing the idea of portents).
86 leave to see forgo seeing.
87 dog him follow Diomedes (an appropriate
phrase for Thersites who is so often called a 'cur').
87 drab whore.
88 uses is used to visiting, regularly visits
(an elliptical usage). Since Cressida has only just
arrived in the Greek camp, the statement cannot be

literally true, but it both answers Thersites' cynical attitude and telescopes the dramatic action in a
way that would go unnoticed by audiences.
89 incontinent varlets promiscuous rogues
('varlet' again chiming with 'harlot' – see 15 and n.).

Act 5, Scene 2
0 SD Although Q has no exit for Thersites at the
end of the previous scene and neither Q nor F has
an entrance for him at 4 in this scene, it seems likely
that he does leave the stage briefly to indicate the
change of location. Productions may nevertheless
want to keep him onstage to emphasise his choric
role.
4 Calchas' vulnerable position as a Trojan traitor
in the Greek camp may account for his readiness to set up his daughter with a powerful Greek
warrior.
5 discover reveal.
5–111 The dialogue from here until Diomedes'
departure and Cressida's return into her father's
tent (111) takes place at three different locations on
the stage, with Diomedes and Cressida somewhere

Enter CRESSIDA

TROILUS Cressid comes forth to him.

DIOMEDES   How now, my charge?

CRESSIDA Now, my sweet guardian, hark, a word with you.

[She whispers to Diomedes]

TROILUS Yea, so familiar?

ULYSSES She will sing any man at first sight.

THERSITES And any man may sing her, if he can take her clef: she's   10
    noted.

DIOMEDES Will you remember?

CRESSIDA Remember, yes.

DIOMEDES Nay, but do then!

    And let your mind be coupled with your words.   15

TROILUS What shall she remember?

ULYSSES List!

CRESSIDA Sweet honey Greek, tempt me no more to folly.

THERSITES Roguery!

DIOMEDES Nay then –   20

CRESSIDA I'll tell you what –

DIOMEDES Fo, fo, come tell a pin! You are forsworn.

CRESSIDA In faith, I cannot – what would you have me do?

THERSITES A juggling trick – to be secretly open.

---

5 SD] F; *after* 'him' *(6)* Q   7 SD] *Rowe (subst.); not in* Q, F   9 sing] Q; finde F   10 clef] Q *(Cliff);* life F   13 SH] F2;
Cal. Q, F   14–15] *Capell; as prose* Q, F   16 shall] Q; should F

near the centre, observed from the side by Troilus and Ulysses and from another vantage point by Thersites, who watches both the central couple and the eavesdroppers. The comments of the various observers are not, of course, overheard by the observed. The fracturing of point of view in the scene is an inventive theatrical metaphor for the breakdown not only of faith but of reality itself that Troilus laments in his great speech at 136 ff. See Introduction, pp. 19–22.

6 charge Diomedes is Cressida's guardian, as she coyly notes in her response.

9 Continuing his derogatory comments on Cressida (see 4.5.54–63) Ulysses says that, like a practised musician who can sight-read any piece, she can quickly and adroitly sound any man she meets.

10–11 Any man can play her tune if he can (1) find the right key, and (2) take possession of her vagina. Thersites elaborates Ulysses' musical metaphor in a more explicitly obscene way,

punning on 'clef' (musical signature) and vaginal 'cleft' (Williams, *Dictionary*). See Textual Analysis, p. 247, for a discussion of F's apparent misreading of Q's 'sing' and 'Cliff'.

11 noted well-known, notorious (with a pun on musical notation).

15 coupled consistent, with a glance at sexual coupling (Diomedes is insisting that Cressida follow through on an apparent sexual promise).

17 List Listen.

22 tell a pin i.e. do not trifle with me. Cressida has started to tell Diomedes something (21) and he replies, tell me nothing ('pin' = trifle).

23 cannot cannot do what I promised.

24 juggling trick (1) engage in sex (juggle = copulate (Williams, *Glossary*), perhaps by association with juggler's balls), (2) pull off a seemingly impossible or self-contradictory feat (juggler = magician, as well as one who deceives). Each sense leads to aspects of the next phrase, 'to be secretly open': (1) open up your private places in

DIOMEDES What did you swear you would bestow on me?   25
CRESSIDA I prithee do not hold me to mine oath.
       Bid me do anything but that, sweet Greek!
DIOMEDES Good night.
TROILUS Hold, patience!
ULYSSES How now, Trojan?   30
CRESSIDA Diomed –
DIOMEDES No no, good night. I'll be your fool no more.
TROILUS Thy better must.
CRESSIDA Hark, a word in your ear.
TROILUS O plague and madness!   35
ULYSSES You are moved, prince, let us depart, I pray,
       Lest your displeasure should enlarge itself
       To wrathful terms; this place is dangerous,
       The time right deadly. I beseech you, go.
TROILUS Behold, I pray you.
ULYSSES   Nay, good my lord, go off;   40
       You flow to great distraction, come, my lord.
TROILUS I prithee, stay.
ULYSSES   You have not patience, come.
TROILUS I pray you stay. By hell and all hell's torments,
       I will not speak a word.
DIOMEDES   And so good night.
CRESSIDA Nay, but you part in anger.
TROILUS   Doth that grieve thee?   45
       O withered truth!
ULYSSES   How now, my lord?

---

27 do] Q; do not F   34 a] Q; one F   36 pray] Q; pray you F   40 Nay] F; Now Q   41 distraction] F; distruction Q   42 prithee] Q; pray thee F   43 all hell's] Q; hell F   44–7] Capell; as prose Q, F   46 How now, my] Q; Why, how now F

secret, and (2) be modest and bold at the same time. Thersites reads Cressida's hesitant behaviour as deliberate provocation.

26 oath Precisely what she has promised Diomedes is never made clear, but in the time since leaving Troy with him she has apparently agreed to some kind of sexual deal, an arrangement from which she now seeks to extricate herself.

28 Diomedes perhaps turns to leave here, since Cressida's next line (31) appears to be an attempt to call him back or dissuade him from leaving. But it is also possible that he embraces her before going, thus prompting Troilus' outcry (29).

32 fool dupe.

33 Thy better Troilus himself.

34 Cressida initiates a whispered colloquy with Diomedes that continues during Troilus' outbursts in the next lines (35–46).

37–8 enlarge . . . terms explode into angry words and a fight.

41 flow . . . distraction are becoming overwrought (the metaphor is of a powerful current or tide).

44 In a subtle irony, the verse line is split between the rival lovers. Lines 45 and 47, shared by Cressida and Troilus, continue the pattern.

TROILUS   By Jove,
    I will be patient.

CRESSIDA   Guardian, why Greek –

DIOMEDES Fo, fo, adieu, you palter.

CRESSIDA In faith I do not; come hither once again.

ULYSSES You shake, my lord, at something, will you go?   50
    You will break out.

TROILUS   She strokes his cheek.

ULYSSES   Come, come.

TROILUS Nay stay, by Jove I will not speak a word.
    There is between my will and all offences
    A guard of patience. Stay a little while.

THERSITES How the devil Luxury with his fat rump and potato finger   55
    tickles these together. Fry, lechery, fry!

DIOMEDES Will you then?

CRESSIDA In faith, I will, la, never trust me else.

DIOMEDES Give me some token for the surety of it.

CRESSIDA I'll fetch you one.   *Exit*   60

ULYSSES You have sworn patience.

TROILUS   Fear me not, my lord.
    I will not be myself, nor have cognition
    Of what I feel. I am all patience.

           Enter CRESSIDA [*with Troilus' sleeve*]

THERSITES Now the pledge, now, now, now!

CRESSIDA Here Diomed, keep this sleeve.   65

---

48 adieu] F; *not in* Q   50–1 You shake . . . out] F2; *as prose* Q, F   56 these] F; *not in* Q   57 Will] Q; But will F   58 la] *Theobald;* lo Q, F   61 my] Q; sweete F   63 SD *with . . . sleeve*] *Bevington; not in* Q, F

48 **palter** trifle, play tricks (see 2.3.216).

51 **break out** erupt into overt anger.

53–4 **There . . . patience** My patience stands guard to prevent my angry feelings or desires ('will') from erupting into offensive action.

55 **Luxury** Lechery, one of the seven deadly sins (personified as a tempting devil).

55 **fat rump . . . finger** Why Lechery should have a fat rump has never been satisfactorily explained, though A. R. Braunmuller, glossing 'rump-fed runnion' (*Mac.* 1.3.5), notes the sexual connotations of 'rump' and cites Marston's *Dutch Courtesan* (1605), where the title character is described as a 'plump-rump'd wench' (4.3.2); potatoes were commonly thought to be an aphrodisiac, so that the devil is pictured as tickling the lovers into sexual excess.

56 **Fry** Burn (both with passion and in hell, the devil having done his job).

58 **la** indeed.

59 **token . . . it** pledge as an assurance of it. What 'it' refers to is left unstated, though during their whispered conversation, she has apparently renewed the sexual promise she has sought to avoid earlier (see 26 n.).

62–3 **I will . . . feel** I will not allow myself even to recognise the feelings I have. Both Ulysses' caution and Troilus' response belie what he says – he is clearly having trouble being patient.

63 **SD sleeve** see 4.4.69 and n.

64 Thersites' voyeuristic excitement at Cressida's pledge (both the sleeve and the implied promise of sex) is taking possession of him.

TROILUS O beauty, where is thy faith?
ULYSSES   My lord –
TROILUS I will be patient outwardly, I will.
CRESSIDA You look upon that sleeve, behold it well:
        He loved me – O false wench! – Give't me again.
DIOMEDES Whose was't?   70
CRESSIDA It is no matter now I have't again.
        I will not meet with you tomorrow night.
        I prithee Diomed, visit me no more.
THERSITES Now she sharpens, well said, whetstone!
DIOMEDES I shall have it.
CRESSIDA   What, this?
DIOMEDES   Ay, that.   75
CRESSIDA O all you gods – O pretty, pretty, pledge,
        Thy master now lies thinking on his bed
        Of thee and me, and sighs and takes my glove
        And gives memorial dainty kisses to it,
        As I kiss thee.
                [As she is kissing the sleeve, Diomedes snatches it]
                        Nay do not snatch it from me;   80
        He that takes that doth take my heart withal.
DIOMEDES I had your heart before – this follows it.
TROILUS I did swear patience.
CRESSIDA You shall not have it, Diomed, faith, you shall not.
        I'll give you something else.   85
DIOMEDES I will have this – whose was it?
CRESSIDA It is no matter.
DIOMEDES Come, tell me whose it was.
CRESSIDA 'Twas one's that loved me better than you will.
        But now you have it, take it.

67] F; *not in* Q 68 SH] F; *Troy:* Q 71 have't] Q *(ha't)*, F 77 on] Q; *in* F 79–80 And . . . thee] F; *as one line* Q
80 SD] *Muir (subst.), after Theobald; not in* Q, F 80 Nay . . . me] *Theobald (conj. Thirlby); assigned to Diomedes* Q, F
81 doth take] Q; rakes F 84 SH] F; *speech continued to Troilus* Q 89 one's] Q *(on's);* one F

69 As in 3.2 and again in 4.5, Cressida's ambiguous behaviour opens up the possibility of multiple interpretations.
74 whetstone stone used for sharpening. As Thersites sees it, Cressida is whetting the edge of Diomedes' sexual appetite through deliberate delay.
78 glove The token she gave him in 4.4.
79 memorial as acts of remembrance.
79 dainty precious.

80 Nay . . . me While Q, F give this sentence to Diomedes, Thirlby's conjecture makes much better sense of the stage action: if the sleeve is snatched back and forth too often, the result could be farcical. Cressida gives Diomedes the sleeve at 65 but demands it back again almost immediately (69). Her kissing it at this point ('thee' = the sleeve) provokes Diomedes to seize it and keep it, despite her protest at 84–5; she finally relinquishes her claim to it at 90.

DIOMEDES   Whose was it?   90

CRESSIDA By all Diana's waiting-women yond,
    And by herself, I will not tell you whose.

DIOMEDES Tomorrow will I wear it on my helm
    And grieve his spirit that dares not challenge it.

TROILUS [*Aside*] Wert thou the devil and wor'st it on thy horn,   95
    It should be challenged.

CRESSIDA Well well, 'tis done, 'tis past, and yet it is not:
    I will not keep my word.

DIOMEDES   Why then, farewell,
    Thou never shalt mock Diomed again.

CRESSIDA You shall not go; one cannot speak a word   100
    But it straight starts you.

DIOMEDES   I do not like this fooling.

THERSITES Nor I, by Pluto, but that that likes not you pleases me best.

DIOMEDES What, shall I come? The hour?

CRESSIDA Ay, come. O Jove! – do come – I shall be plagued.

DIOMEDES Farewell till then.

CRESSIDA   Good night! I prithee, come.   105

Exit [*Diomedes*]

    Troilus farewell, one eye yet looks on thee,
    But with my heart the other eye doth see.

---

91 By] F; And by Q   95 SD] *Oxford; not in* Q, F   98–101 Why . . . you] F; *as prose* Q   102 SH] Q, F; *speech assigned to Troilus / Hanmer*   102 you] Q; me F   105 SD] *Capell; Exit. (after* then) F; *not in* Q

91 Diana's waiting-women The stars (figured as waiting on the goddess associated with the moon and, ironically in the circumstances, chastity).

93 helm helmet.

94 And depress the spirits of whoever fails to challenge it.

101 straight starts you immediately provokes you to abrupt action.

102 Many editors follow Hanmer in giving this speech to Troilus and in doing so turn it into a (rather awkward) verse; they stress its appropriateness to Troilus and the fact that he frequently refers to Pluto; while this is possible, the cynicism suits Thersites, and more to the point, for Troilus to be pleased by what Diomedes dislikes ('likes not you' = 'you do not like') would mean that he approves of Cressida's dallying (though perhaps the emenders wish to suggest that he still desperately wants to perceive her behaviour as motivated by a desire to remain faithful).

104 be plagued suffer. Again Cressida's reaction is hard to read; her comment could be half-jocular,

as with her 'I shall have such a life' (4.2.22–3), but more likely she sees that her action is bound to cause herself pain. The precise nature of that pain is once more ambiguous – is she referring to pangs of conscience, to an awareness that Diomedes will be a much harsher lover than Troilus, to a sense that she will end up a figure of scorn? Also, the word 'plagued' anticipates what most spectators would recognise as Cressida's literary future as a diseased beggar. See Appendix: Sources of the Play, pp. 259–60.

105 SD Diomedes' exit, as Bevington[2] points out, properly occurs not after Cressida's farewell but during it: 'The plaintiveness of her beseeching him to come again is all the more evident if he is disappearing while she speaks.'

106–7 Eyes focused separately on different objects could signal opposing feelings, as in Claudius' 'With an auspicious, and a dropping eye' (*Ham.* 1.2.11); here, the twin feelings, augmented by a pun on eye/I, are Cressida's regretful nostalgia for Troilus and her heart's desire for Diomedes.

Ah, poor our sex, this fault in us I find:
The error of our eye directs our mind.
What error leads must err: O then conclude,   110
Minds swayed by eyes are full of turpitude.   *Exit*
THERSITES A proof of strength she could not publish more,
      Unless she said 'My mind is now turned whore.'
ULYSSES All's done my lord.
TROILUS   It is.
ULYSSES   Why stay we then?
TROILUS To make a recordation to my soul   115
      Of every syllable that here was spoke.
      But if I tell how these two did co-act,
      Shall I not lie in publishing a truth?
      Sith yet there is a credence in my heart,
      An esperance so obstinately strong,   120
      That doth invert th'attest of eyes and ears,
      As if those organs had deceptious functions,
      Created only to calumniate.
      Was Cressid here?
ULYSSES   I cannot conjure, Trojan.

111] F; *quotation marks at left* Q   113 said] Q; say F   113 'My . . . whore.'] *Hanmer (subst.);* my . . . whore. Q, F
117 co-act] F; Court Q   121 th'attest] Q; that test F   122 had deceptious] F; were deceptions Q   123–4 Created . . .
here?] F; *as one line* Q

Victoria Hamilton in the RSC production of 1996 caught the doubleness in her opening phrase: 'Troilus' was a pained cry, and then 'farewell' was tossed curtly off.

109 error wandering.

110 What . . . err Whatever is incited by (moral) wandering must be sinful. Strictly speaking, this is a tautology, but it serves as the premise of a syllogism leading to her conclusion in the next line.

111 turpitude guilt, shame. Cressida's logic is impeccable, though it seems ill-suited to the occasion of her conflicted feelings; she says, essentially, that whatever is led by error is sinful, women's minds are led by error, therefore women's minds are sinful (full of guilt). As with Troilus in 136 ff., Cressida struggles to bring her conflicted feelings in line with reason, but at the same time she strives to distance herself from them through a generalised misogyny.

112–13 Thersites notes Cressida's logic, and applies it specifically to her ('proof of strength' =

powerful proof; 'publish more' = announce more plainly).

115 recordation record.

117 co-act act together.

118 The first of a series of paradoxes that Troilus explores over the next 40 lines in an effort to reconcile his split image of Cressida and, indeed, the rifts in truth itself. Some of the sonnets to the dark lady record a similar paradox (e.g. Sonnet 138: 'When my love swears that she is made of truth, / I do believe her, though I know she lies' (1–2)). Note too the chime with Thersites' use of 'publish' in 112.

120 esperance hope.

121 attest evidence.

122 deceptious deceptive (first *OED* citation).

123 Having been created only for the purpose of misleading. 'Calumniate' (= slander) links the deceptive power of the senses to Time which also calumniates – see 3.3.174.

124 I cannot conjure i.e. I am not a magician able to produce a vision of her.

TROILUS She was not, sure.

ULYSSES   Most sure she was.   125

TROILUS Why, my negation hath no taste of madness.

ULYSSES Nor mine, my lord. Cressid was here but now.

TROILUS Let it not be believed for womanhood.
        Think we had mothers, do not give advantage
        To stubborn critics, apt without a theme   130
        For depravation, to square the general sex
        By Cressid's rule. Rather, think this not Cressid.

ULYSSES What hath she done, prince, that can soil our mothers?

TROILUS Nothing at all, unless that this were she.

THERSITES Will 'a swagger himself out on's own eyes?   135

TROILUS This she? No, this is Diomed's Cressida.
        If beauty have a soul this is not she,
        If souls guide vows, if vows be sanctimonies,
        If sanctimony be the gods' delight,
        If there be rule in unity itself,   140
        This is not she. O madness of discourse
        That cause sets up with and against itself –

---

133 soil] F; spoile Q   138 be sanctimonies] Q; are sanctimonie F   141 is] F; was Q   142 itself] Q; thy selfe F

126 My denial does not smack of madness.

128 for for the sake of.

129–32 Think ... rule Remember that we have honourable mothers, and therefore do not provide an opportunity to inveterate satirists ('stubborn critics' (130), who are ready to denigrate women even without grounds) to judge the entire sex by Cressida's behaviour. 'Square' (from the term for a carpenter's tool for measuring angles – *OED sb* 1) means to 'frame ... according to some standard' (*OED v* 4); the metaphor is continued in 'rule', both an instrument for measurement and a 'standard of conduct'. Like Hamlet and other Shakespearean idealists, Troilus generalises his disillusion with one woman to encompass all.

133 soil taint.

135 Will he, with all this blustering, deny the evidence of his own eyes?

137–41 A self-consciously rhetorical passage with a strictly logical form and an irrational point. Troilus argues on the basis of accepted moral and philosophical truths that the woman he has just seen could not have been Cressida. The repeated 'If' clauses, linked through 'anadiplosis' (a figure in which each succeeding clause begins with the final word of the preceding one), provide the tight structure so at odds with the 'mad' denial of Cressida's presence. For a more extended discussion, see Introduction, pp. 21–2.

138–9 sanctimonies ... sanctimony sacred things ... sacredness.

140 If it is true that unity cannot be divided. 'Rule in unity' refers to the Aristotelian principle whereby one is opposed to many, unity to divisibility. Troilus thus says that if this principle 'rules', then it follows that Cressida, who is one, cannot be divided into two. The language here and in the following lines evokes a dark and threatening version of a mixed self that is celebrated in *The Phoenix and the Turtle*: 'Property was thus appalled, / That the self was not the same; / Single nature's double name / Neither two nor one was called' (37–40). See Adelman, pp. 38–42.

141 madness Troilus recognises the irrationality of his paradoxical discourse, but it is the only way in which he can accommodate the seeming facts and his passionate response to them.

Bifold authority, where reason can revolt
Without perdition, and loss assume all reason
Without revolt! This is and is not Cressid.   145
Within my soul there doth conduce a fight
Of this strange nature: that a thing inseparate
Divides more wider than the sky and earth,
And yet the spacious breadth of this division
Admits no orifex for a point as subtle   150
As Ariachne's broken woof to enter.
Instance, O instance, strong as Pluto's gates,
Cressid is mine, tied with the bonds of heaven.
Instance, O instance, strong as heaven itself,
The bonds of heaven are slipped, dissolved, and loosed,   155
And with another knot, five-finger-tied,
The fractions of her faith, orts of her love,
The fragments, scraps, the bits and greasy relics
Of her o'er-eaten faith, are given to Diomed.
ULYSSES May worthy Troilus be half attached   160
That which here his passion doth express?

---

143 Bifold] Q *(By-fould)*; By foule F   151 Ariachne's] Q *(corr.) (Ariachna's)*, F; *Ariathna's* Q *(uncorr.)*   156 five-finger-tied] F *(hyphens, Pope)*; finde finger tied Q   159 given] Q; bound F

143–5 Bifold . . . Without revolt How absolutely split ('bifold') is the authority of reason when
it can rebel against evident truth without destroying itself ('perdition') and when loss of reason can
assume all the appearances of reason without contradiction.

146 conduce take place.

147 inseparate indivisible (see 140 and n.).

150–1 Allows no opening ('orifex') big enough
even for a fine thread ('subtle . . . woof'), such as
the broken filament of a spider's web, to enter. Ariachne = Arachne, a supreme weaver whom Athena
transformed into a spider and whose web she then
tore up (Ovid, Book VI). Though 'Ariachne' may
be a slip or a spelling invented to fit the metre, it
is more likely that Shakespeare conflated Arachne
with Ariadne, the Cretan girl whose love for The-
seus led her to give him a length of thread to help
him find his way out of the labyrinth (Ovid, Book
VIII). See Freund.

152, 154 Instance Example adduced as proof of
a general proposition.

156 five-finger-tied tied with human hands (she
has, as Johnson notes, given her hand to Diomedes).

The implicit contrast is with the spiritual 'bonds of
heaven' in 153–5 which tie Troilus to her. As Muir
notes, Chaucer's *Parson's Tale* speaks of lechery as
the 'hand of the devel with fyve fyngres' (lines 852
ff.).

157 fractions broken pieces.

157 orts bits, scraps.

159 o'er-eaten chewed up, with the sugges-
tion that she has consumed her faith in betraying
Troilus and hence there are only scraps left for
Diomedes.

160–1 'Can Troilus really feel on this occasion
half of what he utters?' (Johnson). Ulysses' question seems slightly sardonic and sceptical, the word
'worthy' perhaps implying that on this particular
occasion Troilus is acting unworthily. Line 160 is
one syllable short, leading editors to conclude that
either 'Troilus' is trisyllabic (for the only time in
the play) or that a word such as 'but' should be inserted before 'half'; however, a brief interrogative
pause after the name would give an edge to the
tone and also fill out the line.

160–1 attached / With possessed or affected
by.

TROILUS   Ay Greek, and that shall be divulgèd well
                In characters as red as Mars his heart
                Inflamed with Venus; never did young man fancy
                With so eternal and so fixed a soul.   165
                Hark Greek, as much as I do Cressid love,
                So much by weight hate I her Diomed.
                That sleeve is mine that he'll bear in his helm:
                Were it a casque composed by Vulcan's skill,
                My sword should bite it; not the dreadful spout,   170
                Which shipmen do the hurricano call,
                Constringed in mass by the almighty sun,
                Shall dizzy with more clamour Neptune's ear
                In his descent than shall my prompted sword
                Falling on Diomed.   175
THERSITES   He'll tickle it for his concupy.
TROILUS   O Cressid, O false Cressid, false, false, false!

---

166 as much as] F2; as much Q, F   166 Cressid] Q; *Cressida* F   168 in] F; on Q   172 sun] Q; Fenne F   173–5] F; *two
lines (*discent, / Then*) Q

162 **divulgèd** published, written out (the metaphor is continued in 'characters' in the next line).

163–4 as red . . . Venus as blood-red as the heart of Mars when it burned with passion for Venus. The image, which combines the fury of battle (Mars = the god of war) and the fire of love (Mars' passion for Venus being a frequent theme of poetry and art), might also have reminded Shakespeare's audience of the red letters ('characters', 163) used in ecclesiatical calendars to indicate saints' days and Church festivals.

164 **fancy** love.

167 **by weight** in equal measure. The image may recall Diomedes' cynical assessment of Helen's 'weight' in relation to Paris and Menelaus – 4.1.66–73.

168 **in his helm** fixed to his helmet. Q's 'on' seems more idiomatic to modern ears, but, as Malone points out, both texts read 'in' at 5.4.3.

169 **casque** helmet.

169 **composed . . . skill** forged with the skill of Vulcan, the divine blacksmith and Venus' husband, famously cuckolded by Mars (see 163–4).

170 **spout** waterspout, either (1) a violent burst of rain, or (2) a kind of watery tornado, caused by the winds pulling seawater into the air in a furious spiral motion. Cf. *Lear* 3.2.2–3 where both 'spout' and 'hurricano' are associated with the first meaning: 'You cataracts and hurricanoes, spout / Till you have drench'd our steeples.'

172 Densely compressed ('Constringed') by the power of the sun (first *OED* citation under 'constringe'). It is not fully clear why the sun should have this effect.

173 **dizzy** produce a swimming sensation in.

173 **Neptune** The god of the sea.

174 **his** i.e. the waterspout's, which 'descends' either as a cloudburst or as a spiral of water that seems to fall from on high. *OED* (Spout *sb* 6) cites Eden, *Decades* (1555): 'They sawe certeyne stremes of water which they caule spoutes faulynge owt of the ayer into the sea.'

174 **prompted** ready and eager (Muir).

176 'Tickle' can mean 'provoke' or 'chastise' and 'concupy' seems to be Shakespeare's coinage, combining 'concubine' and 'concupiscence', so that Thersites means either (1) He (Troilus) will be provoked to violence because of his whore; or (2) He will chastise Diomedes on account of his whore (or as a result of his – Diomedes' or Troilus' – concupiscence); or (3) He (Diomedes) will 'get it' (be chastised) because of his concupiscence. Exactly which meaning is foremost for Thersites is unclear, though it is obvious he is enjoying Troilus' discomfiture, mocking his furious rhetoric, and looking forward to a knock-down fight between the 'abominable varlet, Diomedes' and the 'young Trojan ass' (see 5.4.2–7).

Let all untruths stand by thy stainèd name
And they'll seem glorious.
ULYSSES   O contain yourself:
Your passion draws ears hither.   180

Enter AENEAS

AENEAS I have been seeking you this hour, my lord.
Hector by this is arming him in Troy;
Ajax your guard stays to conduct you home.
TROILUS Have with you, prince. [*To Ulysses*] My courteous lord, adieu.
Farewell, revolted fair; and Diomed,   185
Stand fast and wear a castle on thy head.
ULYSSES I'll bring you to the gates.
TROILUS   Accept distracted thanks.
                    Exeunt Troilus, Aeneas, and Ulysses
THERSITES Would I could meet that rogue Diomed. I would croak like a
raven, I would bode, I would bode. Patroclus will give me anything
for the intelligence of this whore: the parrot will not do more for   190
an almond than he for a commodious drab. Lechery, lechery, still
wars and lechery, nothing else holds fashion – a burning devil take
them!   *Exit*

<h2>[5.3] Enter HECTOR and ANDROMACHE</h2>

ANDROMACHE When was my lord so much ungently tempered
To stop his ears against admonishment?
Unarm, unarm and do not fight today.

184 SD] *This edn; not in* Q, F   193 SD] Q; *not in* F   Act 5, Scene 3   5.3] *Rowe (subst.); not in* Q, F

178 **stand by** be compared with.
182 **by this** by now.
183 **stays** is waiting.
185 **revolted fair** Cressida, whose treason has caused the revolt of reason within Troilus (143–5).
186 **castle** i.e. (metaphorically) for protection, since a mere 'casque' (169) will not suffice.
189 **raven . . . bode** bode = prophesy. Ravens were traditionally associated with evil omens: cf. *Mac.* 1.5.38–40: 'The raven himself is hoarse / That croaks the fatal entrance of Duncan / Under my battlements' and Dent R33.
190 **the intelligence of** information about. As with Achilles, Patroclus' homoerotic involvement does not preclude an interest in women.
190 **parrot** Proverbially fond of almonds (Dent A220).

191 **commodious drab** accommodating slut.
192 **burning devil** venereal disease, with a suggestion also of the literal sense (may they burn in hell!). Cf. Sonnet 144: 'I guess one angel in another's hell. / Yet this shall I ne'er know, but live in doubt, / Till my bad angel fire my good one out' (12–14). A similar conceit appears in Sonnets 153 and 154.

Act 5, Scene 3

1 The scene begins in mid-conversation: Hector, as we have been told in 5.2.182, is already arming, and Andromache, beset by premonitions, has been trying to persuade him not to go into battle.
1 **ungently tempered** unkindly disposed.

HECTOR You train me to offend you – get you in.

By all the everlasting gods, I'll go.   5

ANDROMACHE My dreams will sure prove ominous to the day.

HECTOR No more I say.

Enter CASSANDRA

CASSANDRA   Where is my brother Hector?

ANDROMACHE Here sister, armed and bloody in intent.

Consort with me in loud and dear petition,

Pursue we him on knees, for I have dreamt   10

Of bloody turbulence and this whole night

Hath nothing been but shapes and forms of slaughter.

CASSANDRA O 'tis true.

HECTOR   Ho! Bid my trumpet sound.

CASSANDRA No notes of sally, for the heavens, sweet brother.

HECTOR Be gone, I say, the gods have heard me swear.   15

CASSANDRA The gods are deaf to hot and peevish vows:

They are polluted off'rings, more abhorred

Than spotted livers in the sacrifice.

ANDROMACHE O be persuaded – do not count it holy

To hurt by being just. It is as lawful,   20

For we would give much, to use violent thefts

And rob in the behalf of charity.

CASSANDRA It is the purpose that makes strong the vow,

But vows to every purpose must not hold.

Unarm, sweet Hector.

HECTOR   Hold you still I say.   25

---

4 in] Q; gone F   5 all] Q; *not in* F   14 SH] F *(Cass.); Cres.* Q   20–2] F; *not in* Q   21 give much, to use] *Rann (conj. Tyrwhitt); count giue much to as* F   23 SH] F *(Cass.); not in* Q   23–5 It . . . Hector] F; *assigned to Andromache* Q *(continued from holy (19))*

4 **train** induce, prompt.
6 **ominous . . . day** foreboding about today.
9 **Consort** Join.
9 **dear** heartfelt (*OED a¹* 7a).
14 **sally** going forth to battle.
16 **peevish** foolish.
18 **spotted** tainted – a sign of an animal that is sick and hence unfit for sacrifice.
20–2 These lines may have been accidentally omitted in Q, they may have been added in revision, or deliberately cut – there is no way of definitively determining. That they were difficult to read for

the F compositor is evident from the tangles in 21 (see collation).
20 **To . . . just** To cause pain merely to remain faithful to an oath.
20–2 **It is . . . charity** It would be equally ethical if, just because we might want to be generous, we were to rob and steal in order to give to charity.
23–4 Because the nature of the cause for which the vow is taken determines its value, vows taken for insufficient reasons are not binding.

Mine honour keeps the weather of my fate.
Life every man holds dear, but the dear man
Holds honour far more precious-dear than life.

Enter TROILUS

How now, young man, mean'st thou to fight today?
ANDROMACHE Cassandra, call my father to persuade.   30

                                   Exit Cassandra
HECTOR No, faith, young Troilus, doff thy harness, youth.
I am today i'th'vein of chivalry.
Let grow thy sinews till their knots be strong
And tempt not yet the brushes of the war.
Unarm thee, go, and doubt thou not, brave boy,   35
I'll stand today for thee and me and Troy.
TROILUS Brother, you have a vice of mercy in you
Which better fits a lion than a man.
HECTOR What vice is that? Good Troilus, chide me for it.
TROILUS When many times the captive Grecian falls,   40
Even in the fan and wind of your fair sword,
You bid them rise and live.
HECTOR O 'tis fair play.
TROILUS   Fool's play, by heaven, Hector.
HECTOR How now? how now?
TROILUS   For th'love of all the gods,
Let's leave the hermit Pity with our mother,   45

---

28 precious-dear] F2; precious deere Q; precious, deere F   45 mother] Q; Mothers F

26 keeps . . . of comes before, takes precedence over (a nautical image – literally, 'stays to windward of').

27 dear man man of true worth.

29 Troilus has just returned from the Greek camp, and is now dressed for battle. Though he does not answer Hector's question, his evident fury prompts Hector's attempt to persuade him to stay home.

31 doff thy harness take off your armour.

32 Hector perhaps means to suggest that he does not need Troilus' help.

33 knots points where the tendons ('sinews') attach to bone and muscle.

34 tempt risk, attempt.

34 brushes skirmishes, encounters.

37 vice of mercy In Troilus' rage, any touch of mercy seems a vice or weakness. The comment, however, accords with Ulysses' assessment of both Hector and Troilus at 4.5.104–7.

38 lion The lion, according to ancient animal lore, manifested his nobility by sparing a submissive foe. Cf. Dent L316.

41 fan and wind whirlwind. Cf. 'the whiff and wind of his fell sword' (*Ham.* 2.2.473), where the force of the wind created by Pyrrhus' sword is said to knock Priam down; here Hector's sword is 'fair' rather than 'fell' since, unlike Pyrrhus, he plays fair, not taking advantage of his fallen enemy.

45 hermit Pity Pity is thought of as hermit-like since it should remain apart and not make an appearance on the battlefield.

45 mother F's 'mothers' may be right, since Troilus could be speaking generally (soldiers

And when we have our armours buckled on
The venomed vengeance ride upon our swords,
Spur them to ruthful work, rein them from ruth.

HECTOR Fie, savage, fie!

TROILUS   Hector, then 'tis wars.

HECTOR Troilus, I would not have you fight today.   50

TROILUS Who should withhold me?
Not fate, obedience, nor the hand of Mars
Beck'ning with fiery truncheon my retire;
Not Priamus and Hecuba on knees,
Their eyes o'ergallèd with recourse of tears;   55
Nor you, my brother, with your true sword drawn
Opposed to hinder me, should stop my way
But by my ruin.

Enter PRIAM *and* CASSANDRA

CASSANDRA Lay hold upon him, Priam, hold him fast;
He is thy crutch – now if thou lose thy stay,   60
Thou on him leaning and all Troy on thee,
Fall all together.

PRIAM   Come, Hector, come, go back.
Thy wife hath dreamt, thy mother hath had visions,
Cassandra doth foresee, and I myself
Am like a prophet suddenly enrapt   65
To tell thee that this day is ominous.
Therefore, come back.

HECTOR   Aeneas is afield
And I do stand engaged to many Greeks

58] F; *not in* Q   60 lose] Q, F *(loose); loose Oxford*

should leave pity behind with their mothers),
though the singular is more personal and forceful.

47 The venomed vengeance 'May the poisonous spirit of vengeance' (Bevington[2]).

48 Spur (our swords) to work that causes grief
and refuses pity or mercy. Though 'ruthful' normally means 'exciting compassion', Shakespeare
seems here to be using it in a slightly different, un-
recorded sense, since Troilus is precisely not calling
on vengeance to excite pity from Hector or the rest
of the Trojans.

53 Waving his fiery staff as a signal for me to
withdraw. In formal chivalric combat, the marshal

used a truncheon to control the proceedings.

55 o'ergallèd . . . tears reddened with contin-
uous weeping.

58 Unless you killed me. Q omits this half-line,
which is not strictly necessary for either the sense
or the syntax, and indeed violates the parallelism of
the speech as a whole, wherein the first two clauses
are given two lines each; it might thus have been
dropped in revision.

60 stay support ('crutch').

62 Fall all Will all fall.

65 enrapt caught up in prophetic fury (first
citation in *OED*).

              Even in the faith of valour to appear
              This morning to them.
PRIAM   Ay, but thou shalt not go.   70
HECTOR I must not break my faith.
              You know me dutiful; therefore dear sir
              Let me not shame respect, but give me leave
              To take that course by your consent and voice
              Which you do here forbid me, royal Priam.   75
CASSANDRA O Priam, yield not to him!
ANDROMACHE   Do not dear father.
HECTOR Andromache, I am offended with you –
              Upon the love you bear me get you in.

                                              Exit Andromache
TROILUS This foolish, dreaming, superstitious girl
              Makes all these bodements.
CASSANDRA   O farewell, dear Hector!   80
              Look how thou diest, look how thy eye turns pale,
              Look how thy wounds do bleed at many vents,
              Hark how Troy roars, how Hecuba cries out,
              How poor Andromache shrills her dolours forth!
              Behold: Distraction, Frenzy, and Amazement,   85
              Like witless antics, one another meet
              And all cry 'Hector, Hector's dead! O Hector!'
TROILUS Away, away!
CASSANDRA Farewell – yet soft; Hector, I take my leave,
              Thou dost thyself and all our Troy deceive.   *Exit*   90
HECTOR You are amazed, my liege, at her exclaim;
              Go in and cheer the town. We'll forth and fight,
              Do deeds worth praise and tell you them at night.

82 do] Q; doth F   84 dolours] Q; dolour F   85 Distraction] F; destruction Q   87 'Hector . . . O Hector!'] *Hanmer*
(subst.); Hector . . . O Hector. Q, F *(subst.)*   89 yet] Q; yes F   90 SD] F; *not in* Q   92] F; *two lines* (towne, / Weele)
Q   93 worth] Q; of F

69 **faith of valour** pledge of faith proper to an   84 **shrills . . . forth** shrieks out her grief.
honourable warrior.   85 **Distraction** Madness.
   73 **shame respect** violate my duty to respect   86 **antics** clowns, grotesque actors. The abstrac-
your wishes (by disobeying). He thus asks for   tions in the previous line are compared to actors in
Priam's consent to go into battle.   a show of lunatics of the kind sometimes presented
   78 **Upon** In the name of.   in contemporary plays, such as *The Duchess of Malfi*
   79 **girl** Cassandra.   (1614) or *The Changeling* (1622).
   80 **Makes . . . bodements** Is behind all these   89 **soft** wait a moment.
ominous prophecies.   90 **deceive** delude (thyself) and betray (Troy).
   82 **vents** openings.   91 **exclaim** outcry.

PRIAM Farewell, the gods with safety stand about thee.
                    [*Exeunt Priam and Hector separately*]
                            Alarum
TROILUS They are at it – hark! Proud Diomed, believe   95
    I come to lose my arm or win my sleeve.

                        Enter PANDARUS

PANDARUS Do you hear my lord, do you hear?
TROILUS What now?
PANDARUS Here's a letter come from yond poor girl.
TROILUS Let me read.   100
PANDARUS A whoreson phthisic, a whoreson rascally phthisic so trou-
    bles me, and the foolish fortune of this girl, and what one thing,
    what another, that I shall leave you one o'these days; and I have a
    rheum in mine eyes too and such an ache in my bones that unless
    a man were cursed I cannot tell what to think on't. What says she   105
    there?
TROILUS Words, words, mere words, no matter from the heart.
    Th'effect doth operate another way. [*Tearing and scattering
        the letter*]
    Go, wind, to wind, there turn and change together.
    My love with words and errors still she feeds,   110
    But edifies another with her deeds.
                                    Exeunt [*separately*]

94 SD.1 *Exeunt . . . separately*] *Malone (subst.); not in* Q, F   **103** o'these] *Rowe;* ath's Q; o'th's F   **108** SD] *Capell (subst.), after Rowe; not in* Q, F   **111** deeds. *Exeunt*] Q; deedes. / *Pand.* Why, but heare you? / *Troy.* Hence brother lackie; ignomie and shame / Pursue thy life, and liue aye with thy name. / *A Larum. Exeunt.* F   **111** SD *separately*] *Malone (subst.); not in* Q, F

94 Priam at last gives his reluctant blessing to his doomed son; ironically, it is not the gods but Achilles' Myrmidons who will 'stand about' Hector.

96 The normal order of the clauses is reversed for the sake of the rhyme (Troilus will either win back his sleeve or lose his arm in the attempt).

101 phthisic bad cough. The word is pronounced 'tizic', as it was in Shakespeare's day (the Q, F spelling is 'tisick(e)').

102 foolish Used here in an unspecific pejorative sense.

104 rheum discharge of mucus. Along with the 'ache' in his bones, this hints at the symptoms of syphilis suggested more openly in Pandarus' epilogue.

105 cursed under a spell (he regards his symptoms, half jocularly, as a sign of having been cursed by a witch).

107 We never find out exactly what Cressida has written, nor are we given any evidence by which to judge Troilus' response to her letter.

108 The facts of the matter (*OED* Effect *sb* 7b, citing this line) point in a different direction from her words (she says she loves me but her deeds prove she loves Diomedes).

109 Go, wind, to wind Fly, mere words (i.e. the letter), into the air.

110 errors lies.

111 edifies builds up (with perhaps a sexual implication).

111 After this line, F adds three lines which are repeated almost verbatim near the end of the play at 5.11.32–4 (see 5.11.30–1 n. and Textual Analysis, pp. 240–2).

[5.4] *Alarum. Enter* THERSITES. *Excursions*

THERSITES Now they are clapper-clawing one another, I'll go look on.
That dissembling, abominable varlet, Diomed, has got that same
scurvy, doting, foolish, young knave's sleeve of Troy there in his
helm. I would fain see them meet, that that same young Trojan ass,
that loves the whore there, might send that Greekish whoremas-   5
terly villain with the sleeve back to the dissembling luxurious drab
of a sleeveless errand. O'th't'other side, the policy of those crafty
swearing rascals – that stale old mouse-eaten dry cheese, Nestor,
and that same dog-fox, Ulysses – is proved not worth a blackberry:
they set me up in policy that mongrel cur, Ajax, against that dog   10
of as bad a kind, Achilles, and now is the cur Ajax prouder than
the cur Achilles and will not arm today; whereupon the Grecians
begin to proclaim barbarism and policy grows into an ill opinion.

Enter DIOMEDES *and* TROILUS

Soft, here comes sleeve and t'other.
TROILUS Fly not, for shouldst thou take the river Styx,   15
       I would swim after.
DIOMEDES   Thou dost miscall retire:
       I do not fly, but advantageous care
       Withdrew me from the odds of multitude –
       Have at thee!

Act 5, Scene 4   5.4] *Rowe (subst.); not in* Q, F   0 SD *Alarum*] F *(at end of previous scene); not in* Q   0 SD *Excursions*]
Q; *in excursion* F   3 young] F; *not in* Q   7 errand] Q *(arrant);* F *(errant)*   7 O'th't'other] F *(subst.);* Ath' tother Q
8 stale] Q; stole F   9 proved not] *Walker (conj. Cam.); not* proou'd Q, F *(subst.)*   13 begin] Rowe²; began Q, F
13 SD] F; *not in* Q   15–16 Fly . . . after] F; *as prose* Q   18–19] F; *as one line* Q

Act 5, Scene 4

0 SD Excursions Sorties; the standard term to
describe the rush of battle on Shakespeare's stage.

1 clapper-clawing grappling with, scratching.
The writer of Q's prefatory epistle apparently
picked up this term and applied it to the noisy
applause of a raucous theatre audience.

3 scurvy knavish.

4 fain gladly.

6 luxurious drab lecherous slut.

7 sleeveless fruitless, futile, with a pun on the
literal sense; 'sleeveless errand' was a common
phrase – see Dent E180.

7 policy trick, stratagem, craftiness (so too in 10).

7–8 crafty swearing given to deceitful claims
and practices that appear truthful.

9 dog-fox male fox, referring to Ulysses'
reputation for cunning.

10 me The old dative form used colloquially as
an intensifier (Abbott 220).

13 proclaim barbarism declare a preference
for anarchy or deliberate lack of 'policy' (in this line
meaning 'proper government', though the previous
sense of 'crafty tricks' remains in play).

15 take enter.

15 Styx The river that serves as the boundary
of the underworld (Troilus will pursue Diomedes
even to death). See 3.2.7 n.

16 miscall retire misinterpret my withdrawal
as retreat.

17 advantageous care concern for my own advantage.

18 odds of multitude the odds against me in
that I was outnumbered.

THERSITES Hold thy whore, Grecian! Now for thy whore, Trojan! –   20
now the sleeve, now the sleeve!

[*Exeunt Troilus and Diomedes fighting*]

Enter HECTOR

HECTOR What art, Greek, art thou for Hector's match?
Art thou of blood and honour?
THERSITES No! No, I am a rascal, a scurvy railing knave, a very filthy
rogue.   25
HECTOR I do believe thee, live.   [*Exit*]
THERSITES God-a-mercy that thou wilt believe me! But a plague break
thy neck for frighting me. What's become of the wenching rogues?
I think they have swallowed one another – I would laugh at that
miracle; yet in a sort, lechery eats itself. I'll seek them.   *Exit*   30

[5.5] *Enter* DIOMEDES *and* SERVANT

DIOMEDES Go, go, my servant, take thou Troilus' horse,
Present the fair steed to my lady Cressid.
Fellow, commend my service to her beauty;
Tell her I have chastised the amorous Trojan
And am her knight by proof.
SERVANT   I go my lord.   [*Exit*]   5

Enter AGAMEMNON

AGAMEMNON Renew, renew! The fierce Polydamas

21 SD.1 *Exeunt . . . fighting*] Capell; *not in* Q, F   22 What art] Q; What art thou F   26 SD] *Rowe; not in* Q, F   Act 5,
Scene 5   5.5] *Capell (subst.); not in* Q, F   0 SD SERVANT] Q; *Seruants* F   5 SH SERVANT] F; *Man.* Q   5 SD.1 *Exit*]
Hanmer (subst.); not in Q, F   5 SD.2 *Enter* AGAMEMNON] F; *after* proof Q

22 art thou . . . match are you worthy of being
Hector's opponent.
26 In accepting Thersites' self-description and
allowing him to continue his filthy existence,
Hector cleverly manages to be both courteous and
insulting.
27 God-a-mercy . . . wilt Thank heaven that
you were willing to.
27 plague blow, affliction (the original Latin
meaning from which the idea of disease is
derived).
30 lechery eats itself lust both consumes itself
in its fulfilment and is self-destructive as one pursues it. There is no doubt an implied reference to
venereal disease. Cf. Sonnet 129: 'The expense of

spirit in a waste of shame / Is lust in action . . .'
(1–2). See also 1.3.121–4.

Act 5, Scene 5
5 proof i.e. I have proved myself in chivalric combat to be the worthier in her eyes.
The courtly language and action contrasts with
Diomedes' harsh and demanding behaviour with
Cressida (5.2).
6–16 Agamemnon adopts a heroic rhetoric, con-
sonant with Diomedes' chivalric language just before, infiltrated but not entirely undermined by
irony. The names of the various warriors and the
'Sagittary' (14) derive from Caxton, though Shakespeare's spellings are sometimes erratic.

Hath beat down Menon, bastard Margarelon
Hath Doreus prisoner,
And stands colossus-wise waving his beam
Upon the pashèd corpses of the kings,   10
Epistrophus and Cedius. Polyxenes is slain,
Amphimachus and Thoas deadly hurt,
Patroclus ta'en or slain, and Palamedes
Sore hurt and bruised. The dreadful Sagittary
Appals our numbers – haste we, Diomed,   15
To reinforcement, or we perish all.

Enter NESTOR [*and others*]

NESTOR Go, bear Patroclus' body to Achilles,
And bid the snail-paced Ajax arm for shame.
There is a thousand Hectors in the field:
Now here he fights on Galathe his horse,   20
And there lacks work; anon he's there afoot,
And there they fly, or die, like scaling schools
Before the belching whale; then is he yonder,
And there the strawy Greeks, ripe for his edge,

---

10 corpses] Q *(corses)*, F *(courses)*   11 Epistrophus] *Steevens; Epistropus* Q, F   11 Cedius] *Capell; Cedus* Q, F
12 Thoas] *Pope; Thous* Q, F   16 SD *and others*] *Walker (subst.); not in* Q, F   22 scaling] Q; *scaled* F   22 schools]
Q *(sculls)*, F *(sculs)*   24 strawy] Q; *straying* F

7 Margarelon Shakespeare's spelling, or perhaps a printer's error, for Caxton's 'Margareton'
(the latter being the preferred form of some recent
editors).

9 colossus-wise with his legs spread wide, like
a colossus (the huge bronze statue of Apollo at
Rhodes that stood astride the harbour).

9 beam huge spear (literally, a massive piece
of timber). Palmer cites 1 Samuel 17.7: 'And the
shafte of his speare *was* like a weauer's beam.'

10 pashèd battered.

14 Sagittary A centaur (half horse, half man).

15 Appals our numbers Strikes fear into our
troops.

17 One way of staging this moment, though one
seen only rarely, would be to have the soldiers who
enter with Nestor carry on Patroclus' body; he
would then direct them to bring the dead youth
to Achilles and they would exit after 18. While
bringing on Patroclus' body could certainly have
a strong theatrical effect, and would vividly prepare for the furious arrival of Achilles, Shakespeare
downplays the whole incident (so crucial to *The
Iliad* and subsequent versions of the story), choosing not to dramatise Patroclus' death nor Achilles'

initial encounter with the body. It seems, then,
more in keeping with the overall ironic tone for
Nestor to direct his command offstage.

19–29 This description of Hector's martial
power parallels that of Coriolanus (*Cor.* 2.2.103–
14), who is likewise irresistible: 'as weeds before /
A vessel under sail, so men obey'd / And fell below
his stem' (105–7).

20 Galathe Like the warriors mentioned by
Agamemnon (see 6–16n.) the name of Hector's
horse derives from Caxton.

22 scaling schools scattering schools of fish;
scale = disperse, scatter, as in Holinshed (1587) II,
499, 'they would no longer abide, but scaled and
departed away' (though this sense is not noted
by *OED*). F's 'scalèd' (= scaly) describes the fish
but misses the active sense, more appropriate to
the context, of them scattering before the whale's
mouth. See Variorum.

23 belching spouting.

24 strawy straw-like (in that they are 'ripe' for
mowing); the epithet was evidently misread by the
F editor or compositor.

24 his edge the sharp edge of Hector's sword
(compared with a mower's scythe).

Fall down before him like a mower's swath.   25
Here, there, and everywhere he leaves and takes,
Dexterity so obeying appetite
That what he will he does, and does so much
That proof is called impossibility.

Enter ULYSSES

ULYSSES O courage, courage, princes, great Achilles   30
Is arming – weeping, cursing, vowing vengeance.
Patroclus' wounds have roused his drowsy blood,
Together with his mangled Myrmidons
That noseless, handless, hacked and chipped, come to him
Crying on Hector. Ajax hath lost a friend   35
And foams at mouth, and he is armed and at it,
Roaring for Troilus who hath done today
Mad and fantastic execution,
Engaging and redeeming of himself
With such a careless force and forceless care   40
As if that lust, in very spite of cunning,
Bade him win all.

Enter AJAX

AJAX Troilus, thou coward, Troilus!   *Exit*
DIOMEDES   Ay there, there!   *Exit*

25 a] Q; *the* F   41–2] *Rowe²; as one line* Q, F   41 lust] Q; *luck* F   42 SD] F; *as SH (43)* Q   43 there! *Exit] Walker;*
SD *after* together *(44)* Q, F

25 **swath** row of cut grain.
26 **leaves and takes** leaves one dead and de-
stroys another (again, as in mowing, one stroke
leads rhythmically to the next – Variorum).
27 His skills so precisely answer to his desire.
28 **will** wills (subjunctive – Abbott 368).
29 (1) That the seemingly impossible is proved
factual; or (2) That what is proved true by indis-
putable visual evidence is nevertheless thought impossible. This second meaning links with Troilus'
refusal to accept the evidence of his senses in 5.2.
33 **Myrmidons** Achilles' own band of soldiers.
Most recent productions have tended to represent
them as violent thugs.
35 **Crying on** Crying for vengeance against.
35–42 **Ajax . . . win all** Ulysses makes explicit
the parallel between Achilles and Ajax: each has
kept to his tent out of pride and now each is roused
to battle by the loss of a friend (though just who
is Ajax's friend is never stated) at the hands of a

valiant and powerful son of Priam.
37–8 **Troilus . . . execution** Troilus' wild violence is in keeping with his feelings in 5.3.44–8 and
later, after the death of Hector (5.11.23–9).
39 Binding himself (to death as a creditor) and
then bailing himself out – the image is of a financial
contract.
40 **careless . . . care** fearless violence and reck-
less unconcern. The phrase relates chiastically
to the previous line – i.e. he 'engages' himself not caring about the consequences ('forceless care') and 'redeems' himself with 'careless
force'.
41 **lust** desire for blood. F's 'luck', meaning Fortune, has been adopted by most editors, but as
Palmer notes, 'it is Troilus' passion for revenge . . .
and not mere chance, which is wholly controlling
him now'.
41 **in . . . cunning** despite the skill of his enemies.

NESTOR So, so we draw together.

Enter ACHILLES

ACHILLES   Where is this Hector?
   Come, come, thou boy-queller, show thy face,   45
   Know what it is to meet Achilles angry.
   Hector! Where's Hector? I will none but Hector.

                                        [*Exeunt*]

[**5.6**] *Enter* AJAX

AJAX Troilus, thou coward Troilus, show thy head!

Enter DIOMEDES

DIOMEDES Troilus I say, where's Troilus?
AJAX   What wouldst thou?
DIOMEDES I would correct him.
AJAX Were I the general, thou shouldst have my office
   Ere that correction. Troilus I say, what, Troilus!   5

Enter TROILUS

TROILUS O traitor Diomed, turn thy false face, thou traitor,
   And pay the life thou ow'st me for my horse.
DIOMEDES Ha, art thou there?
AJAX I'll fight with him alone – stand, Diomed.
DIOMEDES He is my prize, I will not look upon.   10
TROILUS Come both you cogging Greeks, have at you both!

47 SD] *Capell; Exit* Q, F   **Act 5, Scene 6   5.6**] *Capell (subst.); not in* Q, F   **0** SD] F; *as SH* Q   **1** SD] F; *as SH* Q   **4**]
Q; *two lines* (Generall, / Thou) F   **6**] Q; *two lines* (Diomed! / Turne) F   **7** the] *Capell;* thy Q, F   **7** ow'st] *Capell;*
owest Q, F

44 draw together are all pulling together (faction is temporarily forgotten).

45 boy-queller killer of boys (though
Patroclus is, presumably, old enough to bear
arms). Bevington[2] remarks that Achilles uses
the phrase as 'an excuse to call Hector a
coward'.

Act 5, Scene 6
   3 correct discipline.
   4–5 Were . . . correction If I were general, I
would rather give you my high place than allow

you to be the first to 'correct' Troilus.

7 horse Troilus is still smarting from his earlier
defeat at Diomedes' hands (5.5.1–4).

9–10 The faintly ridiculous spectacle of the two
Greek warriors quarrelling over who gets to fight
Troilus suits the satirical bite of the battle scenes
and the play as a whole.

10 look upon stand back and watch.

11 cogging cheating, deceitful (the term is appropriate only to Diomedes, but there was an ancient association between Greeks and 'cheaters' –
see *OED* Greek *sb* 4).

Enter HECTOR

Exit Troilus [fighting with Ajax and Diomedes]
HECTOR Yea Troilus, O well fought, my youngest brother!

Enter ACHILLES

ACHILLES Now do I see thee, ha! have at thee, Hector.
   [They fight; Achilles is subdued]
HECTOR Pause if thou wilt.
ACHILLES I do disdain thy courtesy, proud Trojan.   15
   Be happy that my arms are out of use.
   My rest and negligence befriends thee now,
   But thou anon shalt hear of me again.
   Till when, go seek thy fortune.   *Exit*
HECTOR   Fare thee well.
   I would have been much more a fresher man,   20
   Had I expected thee.

Enter TROILUS

      How now my brother!
TROILUS Ajax hath ta'en Aeneas – shall it be?
   No, by the flame of yonder glorious heaven,
   He shall not carry him. I'll be ta'en too,
   Or bring him off. Fate hear me what I say,   25
   I reck not though I end my life today.   *Exit*

Enter one in [sumptuous] armour

HECTOR Stand, stand, thou Greek, thou art a goodly mark.
   No? wilt thou not? I like thy armour well:

---

11 SD.1 *Enter Hector*] F *(after / Exit Troylus); not in* Q 11 SD.2 *Exit Troilus*] F*; not in* Q 11 SD.2 *fighting . . . Diomedes*]
Rowe (subst.); not in Q, F 12 SD] F*; as SH* Q 13 ha] Q*; not in* F 13 SD] *Oxford (subst.); not in* Q, F*; Fight / Rowe;
dropping his sword / Capell (after 14)* 21 SD] *Cam.; after* brother Q, F 26 reck] Q, F *(wreake)* 26 I end] Q*; thou
end* F 26 SD.2 *sumptuous*] *Malone; not in* Q, F 27] Q*; two lines (Greeke, / Thou)* F

---

11 SD Hector pauses to watch Troilus, who is
apparently a match for both Greeks now that his
bloodlust is fully roused. Hector could be thinking
of going to his brother's aid, but is quickly inter-
cepted by Achilles.

14 An example, and a fatal one, of Hector's lion-
like nobility and courtesy (see 5.3.37–8).

17 **rest and negligence** neglect of battle.

23 **flame . . . heaven** the sun.

24 **carry** maintain power over, defeat.

25 **bring him off** rescue him. Logically, this
clause should precede the previous one – i.e. 'I'll
either free him or be taken myself.'

26 **reck** care.

26 SD **sumptuous** Malone's addition takes account of Hector's later description of the armour as
'goodly' (5.9.2) as well as of the emphasis that both
Caxton and especially Lydgate put on the richness
of the Greek's bejewelled armour. Hector's desire
to claim it as a prize may not necessarily be a sign of
venality, since taking such trophies was a standard
part of Homeric warfare, but Lydgate clearly sees it
as such: '[Hector] sodaynly was brought to his en-
dynge, / Onely for spoylynge of this ryche kinge, /
For of desyre to him that he hadde' (3.5362–4).

27 **goodly mark** handsome target.

I'll frush it and unlock the rivets all,
But I'll be master of it.

> [*Exit the one in sumptuous armour*]

        Wilt thou not, beast, abide?   30
Why then, fly on: I'll hunt thee for thy hide.   *Exit*

[5.7] *Enter* ACHILLES *with Myrmidons*

ACHILLES Come here about me, you my Myrmidons,
    Mark what I say. Attend me where I wheel,
    Strike not a stroke, but keep yourselves in breath;
    And when I have the bloody Hector found,
    Empale him with your weapons round about,   5
    In fellest manner execute your arms.
    Follow me sirs, and my proceedings eye:
    It is decreed Hector the great must die.

> [*Exeunt*]

[5.8] *Enter* MENELAUS *and* PARIS [*fighting, and*] THERSITES [*watching*]

THERSITES The cuckold and the cuckold-maker are at it! Now bull,
    now dog! 'Loo Paris 'loo! Now my double-horned Spartan! 'Loo

---

30 SD] *Walker (subst.); not in* Q, F   31 SD] Q, F; *Exeunt / Malone*   **Act 5, Scene 7** 5.7] *Capell (subst.); not in* Q,
F 1 SH] F; *not in* Q 6 arms] Q; *arme* F 8 SD] *Pope; Exit* Q, F **Act 5, Scene 8** 5.8] *Capell (subst.); not in* Q, F
0 SD] *Capell (subst.); Enter Thersi: Mene: Paris.* Q, F *(subst.)* 0 SD *watching*] *This edn; after them / Capell; not in* Q, F
2, 3 'Loo] F4; *lowe* Q, F *(all four occurrences)* 2 double-horned Spartan] *Alexander (conj. Kellner);* double hen'd spartan
Q; double hen'd sparrow F

29–30 I'll . . . it Even if I have to smash ('frush')
it and tear the rivets off, I'll be master of your
armour.

30 beast The Greek soldier's apparent cowardice prompts Hector to shift his metaphor; he
now sees the Greek not as a worthy opponent, but
as a mere beast to be hunted for his 'hide' (armour).

Act 5, Scene 7
2 where I wheel wherever I range.
3 in breath well rested (opposite of 'out of
breath').
5 Empale Enclose (as with stakes or 'palings').
6 fellest most savage.
7 eye observe.

Act 5, Scene 8
Most editors do not follow Capell in beginning

a new scene here, but the stage is cleared and new
characters arrive, which, as in the previous three
scenes, are the usual criteria for a scene break.
Moreover, as A. R. Braunmuller has pointed out
to me, the previous two scenes both end with a
rhymed couplet, as do all the following scenes, suggesting a break here as well.
0 SD Thersites accompanies the sexual warriors
and provides a running commentary.
1–2 Now bull, now dog This is an 'in'
joke, Paris' name suggesting 'Paris Garden' near
the Globe where bull-baiting contests took place.
Menelaus is the bull because of his cuckold's horns
(cf. 5.1.50–1), and Paris one of the attacking dogs.
''Loo . . .'loo,' a cry of encouragement to the dogs,
continues the mockery.
2 double-horned i.e. as a cuckold and a bull (?).
The Q reading, 'double hen'd spartan' does not fit

Paris 'loo! The bull has the game: ware horns, ho!

[Exeunt] Paris and Menelaus

Enter Bastard [MARGARELON]

MARGARELON Turn, slave, and fight.

THERSITES What art thou?   5

MARGARELON A bastard son of Priam's.

THERSITES I am a bastard too, I love bastards! I am bastard begot,
bastard instructed, bastard in mind, bastard in valour, in everything
illegitimate. One bear will not bite another, and wherefore should
one bastard? Take heed, the quarrel's most ominous to us: if the   10
son of a whore fight for a whore, he tempts judgement. Farewell,
bastard.   *[Exit]*

MARGARELON The devil take thee, coward.   *Exit*

[**5.9**] *Enter* HECTOR

HECTOR Most putrefièd core, so fair without,
    Thy goodly armour thus hath cost thy life.
    Now is my day's work done, I'll take my breath.
    Rest sword, thou hast thy fill of blood and death. *[He
    disarms]*

---

3 SD.1 *Exeunt*] Hanmer; *Exit* Q, F   3 SD.2 MARGARELON] *Capell; not in* Q, F   4, 6, 13 SHS MARGARELON] *Capell (subst.); Bast.* Q, F   7 bastard begot] Q; *a Bastard begot* F   12 SD] *Capell; not in* Q, F   13 SD] Q; *Exeunt.* F   Act 5, Scene 9   5.9] *Capell (subst.); not in* Q, F   3 my breath] Q; *good breath* F   4 SD.1] *Kittredge (subst.); not in* Q, F; *Puts off his helmet and hangs his shield behind him* / *Malone*

---

well with Menelaus, who, despite being Sparta's
king, has no hens at all (though, at a stretch,
'double' could mean 'deceitful, cheating', and refer
to Helen's betrayal); the F reading, 'double hen'd
sparrow' applies best to Paris, who can be said to
have two hens (his abandoned wife, Oenone, and
Helen) and is fittingly called a sparrow by virtue
of his lecherous disposition (sparrows were traditionally so regarded). In the end, Kellner's conjectural emendation makes the best sense and, as
Muir points out, fits with the alternating pattern
of Thersites' satirical thrusts: 'one would expect
the disputed reading, coming as it does between
two references to Paris as a dog, would refer to
Menelaus'.

3 has the game is winning.

3 ware beware of.

9 One . . . another proverbial. Variorum cites

Juvenal, and Muir points to Dent w606, where the
same idea is applied to wolves.

11 tempts judgement invites divine judgement.

Act 5, Scene 9

0 SD Hector either drags the body in or carries
the armour he has won.

1 putrefièd core (1) rotten centre, (2) decaying body (punning on 'corse' and French *corps*).
The image captures a central issue in the play
– the fair outside and the corrupt inner reality. The Greek, now dead, has begun to pu-
trefy, and that corruption at the core stands for
the conduct of the war, the love between Troilus
and Cressida and, in miniature, Hector's desire
for the prizes of war. See 2.1.5, 5.1.5, 6 and
nn.

Enter ACHILLES *and* MYRMIDONS

ACHILLES Look Hector, how the sun begins to set,   5
    How ugly night comes breathing at his heels;
    Even with the vail and dark'ning of the sun
    To close the day up, Hector's life is done.
HECTOR I am unarmed, forgo this vantage, Greek.
ACHILLES Strike, fellows, strike, this is the man I seek.   10
                   [*They kill Hector*]
    So Ilium, fall thou next, come, Troy, sink down.
    Here lies thy heart, thy sinews, and thy bone.
    On Myrmidons, and cry you all amain:
    'Achilles hath the mighty Hector slain.'
                 Retreat [*sounded*]
    Hark, a retire upon our Grecian part.   15
             [*Another retreat sounded*]
A MYRMIDON The Trojan trumpets sound the like, my lord.
ACHILLES The dragon wing of night o'erspreads the earth,
    And stickler-like the armies separates.
    My half-supped sword that frankly would have fed,
    Pleased with this dainty bait, thus goes to bed. [*Sheathes his*   20
    sword]
    Come, tie his body to my horse's tail,
    Along the field I will the Trojan trail.
              Exeunt [*dragging out the body*]

---

4 SD.2 *and*] Q; *and his* F   7 dark'ning] Q; *darking* F   10 SD] *Rowe (subst., after 8); not in* Q, F; Hector *falls* / *Capell*
11 next, come] Q; *now* F   13 and cry] Q; *cry* F   14 'Achilles . . . slain.'] *Hanmer (subst.); Achilles . . . slaine,* Q, F
(subst.)   14 SD sounded] *Malone; not in* Q, F   15 retire] Q; *retreat* F   15 part] F; *prat* Q   15 SD] *Oxford (subst.); not*
in Q, F   16 SH] *Rowe (subst.); One:* Q; *Gree.* F   16 Trojan trumpets] F; *Troyans trumpet* Q   16 sound] Q; *sounds* F
20 bait] Q; *bed* F   20 SD] *Capell (subst.); not in* Q, F   22 SD *dragging . . . body*] *Capell (subst.); not in* Q, F

---

6 his the sun's.

7 vail setting, descent (though with a suggestion
of 'veil' or covering).

9 vantage advantage.

10 SD In performance this is typically one of the
most arresting and powerful moments of the play,
simultaneously brutal and ritualistic. Often the
Myrmidons close in with slow, stabbing motions;
sometimes, as in Dieter Dorn's Munich production (1986), they hoist the still impaled body aloft;
in Barton's 1976 RSC production, they crushed
Hector with huge shields of the size and shape of
double basses.

13 amain loudly.

17 Shakespeare frequently associates night with

dragons: 'For Night's swift dragons cut the clouds
full fast' (*MND* 3.2.379) and *Cym.* 2.2.48, 'Swift,
swift you dragons of the night' (H. R. D. Anders,
cited in Variorum).

18 stickler-like in the manner of an umpire or
arbiter.

19 frankly . . . fed wanted to feed fully (or
freely).

20 dainty bait tasty snack.

21–2 Achilles' barbaric treatment of Hector's
corpse is consistent with his behaviour in Homer,
but fits also with the anti-heroic strain of the play
and his cowardly way of eliminating his enemy. In
Caxton and Lydgate, Achilles accords this treatment to Troilus, not Hector.

[5.10] *Sound Retreat. Enter* AGAMEMNON, AJAX, MENELAUS, NESTOR, DIOMEDES, *and the rest, marching* [*to the sound of drums*]. *Shout* [*within*]

AGAMEMNON Hark, hark, what shout is that?

NESTOR Peace, drums.

SOLDIERS (*Within*) Achilles! Achilles! Hector's slain! Achilles!

DIOMEDES The bruit is Hector's slain, and by Achilles.

AJAX If it be so, yet bragless let it be: 5
　　　Great Hector was as good a man as he.

AGAMEMNON March patiently along; let one be sent
　　　To pray Achilles see us at our tent.
　　　If in his death the gods have us befriended,
　　　Great Troy is ours, and our sharp wars are ended.   10

　　　　　　　　　　　　　　　　　　　　　　　　Exeunt

[5.11] *Enter* AENEAS, PARIS, ANTENOR, *and* DEIPHOBUS

AENEAS Stand, ho! Yet are we masters of the field.

　　　　　　　　　　　　　Enter TROILUS

TROILUS Never go home, here starve we out the night:
　　　Hector is slain.

ALL　　　　　　　　　　　　Hector? The gods forbid!

Act 5, Scene 10   5.10] *Capell (subst.); not in* Q, F   0 SD.1 *Sound Retreat*] F *(at end of previous scene); not in* Q   0 SD.2 *to the sound of drums*] *Muir; not in* Q, F   0 SD.2 *Shout within*] *Capell (subst.); Shout.* F *(at end of previous scene); not in* Q   1 what shout is that] F; what is this Q   3 SD] Q; *not in* F   6 as good a man] Q; a man as good F   Act 5, Scene 11 5.11] *Capell (subst.); not in* Q, F   0 SD *and*] F; *not in* Q   1 SD] Q; *after* 2 F   2 SH] Q; *speech continued to Aeneas* F

Act 5, Scene 10

　4 bruit news (literally, noise, clamour).

　5–10 The couplets here have the ring of finality, as though this were the end of the play, but, characteristically, closure is postponed and attenuated (see 5.11.30–1 n.).

　5 bragless let it be let him not brag about it.

　9 his Hector's.

Act 5, Scene 11

　2 F gives this to Aeneas (delaying Troilus' entry till after the line) and many editors have followed suit. But it seems inappropriate – why should Aeneas desire the Trojans to spend the night out in cold Turkey instead of returning home? As Hillebrand says, 'The invariable routine of battle was that both armies withdrew to their own quarters at dark' (Variorum, p. 342); at 5.9.14–15, retreat is sounded on both sides, and a moment later night, 'stickler-like . . . separates' the armies. At the beginning of this scene, Aeneas is gathering the troops for the march back to Troy. Troilus enters to forestall the return, saying that it would be not only fitting, given Hector's death, to 'starve out the night', but preferable to going back to Troy with the dreadful news – as indeed he makes explicit in 15–17.

　2 starve we out *OED* (*v* 5b) defines 'starve out' as 'endure in perishing cold', with this line as its only evidence, and editors have mostly gone along, citing *OED* in their turn, thus creating a circular argument. But the line is more likely an English version of the medieval Latin phrase *famare noctem*, meaning to defeat or exhaust the night by staying awake, here applied to a kind of vigil for Hector.

TROILUS He's dead, and at the murderer's horse's tail
              In beastly sort dragged through the shameful field.   5
              Frown on, you heavens, effect your rage with speed,
              Sit, gods, upon your thrones and smile at Troy!
              I say at once, let your brief plagues be mercy,
              And linger not our sure destructions on.
AENEAS My lord, you do discomfort all the host.   10
TROILUS You understand me not that tell me so.
              I do not speak of flight, of fear, of death,
              But dare all imminence that gods and men
              Address their dangers in. Hector is gone:
              Who shall tell Priam so, or Hecuba?   15
              Let him that will a screech-owl aye be called
              Go in to Troy and say there, 'Hector's dead.'
              There is a word will Priam turn to stone,
              Make wells and Niobes of the maids and wives,
              Cold statues of the youth, and in a word   20
              Scare Troy out of itself. But march away;
              Hector is dead, there is no more to say.
              Stay yet! You vile abominable tents,
              Thus proudly pitched upon our Phrygian plains,
              Let Titan rise as early as he dare,   25
              I'll through and through you; and thou great-sized coward,

---

7 smile at] Q, F; smite all *Hanmer;* smite at *Warburton*   17 there,] F; their Q   17 'Hector's dead'] *Staunton (subst.);*
Hectors dead Q; *Hector's* dead F   20 Cold] Q; Coole F   21–2 But . . . dead] F; *not in* Q   23 vile] F; proud Q
24 pitched] Q; pight F

---

5 **beastly sort** a brutal, inhuman manner.

5 **shameful** The neutral field is shameful as a result of Achilles' action – Shakespeare frequently transposes epithets in this way.

7 **smile at Troy** be kind to Troy (by bringing about our destruction quickly). Many editors have adopted 'smite at' (after Hanmer/Warburton) but the phrase, as Muir says, is 'feeble'; those who retain 'smile' typically gloss it as 'smile in mockery'. But Troilus means it sincerely, if paradoxically – he wants the gods to both 'frown' (6) and smile in that they should destroy Troy but do so promptly and not 'linger . . . on' the destruction (9); this would be a 'mercy'.

8 **let . . . mercy** be merciful by making your plagues brief.

9 And do not protract ('linger . . . on') our inevitable destruction.

10 **discomfort** discourage, dishearten.

13–14 **all imminence . . . in** any threatening evils that gods or men might be preparing to endanger me with.

16 **screech-owl** harbinger of doom.

16 **aye** forever.

19 **wells and Niobes** fountains of tears. As a punishment for her blasphemy, Niobe was forced to witness the death of her many children and then turned to a weeping statue (Ovid, Book VI). She thus became a figure for maternal grief.

20 **Cold statues** i.e. struck dumb and frozen by grief (perhaps suggested by the image of Niobe, but here the reference is to the immobility of stone).

21–2 'The apparent finality of this couplet might support the theory that the play, in some versions, ended at this point' (Bevington[2]). See 30–1 n.

25 **Titan** The sun.

26 **coward** Achilles (appropriate because of the way he murdered Hector and then treated his corpse).

No space of earth shall sunder our two hates.
I'll haunt thee like a wicked conscience still
That mouldeth goblins swift as frenzy's thoughts.
Strike a free march to Troy, with comfort go: 30
Hope of revenge shall hide our inward woe.

Enter PANDARUS

PANDARUS But hear you, hear you –
TROILUS Hence broker-lackey! [*Strikes him*] Ignomy and shame
Pursue thy life and live aye with thy name.

Exeunt all but Pandarus

PANDARUS A goodly medicine for my aching bones. O world, world –   35
thus is the poor agent despised. O traitors and bawds, how
earnestly are you set a-work and how ill requited! Why should
our endeavour be so loved and the performance so loathed? What
verse for it? What instance for it? Let me see,
Full merrily the humble-bee doth sing   40

---

33 broker-lackey] *Dyce;* broker, lacky Q, F *(subst.)* 33 SD] *Rowe; not in* Q, F 33 ignomy and] F; ignomyny Q 34 SD]
Q; *Exeunt* F 35 my] Q; mine F 35 world, world] Q; world, world, world F 36 traitors] Q, F; traders *Deighton (conj.*
Craig) 38 loved] Q; desir'd F

27 **sunder** keep apart.

28 **still** continuously.

29 That raises demonic images ('goblins' = evil spirits) in the guilty mind as quickly as madness generates frenzied thoughts.

30–1 Editors and critics over the years have frequently seen this couplet (or indeed the couplet at 21–2) as a fitting end to the play, regarding Pandarus' intrusion as both inappropriate and unlikely (what is he doing on the battlefield?). The Oxford edition goes so far as to end the play at this point, printing the Epilogue as an 'additional passage'. The problem is exacerbated by the textual repetition in F only of lines that appear first at the end of 5.3 (see 5.3.111 n.). See Taylor, 'Bibliography', and Textual Analysis, pp. 240–2, for a full discussion.

30 **free** quick and informal.

31–4 As the Trojans prepare to exit (some perhaps already having gone off), Pandarus interrupts; Aeneas and some of the others then watch Troilus as he rejects Pandarus.

33 **broker-lackey** servile bawd, pander.

33 **Ignomy** Ignominy.

35–54 Directors have sometimes brought on Thersites to join forces with Pandarus for the Epilogue, as John Barton did in 1968 and 1976; Trevor Nunn added Cressida as silent observer as well. See Introduction, pp. 54–5.

35 **medicine** the blow he has just received from Troilus.

35 **aching bones** suggesting syphilis (cf. 'Neapolitan bone-ache', 2.3.15).

36 **traitors** both literal and metaphorical. W. J. Craig's conjecture, 'traders' (= pimps, as at 44), accepted by many editors, is certainly possible since Pandarus does not develop his analogy between pimps ('bawds') and traitors. Indeed, 'trader' and 'traitor' derive from a common root meaning 'to hand over' (Latin *tradere*) and are very close in sound. But Pandarus' point is that both political traitors and sexual traders are 'agents' whose work is much sought after but, after it is done, disdained.

38 **endeavour . . . performance** efforts . . . achievements; the pander's efforts are treated exactly as lust itself is: 'Past reason hunted' and then 'Past reason hated' (Sonnet 129, 6–7).

39 **verse** illustrative rhyme (which he then goes on to recite).

39 **instance** example.

Till he hath lost his honey and his sting,
And being once subdued in armèd tail,
Sweet honey and sweet notes together fail.
Good traders in the flesh, set this in your painted cloths:
As many as be here of panders' hall,   45
Your eyes, half out, weep out at Pandar's fall.
Or if you cannot weep, yet give some groans,
Though not for me yet for your aching bones.
Brethren and sisters of the hold-door trade,
Some two months hence my will shall here be made.   50
It should be now, but that my fear is this:
Some gallèd goose of Winchester would hiss.
Till then I'll sweat and seek about for eases,
And at that time bequeath you my diseases.   [*Exit*]

FINIS

41–3 Having once lost his sting (sexual potency, power to move), his honeyed notes (ability to sweet-talk and make assignations) have no more potency either. Like Pandarus' lines just above, his song seems to apply equally to bawds and the lovers who employ them.

44 traders . . . flesh bawds, pimps (addressing the audience).

44 painted cloths wall-hangings painted with scenes and mottoes. What follows is the 'moral' Pandarus would like to see hanging in bawdy-houses, painted on cheap cloth.

45 here in the theatre, but also in the imagined bawdy-house.

45 panders' hall the guild of panders (Pandarus puns on his name and the meaning that has accrued to it since he became notorious – cf. 3.2.178–82).

46 half out already half out from the effects of venereal disease.

49 Brothel-keepers (who have to guard the doors). Again the audience is satirically linked to 'traders in the flesh'.

50 here This word has misled many editors and critics to locate the first performance of the play at the Inns of Court and to elaborate theories about its provenance and revision.

Another, related theory has been that Pandarus' promise of a will means that Shakespeare originally intended a sequel. Both views rest on rather too literalistic a reading. See Textual Analysis, pp. 234, 241–2, and Introduction, pp. 7–9.

51 should would.

52 gallèd (1) diseased, (2) vexed, annoyed.

52 goose of Winchester prostitute (so called because many of the brothels, like the theatres, were in Southwark on the south bank of the Thames, which was under the jurisdiction of the Bishop of Winchester); this reference confirms the location of the speech as the public theatre on the south bank rather than the Inns of Court. Pandarus holds off on making his will, pretending to be worried that some diseased whore in the audience might be annoyed and 'hiss' at him. Since the conventional aim of an epilogue is to invite applause, a hiss would clearly be inappropriate. However, the next two lines effectively take back what he says here, since the promise to bequeath his diseases to a galled audience is tantamount to actually doing it.

53 sweat The conventional cure for venereal disease included inducing a sweat by the application of heat and medication.

53 eases remedies, ways of relieving pain.

TEXTUAL ANALYSIS

The textual situation of *Troilus and Cressida* is complex and intractable. It offers an object lesson in the uncertainties surrounding editorial decision-making. There are two early editions with some claim to authority, the quarto of 1609 (Q) and the Folio of 1623 (F). There are approximately 5,000 differences between Q and F, most of them quite small (punctuation, spelling etc.) but with enough substantive variants (around 500) to complicate the picture. Since the precise sources of these variants remain uncertain, a definitive judgement about their provenance is impossible. Arguments for the primacy of either Q or F are more or less equal, the variants between the two texts are distributed in such a way as to make adjudication extremely tricky (i.e. each text boasts many 'superior' readings), and there are signs of revision in both texts. The revisions probably derive from authorial tinkering of one kind or another, but just for that reason it is impossible to know which reading represents Shakespeare's 'final' thoughts. It is even likely that the idea of a final thought is illusory, since Shakespeare, like most writers, must in certain instances (while copying for example, or after consultation with his fellow actors at rehearsal) have made changes spontaneously, without giving the matter a great deal of attention. Editors have grappled with this situation in a variety of ways, without fully clarifying it, although a generally accepted conclusion, one not without its problems, has been that F was printed from a copy of Q that had been emended to accord with a playhouse manuscript. This MS. would evidently have been different from that behind Q, but there is no reason to assume that it represents a later version of the play.

The 1609 quarto, which was printed by George Eld for Richard Bonian and Henry Walley, exists in two 'states'[1], the second of which prints a virtually identical text but features an altered title page and adds the notorious epistle from a 'neuer writer' to an 'euer reader'. The original title page calls the play 'The Historie of Troylus and Cresseida' and states that the play '*was acted by the Kings Maiesties* / seruants at the Globe'[2], whereas the revised title page adds the word 'Famous' before 'Historie' and, more importantly, makes no mention of performance, substituting instead an enticing description after the main title: '*Excellently expressing the beginning* / of their loues, with the conceited wooing / of *Pandarus* Prince of *Licia*.' The prefaced epistle claims that the play was never 'stal'd with the Stage', i.e. never publicly performed. These facts have given rise to a great deal of speculation about private performance, probably at the Inns of Court, with the further claim that the play was never actually produced at the

---

[1] See Williams, 'Second issue'.
[2] I cite the original spelling throughout the Textual Analysis.

Globe.[1] The precise date of the epistle is unknown – it could have been written back in 1603 when James Roberts entered the play conditionally in the Stationers' Register (though Roberts never printed it, and perhaps never intended to). If the epistle does date from 1603, its statement about the play's non-performance, even if true at the time, would tell us nothing about subsequent stagings. More likely, however, the epistle was written in 1609 for inclusion in the second state of the quarto. Nevertheless, its claims about staging are not necessarily reliable. The preface has to be regarded as a 'blurb' rather than a full statement of the facts. Its author's intent is to sell the book. If he denigrates the 'smoaky breath of the multitude'(line 24), it is to augment the prestige of reading over play-going and hence enhance the book's saleability. Moreover, it would have been extremely odd for the King's Men not to have presented publicly, on a few occasions at least, a new and challenging play by their leading playwright. It seems likely therefore that the play *was* produced at the Globe, and this has important implications for our understanding of the textual situation.[2]

Indeed, the 1603 Stationers' entry hints at performance in the use of the word 'booke', the term typically used for 'playbook', i.e. the text used to manage theatrical presentation. The entry, dated 7 February 1603, reads: 'Entred for his [i.e. that of Roberts, whose name is written in the margin] copie in Full Court holden this day to print when he hath gotten sufficient aucthority for yt. The booke of Troilus and Cressida as yt is acted by my lo: Chamber*l*ens Men.' Greg argued that Roberts may have been making a 'blocking' entry on behalf of the players to prevent an unauthorised edition;[3] but 'authority', as Blayney and others have shown, refers specifically to the need to obtain ecclesiastical permission to print. Roberts, who held a monopoly for the printing of playbills, entered a number of plays without apparently intending to publish them, selling them 'to other stationers rather than taking the financial risk of publishing them himself'[4]. This is probably what happened with *Troilus*, and provides further evidence that the epistle was composed specifically for the 1609 printing.

The rather sloppily printed text of Q lacks a number of necessary stage directions, and is frequently unreliable as to the attribution of speeches, which has led to the conclusion that it derives from an authorial draft or transcript (or at least that it is not of playhouse origin). As for F, bibliographic and typographic evidence have been adduced by Peter Alexander and Philip Williams to show its apparent reliance on Q, although they were also aware that, because of the many added passages and verbal variants, Q alone could not be the source of F.[5] Williams' work essentially corroborated the views of Alexander and of E. K. Chambers, who argued that, in the composing of F,

---

[1] Alexander first raised the possibility of an Inns of Court performance (pp. 278–9) and J. M. Nosworthy has argued the case extensively; they have been followed by Honigmann, 'Date and revision' (who adds Cambridge as a possible venue), Taylor, 'Bibliography' and a number of others. See Introduction, pp. 7–9.
[2] I discuss this matter more fully in the Introduction, pp. 7–8.
[3] *First Folio*, p. 338.
[4] Blayney, p. 387.
[5] See Alexander, and Williams, '*Troilus*'. See Walton for an extensive analysis of common errors and their distribution; Walton supports the view that F was printed from Q and collated with a MS.

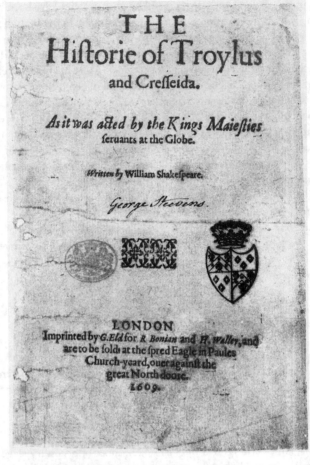

Figure 13. The first 'state' of the 1609 Q title page, featuring the prominent statement that the play was acted by Shakespeare's company at the Globe. This version also lacks the 'epistle'.

a copy of Q was supplemented by reference to a manuscript. This conclusion has gone uncontested since 1950.

The manuscripts behind F and Q

The problem is, what was the nature of that manuscript? The question cannot be answered without considering the nature of Q and its MS., so that we have to approach the two texts simultaneously. The basic issue, which has been much debated, is which text, if either, derives from the 'foul papers' (i.e. Shakespeare's original draft) and which, if either, from a scribal or theatrical copy. Most commentators have noted that F has more theatrical markings than Q, although few have concluded from that observation

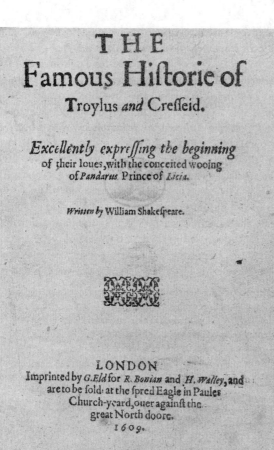

Figure 14. The second 'state' of the 1609 Q title page, from which reference to performance has been omitted, and a note added about the comic mediation of Pandarus; the changes were probably made to entice buyers and to conform with the statement in the epistle, which appears only in this version of Q, that the play had not been 'clapper-clawed' by the 'vulgar'.

that F must derive from a promptbook. But until recently, textual critics tended to think of 'promptbooks' in anachronistic and idealised terms, failing to appreciate the range, messiness, and inconsistency of the playbooks that could be used in the Elizabethan playhouse. (So too, the term 'foul papers,' as used by modern scholars, typically refers to an idealised entity of which no early modern examples have actually survived.[1]) Without going into all the details of the debate about the *Troilus* manuscripts, suffice

[1] On 'promptbooks' see William Long's series of articles about playhouse manuscripts; and for a thorough debunking of the distinctness of the categories implied by both 'promptbook' and 'foul papers', and a cogent critique of the kinds of assumption about the MSS. behind printed texts that the terms encourage, see Werstine, 'Narratives'. While I occasionally use the term 'foul papers' here, I do so mainly for convenience, agreeing with Werstine that the term is imprecise; it merely designates some kind of authorial draft.

it to say that until Gary Taylor re-edited the play for the Oxford edition (basing his judgements on an earlier article), the accepted view was that Q derived from a scribal or authorial fair copy, perhaps specially prepared for a patron, and F from foul papers, which, however, had undergone some amendment.[1] This conclusion, put forward by E. K. Chambers and extended in various ways by Alice Walker, H. N. Hillebrand, and E. A. J. Honigmann, was based initially on the existence of two doubled passages in F (discussed below)[2] and derived from the principle expressed by Greg, that 'textual repetition usually points to foul papers'.[3] Hillebrand and Honigmann also emphasised the role of revision, the latter arguing that the absence of several passages in Q can best be explained as the result of cutting.

The passages which Honigmann regards as 'first shots,'[4] later cut by Shakespeare, Taylor sees as deliberate additions and expansions.[5] Not all of Honigmann's examples are of equal weight, but in some cases he seems to me unquestionably right. Here is one instance (others are discussed in the Commentary). At the end of Nestor's long speech about the dangers of putting their best man forward in the chivalric contest with Hector, we get the following two passages (1.3.354–61; TLN 819–29):

> Q: What heart receiues from hence a conquering part,
>   To steele a strong opinion to them selues.
>   *Uliss.* Giue pardon to my speech? therefore tis meete,
>   *Achilles* meete not *Hector*, let vs like Marchants
>   First shew foule wares, and thinke perchance theile sell;
>   If not; the luster of the better shall exceed,
>   By shewing the worse first:

> F: What heart from hence receyues the conqu'ring part
>   To steele a strong opinion to themselues,
>   Which entertain'd, Limbes are in his instruments,
>   In no lesse working, then are Swords and Bowes
>   Directiue by the Limbes.
>   *Vlys.* Giue pardon to my speech:
>   Therefore 'tis meet, *Achilles* meet not *Hector*:
>   Let vs (like Merchants) shew our fowlest Wares,
>   And thinke perchance they'l sell: If not,
>   The luster of the better yet to shew,
>   Shall shew the better.

[1] Thus, in this account, the F version of the play pre-dates the MS. that stands behind Q, but shows signs of later revision. As Hillebrand puts it, 'the original text underwent some emendment before it appeared in print as Q. And F shows clearly that subsequently to the publication of Q [he means, I believe, the production of the Q MS.] the text had been further emended' (Variorum, p. 344). He concludes that Shakespeare touched up a copy of the play which served as the basis for Q, and that subsequently he made changes to the copy that he retained, but failed to add the revisions made in the Q copy. This retained MS. then found its way to Isaac Jaggard, the publisher of the Folio, perhaps through John Heminge and Henry Condell, Shakespeare's fellow actors who assembled the texts for the Folio printing.
[2] They occur at TLN 2658/2670 and 3328–30/3569–71 (4.5.96 ff. and 5.3.111/5.11.32 ff.). See Chambers, I, 438–49, Walker, *Textual Problems*, Honigmann, *Stability*, and Hillebrand's discussion in Variorum.
[3] *First Folio*, p. 138.
[4] Honigmann, *Stability*, p. 84.
[5] *Textual Companion*, p. 426.

If, as Taylor suggests, we regard Q as foul papers, and F as representing theatrical and authorial revision,[1] we are forced to conclude that Shakespeare added, probably in the theatre, the three very obscure lines absent from Q ('Which . . . Limbes' TLN 821–3). To me, it is much more plausible that the Q text results from a deliberate excision of lines that are almost impossible to decipher the first time through (it may be worth noting, though it doesn't prove anything, that in every modern promptbook I have consulted these lines are cut).[2] Ulysses' response in Q has also, I think, benefited from deliberate revision – eliminating awkward repetition, enhancing clarity (e.g. by adding the word 'First' in 358), and highlighting the antithesis in the final two lines quoted. In this case, then, Q looks strongly like the revised text. Still, and this must be emphasised, it is virtually impossible to decide the matter conclusively; any interpretation of the evidence depends on (fallible and personal) literary judgement.

Other instances are more uncertain. Some F-only passages seem like additions, inserted for clarity or enhanced effect, and there are several cases where variants of single words or short phrases seem to point to F as the revised version. Of the former, probable additions include 3.3.161–3, 4.4.76 (which may be simply restoring a line inadvertently omitted in Q), 4.5.165–70, 5.3.20–2; 5.3.58, 5.11.21–2.[3] And there is at least one passage (2.3.117 ff.) in F which looks like the revised version of the corresponding passage in Q:

> Q: [We] watch
> His course, and time, his ebbs and flowes, and if
> The passage, and whole streame of his commencement,
> Rode on his tide.
> F: [We] watch
> His pettish lines, his ebs, his flowes, as if
> The passage and whole carriage of this action
> Rode on his tyde.   (TLN 1334–7)

Both versions are undoubtedly Shakespeare's, and it is of course possible that in revising he made things less effective, but the elimination of both the vagueness of 'commencement' and the awkwardness of a stream riding on a tide in Q, along with the careful blending of two metaphorical strands in the F passage, point to the latter as the revised.

As for single words and short passages, once again definitive judgements are impossible, but probable F revisions include the following: 'patient' (Q: 'ancient' 1.3.36); 'seekes' (Q: 'feeds', perhaps simply a misreading, 1.3.268); 'shining' (Q: 'ayming' 3.3.100); 'hedge' (Q: 'turne' 3.3.158); 'Knowes almost euery graine of Plutoes gold' (Q: 'Knowes almost euery thing' 3.3.198); 'secrets of nature' (Q: 'secrets of neighbor *Pandar*' 4.2.72); the repetition of 'I beseech you' in 4.2.86 (the Q sentence is less emphatic); 'hem'd' (Q: 'shrupd' 4.5.193).

---

[1] See Taylor, 'Bibliography', p. 109.

[2] Because I regard them as an authorial cut I have omitted them from my text – see also Commentary and collation.

[3] Honigmann (*Stability*) regards the first three of these as deliberate cuts in Q.

More frequently, however, Q readings seem preferable (e.g. in a single scene, 1.3, at 27, 92, 138, 229, 277, 294) and there are also plenty of seemingly indifferent variants, where the direction of revision is impossible to determine: e.g.: 1.2.220: 'such a woman a man knowes not' (Q), 'such another woman, one knowes not' (F); 1.3.19: 'call' (Q), 'thinke' (F); 1.3.264: 'restie' (Q), 'rusty' (F); 3.2.113–14: 'drawes / My very soule of councell' (Q), 'drawes / My soule of counsell from me' (F); 4.1.54: 'deserues . . . best' (Q), 'merits . . . most' (F), etc.

What all this means is that neither text can be confidently described as the 'revised' version. Each variant has to be addressed on its own, in a piecemeal fashion. There can be no certainty about this text, and it therefore seems best to alert readers and performers to the alternatives and encourage them to decide on individual readings for themselves. Nevertheless, the weight of evidence suggests that Q shows more signs of revision than F; this leads us to the view that F was probably printed from some kind of authorial draft, though it had gone through a process of revision and theatricalisation, and may have been recopied by a scribe.

The doubled passages mentioned above support this general conclusion. The first occurs at 4.5.95 ff. where Agamemnon (in F) asks for information about the Trojan knight that 'lookes so heauy'. Here is how the two texts present this moment:

> Q: *Vlisses*: what Troyan is that same that lookes so heauy?
> *Vlis*. The yongest sonne of *Priam*, a true knight,
> Not yet mature . . . [the description extends for ten lines and ends]
> They call him *Troylus* and on him erect . . .
> F: *Aga*. What Troian is that same that lookes so heauy?
> *Vlis*. The yongest Sonne of *Priam*;
> A true Knight; they call him *Troylus* . . .   (TLN 2656–8)

The rest of the F passage parallels Q and repeats 'They call him *Troylus*' (TLN 2670).

The second repeat is more substantial (and more troublesome). Almost identical passages occur at the end of 5.3 in F and just before the Epilogue in both texts. In 5.3, Troilus has just finished tearing up the letter Pandarus has brought him from Cressida, saying 'My loue with words and errors still she feedes, / But edifies another with her deedes.' Q then provides an *Exeunt* and moves to the next scene; F prints the following (TLN 3328–31):

> *Pand*. Why, but heare you?
> *Troy*. Hence brother lackie; ignomie and shame
> Pursue thy life, and liue aye with thy name.
>   *A Larum.*   *Exeunt.*

At the end of the play in both texts, after Troilus' summing-up speech (5.11.11–31), Pandarus enters and there is an almost exact repeat of the short sequence at the end of 5.3, though now Pandarus doubles 'heare you', Q reads 'ignomyny,' for F's 'ignomy, and', and in both Q and F we get 'broker' instead of 'brother' in Troilus' rebuff.

The evidence of these passages has suggested to most scholars that Shakespeare originally wrote what appears in F only, had second thoughts and so lengthened the

4.5 passage, adding a fuller description of Troilus' chivalric qualities (building him up for the finale, perhaps), and removed the 5.3 passage for use at the end, leaving his first thoughts uncancelled. Q, based on a carefully recopied MS. (probably by Shakespeare himself), thus rightly lacks the doubled passages.[1]

Taylor ('Bibliography') turned the consensus upside down, arguing that F derives from the promptbook, and Q from foul papers. He based his view on the putative theatrical markings of F, of which there are certainly more than in Q. They are, however, far from complete, and sometimes mistaken or confused. And, as William Long has shown in a series of articles on theatrical manuscripts from the period, the differences between a 'promptbook' (a term that Long avoids because of its misleading connotations of precision and thoroughness) and an authorial copy are neither clear-cut nor easily discernible. The fact that F shows more attention to theatrical exigency than Q does not rule out the possibility that the F MS. was foul papers. Taylor argues that modern editors should base their editions on F since it was revised by Shakespeare (and/or under his supervision) for productions at the Globe (presumably after the hypothetical first production at the Inns of Court), and hence represents the last version of the play current during Shakespeare's working life.

Facing the dilemma of the doubled passages, Taylor takes the bold step of seeing them as evidence of revision in F of Q's original. The 'bro[k]er lackey'[2] passage in 5.3 is thus for him not a first thought but a revision designed to replace Pandarus' epilogue which, he claims, was written initially for the occasion of an Inns of Court performance and cut for production at the Globe. In the Oxford edition, he therefore cut the Epilogue, relegating it to an appendix.[3]

There is a hard logic to this decision, but it is based on a series of debatable hypotheses. First, that the F MS. is a theatrical copy (it probably is but the evidence is far from water-tight). Second, that the play was originally written for a private performance at the Inns of Court, a view based on no evidence whatsoever. Perhaps it was written for the Globe and revised for private performance (if indeed it ever was shown at the Inns).[4] Taylor's third hypothesis is that the Epilogue is more appropriate for a select audience of young lawyers than for a general audience at the Globe. This is questionable on at least three grounds: (1) the Epilogue is no more 'select' than the rest of the play,

---

[1] Still, the confusion, in the first passage, of Q's speech heading (4.5.95) needs to be explained: F's correction might well derive from the book-keeper, if, as I argue below, the MS. had been marked for theatrical use. Alternatively, Q's error may derive from the compositor.

[2] Taylor regards 'brother' as a simple misreading, but Godshalk argues that it might be a substantive variant.

[3] He did, however, retain both occurrences of 'They call him Troilus.'

[4] One bit of evidence adduced by those who advocate the Inns of Court performance idea is Pandarus' remark in the Epilogue, 'Some two monthes hence my will shall *here* be made' (italics added), which they see as a local allusion to the legal milieu – a rather literal-minded interpretation I think, especially if we compare other epilogues, like those of Puck and Prospero, where 'here' denotes a subtle combination of fictional locale and the stage itself. For an extended critique of Taylor's theory of original (for the Inns of Court) and revised (for the Globe) versions, see Jensen, pp. 417–20. It should be noted that Taylor later apparently abandoned his theory of an Inns of Court performance – see *Textual Companion*, p. 438, where the note on 'Additional Passage' B. 21 explicitly repudiates the idea – even though he did not alter his views about the provenance of the MSS. behind Q and F which depended, to a large degree, on the Inns of Court theory.

which Taylor assumes was presented to the Globe audience; (2) Pandarus addresses the audience as 'Brethren and sisters of the hold-dore trade', a remark that includes everyone in the act of pandering – certainly not a flattering address to the audience but not one confined to lawyers either, and appropriate enough in the circumstances that the play has dramatised; and (3), there were no 'sisters' at the Inns of Court, a fact that no proponent of the Inns of Court theory has ever mentioned.[1] A fourth hypothesis is that the compositor or annotator must have missed the cancellation mark, while picking up on the inserted passage in 5.3. But even a cursory glance at surviving theatrical MSS. from the period will reveal how obvious cancellation marks typically are and how difficult to miss; editorial explanations that rely on missed cancellation marks need to be approached with caution.[2] Overall, then, I have to question the legitimacy of cutting a crucial passage that occurs in both early texts on the grounds of what can only be regarded as highly ambiguous evidence of revision.[3]

The Folio text and the theatre

As William Long has shown, the various theatrical MSS. that have survived from the period make it clear that authorial copy used as a 'Book' and scribal copy are not always distinguishable, and that plays could be mounted and run with what we would regard as very ragged promptbooks, many of which show textual errors that the players and the book-keeper seem to have happily ignored. Thus the existence of the doubled passages in *Troilus and Cressida*, probably left uncancelled by Shakespeare, would not necessarily have posed a problem for the actors, who each had their own 'parts,' nor for the book-keeper, who could apparently do his job without worrying about textual ambiguity. Nor do we have to imagine compositors missing cancellation marks. What I think we are looking at, therefore, in the MS. behind F, is either Shakespeare's 'foul papers' or a transcript of them, but annotated by a book-keeper for performance.[4] The MS. might have looked rather like certain extant theatrical MSS., such as that of Heywood's *The Captives*, though without Heywood's extensive stage directions. While Greg regards *The Captives* as an authorial draft, annotated by a book-keeper 'with a view to having a transcript made' for use as a play-book,[5] it is, despite the problems of

---

[1] I expand on these points in the Introduction, pp. 7–9.

[2] Of course it is possible, as Taylor speculates, that the MS. had no cancellation marks at all. But since Taylor believes that the F MS. is theatrical, not authorial, and theatrical MSS. tend to make cuts obvious, his position is weak and his argument circular, since he assumes what he is trying to prove – that the MS. was produced by a theatrical scribe.

[3] Jensen argues that Taylor's 'interpretive agenda' is to devalue the comic/satiric aspects of the play and upgrade the tragic, creating a generic hierarchy: satire for the Inns of Court, tragedy for the Globe.

[4] Greg's view of the case is somewhat similar, though his reconstruction, done with 'the help of a little imagination', assumes the play was performed only once, at one of the Inns of Court, and that the Chamberlain's Men 'decided to dispense with a formal prompt-copy and make do, for [that] single performance, with the foul papers' which 'turned up' much later 'among the playhouse manuscripts' and were collated with the printed text of Q to form the basis of F (*First Folio*, pp. 347–9).

[5] *Ibid.*, p. 109.

legibility it presents to modern scholars, almost certainly a 'promptbook' in the loose
sense defined by Long.[1]

There are a few places in F where the hand of a book-keeper can indeed be discerned
behind the text. Here are two examples of what I see as non-Shakespearean performance
markings in F:

4.4.47–8

After Troilus' last tearful line to Cressida, 'Distasted [F: "Distasting"] with the salt of
broken tears', F has a direction, *Enter Æneus*, and immediately following, on the next
line, both texts read, '*Æneas within*. My lord, is the lady ready?' Now either Aeneas is
'within' or he is not – he cannot be simultaneously visible and invisible to the audience.
F has it both ways. The best explanation for the confusion is that F's *Enter Æneus*
is a book-keeper's addition, probably marking the need for the actor to be there in
readiness.[2] It is highly unlikely that Aeneas' entry is a revision made by Shakespeare,
since the whole weight of the scene depends on the pressure exerted by Aeneas' invisible
presence and on the calculated delay of his entrance; indeed, he and Paris are still calling
from 'within' (in both texts) at lines 97–8.

4.2.69ff.

Q: *Troyl*. How my atchiuements mock me,
    I will go meete them: and my Lord *Æneus*,
    We met by chance, you did not finde me here.
    Æn. Good, good my lord, the secrets of neighbor *Pandar*
    Have not more guift in taciturnitie.   *Exeunt*.
    Pand. Ist possible: no sooner got but lost, the diuell take *Anthenor*,
    The young Prince will go madde, a plague vpon *Anthenor*. I would
    they had brok's neck.
    Enter Cress. How now? what's the matter? who was heere?

F: *Troy*. How my atchiuements mocke me;
    I will goe meete them: and my Lord *Æneas*,
    We met by chance; you did not finde me here.

[1] In several places in the MS., the book-keeper has inserted a note at the *bottom* of a recto page as an alert
     for a similar direction (in Heywood's hand) that comes at the top of the next verso page (sometimes after
     a cut). This would not be necessary if the intent were to recopy the MS.; but it would be very useful as
     a warning to the book-keeper during the running of the show itself, since he could glance ahead and get
     prepared for what was to follow, without having to turn over the page. Greg noticed these warnings (*First
     Folio*, p. 141), but his conviction that the MS. was too messy to be a promptbook blinded him to their
     significance. His view of *The Captives* MS. led him to note that 'a printed text that shows distinctive marks
     of the prompter may yet have been printed from foul papers' (*First Folio*, p. 109 n.). While his conclusion
     seems apt, his remarks imply a distinction between 'foul papers' and playbook that, as Werstine and Long
     have persuasively demonstrated, does not really hold. See Werstine, 'Narratives', pp. 73, 86, and 'Plays',
     pp. 489–90 for a discussion of the way *The Captives* MS. blurs and undermines the categories established
     by Greg and frequently used by editors.
[2] Or it could be an addition made for a revival with different blocking; a few of the extant playbooks, such
     as *Woodstock*, contain markings that seem to derive from different productions – see Long, 'Woodstock'.

> *Æn.* Good, good, my Lord, the secrets of nature
> Haue not more gift in taciturnitie.   *Exeunt.*
>   *Enter Pandarus and Cressid.*
> *Pan.* Is't possible? no sooner got but lost: the diuell take *Anthenor*;
> the yong Prince will goe mad: a plague vpon *Anthenor*; I would
> they had brok's necke.
>   *Cres.* How now? what's the matter? who was here?

(TLN 2331–40)

F provides the stage direction *Enter Pandarus and Cressid* at a point where Pandarus has been onstage for some time, though he has been silent for the previous twenty lines while Troilus and Aeneas have been carrying on an anxious dialogue. The *Exeunt* in both texts refers to the two of them. Q's next direction, *Enter Cress.*, serves as both entry and speech heading but it is basically sound.[1] Now it is difficult to imagine Shakespeare being unaware that Pandarus is onstage and hence producing the F stage direction and it is conversely easy to imagine a book-keeper coming across the 'Exeunt' in the MS. and, noting that the next lines belong to Pandarus and Cressida, writing in Pandarus' unnecessary entry.[2] Taylor regards it as 'impossible' that F might be wrong here,[3] and hence gives an exit to Pandarus a few lines above (57), where Aeneas tells him to go and fetch Troilus. But Troilus enters immediately (57 SD), before Pandarus has time to exit, and Pandarus' overhearing what follows is psychologically appropriate and dramatically necessary (how else would he know what was up?).[4] Cressida then enters to Pandarus and her line (77) only makes sense in that context.

These examples, together with the often-noticed fact that F provides many necessary entrances and some exits absent from Q,[5] strongly suggest that behind F is a theatrically annotated MS.; and from what we can discern from the extant playhouse MSS., inconsistency in the 'Book' does not seem to have posed a problem to actors or book-keeper. We can thus draw a tentative double conclusion: indications in the text (such as the two doubled passages) that foul papers are behind F, and other indications that some theatrical intervention has taken place, give weight to the view that the F MS. is indeed an authorial draft annotated for use as a promptbook. One immediate corollary is that Q, which must have been printed from a different MS., derives from a copy, whether Shakespeare's own or scribal is impossible to tell, though the changes that must have been made along the way, plus some peculiarities of spelling and speech

---

[1] There are several cases in Q of entry directions serving also as speech headings, e.g. at 5.5.42–3 and 5.6.12–13; indeed this practice is found in many other quartos and throughout F.

[2] The fact that the direction would have to be ignored during an actual production of the play would not, judging from the contradictions in other theatrically annotated MSS., have unduly bothered the book-keeper.

[3] *Textual Companion*, p. 434.

[4] Taylor (in Oxford) begins a new scene to mark Pandarus' 'entry', but there is no indication of any time having elapsed, and indeed any such indication would cut against the dramatic effect – the sense of urgency and dismay.

[5] Because some of the theatrical untangling discernible in F could in principle be authorial, I've built my argument for book-keeper markings on cases of error or potential confusion, where the author was unlikely to have been involved. Other such cases include F's *Exit* at 4.4.100 and *Enter the Greekes* five lines later.

headings,[1] suggest Shakespeare's hand. I therefore accept the general view of Q put forward by Hillebrand and Honigmann, that Shakespeare at some point made a copy (perhaps after interest was stirred up by an Inns of Court performance), introducing changes as he went. The copy found its way to print in Q (unauthorised by the players)[2] at exactly the same time that another unauthorised Shakespearean MS., and one with many thematic affinities with *Troilus and Cressida*, was printed in the same shop, dedicated to a mysterious Mr. W. H.;[3] the foul papers (or perhaps a copy) were meanwhile delivered to, and revised in, the playhouse.

In some instances, then, Q provides a revised reading and in other instances F does, and it is impossible now to determine in many cases which text offers the 'original' reading and which the revised. But that there were revisions, made perhaps over a number of years, can hardly be doubted. Which text is closer to Shakespeare's hand and intentions? This is the question that many have puzzled over and it is, in the end, insoluble. Neither text can confidently be deemed the 'final' version. Educated guesses about the nature of the manuscripts behind each text help, but they don't eliminate the quandary – in some ways they even augment it. For those few sections of the text where F seems to rely directly on Q (discussed below), clearly the latter will have priority. But for the bulk of the play, we are without firm guidance.[4]

The relation between Q and F

There is one more vexed and uncertain textual question to deal with and that is the relation between Q and F. It has been noticed that the first three pages of the F version conform quite closely to Q, suggesting that publisher and printer Isaac Jaggard's compositors had an unmarked copy of Q from which they began to set up their version.[5] Since these pages display only the same kinds of minor variant noticeable in other texts printed directly from 'good' quartos, it is safe to conclude that the initial intention was to print F directly from Q, as was the procedure with *Romeo and Juliet*, the play Troilus was originally designed to follow. That this was the original design is proven by the chance survival, in a few copies of the Folio, of the final (cancelled) page of *Romeo* with the first page of *Troilus and Cressida* on the verso. But the printing of F was broken off after the first three pages and the position that *Troilus* was meant to occupy was filled by a different play, *Timon of Athens*.[6] When *Troilus* was finally printed, it was squeezed

---

[1] See Alexander, pp. 279–80, Honigmann, *Stability*, pp. 88–91, and Taylor, 'Bibliography', pp. 131–2 (nn. 15–17).

[2] The epistle makes this lack of authorisation tolerably clear: 'thanke fortune for the scape it [i.e. the text] hath made amongst you' (25).

[3] Honigmann makes this interesting, if conjectural, connection between *Tro.* and the Sonnets – see 'Date and revision', p. 54.

[4] This question of insolubility is linked to the radical scepticism inherent in the play (and discussed in the Introduction), as well as to post-modern uncertainties about the stability of knowledge, whose effect on textual studies has been profound.

[5] See Walker, *Textual Problems*, pp. 71–2.

[6] The precise timing and order of the printing is discussed at length by Hinman. See especially vol. II, pp. 231–7, 261–4, 326–40.

in at the beginning of the Tragedies section, with a previously unpublished Prologue but without pagination (except for leaves two and three which had been retained from the earlier setting and reused);[1] nor was it mentioned in the 'Catalogue' of plays at the beginning. When printing was resumed, a manuscript (different from that behind Q) was introduced into the process and played a key role in the composition of the F text. Such are the facts, as nearly as scholars have been able to confirm them. The most plausible explanation for the interruption of the F printing is that there was trouble over copyright with the surviving Q stationer, Henry Walley (his partner in the publication of Q, Richard Bonian, having died).[2] This dispute, if that's what it was, seems to have lasted a good while; somewhere late in the process Jaggard, having abandoned the idea of printing *Troilus*, got hold of a manuscript which he could use in tandem with (or instead of) Q. Greg suggested that Jaggard could then claim that he was not simply reprinting Q and was thus 'in a position to snap his fingers at Walley', but Blayney has recently shown that holding 'copy' as it was then understood, would have given Walley 'not only the exclusive right to reprint the text, but also the right to a fair chance to recover his costs', meaning that he could reasonably oppose the production of '*any* book . . . [that] threatened his ability to dispose of unsold copies'.[3] Though we do not know how, Jaggard must have acquired the right to print. A crucial point here is that *Troilus and Cressida* was printed at the very end of the process; it was, as Hinman shows, not only the last play to be set into type, but was composed even after all the preliminary material and the Catalogue had been set. In addition, a new workman, 'Compositor H', seems to have been engaged to speed along the work and he was responsible for a large proportion of the text.[4] Perhaps the other compositors were busy with a new project. Whatever the case, it seems evident that it was important to complete the setting of *Troilus and Cressida* as quickly as possible so as not to delay any further the publication of the finished book, which Jaggard had originally intended to have completed the previous year. This hurry might have affected the choices about the nature of copy; in particular it probably led, as I suggest below, to the unusual practice of using dual copy.

Exactly what role Q played in the process of setting F is difficult to determine. The usual explanation has been that someone (variously referred to as an 'editor', 'annotator', or 'collator') marked up the quarto by reference to the manuscript that had recently come to light. The compositors then worked from that marked copy. This theory, first advanced by Alexander and later buttressed by Philip Williams ('*Troilus*'), is based on evidence that is largely typographical and bibliographic, and thus has been regarded as definitive. It accounts for the existence in F of many incidental similarities between the two texts as well as for the existence of common errors. It could also account

---

[1] The Prologue was set in large type to take up the whole of the recto page formerly occupied by the last leaf of *Rom.* The first page of *Tro.* was, necessarily, reset on the verso, to enable the reuse of the two, now anomalously paginated, following pages. The first page of the text therefore exists in two states, 'uncorrected' (that on the verso of the cancelled final page of *Rom.*) and 'corrected' (the reset page).

[2] See Greg, *First Folio*, pp. 448–9.

[3] *Ibid.*, p. 449 and Blayney, p. 399.

[4] See Taylor, 'Compositor A' and the tables in *Textual Companion*, pp. 149–54.

for the presence in F of several passages not in Q, though these could certainly not all have been squeezed into the margins of Q; some kind of interleaving would have been necessary. Substantive variants of single words or short phrases are also easily explicable in terms of this theory. Even the few short Q-only passages do not contravene it – they could have been left out either inadvertently, because of the difficulty of reading the marked-up copy, or deliberately, if (though this is unlikely in most cases) they had been cut in the MS. presumably used by the collator. But at the same time, all scholars who have looked at the two texts have had to face the mysterious fact that there are many instances of apparent misreading in F, of the kind that can only be the result of setting from manuscript copy (instances, that is, where Q apparently got it 'right').

How, then, could a compositor, or an editor, collator, or scribe, have possibly come up with some of the aberrant readings evident in F when the 'correct' readings were right in front of him, in the printed text of Q? As William Godschalk has pointed out, no one who accepts the theory of the annotated quarto has offered a satisfactory explanation as to how or why the many obvious errors in F might have crept into the text.[1] Taylor, in his eagerness to prove that the MS. behind F was a theatrical copy, simply sidesteps the problem, even though he carefully lists the problematic passages. There are only two ways of dealing with this dilemma: either amend the theory of the annotated quarto, or imagine an annotator deliberately altering lines that make excellent sense in the printed copy, rendering them less intelligible or altogether meaningless, on the basis of passages in his MS. that are difficult to decipher. Can we imagine an annotator, for example, deliberately crossing out the printed word 'sunne' in the phrase 'the almighty sunne' (Q) and substituting for it the word 'Fenne', in order to give us F's peculiar phrase, 'the almighty Fenne' (TLN 3170)? Or changing 'violenteth' to 'no lesse' (TLN 2392) in the phrase 'And violenteth in a sence as strong', or 'ioyes' to 'eyes' (TLN 2269) in 'And dreaming night will hide our ioyes no longer'? Or, to turn to an example singled out by Godshalk, making the changes in 5.2.8 ff.:

    Q: *Troy.* Yea so familiar?
       Vlis. Shee will sing any man at first sight.
       Ther. And any man may sing her, if hee can take her Cliff, she's noted.

    F: *Troy.* Yea, so familiar?
       Vlis. She will sing any man at first sight.
       Ther. And any man may finde her, if he can take her life: she's noted.

In Q there is a series of bawdy jokes turning on the musical/sexual pun on 'Cliff' (= 'clef' and 'cleft')[2] but, as Godshalk notes, F misses most of this verbal play by substituting 'finde' for 'sing' and 'life' for 'Cliff'.

---

[1] Taylor ('Bibliography', p. 106) notes twenty-eight such errors and his list could be extended by at least five others. Godschalk, whose article on the problems of the *Tro.* text I have found particularly helpful, tackles this problem of F errors directly. I examine a number of his suggestions in what follows, and add supplementary evidence for some of his hypotheses.
[2] See Commentary.

To sum up my point here: F does not seem to have been printed directly or exclusively from an annotated copy of Q. What annotator would deliberately change the printed text of Q to come up with these F readings (most of which are best explained as graphic errors of the sort typical of setting from MS.)? If there were only one or two such readings, carelessness or chance might come in as explanations, but with more than thirty, it seems very unlikely. Hence I propose, with William Godschalk, that we rethink the idea of the annotated quarto.

But what about the bibliographic evidence adduced by Alexander and especially Williams and accepted by all editors? Here we come to another conundrum – for there are segments of F, in addition to the first three pages, which bear a startling resemblance to the corresponding parts of Q, most notably from 2.2.106 to 2.3.41, and parts of 3.1 and 3.3.[1] For these sections, Q seems to have been used directly (and I have accordingly granted it greater authority in my own text). But what of the rest? Does the whole of F depend in the same way on Q? Close examination of the bibliographic evidence suggests that it does not.

Let me illustrate briefly. Alexander points to a number of common errors and/or peculiarities to make his case. One of the most intriguing is 'That doth inuert th‚attest of eyes and eares' in Q, which becomes in F 'That doth inuert that test of eyes and eares' (5.2.121), where the inverted apostrophe in Q *might* have been misinterpreted by the F compositor (as Alexander suggests).[2] But the far more likely explanation of the variant is that the compositor was working from a manuscript which read 'thattest'; in Hand D's section of the MS. of *Sir Thomas More* (Hand D probably being that of Shakespeare) we get two comparable readings: 'thipp' (for th' hip) and 'thappostle' (th' apostle).[3] Thus Alexander's evidence for F's reliance on Q actually suggests paradoxically that at this point at any rate, the compositor was working not from Q but from MS. Of Alexander's other examples, the following, I think, are the strongest:

1. 2.3.82 where 'Achillis' instead of 'Achilles' appears uniquely in both texts
2. 4.5.143 where both Q and F print '(O yes)' instead of 'Oyes' (i.e. the town crier's 'Oyez') in the phrase 'her lowdst [F: lowd'st] (O yes)'.

It is possible though unlikely that 'Achillis' goes back to aberrant spelling in the foul papers[4], but the parentheses around 'O yes' seem to indicate a misreading on the part of the Q compositor or scribe which was simply repeated in F. There are then really only a couple of bits of evidence from Alexander that suggest the direct influence of Q.

The evidence adduced by Williams ('*Troilus*') is of three kinds: the forms of speech headings, the use of roman and italic type, and variant spellings of common words

[1] See Muir, 'Note', although he doesn't mention 3.1, where the unusual lineation of the song is the same in both texts and there are other marked similarities (see note to 3.1.134), and his evidence for the first hundred lines of 3.3 is not entirely persuasive. There are also indications that in the first part of 4.5 (corresponding to page ¶¶3*b*) Q might have exerted unmediated influence.
[2] Walton regards this example as 'enough to show that F was printed from Q' (p. 197).
[3] See lines 18 and 94 of Evans' transcription in Riverside (pp. 1780, 1786).
[4] But note too that this unique spelling occurs in a section where there are many variants, including the impossible 'flight' for 'flexure' (2.3.94).

(such as do/doe, go/goe, O/Oh etc.). His argument rests on the view that when there is correspondence between the two texts in cases where, on the basis of ordinary practice, we would not expect it – i.e. when a later text, abnormally (given, for example, the usual practice of particular compositors), reproduces an earlier text's incidentals – then the correspondence points to direct influence. He produces a goodly number of instances of such correspondence, but he neglects to provide the full context for them. For example, in his analysis of speech headings, he identifies at TLN 270 an instance where Q and F both have *Pand.* (though F normally has *Pan.*) but he ignores six instances on the same page where F has *Pand.* and Q has *Pan.* Moreover, on the same page again, Q (unusually) reads *Helen* (263) where F has the more normal *Hellen* and between 375 and 81, F spells *Hellenus* five times and *Helenus* once, while Q is consistent with a single 'l' in all six instances. This, I should emphasise, is on a page that we now can be fairly certain was printed from Q, and if even there the pattern of correspondence is so haphazard, what certainty can occasional correspondence carry in circumstances where we are trying to prove influence? Other examples could be adduced to support the conclusion that, given so much uncertainty and variation in relation to speech headings, occasional correspondence proves very little.

What about the use of italics? Again here, the evidence is much more ambiguous than Williams allows. He cites cases where proper names, normally in italics in both texts, occur in roman. He leaves out cases, such as 'Ioue' (i.e. Jove), 'Charon,' or 'Genius' (1.3.20, 3.2.8, and 4.4.49), where Q uses roman and F italic or vice versa. He cites the stage direction at 3.3.37: 'Achilles *and* Patro *stand in their tent*' (Q) and '*Enter* Achilles *and* Patroclus *in their tent*' (F) without explaining the obvious variants which a compositor would surely notice were he attending closely to Q as his copy. Some of Williams' examples rely on the identification of compositors as understood at the time (1950) but with the work of Hinman and others since then, much of what Williams says needs to be adjusted; further instances are derived from the first three pages of the F text which we are now fairly certain were set from Q, so those too need to be discounted. Of his other examples, the most telling are the stage direction at the beginning of 2.3, which is identical in both texts ('*Enter* Thersites *solus.*'), and the three instances of 'Troy' (at 3.1.119, 3.2.166, and 3.3.141) where, in each text, the word is set in italics (in fact, though Williams does not note this, the intial T in Troy is in roman in all three cases in Q), when the other forty-nine instances in each text are in roman. Of the three, the first is in a section of the play where other evidence also suggests the direct influence of Q; the third is in a line with a substantive variant (Q: 'And great T*roy* shriking'; F: 'And great *Troy* shrinking'), explicable certainly as either error or unnecessary correction[1] but nevertheless complicating the hypothesis of close compositorial attention to the details of Q.

Finally, there is the evidence of spelling of common words; even more than with italicisation, this evidence has been vitiated by advances in work on compositors. As mentioned earlier, more than half of *Troilus and Cressida* was set by a new, relatively

---

[1] Honigmann (*Stability*, p. 88) argues cogently that 'shriking' (i.e. shrieking) is the right reading here.

inexperienced compositor, H, who played no other role in the printing of F, who may indeed have been a new recruit or a journeyman hired for the occasion (Taylor, 'Compositor A'). His habits can therefore not be traced in other texts. Indeed, as Howard-Hill has argued, evidence based on the spelling of common words in such circumstances is not very helpful since sparseness of evidence can lead to 'so many qualifications of argument that conclusions become unconvincing'.[1] Moreover, a new compositor's spelling may easily undergo changes in the course of his learning the ropes. Despite this, the fact that H seems to prefer the final 'e' spellings of 'goe' and 'doe' and yet sometimes corresponds with Q's shorter forms might count for something.[2] Of Williams' other orthographic examples, the occurrence of 'ie' endings on polysyllabic words is unpersuasive; by Williams' own count barely more than half of F's 'ie' endings correspond with Q. A simple comparison of a few lines in 2.3 (90, 93–4) can indicate the perils of this kind of 'proof':

> Q: The amity that wisdom knits not, folly may easily unty . . .
> The Elephant hath ioynts, but none for courtesie,
> His legs are legs for necessity, not for flexure.

> F: The amitie that wisedome knits, not folly may easily untie . . .
> The Elephant hath ioynts, but none for curtesie:
> His legge are legs for necessitie, not for flight.

And the inconsistency of the spellings 'O' and 'Oh' are similarly unconvincing. Overall, then, the evidence from spelling is seriously ambiguous.

Conclusions

The precise relation between Q and F, despite the scholarly investigation and controversy that has been directed at determining it, thus remains uncertain. Since no definitive explanation is possible, plausibility is the most we can hope for. What seems the most plausible explanation for the plain, if frustrating, fact that F exists in the state it is in (it must have been produced somehow)? Godschalk has outlined some of the possible scenarios, of which two seem less unlikely than the others: either F was set from dual copy (Q and the MS.), an explanation which, although awkward (both in itself and because of the obstacles it would pose for proof-reading) seems reasonably plausible; or F was set from a specially prepared scribal copy (commissioned by Jaggard) which was influenced somehow by Q. The dual-copy idea, despite its difficulties, is the simplest and explains certain features of both texts best. Added corroboration might be adduced if we consider the probable rush to finish the volume, the fact that there is little evidence of proof-reading for this text, and the apparent reliance of only certain sections of F on Q. However, there is no discernible pattern to this reliance, nor any relation that I can find between a particular compositor and an apparent use of Q rather than MS. A scribal

---

[1] Howard-Hill, p. 6.
[2] But as Taylor's discussion clearly, if inadvertently, implies, such evidence is highly uncertain ('Compositor A', pp. 102–3).

copy is also possible, though one would have to question why there is so much variation in the influence of Q. We would have to postulate that the scribe, specifically charged with providing copy for print, and having a copy of Q (perhaps unbound) as a kind of check, might easily (though very haphazardly) have reproduced some of the incidental features of Q. Errors in F might then either derive from compositorial misreading or from the scribe having misread his MS. and not having checked Q. Faced with these two hypotheses, I would choose dual copy, but not with a great deal of confidence.

Given the complexity, even insolubility, of the textual situation, there is ample justification for an eclectic text, though the fact that Q overall boasts more 'superior' readings gives it a slight edge. So, hesitantly and with due caution, I have selected Q as my copy-text of this edition. In doing so, I have worked from the following assumptions: (1) that the obscure relation between Q and F, however we may explain it (and, as I said, I think dual copy the least unlikely possibility) suggests a situation in which it is probable that more errors and 'corruption' could creep into F than Q in the various processes of transmission and printing; (2) that an author doing a fair copy (which, as I have argued, is the source of Q) is more likely to be careful about the revisions he makes than an actor in the theatre, even when they are one and the same person; and (3) that the theatrical provenance of F, while it may contain revisions and final thoughts, also makes it subject to book-keeper error and actorly substitution. All this means, however, is that I think of Q as having marginally more weight. Because of the complexity of the textual situation, I have not hesitated to conflate when I felt it necessary or justifiable. Because of the current awareness in textual circles of the pitfalls of conflation and the vogue for separate or parallel texts, one has to approach the task with caution; but I would argue that, with *Troilus and Cressida*, to refuse conflation altogether would be to shirk one's editorial responsibility.

Finally, after all this scholarly investigation, it needs to be said that the differences between the texts we are considering are fairly negligible. Of the 500 or so substantive variants, recent editors have agreed on the preferred reading in a large majority of cases. Furthermore, the textual problems make much less difference to the overall meaning of the play than analogous discrepancies between quarto and Folio in the texts of plays such as *Hamlet* or *King Lear*, where both action and character are affected in small but significant ways, depending on whether one follows Q or F, a feature that has led some editors to promote the publication of separate editions.[1] In the case of *Troilus and Cressida*, such a strategy would not pay off: whether one chooses Q or

---

[1] Since the publication of Gary Taylor and Michael Warren, eds., *The Division of the Kingdom: Shakespeare's Two Versions of King Lear* (1983), a minor textual industry has developed in relation to these kinds of problem. Separate texts of *Lear* and *Ham.* (including Q1) have been published as well as a whole raft of articles and books devoted to related questions in a variety of plays, many of them deeply critical of the ideological and interpretive assumptions of the 'new bibliography' of Greg, Bowers, and co. See, for example, Laurie Maguire, *Shakespearean Suspect Texts: The 'Bad' Quartos and Their Contexts*, 1996; Steven Urkowitz, 'Good news about "bad quartos"', in *Bad Shakespeare*, ed. Maurice Charney, 1988, pp. 189–206, and 'Well-sayd olde mole': burying three *Hamlets* in modern editions', in *Shakespeare Study Today* ed. Georgianna Ziegler, 1986, pp. 37–70; Grace Ioppolo, *Revising Shakespeare*, 1991; Leah Marcus, *Unediting the Renaissance*, 1996; and, for a general account, Jerome McGann, *A Critique of Modern Textual Criticism*, 1983.

F as copy-text, the resulting editions will, in general terms, be quite similar. It is the maddening uncertainty of the textual situation that raises the latent detective in the soul of the editor, rather than a perception of earth-shaking difference. In this, the textual situation mirrors the play itself: both enact the paradox that I identify and discuss in the Introduction – that the conundrum of identity and difference depends for its solution entirely on perspective, but at the same time, perspective does not altogether erase the bitterness or gaiety of plain fact. We both construct meanings *and* discover them. The play dramatises the struggle, and it is thus supremely fitting that the difficult process of sorting out truths begins, but certainly does not end, with its material texts.

APPENDIX: SOURCES OF THE PLAY

The story of the Trojan War and the sad romance of Troilus and Cressida were both well known in Shakespeare's England, so that when we talk of 'sources' of the play[1] we need to keep in mind that the basic narratives were already established and apparently inevitable: the Trojans would suffer as a result of their determination to hold on to Helen, Achilles would kill Hector and desecrate his body, Cressida would betray Troilus and take Diomedes as a lover. Both the war and the love stories had been told and retold numerous times. This is not to say that when Shakespeare took over the traditional material he could not have changed the basic plots – he often did so with other traditional narratives. But he chose not to, no doubt because the various failures that the old stories recorded could be reconfigured to suit his critical and satirical purposes. As was his habit, he read widely in the literature available, and probably spoke with his colleagues and friends about the story. He had an extraordinary capacity to absorb what he read and heard (a characteristic that was comically rendered in the film *Shakespeare in Love*) and was adept at transforming it for his own purposes. For all these reasons, it is difficult to say with precision exactly what sources he used for *Troilus and Cressida*, though the main outlines are clear.

Three texts are primary – Chaucer's *Troilus and Criseyde*, Homer's *Iliad* (especially the seven books translated and published by George Chapman in 1598), and William Caxton's *Recuyell of the Historyes of Troye* (published in 1474, the first English-language book ever printed); two others also played a significant, if minor, role – John Lydgate's *The Troy Book* (1513) and Robert Henryson's *The Testament of Cresseid* (1532).[2] Chaucer, Caxton, Lydgate, and Henryson all based their work on earlier texts, so that each was participating in a long process of passing along a literary tradition. In thinking about Shakespeare's use of these and other texts, we need not imagine him at his desk surrounded by a scattering of open books, looking into one or the other as he wrote. More likely, he read and absorbed, stored material in his capacious memory, and, when he began to write, simply used what came to mind. There are some cases (such as Plutarch for *Antony and Cleopatra* or *Julius Caesar*) where, judging by the close and extensive verbal parallels, he seems to have had a particular book beside him as he

---

[1] Thorough analysis of the sources of the play may be found in Variorum, Bullough, Muir '*Sources*', Bevington[2], and Palmer. The first two of these reprint large selections of the relevant texts. What follows here is a somewhat more selective account, though I have tried to cover all the important material that Shakespeare consulted and to provide an array of pertinent examples.

[2] The dates given are those of first publication; Lydgate's *Hystorye Sege and Dystruccyon of Troye* (to give it its 1513 title) was written under the direct patronage of Henry V in the early fifteenth century, though not published till a century later, and Henryson's poem was written in the late fifteenth century (he died around 1500).

wrote. Such is not the case with any of the books he relied on for *Troilus and Cressida*, where verbal parallels are relatively few.

Chaucer

Troilus and Cressida is in many ways very different from Chaucer's great poem; for this reason, it used to be thought that Shakespeare might not even have read Chaucer, but that view has quite rightly been discredited. As E. Talbot Donaldson has shown, we can see if we look closely at the two texts how one great writer engaged the other and what imaginative transformations that engagement involved.[1] The earlier poet focuses almost entirely on the lovers, paying attention to the war only insofar as it impinges on the lives of his main characters. Shakespeare gives more time to the war than to his eponymous lovers, covering far more material in far less space. This necessitates a fair bit of compression. Still, he adopts and adapts the main characters from Chaucer and follows his precursor's general scheme with regard to the love plot. The play's opening scene stages an important episode of Chaucer's Book I, in which a sententious Pandarus alternately consoles Troilus and praises Criseyde's beauty. Shakespeare's second scene (1.2) combines two separate incidents in Book II: in the first Pandarus chats expansively with Criseyde, trying to win her heart for Troilus, whom he compares to Hector; after he leaves, she observes Troilus returning from battle. On a later occasion, Pandarus is with her at the window, prompting, when Troilus again rides by, this time (it seems) on purpose to see and be seen. The play's 3.2 and 4.2 dramatise the tryst and the morning after, the main subject of Chaucer's Book III. In both texts, Calchas' request for the exchange comes immediately after the consummation of the lovers' desires, which then leads to the painful scene of parting, marked in both works by vows of fidelity, by Troilus' worry about the amorous Greeks, and by Cressida's irritation at Troilus for doubting her (4.4 and IV.1128 ff.). Lastly come the betrayals, though the final act of the play, in which Troilus observes Cressida with Diomedes and the battle comes to a kind of climax with the brutal slaying of Hector, moves further away from the concerns of the poem. Chaucer stresses Criseyde's sorrow, vulnerability, and isolation in the Greek camp ('And this was yet the werste of al hire peyne, / Ther was no wight to whom she dorste hire pleyne' (V.727–8)) and he extenuates her guilt as much as he can ('For she so sory was for hire untrouthe, / Iwis, I wolde excuse hire yet for routhe' (V.1098–9)).[2] He handles all the events of the poem at a leisurely pace, concentrating on character and psychology and the ideology of courtly love. Shakespeare compresses and highlights: he begins after the lovers are already in love (though at a distance), while Chaucer begins with their first sight of each other (Troilus, like Shakespeare's

---

[1] Donaldson's discussion of the relation between the two texts is brilliant and indispensable – as both source study and criticism.

[2] Chaucer never dramatises the actual betrayal, and indeed distances himself and the reader from it by reverting to his own sources: the reader is brought close to Criseyde in the presentation of her conflict and Diomede's subtle wooing, but then for three stanzas Chaucer turns to what 'the storie telleth us' (V.1037–57). The inevitability of Criseyde's fall thus becomes a result of the tyranny of the ancient narrative.

Benedict, is scornful of love and lovers, but then spots Criseyde in a temple and falls head over heels); Shakespeare gives the lovers one night together instead of three years, and he makes the betrayal cruelly quick, while Chaucer's Diomede, who is (in contrast to Shakespeare's predatory opportunist) an honourable, if also sly and 'sodeine', courtly lover, has to go to some pains to finally win Criseyde.

More important than any of the shifts or compressions is the change of tone. Chaucer's attitude mixes sympathy with genial detachment; his irony is softer and sub-tler than Shakespeare's and he provides no precedent for Shakespeare's bitter satire. Shakespeare shifted the characters of all three of the central personages, in every case darkening aspects already there in the earlier work. This is most obvious with Pandarus who, in Chaucer, is cheerful and sententious, himself a failed lover who acts to bring Troilus and Criseyde together because he likes them and wants to see them happy. There is none of the sleazy voyeurism and worn-out, cynical gaiety of Shakespeare's go-between, aspects that have been energetically projected in much recent performance; nor is there anything to match Pandarus' poisonous epilogue and his spreading disease. There is, however, a voyeuristic streak in Chaucer's Pandarus that Shakespeare seems to have exploited; and there is an ambiguous hint in Chaucer that even Shakespeare seems to have shied away from, i.e. that Pandarus may himself be enjoying Criseyde's favours (III.1555–1582); at the very least, Pandarus' relation with Criseyde is flirtatious in the extreme, whereas in Shakespeare he appears more taken with Troilus.

Troilus is Chaucer's hero, sympathetically treated as passionate, faithful, and high-minded, devoted to the honour of his beloved (since secrecy is a crucial part of the code of courtly love, he is careful to guard Criseyde from discovery). In the play, Troilus is still faithful, but his self-regard undermines the value of his loyalty; his mind typically turns to his own needs, his own constancy, his own hopes, so much so that he shows little concern for Cressida as an independent person. His passion too seems closer to simple lust, although his pain is real and can evoke empathy. Since Shakespeare was writing within a cultural framework that favoured marriage (as in the comedies and *Romeo and Juliet*), Troilus' failure to mention marriage is both noticeable and a little contemptible, whereas in Chaucer it is part of the ideology of a courtly love tradition that eschewed marriage.

Cressida is enigmatic in both texts. Chaucer doesn't condemn his heroine though ever since Benoît de Ste Maure invented her in the twelfth century she had provided an excuse for misogynistic discourse. By the time Shakespeare turned his attention to her, she had degenerated into a cliché, an anti-feminist paradigm of faithlessness.[1] Surprisingly, given tradition and cultural context, Chaucer is sympathetic to her plight, and suggests, though ambiguously, that she surrenders to Diomede out of loneliness rather than wantonness. In his main source, Boccaccio's *Il Filostrato*, she is a widow, all too easily led by sexual desire (the stereotypical propensity of widows); Chaucer

---

[1] This was at least partly a result of the influence of Robert Henryson's *The Testament of Cresseid* (see below) which continues her story after Diomedes deserts her – she becomes a leper and a beggar (Pistol in *H 5* 2.1.76 refers to a prostitute as a 'lazar kite of Cressid's kind'). As I argue in the Introduction, Shakespeare actually makes the traditional literary identities of his characters a *subject* of his play.

too makes her a widow (though Shakespeare does not), but he avoids the anti-feminist connotations. Her surrender to Troilus seems to flow as much from Pandarus' persuasiveness as from anything else. Chaucer deliberately avoids giving us a clear sense of her motivations. As a character she is ambiguous, both timid and bold, calculating and spontaneous, sexy and modest, as well as vulnerable – a lot like Shakespeare's heroine in fact, though more hidden and less subject to the bitter inconstancies of the world as Shakespeare portrays them.[1] Shakespeare's two added scenes, the arrival in the Greek camp (4.5) and the betrayal scene itself, watched by Troilus (5.2), offer the possibility of a much more negative view of the character than anything in Chaucer, though those scenes can also be treated in such a way as to provide a portrait of Cressida as subjected to male aggressiveness, or at least deeply conflicted about what she feels herself falling into. Like Criseyde, she is 'tendre-herted, slydynge of corage' (v.825); she feels the intensity of the present moment but tends towards passive acceptance, allowing herself to slide into a kind of self-destructive ease. Donaldson suggests that Shakespeare, reading Chaucer, was 'particularly struck by the vulnerability of [Criseyde], her precariousness, as the daughter of a traitor, in a city at war' (p. 84). He made her more vulnerable, more alone, more ambiguous, and kept more distance from her than Chaucer (or his narrator) was willing to maintain, thus setting up the harsh judgements of many critics, but at the same time providing, if we look closely, a complex uncertainty and sense of internal conflict.

Homer

While Shakespeare was probably familiar with the whole of *The Iliad* in one or more of the Latin or French translations available in the sixteenth century, or at least with the first ten books rendered into English verse by Arthur Hall in 1581 (translating from the French), he seems to have focused his attention primarily on the seven books of *The Iliad* (I and II, and VII–XI) translated by his fellow playwright and rival George Chapman in 1598.[2] Most of the events of the first four acts of the play (those not concerned with the love plot) correspond with material in those seven books – e.g. the Greek council, and Hector's challenge – though they are frequently given a different twist. 'Blockish' Ajax[3] is a heroic warrior in *The Iliad* and the choice that he should answer Hector's challenge is decided by a true lottery, unlike in Shakespeare where the whole episode is manipulated by Ulysses. But, in thinking through the whole narrative, Shakespeare seems to have had all of Homer rather than only Chapman's seven books in mind – like Homer, he begins 'in the middle' (Prologue 28), with the dissension in the Greek

[1] Donaldson, pp. 81–2.
[2] Tatlock, p. 742, lists the translations available to Shakespeare: Hall translated from Hugues Salel (whose verse translation came out in segments, with a complete version in 1580); there was another French version in prose by Jehan Samxon (1530); in Latin there were versions by Lorenzo Valla (1474, 1502, 1522), Eobanus Hessus (complete text in 1549), V. Obsopoeus and others (1573), and Spondanus (1583), plus a two-language version (Greek and literal Latin, frequently reprinted after 1551).
[3] The depiction of Ajax might owe something to his characterisation by Ovid in Book XIII of the *Metamorphoses*, a book Shakespeare knew well.

camp and Achilles' withdrawal, and he ends right after the death of Hector. Of course, the different tone persists – where Homer ends on a sombre note, with the mourning, cremation, and burial of Hector, Shakespeare ends with Pandarus, casting a savagely ironic shadow on the death of the Trojan hero. There are also incidental references scattered throughout the play to events from sections of *The Iliad* not published by Chapman till after the play was written (five more books were added in 1608 and the whole poem eventually appeared in 1611); examples include Menelaus' bout with Paris (1.1.103–5), or Ajax's 'coping' of Hector (1.2.29–31). And as he does with Chaucer, Shakespeare adopts features of character from Homer – 'crafty' Ulysses, 'wrathful' Achilles – and darkens them. Hence, while relying primarily on Chapman for the Homeric elements in his story, Shakespeare cast his net more widely.

Where Chapman seems to have influenced Shakespeare directly is in the depiction of Thersites, and to some degree in his rendering of the Greek war council. Of Thersites, Chapman writes:

> A man of tongue whose ravenlike voice a tuneles jarring kept,
> Who in his ranke mind coppy had of unregarded wordes . . .
> The filthiest Greeke that came to Troy, he had a goggle eye;
> Starcke-lame he was of eyther foote; his shoulders were contract
> Into his brest and crookt withall; his head was sharpe compact

He loves to 'chide' and 'raile' (the word is used recurrently in the play as well), disdaining Ulysses and Achilles. Shakespeare seems to have adopted some of the vocabulary here ('rank Thersites' 1.3.73, 'I would croak like a raven', 5.2.188–9, 'rail', etc.), and the general sense of Thersites' verbal sharpness and misshapen deformities, often exploited by actors and producers, might also be indebted to Chapman's vivid description. As for the council, the whole sequence in *The Iliad*, Book II, was much referred to and used in political debates in the late sixteenth century,[1] and so Shakespeare hardly needed Chapman to suggest it to him. But his reading of the poem might easily have contributed to the way he depicts the whole issue of political authority.

Caxton and Lydgate

Caxton's book on the history of Troy is very long, and Shakespeare used only a small part of it. That he did use it is fairly certain – there are some verbal echoes, especially concerning proper names, and many of the incidents of the war in the play are not to be found in Homer, but they are prominent in the *Recuyell*. Caxton's work is a translation of a French text by Raoul Lefèvre, the *Receuil des Histoires de Troie*, itself a translation of the most widely disseminated medieval redaction of the ancient story, Guido delle Colonne's Latin *Historia Trojana* (1287). Guido's work was, in turn, a translation of Benoît de Ste Maure's twelfth-century French poem, which was the first text to bring Troilus, Cressida (called Briseida in the poem), and Diomede into an amorous triangle,

---

[1] See Introduction, pp. 44–6, and Norbrook.

though this only occupied a small fraction of the complete work. Boccaccio used both Guido and, especially, Benoît, in *Il Filostrato* (Chaucer's major source), which was the first work to focus exclusively on the Troilus and Cressida story.[1]

Complicating Shakespeare's debt to Caxton is the existence of Lydgate's *Troy Book*, which covers much of the same ground and which Shakespeare seems also to have used, if only incidentally. Both present the story of the siege, a Trojan council of war, Calchas' request for the exchange, Hector's visit to the Greek camp, Cassandra and Andromache pleading with Hector to avoid battle on the fateful day; in both Hector attacks a well-dressed Greek warrior, and Diomede captures Troilus' horse and sends it to Cressida. Overall, Shakespeare follows Caxton in many verbal and narrative details. Verbal parallels include 'sixty and nine', 'orgulous',[2] the names of the city gates in the Prologue and both the form and the clustering of several proper names: warriors and kings named in 5.5, Polyxena, the 'Sagitarry' (5.5.14). Many of the incidents of the war plot also resemble Caxton's treatment: e.g. the Trojan debate, though transposed to later in the story and focusing on returning Helen instead of abducting her as revenge for the Greek abduction of Hesione.[3] In Caxton's debate, as in the play, Hector is the voice of reason, Paris and Troilus are aggressively chivalric, and Helenus is characterised by Troilus as a 'coward preste'[4] (cf. 2.2.37–8). In Caxton, Hector meets Ajax, his 'coosin Germaine' in battle (compare 4.5.121 where Hector embraces Ajax after the tournament and calls him 'cousin-german'); and, after the exchange, Cressida is greeted by a number of the Greeks instead of being brought directly to her father as in Lydgate and Chaucer. We may note here Shakespeare's characteristic procedure: he seizes on certain details but frequently transposes them, bringing together bits that may be quite distant from each other in Caxton's account. The battle scenes especially condense and fuse different moments in Caxton's much more extended and leisurely treatment. The most salient instance of this is the surrounding and then the killing of Hector by Achilles and his Myrmidons, an event that Shakespeare transposes from Caxton's description of the death of Troilus.

Because Caxton and Lydgate are following the same sources and telling the same stories, and because there are no clear instances of verbal parallels with the latter, it is difficult to tell how much Shakespeare may have relied on Lydgate – if at all. But there are a few hints that he did: in both source texts, Hector goes after the fine armour of the well-outfitted Greek but only in Lydgate does he actually kill him, and the moral implication of the scene, while made sententiously explicit by Lydgate, is clearly present

[1] See Bullough, pp. 90–4, for an account of this narrative genealogy. The history of the Troy material provides a vivid picture of how mediaeval writers and readers regarded stories – their preference for traditional over original narratives.
[2] Bullough, p. 94, points out that 'orgulous' had been changed to 'proud' in the most recent edition available to Shakespeare (1596), suggesting that he used an earlier edition.
[3] The original abduction of Hesione and her subsequently becoming the mother of Ajax is mentioned several times in the play (see, for example, 2.2.77–9 and 4.5.120). Caxton and Shakespeare got this detail confused – in the original story Hesione was Ajax's step-mother. Shakespeare also conflates two different Ajaxes, from *The Iliad* and from later accounts, which might help to explain the contradictory nature of the character as he appears in the play.
[4] Bullough, p. 191.

in Shakespeare as well. Also, the scene in which Hector's wife, sister, and father try to keep him from fighting on the day he will meet death (5.3) is closer in its outlines to Lydgate; and Lydgate also provides fuller portraits of some of the main characters (for example, Ulysses' description of Troilus in 4.5.96–109 echoes Lydgate's description at ii.4861 ff.: "The seconde Ector for his worthynesse / He called was and for his hyeprowesse").[1]

But if one reads either of these earlier texts, it is immediately apparent that Shakespeare has borrowed only incidents and the occasional word. The flavour and structure of the play are utterly different. Most obviously, the harsh critique of all the Greek and most of the Trojan warriors, the disillusionment with chivalric values, the satirical attitude of Thersites, the sense of inconstancy and futility that hovers behind the play's martial action – all this is Shakespeare's own. So too is the philosophical speculation (though it has its source in Renaissance debates about value and government) and the suspicion of idealism. Also, crucially, Shakespeare has balanced the various incidents he has borrowed, bringing them into astringent relation with one another, prodding audiences to think about the juxtapositions and the meanings they generate. He weaves together scenes from a number of Caxton's battles to stage the action in Act 5, and he provides a variety of perspectives on it. Basically, he uses whatever is to hand that might suit his purposes, but his strategy is highly selective and, since he is writing drama, necessarily more concise and economical than Caxton or Lydgate.

Henryson and others

It is possible that some of the thematic selection discernible in the play had already been achieved by previous writers, and it is certainly the case that darker attitudes towards both the love and the war plots existed before Shakespeare sat down to compose. One of the most famous versions of the Cressida story was that of Robert Henryson, a Scots poet whose *The Testament of Cresseid*, is a kind of sequel to Chaucer, and tells the sad tale of Cressida's life after she is abandoned by Diomedes. (When, near the end of the 'betrayal scene', Cressida speaks clairvoyantly of the sleeve she has just relinquished to Diomedes "Twas one's that loved me better than you will' (5.2.89), Shakespeare seems to be remembering Henryson.) *The Testament* was widely disseminated in the sixteenth century since it was appended to all editions of Chaucer's poem. Many readers were apparently unaware that it was a different poem by a different poet (though one would have thought that the fact that it is written in a Scots dialect and mentions 'worthy Chaucer glorious' (p. 352) as the author of the earlier narrative would have alerted the perspicacious reader). In it, Cresseid becomes a leper and a beggar, and there is a poignant moment when, moving along the road with her fellow sufferers, she meets Troilus on horseback – out of pity and a haunting reminiscence he gives her alms but fails to recognise her. She dies of both the pain of this encounter and her recognition of her own inconstancy, leaving the gold Troilus had given her to her fellow lepers

---

[1] *Ibid.*, pp. 159–60.

and a ring to Troilus, who, when he hears her story, builds her a marble monument. Shakespeare took nothing direct from Henryson, but *The Testament*'s moving evocation of loss and vicissitude seems to have touched him; in addition, its emphasis on disease and the relation between physical and moral decay might well have influenced the play's language, with its recurrent evocation of corruption and sickness, both venereal and otherwise (some see Cressida's 'I shall be plagued' (5.2.104) as a direct allusion to Henryson, but more probably it reflects a general influence).

There were a number of plays, no longer extant, written on Trojan themes prior to *Troilus and Cressida*, two of which might have contributed in unknown ways to Shakespeare's work. The first, simply listed as 'troye', is mentioned in Henslowe's Diary as a 'new' play presented on 22 June 1596, but nothing else is known about it.[1] Later in the Diary, Henslowe notes two payments to Dekker and Chettle for a play on Troilus and Cressida ('Troyeles & creasse daye').[2] This is probably the play that is represented by the fragmentary 'plot' dating from 1599–1600 now in the British Library.[3] The fragment begins with a Trojan council scene (equivalent to 2.2) and generally seems to alternate scenes between the love and war plots as in Shakespeare, though some different parts of the story are dramatised. The plot seems to indicate more emphasis on the war (there are two battle sequences and only two scenes involving Cressida), though the missing parts no doubt would have filled in the gaps in the love story; there are no scenes indicating the exchange or the betrayal though there is a scene, adapted from Henryson, that shows Cressida among the beggars. Achilles' refusal to fight and then his joining battle as a result of the death of Patroclus (as in Homer, but not Caxton or Lydgate) seem to be the most prominent aspects of the war plot. There is no sign of the lottery or the tournament, nor of the Trojan visit to the Greek camp.[4] It is, of course, impossible to say whether or how Shakespeare might have been influenced by this play at a rival theatre, but it seems likely that he and his company were aware of it and perhaps produced *Troilus and Cressida* as a kind of riposte. We might also speculate that the Dekker–Chettle play, like some of the other (non-dramatic) texts of the period on the same subject (such as Peele's 'The Tale of Troy'), might have introduced critical or satirical elements that Shakespeare then exploited in his more scathing exposé.

Lastly, there are two other texts that should be mentioned: Robert Greene's *Euphues his Censure to Philautus* (1587), in which a number of Trojan ladies and knights visit the Greek camp for a banquet; they use the occasion to tell long stories and debate abstract subjects, such as the ideal qualities of a soldier. A discussion of whether Helen should be returned has a few details that Shakespeare might have picked up for the Trojan council

[1] Foakes and Rickert, p. 47. (I am assuming that Henslowe's repeated notation, 'ne', refers to a new play or to one that had been revived after being out of the repertory for some time.) The play was repeated on 2, 7, and 16 July. Tatlock (p. 710) thought that this entry might have referred to Heywood's *Iron Age*, but that view has been effectively refuted – see below.
[2] Foakes and Rickert, pp. 106, 107.
[3] See Greg, *Documents*, vol. I, item 5, and II.138.
[4] See Tatlock, p. 702.

(especially Hector's double attitude, though in Greene there is no abrupt reversal).[1] And finally there is Thomas Heywood's play *The Iron Age* which Tatlock argued was written around 1594–6 but which later scholars have agreed must be, along with Heywood's other 'Age' plays, dramatisations of his long poem *Troia Britannica* (1608/1609).[2] There are several parallels with Shakespeare's play, most especially the characterisation of Thersites, but as Hillebrand suggests, the 'impression one gets is of apparent pains taken to avoid duplication'. Even Heywood's Thersites is 'as unlike Shakespeare's . . . as two snarling cynics can be'.[3] Heywood probably had both Shakespeare's play and that of Dekker and Chettle in mind when he wrote, but the rather bland feel of his play is utterly different from Shakespeare's.

What then can we say in general of Shakespeare's use of the massive amount of traditional material that he pulled together for *Troilus and Cressida*? The most important point is that he was a playwright not a scholar, and his attitude to earlier work was pragmatic and even mercenary. He took what he could use and did with it what he pleased. Confronting a great writer like Chaucer, he entered into an imaginative relation with his precursor, mining for both character and structure at a deep level. He raided Caxton for elements of the plot, remembering the odd detail that he could highlight or reconfigure; he ignored Lydgate's moralising but pounced on a few moments that he exploited for different emotional or moral purposes. He might well have been impressed by the grandeur of Chapman's Homer, but he was certainly not intimidated, transforming the heroically wrathful Achilles into a lazy, arrogant, and murderous thug with an oddly paradoxical penchant for philosophy, and building his Thersites out of the most caustic verses of Chapman's poem. In the end, though he had cast his eye over a wide range of texts, he made something unique and original, casting a pattern of light and shadow over the famous events of Troy that had never been seen before.

---

[1] For other examples see Muir, *Sources*, pp. 150–1; Muir suggests that Shakespeare might have derived 'a good deal of atmospheric detail' from Greene (p. 151).
[2] See Variorum, pp. 462–3.
[3] *Ibid.*, p. 462.

READING LIST

This list includes details of certain books and articles which may serve as a guide to those who wish to undertake a further study of the play.

Adams, Howard C. 'What Cressid is', in *Sexuality and Politics in Renaissance Drama*, ed. Carole Levin and Karen Robertson, 1991, pp. 75–93

Adelman, Janet. *Suffocating Mothers: Fantasies of Maternal Origin in Shakespeare's Plays, 'Hamlet' to 'The Tempest'*, 1992

Alexander, Peter. '*Troilus and Cressida*, 1609', *Library* 9 (1929), 267–86

Bayley, John. 'Time and the Trojans', *Essays in Criticism* 25:1 (1975), 55–73

Beale, Simon Russell. 'Thersites in *Troilus and Cressida*', in *Players of Shakespeare 3: Further Essays in Shakespearean Performance*, ed. Russell Jackson and Robert Smallwood, 1993, 160–73

Bednarz, James P. *Shakespeare and the Poets' War*, 2001

Bowen, Barbara E. *Gender in the Theatre of War: Shakespeare's 'Troilus and Cressida'*, 1993

Bradshaw, Graham. *Shakespeare's Scepticism*, 1987

Charnes, Linda. *Notorious Identity: Materializing the Subject in Shakespeare*, 1993

Donaldson, E. Talbot. *The Swan at the Well: Shakespeare Reading Chaucer*, 1985

Dryden, John. *Troilus and Cressida*, ed. Maximillian Novak and George Guffey, in *The Works of John Dryden* (California Edition, 20 vols., 1956–94), vol. xiii, 1984

Elton, William R. *Shakespeare's 'Troilus and Cressida' and the Inns of Court Revels*, 2000

Engle, Lars. *Shakespearean Pragmatism: Market of His Time*, 1993

Freund, Elizabeth. ' "Ariachne's broken woof": the rhetoric of citation in *Troilus and Cressida*', in *Shakespeare and the Question of Theory*, ed. Patricia Parker and Geoffrey Hartman, 1985, pp. 19–36

Girard, René. 'The politics of desire in *Troilus and Cressida*', in *Shakespeare and the Question of Theory*, ed. Patricia Parker and Geoffrey Hartman, 1985, pp. 188–209

Godschalk, William. 'The texts of *Troilus and Cressida*', *Early Modern Literary Studies* 1 (1995), 1–54

Greene, Gayle. 'Shakespeare's Cressida: "a kind of self" ', in *The Woman's Part: Feminist Criticism of Shakespeare*, ed. Carolyn Lenz, Ruth Swift, Gayle Greene, and Carol Thomas Neely, 1980, pp. 133–49

Hodgdon, Barbara. 'He do Cressida in different voices', *English Literary Renaissance* 20 (1990), 254–86

Honigmann, E. A. J. 'The date and revision of *Troilus and Cressida*', in *Textual Criticism and Literary Interpretation*, ed. J. McGann, 1985, pp. 38–54

Myriad-Minded Shakespeare: Essays, Chiefly on the Tragedies and Problem Comedies, 1989

James, Heather. *Shakespeare's Troy: Drama, Politics, and the Translation of Empire*, 1997

Jensen, Phebe. 'The textual politics of *Troilus and Cressida*', *SQ* 46 (1995), 414–23

Kennedy, Dennis. *Looking at Shakespeare: A Visual History of Twentieth-century Performance*, 1993

Kermode, Frank. ' "Opinion" in *Troilus and Cressida*', in *Teaching the Text*, ed. Susanne Kappeler and Norman Bryson, 1983, pp. 164–79

Kimbrough, Robert. *Shakespeare's 'Troilus and Cressida' and Its Setting*, 1964

Lancashire, Ian. 'Probing Shakespeare's idiolect in *Troilus and Cressida*', *University of Toronto Quarterly* 68 (1999), 728–67

Mallin, Eric S. *Inscribing the Time: Shakespeare and the End of Elizabethan England*, 1995

Norbrook, David. 'Rhetoric, ideology, and the Elizabethan world picture', in *Renaissance Rhetoric*, ed. Peter Mack, 1994, pp. 140–64

Nosworthy, J. M. *Shakespeare's Occasional Plays: Their Origin and Transmission*, 1965

Parker, Patricia. *Shakespeare from the Margins: Language, Culture, Context*, 1996

Rutter, Carol. *Enter the Body: Women and Representation on Shakespeare's Stage*, 2001

Taylor, Gary. '*Troilus and Cressida*: bibliography, performance and interpretation', *Shakespeare Studies* 15 (1982), 99–136

Tylee, Claire M. 'The text of Cressida and every ticklish reader: *Troilus and Cressida*, the Greek camp scene', *S.Sur.* 41 (1989), 63–76

Williams, Philip. 'Shakespeare's *Troilus and Cressida*: the relationship of quarto and folio', *Studies in Bibliography* 3 (1950), 131–43

'The "second issue" of Shakespeare's *Troilus and Cressida*, 1609', *Studies in Bibliography* 2 (1949), 25–33